FLORIDA EXPLORED

Academy of Natural Sciences of Philadelphia (ANSP) through time: a) 1812;
b) Gilliams Hall; 1817; c) 1826; d) 1845; e) 1876; f) 1915; g) 2012. Founded in
1812, the ANSP became affiliated with Drexel University in 2012 and became the
Academy of Natural Sciences of Drexel University. Throughout its history it has
been often referred to as the Philadelphia Academy of Natural Sciences.

ANSP Archives, Collection 49, Courtesy of the Academy of Natural Sciences of Drexel University.

FLORIDA EXPLORED

The Philadelphia Connection in Bartram's Tracks

THOMAS PETER BENNETT

MERCER UNIVERSITY PRESS

Macon, Georgia

1979–2019

40 Years of Publishing Excellence

MERCER UNIVERSITY PRESS

Endowed by

TOM WATSON BROWN
and
THE WATSON-BROWN FOUNDATION, INC.

MUP/ H969

© 2019 by Mercer University Press
Published by Mercer University Press
1501 Mercer University Drive
Macon, Georgia 31207
All rights reserved

9 8 7 6 5 4 3 2 1

Books published by Mercer University Press are printed on acid-free paper that
meets the requirements of the American National Standard for Information
Sciences—Permanence of Paper for Printed Library Materials.

Printed and bound in the United States.

This book is set in Adobe Garamond Pro

ISBN 978-0-88146-693-5

Cataloging-in-Publication Data is available from the Library of Congress

CONTENTS

ILLUSTRATIONS

Frontispiece

Academy of Natural Sciences of Philadelphia (ANSP) through time. Founded in 1812, the ANSP became affiliated with Drexel University in 2012 and became the Academy of Natural Sciences of Drexel University. Throughout its history it has been often referred to as the Philadelphia Academy of Natural Sciences. (ANSP Archives, Collection 49, Courtesy of the Academy of Natural Sciences of Drexel University.)

Chapter 1

Map of John and William Bartram's journey to Florida. (Courtesy of Brad Sanders.)

Chapter 2

Bartram's Southeastern travels (1773–1776) into East Florida and Bartram's Southwestern travels (1773–1776) into West Florida. (Courtesy of Brad Sanders.)

Chapter 3

William Bartram (1739–1823) by Charles Willson Peale, 1808. (Courtesy of Independence National Historical Park.)

Chapter 4

THE FLORIDA FOUR: William Maclure, George Ord Thomas Say, and Titian Peale. (Courtesy of Academy of Natural Sciences of Drexel University.)

Chapter 5

The Florida Rat (Neotoma floridana), described by Ord on his return from Florida. (Courtesy Academy of Natural Sciences of Drexel University.)

Chapter 8

John James Audubon by John Syme, 1826. (Courtesy of White House Collection/White House Historical Association.)

Map of Audubon's travels in Florida. (Courtesy of Brad Sanders.)

Egg specimen of Peale's Egret (reddish egret) from Florida with Audubon's handwriting. (Courtesy of ANSP Ornithology Department.)

The "Florida" common moorhen (Gallinula chloropus) egg, also collected by Audubon. (Courtesy of Nate Rice, Academy of Natural Sciences of Drexel University.)

Chapter 11

Young Joseph Leidy with Edgar Allan Poe and member in a top hat, at the Academy. (Courtesy of the Academy of Natural Sciences of Drexel University.)

Joseph Leidy next to the tibia of *Hadrosaurus foulkii*, Philadelphia, Pennsylvania, taken in the museum, ca. 1859. (Courtesy of the Academy of Natural Sciences of Drexel University.)

Chapter 12

Southwest coastal map showing Key Marco and other locations. (Courtesy of Brad Sanders.)

Chapter 13

Ernest Hemingway shows off two of his catches in 1934. (Courtesy of the Academy of Natural Sciences of Drexel University.)

End Piece

Montage of Bartram Trail signs. (Courtesy of Gudrun Dorothea Bennett and Thomas P. Bennett.)

FOREWORD

For many years, popular historians of science, from Joseph Ewan (*A Short History of Botany in the United States*) and John Bakeless (*The Eyes of Discovery*) to Joseph Kastner (*A Species of Eternity*) and Andrea Wolf (*Brother Gardeners*), have celebrated Philadelphia's central role in the eighteenth- and nineteenth-century nexus of exchange in plants and wildlife between North America and England. *Florida Explored: The Philadelphia Connection in Bartram's Tracks* is the first book to explore in detail the many lines of contact between Philadelphia and Florida that provided a vital part of that international trade in specimens and ideas.

The English naturalist Mark Catesby first drew scientific attention to Florida with his pioneering color plate book, *Natural History of Carolina, Florida and the Bahama Islands* (1729–1747). This stimulated John and William Bartram's interest in the biological diversity of Florida. During winter 1765–1766, after John was named Royal Botanist to North America by King George III, he and William made an extensive trip into the northern part of East Florida. Several years later, William explored both East and West Florida on his own. Using the collections of seeds and live plants made on these and other trips and propagated in their Philadelphia garden, the Bartrams played a critical role in opening botanical links within North America and beyond. Other naturalists, following in their footsteps, reinforced their efforts, and expanded the focus of attention into many other fields of natural history.

The institutional base behind some of the post-Catesby, post-Bartram expeditions to Florida was the Academy of Natural Sciences of Philadelphia (now part of Drexel University), where many of the specimens collected now reside, and in whose journal many of the new discoveries were first described. Founded in 1812 for the systematic study of nature and the "dissemination of useful knowledge," the Academy quickly established itself as the preeminent natural history institution in North America. It maintained that position through most of the nineteenth century, encouraging, by example and from its leadership position, the creation of similar institutions in Washington, New York, Chicago, and elsewhere.

The Philadelphia-Florida connection, initiated by the Bartrams, was continued by Academy members (and Bartram protégés) William Maclure, Thomas Say, Titian Ramsay Peale and George Ord (the "Florida Four"), and then by John James Audubon, Joseph Leidy, Joseph Willcox and many others with close Academy connections. In the twentieth century, still more Academy of Natural Sciences members and professional staff focused their research on Florida. They included Timothy Abbot Conrad, Francis Harper, Henry Pilsbry, Henry Weed Fowler, and R. Tucker Abbott, among others. Leaders of their respective fields of study, these men continued to broaden, deepen, and further stimulate Philadelphia's ties to Florida. This connection took more tangible and popular form in the 1970s when the Academy became involved, tangentially, with the planning and establishment of an official Bartram Trail throughout the South. Following William Bartram's eighteenth-century travels, the trail traced much of its course through Florida.

Thomas Peter Bennett, a lifelong Floridian with deep roots in the natural sciences, embodies the intellectual and physical links between these two parts of the country. He served as president of the Academy of Natural Sciences from 1976 to 1985, the critical period in which William Bartram was regaining public recognition in Florida and throughout the Southeast. He enthusiastically supported my own participation in the federally funded creation of a National Scenic Trail designed to commemorate William Bartram's travels on the eve of the American Revolution. That trail, and its related historic sites, continues to inform the public about Bartram's travels and celebrate the Philadelphia-Florida links that Peter Bennett has championed throughout his career.

After a decade of leadership at the Academy, Peter returned to Florida to head up the Florida Museum of Natural History in Gainesville for a decade, and later the South Florida Museum. In Florida he undertook a series of exploration and writing projects that have further revealed the important connections between Florida and Philadelphia. In his 2011 book, *The Legacy*, Peter traces the history of the South Florida Museum and the public understanding and exhibition of all things Floridian, beginning with the area's prehistoric creatures, native inhabitants, and European contact with De Soto's arrival in 1539 and to the present day. With this book he has both narrowed his focus to tell the rich Florida-Philadelphia story that has fascinated him for so long and expanded it by revealing the depth, breadth, and continuing significance of that connection.

Building on its deep Quaker roots and its pioneering role in American natural history, nineteenth-century Philadelphia, the "Athens of America," was a center not just for the study and interpretation of the natural world but also for the dissemination of that information. William Maclure, the Academy's president who organized and helped pay for the institution's first research expedition to Florida in 1817, was also the person who helped to publicize the findings of the trip through the Academy of Natural Sciences' *Journal,* which he had helped to launch in that very same year. Like Maclure, who was both a scholar and a philanthropist dedicated to science, Peter Bennett is making his research accessible to a wider audience through *Florida Explored: The Philadelphia Connection in Bartram's Tracks.*

For those nineteenth- and early-twentieth-century scientists studying prehistoric life (Joseph Leidy and Joseph Willcox), indigenous peoples (George Morton, Clarence Moore, and others), or almost any subject of natural history (the rest of the figures profiled in this book), Florida was an ideal destination. Its rich history and its unspoiled habitats (until relatively recent time) made it a paradise for naturalists of all stripes. Introduced to the region by the paintings of Mark Catesby and the evocative descriptions of John and William Bartram, subsequent researchers were irresistibly drawn to the area and willing to undertake any hardship to immerse themselves in its rich diversity of life. Some did so consciously following in the footsteps of their admired colleagues. Others "discovered" Florida on their own. All came away from their experiences forever changed by them. Peter Bennett's book will have the same effect on its readers, enabling us to see Florida again with fresh eyes and a renewed appreciation for the study of its wildlife, past and present.

A disproportionate number of Philadelphians may have dominated Florida's early study, but they were by no means the only scientists to visit and research the flora and fauna of the area. The information that was collected there was shared between like-minded scholars and published in a number of venues. Today, as the region's habitats face increasing threats from agriculture, population spread, and rising ocean levels, the continuing study of Florida's ecosystems is more urgent than ever. This is being carried out by experts from across the country and around the world. Fortunately, new generations of scholars with new questions to ask and new technologies at their disposal will have a strong baseline from which to work. That baseline, and many of the people who created it, are recorded in *Florida Explored.* Thus, the legacy of Bartram—and so many others—is transported to the present day.

Robert McCracken Peck
Senior Fellow
The Academy of Natural Sciences of Philadelphia
Drexel University

PREFACE

Florida Explored: The Philadelphia Connection in Bartram's Tracks is a time capsule of the exploration and discovery of Florida's natural history by the eminent scientists associated with America's oldest natural history museum, Philadelphia's Academy of Natural Sciences. *Florida Explored* presents an account of their expeditions and findings, including many of Florida's unique nature icons, from the rare scrub jay and Torreya tree to the more familiar anhinga and sabal palm. These scientists' collections of new plants, animals, fossils, and artifacts filled research databases and expanded our knowledge of Florida's botany, zoology, geology, and anthropology. *Florida Explored* offers a scientific chronicle of these naturalists' contributions to our modern understanding of Florida's geographic and natural history, along with developments that have taken place at the Academy of Natural Sciences since its founding in 1812.

Florida Explored begins in 1764 with John Bartram's appointment as royal botanist for British Colonial Florida. Bartram and his son, William, soon set out from Philadelphia to explore East Florida along the St. Johns River. William returned to Florida alone a decade later; his discoveries were published in 1791 in *Travels through North & South Carolina, Georgia, East & West Florida.* William Bartram's descriptions of Florida's plants and animals and their ecosystems electrified the international scientific and literary worlds and stirred considerable controversy. Some believed his accounts of the flora and fauna, battles with alligators, and encounters with natives; others thought them to be exaggerated or imaginary. Nevertheless, all were inspired by Bartram's awe at the beauty of Florida.

William Bartram became America's preeminent naturalist. His students founded Philadelphia's Academy of Natural Sciences and elected Bartram to membership shortly thereafter. Bartram's *Travels* and the scientific questions it raised also inspired the Academy's first major scientific expedition to Spanish Florida by the "Florida Four"—William Maclure, George Ord, Thomas Say, and Titian Peale—in 1817.[2]

Thomas Say wrote that their mission was "pursuing pretty much the track of Bartram...but whether or not we shall go further than he did will

---

[2] This group has also been referred to as the "Florida Party."

entirely depend on circumstances...." These four Academy members made observations and collected specimens of plants, animals, fossils, and ancient artifacts, which they brought back to Philadelphia for study, preservation, presentation to assembled members, and description in the newly founded *Journal of the Academy of Natural Sciences of Philadelphia.*

In the two hundred years since, Academy members and correspondents such as Louis Agassiz, John James Audubon, Asa Gray, and Clarence Moore have followed the Florida Four by using Bartram's *Travels* to guide their explorations in Florida. Some participated in organized expeditions, some traveled solo or led small groups with paid or volunteer assistance; a few wintered there or were part-time Florida residents. Others in Philadelphia, often called "closet naturalists," simply requested that Florida specimens be sent to them at the Academy for study. This book is a group biography that chronicles their adventures and scientific discoveries as they systematically followed Bartram's tracks and contributed to our understanding of Florida's natural history.

Florida Explored is a time capsule of researched, narrated, and illustrated contents that provide a glimpse into scientists' lives during specific Florida expeditions as well as descriptions of their discoveries presented at scientific meetings, in publications, and through deposited data specimens for curation, future study, and reference. Many plants and animals they gathered remain in the Academy's collections, and new methodologies in molecular biology and digital technology continue to reveal more details about the origins and future of Florida's ecosystems.

This Book and Many Thanks

This book has been a long Florida journey "in Bartram's tracks" with many Philadelphia, Florida, and other Southern connections, and I thank Gudrun Dorothea Bennett and all whom I met along the way for contributing and inspiring me to continue.

Born in Florida, I grew up rambling, camping, and studying nature in Florida's piney woods, hammocks, and then-pristine lakes and springs. The spirit and imagery of Bartram's own travels from Mrs. Gray's fourth-grade Florida history class and Helen and Alan Cruickshank's public Audubon travel talks sparked my William Bartram interests, which only grew during Boy Scout explorations and university studies in Florida. In Tallahassee, as an undergraduate during the 1950s and as a professor in the 1970s, I became familiar with Bartram's influence in the panhandle and western Florida and the adjacent states. In the late 1970s, my curiosity was piqued by rambles in the collections and library of Philadelphia's Academy of Natural Sciences and visits to nearby Bartram's Garden, American Philosophical Society, and Wagner Free Institute. Discovering manuscripts, specimens, and artifacts related to the Academy's 1817 expedition to Florida and those related to a later expedition, tweaked my interest in the links between Philadelphia and Florida explorations; they seemed related to Bartram's travels. As Academy members and correspondents had been doing for two hundred years, I decided to follow in Bartram's Florida tracks on foot, by car, and by boat. The Florida stories of the Academy-related explorers that I found in their publications, letters, and accounts, along with their natural history discoveries for the "gentle reader," amateur, and professional, are the origins of this book.

Further study, exploration, and discussions that took place in Bartram's Alachua haunts during the 1980s–1990s with the curators and staff of the Florida Museum of Natural History (FLMNH) and colleagues at the University of Florida fueled my interest in Bartram and his Florida explorations. The scientific outreach into this region during the mid-nineteenth century by members of the Academy and the Wagner Free Institute of Science in Philadelphia maintained the link to the curators and staff of those institutions.

In following Bartram's and the Florida Four's 1817 Academy expedition tracks through Georgia and the Sea Islands, my study and exploration extended (as did my friends and colleagues) into Georgia haunts that were familiar to me from my childhood summers in and around Macon and Milledgeville. I became aware of the Academy's influence and central role as a scientific resource and collection and publication outlet for its Southern members and correspondents in their contributions to Florida exploration, particularly William Baldwin, members of the Le Conte and Harper families, as well as many more contemporary writers, scientists, and artists in Georgia, Alabama, Mississippi, and Louisiana with ties to Bartram and Florida.

Later, in the non-Bartram-traveled territory of south Florida, which held great scientific interest to nineteenth- and twentieth-century Academy members and correspondents, I had the opportunity to explore their Bartram-inspired tracks from Florida's Gulf west coast to the Keys. Many colleagues and friends at the South Florida Museum in Bradenton and the Bailey-Matthews National Shell Museum in Sanibel inspired my later explorations.

I thank all those who inspired, advised, criticized, patiently listened, and in so many ways continue to contribute to *Florida Explored: The Philadelphia Connection in Bartram's Tracks.*

Thomas Peter Bennett

ABBREVIATIONS

AJS—*American Journal of Science*, founded in 1819; it became the *American Journal of Science and Arts* in 1820, and back again to the original name in 1880.

APS—American Philosophical Society

ANSP—The founding (1812) and legal name of the Academy of Natural Sciences of Philadelphia until its affiliation with Drexel University in 2012 when the "of Drexel University" replaced "of Philadelphia." I have used ANSP in this book because the text and references all refer to the period prior to 2012. "Philadelphia Academy" and "Academy of Natural Sciences in Philadelphia" are sometimes used in publications.

CPP—Founded in 1787, the College of Physicians of Philadelphia is the oldest private medical society in the United States.

FHBT—*The Travels of William Bartram: Naturalist's Edition.* Annotated and indexed by Francis Harper. Athens: University of Georgia Press, 1998. First published 1958 by Yale University (Cambridge).

FLMNH—Florida Museum of Natural History, Gainesville, Florida

HH—Thomas Hallock and Nancy E. Hoffmann, eds. *William Bartram: The Search for Nature's Design: Selected Art, Letters, and Unpublished Writings.* Athens: University of Georgia Press, 2010.

HSP—Archives of the Historical Society of Pennsylvania, Philadelphia, Pennsylvania.

JANS—*Journal of the Academy of Natural Sciences of Philadelphia.* Founded in 1817.

JB—John Bartram

NYBG—New York Botanical Garden

PANS—*Proceedings of the Academy of Natural Sciences of Philadelphia.* Started in 1843 as a replacement for the *JANS*.

PAPS—*Proceeding of the American Philosophical Society*

PDANS—*Proceeding of the Davenport Academy of Natural Sciences*

PENN—Archives of the University of Pennsylvania

PH—Philadelphia Herbarium. Located at the Academy of Natural Sciences.

WBT—William Bartram, *Travels through North & South Carolina, Georgia, East & West Florida, The Cherokee Country, The Extensive Territories of the Muscogules, or Creek Confederacy, and the Country of the Chactaws: Containing an Account of the Soil and Natural Productions of those Regions, together with Observations on the Manners of the Indians* (Philadelphia: James and Johnston, 1791).

TWFIS—Transactions of the Wagner Free Institute of Science

WB—*William Bartram*

WFIS—Wagner Free Institute of Science

FLORIDA EXPLORED

PART 1

INTRODUCTION TO PART 1

An Overview

This introduction to Florida's cultural[1] and natural history,[2] sets the stage for the first five chapters of *Florida Explored*.

The travels of John Bartram and his son, William, to the British colonies of East Florida and West Florida and their discoveries while there are described in chapter 1. Chapter 2 covers William's solo exploration of British Florida, which he detailed in his classic *Travels*.[3] Soon afterward (chapter 3), William returned to Philadelphia to write and also mentor those who founded America's first natural history museum, the Academy of Natural Sciences of Philadelphia (chapter 4). From 1817–1818, four other Academy members traveled to what had become again Spanish Florida "in Bartram's tracks" on their museum's first expedition to a foreign land (chapter 5).[4]

Florida has the longest recorded history of any American state and also

---

[1] See Gannon's *Florida: A Short History*, *Michael Gannon's History of Florida in 40 Minutes*, and *The New History of Florida*; see also Tebeau and Marina, *A History of Florida*.

[2] Daniels, *American Science in the Age of Jackson*, 38–9, 112–15; Oleson and Brown, *The Pursuit of Knowledge in the Early American Republic*; Hagen, "The History of the Origin and Development of Museums," 80–90; Meyers and Pritchard, *Empire's Nature*; Brown, *Florida's First People*; Milanich, *Florida's Indians from Ancient Times to the Present*; Johnston, "Additional 16th-Century Bird Reports from Florida," 1–20.

[3] William Bartram's *Travels through North & South Carolina, Georgia, East & West Florida, The Cherokee Country, The Extensive Territories of the Muscogulges, or Creek Confederacy, and the Country of the Chactaws: Containing an Account of the Soil and Natural Productions of those Regions, together with Observations on the Manners of the Indians* (Philadelphia: James and Johnson, 1791). This 1791 work hereafter will be cited as *WBT*. The closely related title *The Travels of William Bartram: Naturalist's Edition*, annotated and edited by Francis Harper (Athens: University of Georgia, 1998), will hereafter be cited as *FHBT*.

[4] "Bartram's Garden" still refers to "John Bartram's Garden." Francis Harper's writings and publications (described in ch. 14 of this book) led to the mixed use (John and William) and meaning of the "Bartram Trail," which now generally indicates the trail of William Bartram. The plural possessive "Bartrams' Trail" refers to the overlap of John's and William's respective trails; "Bartram's Trail" (singular possessive) refers to William's travels from 1773–1776. Because William's Florida exploration and travels extended beyond those of his with John, the term "in Bartram's tracks" is used in this book. The phrase was coined by Thomas Say during the 1817 Academy expedition to Florida.

one of the most complex; it extends to the 14,000-year-old archeological record linking the ancient peoples to Florida's exploration and settlement and also to earlier records in geological and climatic time.

Spanish Discovery and Settlement (c. 1513–1763)

Spanish explorer Juan Ponce de León sailed from Puerto Rico during the season of *La Pascua de la Florida* ("Passion of the Flowers"); he landed in an unexplored region along the Atlantic coast between present-day St. Augustine and Melbourne, which he named La Florida, on 2 April 1513.

At the time, numerous native tribes inhabited the region. The Spanish identified nearly one hundred group names, ranging from organized political entities, such as the Apalachee, with a population of around 50,000, to villages with no known political affiliation. There were an estimated 150,000 Timucua people and other smaller tribes: the Ais, Calusa, Jaega, Mayaimi, Tequesta, and Tocobaga.

By the 1540s, the Spanish had explored the New World's southeastern coastline and made incursions inland; French explorers soon followed. Although navigational notes and maps survive, the expedition records seldom mentioned the region's natural history or agriculture. The Spanish explored La Florida but did not attempt permanent settlements until after the French had already established a colony.

In 1564, French settlers founded Fort Caroline (near modern-day Jacksonville) as a safe haven for Protestant Huguenots who had first arrived in 1562. In 1565, the Spanish crown dispatched Menéndez de Avilés with troops to attack and destroy Fort Caroline. De Avilés succeeded in his campaign, then traveled south and built a fortified settlement, which he named St. Augustine. It became the most important settlement in Spanish La Florida and proved key to the further exploration and development of the area.

Although Spanish explorers and settlers imported "exotics," such as horses, pigs, cattle, along with citrus and other plants and animals, Spanish Florida never developed agricultural self-sufficiency; other than the unsuccessful quest for gold, its natural resources were also never exploited. After establishing many Catholic missions, the Spanish abandoned the idea of settling Florida to focus on more profitable areas in the New World. However, due to Florida's militarily strategic location for shipping from South and Central America along the Straits of Florida, the Spanish maintained fortifications and continued to occupy Florida. Nevertheless, by 1763, Spain's interest in and hold on La Florida was marginal, and it was transferred to British control.

British Period (1763–1783)

The Treaty of Paris of 1763 concluded the French and Indian War, and Spain ceded La Florida to Great Britain in exchange for Cuba. The changing of flags drove most of the Spanish settlers to Cuba, and much of the remaining indigenous population followed. The British ambitiously planned their fourteenth and fifteenth British colonies, East and West Florida, which were separated by the Apalachicola River.

West Florida included the former Spanish Florida region located west of the Apalachicola River plus sections of French Louisiana earlier acquired by the British. Thus, British West Florida comprised all the territory between the Mississippi and Apalachicola Rivers, with a northern boundary arbitrarily set at the 31st parallel north. It included areas that would later become parts of Alabama, Louisiana, and Georgia. Although Mobile was the major western settlement, Pensacola was chosen as the capital of British West Florida; St. Augustine served as East Florida's capital. During the British Colonial period, most settlers headed for East Florida's St. Johns River and the St. Augustine region, which were easily accessible.

Throughout the American Revolutionary War (1775–1783), East and West Florida's colonists remained loyal to Great Britain. East Florida's population of approximately 3,000 individuals swelled to 17,000 as British Loyalist refugees flooded in from other British colonies during the war.

The American Revolutionary cause was strengthened in 1781 when the West Florida capital of Pensacola was captured from the British by Spain, which had entered the war indirectly as an ally of France. By 1782, George Washington had achieved substantial victories over the British with French and Spanish aid, and the thirteen British colonies became the United States of America. The Treaty of Paris in 1783 ended the Revolutionary War and returned all of British East and West Florida to Spanish control, but it did not specify their precise boundaries.

Second Spanish Period (1783–1821)

During Spain's second reign over Florida, the Spanish presence was minor, marked by intrigue, border disagreements, Indian trade disputes, and population turnover as the motherland's attention was diverted to problems in its other New World holdings. In 1810, President James Madison claimed sections of Spanish West Florida as part of the Louisiana Purchase.

Although Spain did not enter the War of 1812 between the United States and Great Britain, the country permitted the British to freely use the Spanish Floridas to attack America. In 1813, Major General Andrew Jackson turned the tables and captured the British base in Spanish Pensacola. Two years later, Jackson was again victorious at the Battle of New Orleans, the final major clash of the War of 1812.

Although the war ended with relations between the United States and Great Britain largely restored to *status quo ante bellum*, America asserted its aroused sense of nationalism against Spain and the British loyalists in Florida during the years that followed. In 1818, Jackson again invaded the Spanish Floridas while pursuing the Seminoles and their British loyalists. After rousting some Seminoles, he occupied Pensacola, ending the so-called First Seminole War. The Floridas remained an increasing burden for Spain, and in 1819 Spain ceded the territory to the United States in the Adams-Onís Treaty, also known as the Purchase of Florida, which was ratified in 1821. Spanish East and West Florida became the United States' Territory of Florida on 10 March 1821, and Andrew Jackson was named its first territorial governor.

Natural History

By geological standards, the Florida state peninsula as we know it today (the emergent part of the Florida Platform) is young.[5] The state abounds with both invertebrate and vertebrate fossil evidence of its marine past. Having had no significant tectonic upheavals, Florida has little topographic relief; its high point is 345 feet above sea level, the lowest of all fifty states. Azure waters from Florida's porous limestone aquifers, the most productive in the world, supply more than six hundred freshwater springs that dot Florida's interior. Its cool "boiling springs," with water temperatures between 68–75°F, flow into networks of 1,700 rivers, streams, swamps, and outlets along the 1,350 miles of Florida's climate-moderating Atlantic-Gulf coastline. These climatic and geologic features create Florida's many rich ecosystems, a north-south crossroads of biological exchange, along with great floristic and zoological diversity.

Early explorers often noted various indigenous animals and plants; the Spanish also introduced new ones into the environment for agricultural and medicinal purposes. Florida's native species were in turn shipped back to Europe for study and horticulture. By the eighteenth century, the British had substantial economic and scientific interest in the Southern flora and fauna of the Florida colonies.

The first notable contributor to collecting and describing Southern

---

[5] Randazzo and Jones, *The Geology of Florida*, 1–12.

plants and animals to have an influence on eighteenth-century colonial explorers was self-taught British artist-naturalist Mark Catesby. Catesby arrived in Williamsburg, Virginia, in 1712 to visit relatives. Obsessed with describing Southern plants and animals, he explored Virginia and then moved south into the Crown Colony of Carolina before sailing back to England with his portfolio of work in 1719. Three years later, he returned to America under the auspices of London's Royal Society to travel and publish the first scientific descriptions of the New World's plants and animals based on his firsthand observations and art. He journeyed as far south as the new British colony of Georgia (formerly La Florida) but not into modern-day Florida as we know it. His second expedition started in Charles Town, West Virginia. Catesby explored the mainland as far south as Savannah, in an area that was in transition and had been termed La Florida. Although he did not venture into what later became British East Florida and present-day Florida, many of the plants and animals he illustrated and described were also present in the Floridas, including birds, fishes, flowers, trees, and bison.

Catesby spent the next two decades writing and illustrating his book in sections of twenty plates, which he later bound in two volumes as *The Natural History of Carolina, Florida and the Bahama Islands: containing the figures of birds, beasts, fishes, serpents, insects, and plants: particularly, the forest-trees, shrubs, and other plants, not hitherto described, or very incorrectly figured by author.* This work was the first comprehensive study and illustration of the flora and fauna of English colonies in the New World and the earliest work of natural history art that placed animals alongside plants within the context and setting of their natural habitats. Catesby's accounts and illustrations informed and inspired the first two generations of American naturalists, including John and William Bartram (chapter 1).

While Catesby was describing American plants and animals, Swedish scientist Carolus Linnaeus and his students and foreign collaborators were creating a uniform scientific system for naming and defining living organisms and minerals.[6] *Systema Naturae*, which was published in 1735, outlined the Linnaean system; each organism had a two-part Latinized name of genus and species (for example, *Homo sapiens* for modern-day humans). In 1753, Linnaeus recorded "printed instructions" for arranging specimens and collections. As preservation methods were developed and museums constructed to house reference specimens, the original reference specimen used for naming

[6] Isely, *One Hundred and One Botanists*, 86–93.

became known as the "type," with the scientific name and its discoverer insured by a publication and often also accompanied by an illustration. Thus, Linnaeus created a worldwide scientific system of botanical and zoological nomenclature for communicating about organisms. Soon, Linnaeus's disciples in many countries were working on curiosities and collections of organisms, competing for the highest quantity and quality of well-preserved and identified type specimens.

During its British and Second Spanish Periods, Florida was first systematically explored by British Colonials and Americans linked to Philadelphia and the newly founded Academy of Natural Sciences of Philadelphia. They followed "in Bartram's tracks" using Linnaeus's guidelines for taxonomy and systematic study.

CHAPTER 1

THE BARTRAMS' EXPLORATION

"Fine pleasant clear morning therm 70"[1]

—John Bartram

A new chapter in Florida history and in the life of John Bartram, owner of one of America's first and oldest continually operating botanical gardens near Philadelphia, Pennsylvania, began in 1763 when Great Britain's King George III acquired Spain's Florida territories and created the fourteenth and fifteenth British colonies of East and West Florida, which stretched from St. Augustine on the Atlantic Ocean to the Mississippi River. St. Augustine was the capital of East Florida, while Pensacola became West Florida's capital. Two years later, in 1765, King George appointed John Bartram, the American colonies' most distinguished botanist, to be Botanist to his Majesty for the Floridas.

With Spanish Florida now East and West Florida, the British government faced many questions related to the new colonies' natural history and its impact on their potential for development. How could this vast, unexplored region be used to increase naturalists' knowledge? What botanical resources did Florida hold for physicians, apothecaries, and agriculturists? Were food plants available, or natural products of interest to European buyers? The survival and economic interests of the colonists, the Crown, and British merchants relied on the answers to these questions.

During the early eighteenth century, great interest arose in the traffic of seeds and plants from America to England. Many wealthy merchants in England built conservatories to grow imported plants and conduct experiments. Agriculturists sought to raise crops to readily feed more people and animals while herbalists desired to explore both the known and experimental properties of these new plants for medicinal purposes. Additionally, collectors of exotica were often interested patrons.

---

[1] JB, "Diary of a Journey," 33. This entry is similar to the beginnings of his daily entries.

For these pursuits, the British required the experience of Quaker farmer John Bartram (1699–1777). Bartram's expertise was derived from his export enterprise in botanicals, which he had successfully established by the mid-eighteenth century at his farm and garden near Philadelphia. Indisputably the first native-born American botanist, Bartram was also considered the greatest natural botanist in the world by eminent Swedish botanist Carolus Linnaeus, who published *Systema Naturae*, a uniform scientific system for naming and describing creatures, in 1735. John Bartram made his first serious exploration of the natural history of Florida during its early British period and began by exploring the natural history of the St. Johns River in East Florida with the aid of his son, William.

John Bartram

John Bartram's eight-acre botanical garden was located in Kingsessing on the west bank of the Schuylkill, about three miles from the center of Philadelphia, and was named Bartram's Garden. This was the first living botanical collection of widely collected and scientifically studied North American plants. Bartram's house, which he built himself for his growing family and botanical enterprise, shared the same land as the garden.

As early as the 1740s, the house and garden adjacent to Bartram's one hundred-acre farm became internationally known as a "must visit" destination for botanists and horticulturalists. Furthermore, Bartram's botanical interests allied him with Philadelphia's businessmen by day and scholars by night; in 1743, Bartram and Benjamin Franklin co-founded the Philosophical Society, which later became the American Philosophical Society of Philadelphia.

Bartram, a skilled horticulturalist, traveled throughout Pennsylvania and New York and south into North Carolina seeking plants from other localities. His business flourished by exporting to interested merchants in England roots, seeds, and plants gathered using the necessary collecting paraphernalia: cutting and digging equipment, grapnels for aquatic plants and roots, magnifying glasses, portable plant presses, drying papers, labels for specimens, notebooks, maps, and identification books. He carefully dried and labeled the leaves, stems, roots, flowers, and seeds of plant specimens that often accompanied live plants that he potted.

In 1733, Peter Collinson (1694–1768), a distinguished English Quaker merchant, botanist, and gardener, commissioned Bartram to package and send him collections of plants, insects, and other examples of America's nature in exchange for packets of seeds and bulbs from Collinson's own collections.[2] This relationship with Collinson aided Bartram in developing a network of friends and correspondents among leading Englishmen of the eighteenth-century scientific community. Bartram's appointment as royal botanist in 1765 was based on recommendations by Peter Collinson and Benjamin Franklin. Bartram received a stipend of £50 per annum from the Crown and held the position until his death in 1777.

Bartram's first assignment as royal botanist was to define the botanical and agricultural potential surrounding the St. Johns River in East Florida. Within the two new English colonies, this region was deemed the most practical to develop as the St. Johns River provided transportation and access to vast, unexplored East Florida. Since the river's origins were unknown, an additional challenge for Bartram was to determine the river's Southern source in the unexplored wilderness of East Florida. The river ran north, with its mouth to the Atlantic near Cowford (present-day Jacksonville) and was called a "River of Lakes." This task was indeed a challenge for Bartram, who was sixty-five years old at the time.

The previously created Spanish and English maps of the New World revealed very little about the interior geography of Florida. Available publications contained only a few natural history observations.[3] They recorded scattered Spanish mission sites and indicated that the St. Augustine region was the most inhabited area of East Florida. The royal assignment, as explained by Collinson, included preparing a detailed report of Bartram's Florida travels and collecting specimens for the King's collections: plants, ores and fossils. Collinson also requested specimens of land snails, river mollusks, and insects for himself.

John's Son Billy

John Bartram was born to Quaker parents on 23 March 1699, in Darby, Pennsylvania (now a suburb of Philadelphia). Bartram was married to his first wife from 1723 until her death in 1727, and the couple had two sons together. Two years later, he married Ann Mendenhall; they had four daughters

---

[2] Commemorative papers regarding celebrations, schools, expeditions, garden clubs, etc., named in his honor were displayed in the collection at the Academy of Natural Sciences' Bartramania exhibit in 1941 (Peck and Stroud, *A Glorious Enterprise*, 285).

[3] Oviedo y Valdes resided in the West Indies from 1526 until 1546. Bartram may have had access to his writing and also that of John White from Virginia. Later works by earlier southern colonial explorer Mark Catesby and other naturalists were available to Bartram. See Reveal, *Gentle Conquest*.

and five sons. William Bartram (20 April 1739–22 July 1823) had a twin sister named Elizabeth and was the third son of John Bartram's second marriage. John called him Billy and allowed Billy to shadow his botanical and horticultural activities at Bartram's Garden. Billy, who was self-taught and talented in drawing and painting, found his subjects in the garden and nature. As a youthful assistant, Billy accompanied his father on his many botanical travels to the Catskill Mountains in New York, to the New Jersey Pine Barrens and, later, to Florida.

Unlike his self-educated father, Billy grew up in a highly intellectual atmosphere. John Bartram's botanical garden was a center for those with horticultural interests; many of the intellectual, social, and political leaders of the day visited. Beginning at thirteen years of age, Billy was schooled at Benjamin Franklin's recently established Philadelphia Academy, where he received a classical education for about four years. According to John Bartram, despite his studies in the classics, drawing and botany remained Billy's "darling delights."[4] Although John had other plans for Billy that did not involve art and botany, he also proudly shared Billy's artwork and acquired commissions for Billy from English patrons, who were frequently impressed with Billy's work. All the while, John planned for Billy to become a merchant and leave his "darling delights" behind.

When Billy was eighteen, Benjamin Franklin offered him a position as an apprentice printer. After Billy failed in this pursuit, he then began training as a merchant, where he also failed. He also tried to establish a career as an independent trader while living at his uncle's plantation named "Ashwood" on the Cape Fear River in North Carolina. Billy was unhappy and unsuccessful in this work, and he continued studying natural history and creating artwork with the hope of attracting support from financial backers and escaping his life as a merchant. When John became the royal botanist, Billy happily accepted his father's offer to assist in exploring Florida to pursue his "darling delights."

Royal Botanist Travels to Florida

On 1 July 1765, royal botanist John Bartram sailed on the schooner *East Florida* from Philadelphia to Charleston, South Carolina, where he explored Southern botanicals and horticulture. He also conducted meetings and local excursions with his friend and colleague Dr. Alexander Garden, as well as other prominent local gardeners and botanists. This was the first stop along

---

[4] See Slaughter, *The Natures…*, 120.

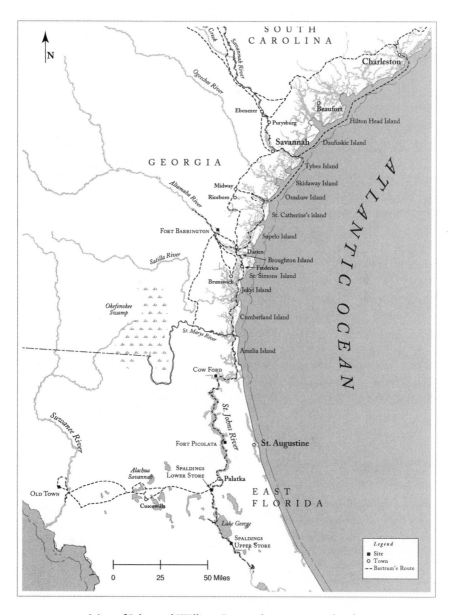

Map of John and William Bartram's journey to Florida.
Courtesy of Brad Sanders.

Bartram's journey to his detailed assignment in East Florida. A week later, Bartram rode over a hundred miles northward to his brother's home near Cape Fear, North Carolina, where twenty-six-year-old Billy was also living. John and Billy then spent several days on long excursions exploring elements of the local natural history, including plants, animals, and fossils, after which time Billy returned with John to Charleston. Late that August, the *South Carolina Gazette* announced, "Mr. Bartram, his Majesty's botanist for North America...set out, accompanied by his son (who is an excellent draughtsman), for Georgia, and East and West Florida, intending also to go as far back of those countries as the Indian nations may permit him."

Over the next three weeks, John and Billy traveled to Savannah by way of Cowpens, South Carolina. They made several observations along river bluffs and a silk farm, where John collected plant specimens, fossils, and various insects and mollusks while Billy drew. After catching up on their writing, art, and mail in Savannah, they made several informational side trips at Collinson's and Franklin's request. By the end of September, John and Billy were on their way to St. Augustine.

To St. Augustine

On the journey from Savannah to St. Augustine, the Bartrams made their most noteworthy discovery at a site several miles from Fort Barrington near the Altamaha River although they did not know it at the time. In detailed diary accounts largely concerning plant life (along with notes about the weather, soils, fossils, and social events), John Bartram mentions in a single entry[5] on 1 October 1765, "this day we found several very curious shrubs."[6] The plants were not in bloom, making identification difficult. It would be another decade before Billy collected their flowers during a return visit and named one of the "curious shrubs."

John and Billy continued their journey with a three-day stopover at Fort

---

[5] JB, "Diary of a Journey," 13–49. The three editions of Stork's work on East Florida (1767, 1769, and 1774), *An Account of East-Florida* served as Harper's source for entries from 19 December 1765 to 12 February 1766.

[6] One of these "shrubs" is now known as "Franklinia" or "The Franklin Tree" (scientifically, *Franklinia altamaha*). During Billy's later solo exploration of the Southeast from 1773–1776, Billy returned to this location on the Altamaha River to draw the blooming Franklinia's elegant white flowers and to collect its seeds for propagation in Bartram's Garden (see *WBT*, 467–68, and chapter 2 of this book). By 1781, he had grown flowering plants and later assigned the "rare and elegant flowering shrub" to a new genus *Franklinia* in honor of his deceased father's friend, Benjamin Franklin.

Barrington on the Altamaha River. As part of his assignment, John assessed the rice-growing conditions of that area and also in other locations during their travels. He observed a "rare tupelo with large red acid fruit called limes which is used for punch," likely the earliest botanical reference to the white tupelo or Ogeechee lime tree (*Nyssa ogeche*).

On 8 October, the Bartrams crossed the St. Mary's River, which separated the Georgia and East Florida colonies, and continued on, observing the landscape's transition to groves of cabbage palm trees (*Sabal palmetto*), which John called "tree palms." Two days later, they crossed the St. Johns River at Cowford, a cattle crossing near the mouth of the river, and "lodged under a big pine" in the sparsely settled area that is now Jacksonville, Florida. Finally, they reached the primary site of their future explorations: the St. Johns River and its surrounding valley, which they would soon survey while seeking the river's Southern origins.

In St. Augustine

John and Billy Bartram continued along the St. Augustine Road, which ran parallel to the east bank of the St. Johns River. The land became poorer, with stunted trees and miserable grass, all of which John mentioned in his journal. On 11 October they reached St. Augustine. The following day, they dined with East Florida Royal Governor James Grant and discussed their plans to explore the local area and the St. Johns River. During the next several days, they caught up on their correspondence, explored the town and the main fort of Castillo de San Marcos, and botanized several miles northwest to the old Fort Mose (or Mosa, as it was called at the time).[7]

Several days later, John Bartram unexpectedly became ill, shaking with the chills and fevers of malaria. He was ill for a few weeks and suffered a relapse following a day in the field on 21 October. By 1 November, he was feeling much better; his fever did not recur, but he was cautious. Throughout his recovery, John dined frequently with the governor and made only short field trips with Billy. John arranged to attend a meeting on 13 November at Fort Picolata, some eighteen miles from St. Augustine on the St. Johns River, with the governor and others at a congress with the Creek Indians. During their stay at Picolata, John and Billy attended the treaty meeting, often taking breaks to explore areas near the St. Johns River by canoe and to look for plants in the coves and swamps connected to the river. On the last day's jaunt, Billy

---

[7] This fort was fortified by free runaway slaves during the First Spanish Period. Fort Mose was rediscovered in the 1980s by Kathleen Deagan and Jane Landers and has become a Florida State Historic Park (see Deagan and MacMahon, *Fort Mose*).

killed a monstrous rattlesnake. They carried it back to the Fort at Picolata and enjoyed a hearty meal of snake meat at dinner that night with the governor.

For the next several weeks, the Bartrams lingered at St. Augustine as John regained his strength and prepared for the strenuous exploration that Governor Grant was eager for him to undertake: discovering the unknown headwaters of the St. Johns River. The governor, in turn, offered to cover all the trip's expenses, including the cost of a boat, guide, and cook.

Up the St. Johns River

While the Bartrams were eager to proceed on their journey, they prudently waited until John had regained his strength completely. John noted in his journal:

> December 20th. Set out for Robert Davis's, whose son the Governor had ordered to take us up to search for the head of the river St. John's; and having necessaries provided, I, my son William, Mr. Yates, and Mr. Davis, embarked in a battoe; Mr. Davis was not only to conduct us, but also to hunt venison for us, being a good hunter, and his Negro was to row and cook for us all, the Governor bearing our expenses.[8]

By 28 December, the Bartrams had explored several springs that fed the St. Johns, evaluated the land for which individuals who hoped to undertake farming had petitioned the king, and stayed overnight at Spalding's Lower Trading Store, six miles south of Palatka. The following day, as they entered Little Lake George, they passed by a huge shell mound that John named "Mt. Hope." He noted that shells were evidence of "the common planting grounds of the former Florida Indians."[9] On the St. John's west bank, they investigated a more imposing Indian mound with a view upriver to Lake George, which John named "Mount Royal." Later, they found groves of bittersweet oranges. John's diary entries during this portion of the Bartrams' exploration were very detailed about agricultural and economic development issues, with a natural history flair: "saw many alligators, and killed one; 'tis certain that

---

[8] JB, "Diary of a Journey," 36. A "battoe" or bateau or batteau is a shallow-draft, usually flat-bottomed boat. The Bartrams' was a large "dugout" canoe shaped from a cypress log. Also, when Bartram indicates travel "upriver" or when he refers to a site as "above," he means the direction generally to the south; similarly, when reference is made to "downriver" or "below," the direction is to the north. The St. Johns is one of the several major rivers in the world that runs north.

[9] Ibid., 38.

both jaws open by a joint nearly alike to both."[10]

Through rain, fog, and chilly days, the Bartrams made their way up the river, surveying its meandering coves, measuring its temperature and depth, and making onshore observations about the plant life and soils: essentially a preliminary ecological survey. By New Year's Day, they had reached Spalding's Upper Trading Store, about fifty miles upriver from the Lower Trading Store. As they continued, the river narrowed with many incoming tributary streams. They took a detour to explore a creek, ending up at what is now called Blue Springs. John named a nearby shell mound "Mount Joy," at present-day Blue Springs landing.[11]

By 10 January 1766, it was becoming more difficult for the Bartrams to determine the course of the main river, except by its gentle current flow. At their stop overnight near Lake Harney, Bartram noted:

> The wolves howled, the first time I heard them in Florida; here we found a great nest of a wood rat, built of long pieces of dry sticks, near 4 foot high and 5 in diameter, all laid confusedly together; on stirring the sticks to observe their structure, a large rat ran out, and up a very high sapling with a young one hanging to its tails.[12]

Two days later, the Bartram party reached a cluster of lakes along the St. Johns, including Ruth Lake and Clark Lake. Here they found that reeds and water plants blocked their further passage. John wrote, "January 12. Fine clear morning; thermometer 44. Set out, and rowing…shoaling gradually until the weeds and reeds stopped our battoe in such a manner, that it was impossible to push her any farther.… We returned to the rich hammock where we lodged last night." The next morning, John wrote, "January 13th. Fine pleasant morning; thermometer 54. Set out homeward from the rich hammock, the highest up the river we could land at."[13]

John mistakenly thought that Ruth Lake and Clark Lake were one body of water with several islands on its south end. Soon after they rowed out into the main channel of the St. Johns, their battoe came to an obstructed area, which forced them to return to the previous night's campsite (Baxter Mound). John wrongly assumed that they had reached the point of origin for the St. Johns River; the following morning, they began their return journey.

---

[10] Ibid., 39.

[11] Ibid., 40.

[12] Ibid., 41. The Florida rat was the subject of future scientific study by William Bartram in *WBT* (1791) and Academy of Natural Sciences members George Ord and John Audubon during their respective Florida expeditions in 1818 and 1831.

[13] JB, "Diary of a Journey," 42.

Today, Bartram's impassable point is found near a highway running between Indian River City and Orlando. The true source of the St. Johns is much further south, along a winding channel and wetlands that are still impenetrable (except by airboat) in an unnavigable, unpopulated area called St. Johns Marsh located in Indian River and Okeechobee Counties, north of Lake Okeechobee. The Bartrams were among the first Americans or English to explore this area of the upper St. Johns.

After further exploration of the lakes and their tributaries, the Bartrams returned by way of the St. Johns' western riverbanks, with occasional river crossovers, since they had come up on the eastern side. At some locations, such as Mount Royal, they lingered to expand upon their earlier observations; at others, John's diary entries recorded entirely fresh findings. Near Picolata, a familiar place, they explored the nearby navigable creeks and local vegetation before traveling further downriver to Cowford, the narrow river cattle crossing, arriving on 8 February. After a few days in Cowford, they resumed their travels to the mouth of the St. Johns near Fort George Island, where they visited a planter friend for two days. Following this detour, they returned upriver to the home of their guide, John Davis. From there, John and Billy rode on horseback to St. Augustine, completing their eight-week journey.

In St. Augustine Again

For the next month, with the support of Governor Grant, John converted his diary entries and many of Billy's observations of natural history information into a travel diary, spanning 19 December 1765 to 12 February 1766. Their finds included a unique Florida rat, rattlesnakes, alligators, pests, and geographic information that would prove useful for future landholders of Florida plantations. John prepared a map of the St. Johns to guide prospective investors to choice sites. He shipped 259 plant specimens to England for the king's herbarium. The governor sent John's journal to London where it was incorporated into the second edition of Dr. William Stork's *A Description of East-Florida, with a Journal Kept by John Bartram of Philadelphia, Botanist to His Majesty for the Floridas; upon A Journey from St. Augustine up the River to St. John's as far as the Lakes*, published by the Board of Trade and Plantations in 1766.[14] The manuscript was widely read in Britain and fanned the flames of "Florida Fever" that prompted numerous aristocrats and merchants to acquire land for plantations in East Florida.

---

[14] A copy later owned by Clarence B. Moore is now in the library of the Academy of Natural Sciences.

While John planned to return to Philadelphia by way of Charleston, Billy had other ideas; he wanted to stay in East Florida, become a planter, and pursue his interests in nature and art. The following month, John and Billy took several short trips around the area, looking for more plants to document and identifying places where Billy might start a plantation. Although Gerard de Brahm, a cartographer surveying the area, offered Billy work as a draftsman as an alternative, he was set on the idea of becoming a planter. Billy was mesmerized by the opportunities for Florida farming and further exploration although he had no aptitude or previous experience. As in the past, however, John was supportive, though he groused to others about Billy's "frolic."

Billy in Florida

John Bartram sailed for Charleston, arriving on 22 March. He spent twenty busy days caring for his plant collections, completing other parts of his journal, and studying the plant specimens and seeds in preparation for shipping to Peter Collinson. John also purchased six slaves for Billy and arranged for their passage to Florida. In addition, John secured seed crops for Billy and sent him cash, along with detailed instructions for preparing twenty-five acres for planting. John ordered barrels of provisions to support Billy and his slaves during their startup period. Before leaving St. Augustine, John had ordered common garden seeds, two cows, a mare, and a colt for Billy's enterprise. John relied on Collinson for financial credit, and as he wrote later, after returning to Philadelphia, "I have left my son Billy in Florida. Nothing will do him now, but he will be a planter upon St. John's River. This frolic of his, and our maintenance, hath drove me to great straits; so that I was forced to drawn upon thee, at Augustine, and twice at Charleston."[15]

Billy remained in Florida as the owner of a five-hundred-acre British Land Grant plantation on the east side of the St. Johns River, across from present-day Green Cove Springs.[16] John received regular accounts about Billy, who seldom wrote himself. Stories often conveyed concerns about Billy's health and his plantation enterprise. The most reliable was that Billy had abandoned his plantation after six months, worked briefly for de Brahm on a survey near New Smyrna, and was then shipwrecked and missing after trying to sail to Philadelphia. This information left John Bartram and his

---

[15] John Bartram to Peter Collinson, June 1766, Berkeley and Berkeley, *The Life and Travels of John Bartram*, 265.

[16] Billy's plantation on the St. Johns is now marked by an historic Bartram Trail marker.

family in a state of uncertain grief until news arrived months later that Billy had abandoned his plantation and was safe in St. Augustine.

Billy in Transit; Again to Florida

After less than a year in Florida, Billy returned to Philadelphia and confirmed his ill-fated experiences. He settled in at his father's home and garden, where he pursued his art and botanical work while also attempting various types of manual and business-related work. During this time, Billy's financial indebtedness became very serious, and he left home two years later in an attempt to flee his debtors, returning to his uncle's plantation in North Carolina. In mid-1772, Billy wrote to his parents that he had spent the year there reviewing his past and planning his future. He had concluded that his interests, namely, drawing and studying nature, were the business pursuits he should follow. He was therefore determined to get back to Florida. John replied, in no uncertain terms, that the idea was ridiculous and that Billy should return home where family and friends could help him find a way to support himself.

Billy sent a similar letter with his new plans and some enclosed drawings to Dr. John Fothergill in England. This letter fell on more receptive eyes. Fothergill was a close friend and associate of Collinson and had been a patron and customer of John Bartram for a very long time. Fothergill's gardens were among the most highly regarded in England, and John Bartram was his principal plant supplier. Fothergill admired Billy's artwork and had often purchased or commissioned his drawings. Although Fothergill was always supportive of Billy, he was cautious to ensure that his funding advanced Billy's talents rather than his seemingly romantic ideas. He commissioned Billy to return to the Floridas to collect seeds and plants offered him an annual allowance and oversight by a mutual colleague in Charleston. Fothergill separately paid for many incidentals, such as shipping costs and the cost of many of Billy's accurate drawings from life as well as of animals and plants. Enthusiastic about the opportunity, Billy briefly returned to Philadelphia to prepare for his new enterprise. On 20 March 1773, at the age of thirty-four, he sailed from Philadelphia to Charleston to begin his assignments and to return to the Floridas.

CHAPTER 2

DO YOU KNOW BARTRAM'S *TRAVELS*?

"The attention of a traveller, should be particularly turned,
in the first place, to the various works of Nature."[1]

—William Bartram

An eager William Bartram left Philadelphia in 1773 determined to explore East and West Florida and unaware that his exploration, writings, art, and the 1791 publication of his famous *Travels through North & South Carolina, Georgia, East & West Florida...* would influence more than two centuries of Southeastern United States explorers.

Bartram's eloquent descriptions of Florida's natural history comprise about half of *Travels* and have made it a classic. The frontispiece engraving of "Mico Chlucco, the Long Warrior or King of the Siminoles" is among the first published portraits of a Native-American chieftain. A map of the East Florida coast is depicted on the opposite page of the opening chapter, and the illustrations in *Travels* display many engravings of Florida's plants and animals. These salient features and Bartram's rapturous accounts of Florida contributed to Thomas Carlyle's later inquiry of Ralph Waldo Emerson, "Do you know Bartram's *Travels*? Treats of Florida chiefly, has a wondrous kind of floundering eloquence in it; and has grown immeasurably old.... All American libraries ought to provide themselves with that kind of book; and keep them as a future biblical article."[2]

When published, Bartram's remarkable work embodied the cutting edge of science reporting and offered detailed Linnaean taxonomies of plants and animals, narrative adventure, and poetic overtones. The images of Florida in particular enchanted an international readership. Young American naturalists were intrigued and inspired by Bartram's scientific descriptions of plants, animals, and their habitats, and the questions he raised in *Travels* continue to stimulate new generations.

---

[1] *WBT*, li.

[2] *Correspondence of Thomas Carlyle and Ralph Waldo Emerson*, 2:198.

Patron of William's Florida Exploration

Due to his talent and interest in drawing, William Bartram's observations from fieldwork conducted in 1765–1766 with his father, Royal Botanist John Bartram, during their Florida exploration (1765–1766) were so effective that they impressed Peter Collinson and Dr. John Fothergill. These distinguished British patrons and friends of John Bartram had long observed and admired "Billy" Bartram's developing talents in natural history art. Fothergill, in particular, responded favorably to William's proposal to return to Florida, an idea that John Bartram had found ridiculous.[3] Dr. Fothergill agreed to pay William "any sum not exceeding 50 £ per Ann…to collect and send to me, all the curious plants and seeds, and other natural productions that might occur to him…I would make him allowance for his drawings, proportional to their accuracy. Birds, reptiles, insects, or plants should be drawn on the spot."[4] William noted that Fothergill requested he "search the Floridas and the western parts of Carolina and Georgia, for the discovery of rare and useful productions of nature, chiefly in the vegetable kingdom."[5]

Compared to his father, William was a more romantic observer who celebrated wild nature and its creatures. He applied a literary approach to observation and writing gained from his classical education to the study of animals, the relationships between living organisms, and their interactions with the natural or human-altered environment. By contrast, John Bartram used his self-taught business style to focus his interests on the more practical horticultural and agricultural aspects of plants and botany, which required accurate soil and climate observations along with taxonomic expertise. Their notes and reports reveal William's broad biological interests; his true genius was transforming his notes and reports into his classic *Travels,* a project that was neither on Dr. Fothergill's agenda nor a requirement.

At the beginning of William's journey, Fothergill provided detailed instructions to "draw the flower and a leaf or two, carefully on the spot, and mark the outline of the branch or shrub. The rest may be finished at leisure. The same may be done with any other article of Natural history that deserves

---

[3] Hallock and Hoffmann, *William Bartram: The Search for Nature's Design*, 82–86. This work is hereafter abbreviated as HH.

[4] Dr. Fothergill to Dr. Lionel Chalmers, 23 October 1772, in WB, "Travels…: A Report," 126. Dr. Chalmers of Charleston was the fiscal agent in Fothergill's dealings with William (HH, 87–88).

[5] *FHBT*, 1; WBT, 1.

notice."[6] As was William's spirit, he corresponded and traveled at will. Fothergill often queried John Bartram and others about William's whereabouts as William was available only when he contacted Dr. Lionel Chalmers, Dr. Fothergill's agent in Charleston, South Carolina, when in need of funds.

In addition to collecting specimens, illustrating, and making notes, Fothergill asked William to "keep a little journal, marking the soil, situation, plants in general, remarkable animals, where found, and the several particulars relative to them as they cast up.—Land & river shells will be acceptable, as also any rare insects,"[7] and also expected a written report. However, Bartram had complete freedom in the style of his notes and report and sent the collected specimens, brief reports, and illustrations to Dr. Fothergill but often kept duplicates for himself.

William followed his inclinations and interests while exploring the Southeast, employing a "seize the opportunity" approach. For example, he observed about his brief trip to the West Florida capital of Pensacola, "My arrival…was merely accidental and undesigned."[8]

There are many conflicts in the dates and the chronology of Bartram's excursions among his several narrations as reported in *Travels,* in William's report to Dr. Fothergill; a letter to his father, and a draft manuscript.[9] Bartram's original field notes might clarify the differences, but they have not been found. However, Francis Harper and many scholars have confirmed that the timetable and course of Bartram's Florida exploration differed from the account published in *Travels.*[10] In *Travels,* Bartram often combined the details of several "short excursions" with great narrative effectiveness and presented the story as one long expedition. At times, Bartram's ill health and fevered confusion or mistakes about his exact location also may have produced inaccuracies about dates and places, or he, his editor, or publisher may have lacked interest in the detail. Fortunately for those today who wish to follow Bartram's tracks chronologically, Harper and others have provided annotated guides and dates.[11]

---

[6] WB, "Travels…: A Report," 121–42; HH, 84–86.

[7] HH, 84–86.

[8] *FHBT,* 262; *WBT,* 414.

[9] WB, "Travels…: A Report," 121–42; *FHBT,* 353; HH, 110–12, 302–39.

[10] Harper's scholarly and field work about Bartram's exploration are presented in ch. 14. Pertinent references for the current chapter are *FHBT, WBT.*

[11] Peck, *Bartram Heritage*; Sanders, *Guide to William Bartram's Travels*; Kautz, *Footprints Across the South*; Spornick, Cattier and Greene, *An Outdoor Guide to Bartram's*

Bartram's Travels Begin

William Bartram left Philadelphia on 20 March 1773, for Charleston to meet Dr. Fothergill's representatives before sailing to Savannah.[12] From there, Bartram continued south to the St. Mary's River and then northwest to Augusta, returning to Savannah first each time.[13] His year of exploration in East Florida began in late March or early April 1774.

Either before or after traveling to East Florida, William explored the vicinity of the Altamaha River and Fort Barrington. This was the site where he and his father had collected and "observed a curious shrub" (see page 13), which William now found to be "in perfect bloom!" These plants produced camellia-like, cup-shaped, five-petaled, sweetly fragrant white flowers; some were even "bearing fruit."

Bartram collected appropriate specimens for his herbarium—branches, flowers, leaves, seeds, seed pods/capsules—and made many sketches and drawings. He kept some samples himself and sent the rest to Fothergill. William later named the plant *Franklinia*, in honor of Benjamin Franklin.[14] Bartram's herbarium sheet for the species eventually became housed at the British Museum as the "type" specimen.[15] The plant was last reported in its native

---

Travels; *The Bartram Trail, National Scenic/Historic Trail Study,* 2012, National Park Service (NPS).

[12] Sanders, *Guide to William Bartram's Travels*, is an unparalleled book of detailed site descriptions and detailed maps covering all of Bartram's travels in East, West, and contemporary Florida. One of William's final acts before sailing involved executing a slave deed on this date. It was exhibited at the Academy in 1941–1942 and is in ANSP Archives, coll. 15, JB Papers.

[13] The St. Mary's River is a remote black water stream located in southeastern Georgia and northeastern Florida that forms the easternmost border between the two states.

[14] In chapter 9 (*WBT*, 467–68), William discusses the rediscovery of Franklinia in bloom and its elegant white flowers, the "rare and elegant flowering shrub" to a new genus *Franklinia*, named in honor of his deceased father's friend Benjamin Franklin. The new plant name *Franklinia altamaha* was first published by his cousin, Humphry Marshall, in *Arbustrum Americanum* ([Philadelphia: Joseph Cruikshank, 1785] 48–50). William later wrote in his *WBT* about the discovery of Franklinia.

[15] In biology, a "type" is one particular specimen (or in some cases, a group of specimens) of an organism to which the scientific name of that organism is formally attached. The type is the reference specimen for all characteristics of the organism, many of which are published over time as new discoveries in microscopy, molecular biology, and other techniques for examination become available to investigators. Every attempt is made to deposit and curate a type specimen over time in a museum for future studies.

habitat in southern Georgia in 1803 and is now extinct in the wild. Fortunately, William propagated some of the seeds that he had collected in Bartram's Garden, rescuing Franklinia for posterity as a cultivated plant. There are several current theories about the extinction of Franklinia in the wild.[16]

In March 1774, William did not follow the overland route he and his father had taken from Savannah to Florida in 1765. Instead, he writes, "I left my horse in Georgia, & went down the Alatamaha, to Frederica on the Island St. Simons.... Mr. Spalding who was pleased to give me Letters to his Agent in East Florida & in a few days went onboard his Vessell bound to his Store on St. Johns."[17]

Bartram's expedition and his observations in East Florida are well documented in his report to Dr. Fothergill and in part 2 of *Travels*.[18] He explored West Florida in fall 1775. As Bartram reflects in the opening section on his Florida travels, his plans often went amiss: "We are, all of us, subject to crosses and disappointments, but more especially the traveller."[19]

To Florida

While in Georgia in 1774, Bartram sent most of his belongings ahead in a "Chest onboard a small vessel bound for the River St. John" before embarking for East Florida. Although his ship was delayed, he arrived at Amelia Island and set out on foot to explore East Florida, observing, sketching, writing, and collecting.[20] Upon reaching Cowford, on the St. Johns River, he

---

For some of Bartram's discoveries, no specimen is available; therefore, his drawings and illustrations have been designated as the "type."

[16] It is not known why Franklinia disappeared in the wild. One theory is that a cotton pathogen in the soil caused the plant's extinction. Other extinction theories include a decline because of past climate change, destruction by man, a lack of genetic diversity in the colony of plants to withstand pathogens, or changing conditions, or a local disaster (flood or fire).

[17] James Spalding entertained Bartram at his plantation in Frederica on St. Simon Island. Spalding was a "gentleman carrying on a very considerable trade...furnished me with letters to his agents residing at this trading house, ordering them to furnish me with horses, guides and every other convenient assistance" (*WBT*, 57–8; *FHBT*, 37); WB to JB, Charleston, 27 March 1775, Archives, Bartram Papers 1:78, HSP; WB, "Travels...: A Report," 181. Bartram made collecting excursions around the island.

[18] *FHBT*, li–lxi, 37–194; WB, "Travels...: A Report," 121–241.

[19] *WBT*, 57; *FHBT*, 37.

[20] Sanders, *Guide to William Bartram's Travels*, 96–134.

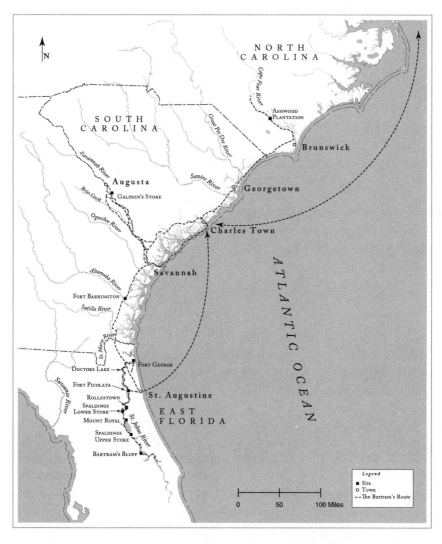

Bartram's Southeastern travels (1773–1776) into East Florida.
Courtesy of Brad Sanders.

purchased a small sailing skiff. Bartram wasted no time in continuing his up-river trip, and he wrote, "My little vessel being furnished with a good sail, and having fishing tackle, a neat light fusee, powder and ball, I found myself well equipped, for my voyage, about one hundred miles to the trading house."[21]

He traveled southward up the St. Johns River, with brief side ventures, to his first base camp, Spalding's Lower Store. Along with other traders, William made two longer trips from the Lower Store to Spalding's Store near the Alachua Savanna (or Payne's Prairie, as it is now generally called) and to Spalding's Store in Talahasochte, near the Suwannee River ("Little St. Johns") and Manatee Springs. He also made excursions to Spalding's Upper Store on the St. Johns River and beyond, exploring many locations that he had previously visited with his father during their expedition. William collected, sketched, and wrote extensive notes about the creatures he saw and their habitats for his report to Dr. Fothergill.

During Bartram's voyage along the St. Johns River, his meager provisions were supplemented by food he procured through hunting, fishing, and stopovers at welcoming plantations.[22] "Oranges and evergreens...evergreen commonly called wild lime" grew profusely along the river banks. At his overnight stops, turkey cocks and hens were abundant, and he "barbecued them for provisions." He also encountered a few Indian settlements and English plantations along the way, which often had orange groves with hundreds of trees "in perfect bloom, and loaded with ripe golden fruit," and acres of indigo, corn, and potatoes. Bartram was always diligent in his scientific responsibility to Fothergill, "having in the course of the day collected a variety of curious specimens of vegetables, seeds and roots"[23] at various river stops and "making drawings of such curious subjects as could not be preserved in their native state of excellence."[24]

When reading and following Bartram's travels, one must keep in mind that Bartram's official job was to explore and collect primarily botanical specimens to be forwarded to Dr. Fothergill, who assigned the task of identifying and describing them to Daniel Solander, an accomplished Swedish botanist residing in England.[25] Bartram and Fothergill agreed that Bartram could keep

---

[21] *WBT*, 74; *FHBT*, 48.

[22] *WBT*, 76–78; *FHBT*, 49–51.

[23] *WBT*, 304; *FHBT*, 193.

[24] *WBT*, 48; *FHBT*, 31.

[25] Daniel Carl Solander (1736–1782), a student of Linnaeus, traveled to England

duplicate specimens and sketches as he wished, along with his other collections, which he later shipped to Philadelphia.[26]

To the Lower Store

While sailing up the St. Johns River to Spalding's Lower Store, Bartram stopped at Fort Picolata, where he and his father had witnessed the Congress of the Creek Indians during their first stay in St. Augustine (page 15). William and his father had briefly explored the area by boat, and William killed his first "monstrous rattlesnake." However, during his current visit, as he noted in *Travels*, "but to my disappointment, [I] found the fort dismantled and deserted."[27] Walls and ruins were all that remained of the buildings that had been made of carved coquina rock quarried from Anastasia Island near St. Augustine.

Continuing upriver on the "West or Indian shore," Bartram passed an Indian settlement at the present site of Palatka. He later observed that the "Live Oaks are of an astonishing magnitude," and he weaved an enchanting scientific and cultural narrative about the trees and their importance: "wood almost incorruptible...the acorn...is food for almost all animals...Indians...eating them as we do chestnuts."[28] He documented vast islands of floating water lettuce: "Pistia stratiotes, a very singular aquatic plant."[29] In *Travels*, William's unique scientific yet literary narrative flows like river breezes, infused with scientific summaries of plants.

After describing the abandoned towns of Charlotia and Rollestown on a high eastern bluff, William arrived at his destination: Spalding's Lower Store, which was on the west side of the river, about six miles southwest of present-day Palatka at the current Stokes Landing.[30] The Lower Store,

---

in 1760 to promote the new Linnaean system of classification. In 1763 he began cataloguing the natural history collections of the British Museum and was elected Fellow of the Royal Society the following year. He served as a librarian at the British Museum, identified plants for John Bartram, and worked for Dr. Fothergill on the curation and taxonomy of William Bartram's plants. Solander's work on the Bartram collections was interrupted by his travels with Joseph Banks and Captain Cook. William Bartram's specimens became part of the collections of the Natural History Museum (London).

[26] WB, "Travels... A Report," 130.

[27] *WBT*, 80; *FHBT*, 52.

[28] *WBT*, 85; *FHBT*, 54–55.

[29] *WBT*, 88; *FHBT*, 57.

[30] Rollestown was founded in 1765 by a wealthy eccentric, Denys Rolle, who attempted to develop the area with imported indentured servants and later slaves. It is now East Palatka.

managed by Charles McLatchie, served as a distribution point for Spalding's inland trading houses at Alachua and Talahasochte and for the river's Upper Store, which was managed by Job Wiggens and his Indian wife. At the Lower Store, Bartram received his trunk, which he had forwarded with Spalding's traders. In the months ahead, the Lower Store would serve as his headquarters as he explored the upper St. Johns River, the Alachua Savanna region, and the Suwannee River near Talahasochte.

Complexities of Bartram's Travels

The chronological course of Bartram's exploration differed from the account published in *Travels*. In late April, soon after William arrived at the Lower Store, he traveled over land with several traders to the Alachua Savanna (as he described later in part 2, chapter 6). He returned to the Lower Store weeks later and, from mid-May to June, explored the St. Johns River to Mount Royal, Lake George, and Spalding's Upper Store, and then arrived once more at the Lower Store (as detailed in *Travels'* part 2, chapters 4 and 5). From mid-June until July, starting from the Lower Store, he went over land with traders, returned to the Alachua Savanna (his second visit to the area), and then proceeded on to the Suwannee River, the Seminole town of Talahasochte, and Manatee Springs (in *Travels'* chapters 6 and 7), finally returning to the Lower Store. From August through September, he further explored the St. Johns River to the vicinity of Lake Beresford (also in chapters 4, 5, and 8) and returned to the Lower Store. Rather than following in Bartram's chronological tracks (as in his report to Dr. Fothergill and various correspondence), our story continues Bartram's exploration as he narrates it in *Travels*, including information and quotes from the report and correspondence with various recipients that describe the separate trips.

To the Upper Store

In part 2, chapter 4 of *Travels*, Bartram left Spalding's Lower Store in May and traveled upriver on the St. Johns.[31] On this expedition, as on others, Bartram accompanied traders or, occasionally, traveled with a companion. The traders were a varied group; some worked for Spalding, transporting goods from the Lower Store to other Spalding stores, and also independently traded goods with natives, explorers, and settlers. At times, Bartram was

---

[31] The present account from *WBT* must be considered a composite of two trips up the St. Johns to the vicinity of Lake Beresford. The first trip was in May and June; the second took place in August and September 1774. These two trips are described separately in "Travels... A Report."

towed along the river by a trader's larger boat, but he often broke away and journeyed solo, rejoining the traders at a later date. His river travels reminded William of his earlier exploration with his father:

> The traders with their goods in a large boat, went ahead, and myself in my little vessel followed them...ran by Mount Hope, so named by my father John Bartram, when he ascended the river, about fifteen years ago...a very high shelly bluff...at that time a fine Orange grove...now...a large Indigo plantation...In the evening we arrived at Mount Royal.[32]

William's description of Mount Royal in *Travels* incited great interest in the archeological site, which continues to this day[33]:

> About fifteen years ago I visited this place, at which time there were no settlements of white people, but all appeared wild and savage; yet in that uncultivated state it possessed an almost inexpressible air of grandeur, which was now entirely changed. At that time there was a very considerable extent of old fields round about the mount...what greatly contributed towards completing the magnificence of the scene, was a noble Indian highway...about fifty yards wide.... Neither nature nor art could anywhere present a more striking contrast.... The glittering water pond played on the sight, through the dark grove.... But the venerable grove is now no more. All has been cleared away and planted with indigo, corn, and cotton but since deserted.... It appears like a desert to a great extent.

Bartram, however, offered future hope in his musing: "...that the late proprietor had some taste, as he preserved the mount and this little adjoining grove inviolate. The prospect from this station is so happily situated by nature, as to comprise at one view the whole of the sublime and pleasing." Bartram concluded with one of his many lengthy epiphanies (and extended prayers) in *Travels*: "May these my humble and penitent supplications, amidst the universal shouts of homage from thy creatures, meet with thy acceptance! ...Thus may we be worthy of the dignity and superiority of the high and

---

[32] *WBT*, 98–101; *FHBT*, 64–65. Mount Royal is one of the Southeast's most famous archeological sites and, along with Crystal River, among the most well-known sites in Florida. The two Timuncuan mounds were first named "Mount Royal" by John Bartram in 1766. His and William's observations stimulated scientific interest in the site over time, and extensive excavations late in the nineteenth century by ANSP archeologist Clarence B. Moore were continued by others into the twenty-first century. Moore's early artifacts were deposited at the ANSP and most recently became treasures of the Smithsonian's National Museum of the American Indian.

[33] Milanich, *Famous Florida Sites*; Milanich, "Clarence B. Moore," 113–33.

distinguished station in which thou hast placed us here on earth."[34]

William included detailed estimates about the size of the mound and the length and placement of the road in his correspondence and report to Dr. Fothergill. He also provided descriptions of the vegetation, the lake, and its origins, "& seems to have been dug out by the Indians, & perhaps the earth came a way to raise the mound with."[35]

Bartram's departure from Mount Royal was delayed a day due to heavy storms, which intermittently continued for two days as he navigated Lake George to arrive at Spalding's Upper Store. Today, the site of the Upper Store is at present-day Astor, on the west side of the St. Johns, about five miles upstream from Lake George.

Further Up the St. Johns

After a two-week stopover at the Upper Store, William Bartram began his sixty-mile journey upriver to the Beresford Plantation at the invitation of its gentleman agent and resident. Bartram "resolved to pursue my researches to that place."[36] His research focused on what he termed "ferocious crocodiles" and rich natural areas with many unique plants and birds.

Bartram's first campsite was about three miles upriver, near Lake Dexter. He noted in his writings, "crocodiles began to roar and appear in uncommon numbers along the shores and in the rivers." Upon discovering that his provisions were low, he decided to fish among a grove of aquatic plants that "were excellent haunts of trout."[37] In his quest for food, he found himself competing with "the subtle greedy alligator. Behold him rushing forth from the flags and reeds."[38] When the alligator discovered another alligator, "his rival champion," Bartram notes, "a terrible conflict commences…folded together in horrid wreath…their jaws cling together." His "apprehensions were highly alarmed after being a spectator of so dreadful a battle."[39]

As he attempted to make his way back to camp from his fishing expedition, Bartram "was attacked on all sides, several [alligators] endeavoring to overset the canoe…two very large ones attacked me closely, at the same instance, rushing up with their heads and part of their bodies above the water, roaring terribly and belching floods of water over me." Bartram used a club

---

[34] *WBT*, 98–101; *FHBT*, 64–65.

[35] WB, "Travels… A Report," 151.

[36] *WBT*, 114; *FHBT*, 73.

[37] Based upon his earlier description, the trout were actually largemouth bass.

[38] *WBT*, 117–22; *FHBT*, 75–77.

[39] *WBT*, 123–28; *FHBT*, 78–81.

to fight the alligators off but, as he made his way back, he was harassed as he landed and tried to secure his fish. Retrieving his gun, Bartram "dispatched him [the alligator] by loading the contents of my gun in his head." Later, after starting his fish boiling for supper, from a river inlet promontory William observed a school of fish being caught and swallowed by alligators. Bartram's drawing of alligators, along with his descriptions of bellowing and the text in *Travels*, remained controversial into the twentieth century.[40] Early readers of *Travels* regarded the "clouds of smoke" from the animal's nostrils and the savage attack on Bartram as his fanciful exaggeration. However, later observations confirmed these descriptions were not improbable.[41]

Returning to camp, Bartram encountered two bears helping themselves to the dinner that he had started cooking earlier and left simmering and warm. Fortunately, the flash of fire from his gun, which had misfired, frightened the beasts away. On a quieter note, that night his sleep was disturbed by "wood-rats running amongst the leaves." Bartram's descriptions of the Florida wood rat[42] and its dwelling had been mentioned by his father during their earlier trip (page 16); in 1818, the Wood rat would be detailed in the scientific literature (pages 89–91) stimulated by the observations of and with reference to the Bartrams.

As William Bartram continued upriver, he remarked many times about alligator nests and eggs as he explored their general breeding places and nursery grounds.[43] These observations gave way to his descriptions and collections of plant materials as well as "resting and refreshing myself in these delightful shades."[44] As he "left them with reluctance," Bartram spotted "here in this river and in the waters all over Florida, a very curious and handsome species of birds; the people call them Snake Birds."[45] In addition to the snake bird, or anhinga, William's descriptions included, "types"[46] of Florida birds, such as the Florida Limpkin, "two species" of "Spanish curlews," the "wood pelican," Bartram's still unknown "Vultur sacra," and many others.[47]

---

[40] Magee, *The Art and Science of William Bartram*, 108–109.

[41] *FHBT*, 356.

[42] *WBT*, 124–25; *FHBT*, 79; WB, "Travels…: A Report," 41. Nest with young as described by John Bartram.

[43] *WBT*, 126–31; *FHBT*, 80–83.

[44] *WBT*, 132–33; *FHBT*, 84.

[45] *WBT*, 132; *FHBT*, 84.

[46] "type" (see note 15 above).

[47] Florida birds are frequently cited. A cluster of descriptions occurs (*FHBT*, 93–97), including limpkin, Spanish curlew, wood pelican (wood ibis), and two species of

While in Lake Beresford, Bartram weathered a violent storm ("hurricane") and arrived at the Beresford Plantation in such condition that "my friend was affrighted to see me."[48] He remained at the plantation for three days: "indeed it took most of the time of my abode with him, to dry my books and specimens of plants."[49] In *Travels*, Bartram digresses from Beresford to describe his earlier visit to New Smyrna, about thirty miles east of the plantation.[50] Bartram also had time for a trip from Beresford to Blue Springs (about four miles), which Bartram had visited in 1765 with his father. Blue Springs, the southernmost stop of Bartram's journey, remains the largest spring in the St. Johns River Basin. As Bartram reported, "It boils up with great force.... This tepid water has a most disagreeable taste, brassy and vitriolic, and very offensive to the smell...."[51] He correctly identified the cause of the odor as "owing to vitriolic and sulphureous fumes." From Blue Springs, Bartram began his return downriver.

Downriver Return

Enchanted by the green meadows during his passage downriver, Bartram was "determined not to pass this Elysium without a visit."[52] The sight was spectacular: "Behold the loud, sonorous, watchful savanna cranes (grus pratensis) [Florida sandhill crane] with musical clangor, in detached squadrons." He described in an eloquent narrative the flight of the sandhill cranes, which he later observed near the Alachua Savanna.

Further along, he saw and again reported (this time in more detail) the Florida limpkin, "a very curious bird...called...the crying bird. I cannot determine what genus of European birds to join it with."[53] Earlier on his voyage, he had named and eaten the "type" specimen of limpkin. Bartram's drawing

---

vultures. A list of birds (with notes) seen from Pennsylvania to Florida (*FHBT*, 180–88) includes "the little jay of Florida" (scrub jay) and jackdaw (grackle), among others. Bartram's "*Vultur sacra*" or painted vulture, has continued to stimulate ornithological interest since the bird has never been observed by anyone other than Bartram. See Snyder and Fry, "Validity of Bartram's Painted Vulture (Aves: Cathartidae)," 61–82.

[48] *WBT*, 141–43; *FHBT*, 89–90.

[49] *WBT*, 143; *FHBT*, 91.

[50] After abandoning his Florida plantation in 1766, Bartram spent time there while he was briefly employed by Gerard De Brahm and subsequently shipwrecked near the coast.

[51] Blue Springs is now Blue Springs State Park (*FHBT*, 92).

[52] *WBT*, 146; *FHBT*, 93.

[53] *WBT*, 147; *FHBT*, 93.

of "The Crying Bird," published by W. P. Barton in 1818, serves as the type.

Near Lake Dexter, Bartram observed, "What a beautiful display of vegetation is here before me! Seemingly unlimited in extent and variety…behold the azure fields of cerulean Ixea!"[54]

Bartram's seven-word description of the Ixia—"behold the azure fields of cerulean Ixea"—and his illustration with descriptive notes in *Travels* constitute the original reference for the plant now known as *Salpingostylis coelestinum* (Bartram) Small.[55] The "Bartram's Ixia" was apparently first discovered by the Bartrams in 1765–1766, drawn by William, and circulated by his father with a descriptive essay, "Purple Flower'd Ixia of St. Johns River East Florida."[56] However, after William's second visit, it was not until 1931 when Dr. John K. Small rediscovered the rare endemic near Lake Dexter where other explorers located the plant. Even today, the species is difficult to find and seldom seen because of its rarity and unusual blooming habits. The type locality has now been fixed near the shores of Lake Dexter.

At one stop, before reaching the Upper Store, Bartram "made ample collections of specimens and growing roots of curious vegetables, which kept me fully employed the greatest part of the day."[57] At Spalding's Upper Store, he "continued a few days at this post, searching its environs for curious vegetable productions, collecting seeds and planting growing roots in boxes, to be transported to the lower trading house."[58]

Bartram's return to the Lower Store included his "Elysian" encampments along the way. "I found myself alone in the wilderness of Florida, on the shores of Lake George,"[59] he wrote, interrupted one night by wolves that snatched the fish hanging over Bartram's sleeping head near Silver Glen Springs.

As a preface to his extended on-shore observations and lists of plants and trees in "the open forests," William noted, "As I intended to make my most considerable collections at this place, I proceeded immediately to fix my encampment but a few yards from my safe harbor."[60]

---

[54] *WBT*, 155; *FHBT*, 98.

[55] *WBT*, 360; *FHBT*, 155.

[56] *WBT*, 98, 360; HH, 68–69; Small, "Bartram's *Ixia coelestina* Rediscovered," 57–66. This is discussed in detail in ch. 14 along with other references.

[57] *WBT*, 155; *FHBT*, 98.

[58] *WBT*, 156; *FHBT*, 99.

[59] *WBT*, 158; *FHBT*, 100.

[60] *WBT*, 160; *FHBT*, 101.

In *Travels,* Bartram blended his account of Silver Glen Springs ("Johnsons Springs") and Salt Springs ("Six-mile Springs"), with details from his first and second trips and, undoubtedly, memories of his earlier visit with his father.[61] The result was Bartram's "amazing crystal fountain [Salt Springs]…a continual and amazing ebullition, where the waters are thrown up in such abundance and amazing force, as to jet and swell up two or three feet above the common surface."[62] Bartram described the wonders of life in which "the water or element in which they live and move, is so perfectly clear and transparent." Bartram's description of Salt Springs influenced the poet Samuel Coleridge's imagery in "Kubla Khan."[63]

The following day, William Bartram "employed the fore part of the day in collecting specimens of growing roots and seeds." In the afternoon, he "left these Elysian springs, and the aromatic groves" for his return; "called at Mount Royal, where I enlarged my collections…arrived in the evening at the lower trading house."[64]

To Alachua Savanna

Bartram's description of his exploration of the Florida interior in chapter 7 of *Travels* combined his two trips to the Alachua Savanna with his trip to Talahasochte.[65]

Unlike his St. Johns exploration, which was primarily a solo venture, his land travels usually included "an old trader, whom Mr. McLatchie had delegated to negotiate with Cowkeeper and other chiefs of the Cuscowilla, on the subject of reestablishing trade."[66] The "old trader" was one of five traders in the party en route to the destination trading stores that Spalding had established in Alachua and Talahasochte.

---

[61] *WBT,* 157–68; *FHBT,* 99–107, 361.

[62] *WBT,* 165–6; *FHBT,* 103–104. The springs described by Bartram are groundwater that gushes into basins of white sand and limestone, partly free of vegetation except for underwater gardens. The force of the groundwater at the spring's opening creates loose sand "boils" as the water shoots forth, and concentric ripples form at the spring's surface water. Water flows from the spring basin, which varies in size up to a small lake, in a "run" to a nearby waterway. Florida has more freshwater springs than any other area of comparable size in the world. See Whitney, Means, and Rudloe, *Priceless Florida,* 233–44.

[63] Magee, *The Art and Science of William Bartram,* 135–37.

[64] *WBT,* 169; *FHBT,* 107.

[65] See Sanders, *Guide to William Bartram's Travels,* 122–29.

[66] *WBT,* 179; *FHBT,* 108.

Bartram's route to the Alachua Savanna was through dry pine barrens with its rolling sand hills. As he observed, many plants and animals were well adapted to the Florida scrub and sand hills. One of his first sightings was a species of jay; "they are generally of an azure blue color, have no crest or tuft of feathers on the head, nor are they so large as the great created jay of Virginia, but they are equally clamorous...."[67]

Bartram's "jay without a crest" or "Bartram's Little Jay," as it was initially commonly called, is now known as the Florida scrub jay and was scientifically named and studied in detail (page 85) in 1818." Like many of the plants and animals mentioned in *Travels*, the Florida scrub jay is endemic to the unique Florida habitat that Bartram described. With the disappearance of this scrub habitat through modern development, many of the plants and animals that relied on scrub have now become threatened, endangered, or extinct.

The scrub habitat once occurred throughout Florida on ancient sea and river dunes of well-drained sand—similar to beach sand. Rain easily percolates the soil into aquifers. Development has now restricted the scrub to small patches.[68] As Bartram noted, the scrub has a similar appearance to deserts. However, unlike a desert, the subtropical rains make the climate very humid and permeate the sand where they drain through the limestone substructure. Several types of scrub are characterized by their predominant plants: rosemary, oak, and pine. Bartram described the open patchy rosemary scrub, where only drought-resistant plants and burrowing animals can survive: the partially shaded twisted oak scrub, and the forested, shady sand pine scrub. Snakes, skinks, and lizards swim through the beach-like scrub sand. The gopher tortoise, described by Bartram as a "great land tortoise, called gopher," creates burrows that provide homes for mice and frogs. About half of all the plant and animal species in the scrub areas Bartram explored are endemic to Florida and are among the region's rarest species. In fact, today the central Florida ridge has more rare and endangered species than any other habitat in North America.[69]

The account Bartram gives in *Travels* of proposing to name the "gopher" as "Testudo Polyphaemus" constitutes the type description of the gopher tor-

---

[67] *WBT*, 172–73; *FHBT*, 109.

[68] Ocala National Forest and the Central Florida Ridge are the largest interior scrubs remaining. Remnant spits and dunes occur in the Florida Panhandle and along the coasts.

[69] Whitney, Means, and Rudloe, *Priceless Florida*, 67–83.

toise (*Gopherus polyphaemus*). Southeastern Alachua County is the type locality established by Bartram's writing for this ancient burrowing land tortoise.[70]

The ease Bartram had in observing reptiles, amphibians, and fishes along
his overland route—in scrub, sand hills, lakes, and sinkholes—provided
many plant and animal lists and reports, but difficulties in preserving the
specimens limited their collection. However, he captured many animals, as
well as plants, in his artwork. Bartram's written descriptions of color and illustrations of live or fresh specimens are still valuable today; the colorful, soft
body parts of animal and plant specimens in museums discolor over time,
and often the artwork and notes are the only surviving records of uncollected
specimens. In addition to his detailed drawings, he mused in detail about the
"Great Yellow Bream of the St. Johns": "What a most beautiful creature is
this fish before me! gliding to and fro...of a pale gold (or burnished brass)
colour, darker on the back and upper sides; the scales...powdered with red,
russet, silver, blue, and green specks...a warrior in a gilded coat of mail."[71]

In many cases, for example, the "Soft-shelled Tortoise" and the "great
land tortoise, called gopher," Bartram described the creatures in scientific detail and commented on their edibility. Interspersed with these scientific descriptions and culinary observations are Bartram's musings:

> At the return of the morning, by the powerful influence of light, the pulse
> of nature becomes more active, and the universal vibration of life insensi-
> bly and irresistibly moves the wondrous machine. How cheerful and gay
> all nature appears! Hark! the musical savanna cranes, ere the chirping spar-
> row flirts from his grassy couch, or the glorious sun gilds the tops of the
> pines, spread their expansive wings, leave their lofty roosts, and repair to
> the ample plains.[72]

As Bartram and the traders continued on to Alachua Savanna, the group
arrived in the Indian village of Cuscowilla (near Lake Tuscawilla and present-

---

[70] *WBT*, 182–83; *FHBT*, 116. The gopher tortoise is a large terrestrial turtle that
possesses forefeet adapted for burrowing and elephantine hind feet, features common to
most tortoises. Still widespread in Florida and the southeast, they are a threatened species
due to habitat destruction and disease. They are a "keystone species" since their burrows
provide shelter and homes for between 300–400 other animal species such as frogs,
rodents, insects, and other creatures living in similar habitats.

[71] *WBT*, 153–54; *FHBT*, 97.

[72] *WBT*, 179; *FHBT*, 114. Another muse captures the questions naturalists raise
about Bartram's scientific observations in his musing. See Bennett, "Flight of Savanna
Cranes," in *A Celebration of John and William Bartram*, 14–15.

day Micanopy). They were warmly greeted and invited to pursue their business with the council and the chief called Cowkeeper. On learning of Bartram's mission, Cowkeeper "saluted me by the name of PUCPUGGY, or the Flower Hunter, recommending me to the friendship and protection of his people."[73]

In the following days, Bartram experienced another great epiphany when he beheld the Alachua Savanna.[74] He returned to Cuscowilla and described the village in considerable detail, an action later appreciated by generations of ethnologists and anthropologists.

Bartram studied the Alachua Savanna (now Payne's Prairie) on several passes and on many paths while visiting the traders' various destinations, "enjoying the like scenes we had already past." He rhapsodized, "On the first view of such an amazing display of the wisdom and power of the supreme author of nature, the mind for a moment seems suspended, and impressed with awe."[75] His writing and drawings of the savanna are among his finest and most detailed about any area.[76]

Bartram wrote the first description of the Florida wolf, along with observations about snakes, birds, deer, and their behavior. The "Great Sink," located on the northeastern border of the savanna, about three miles southeast of present-day Gainesville, was of geological interest to Bartram, who documented it as follows:

> These hills, from the top of the perpendicular, fluted excavated walls of rock, slant off moderately up to their summits, and are covered with a very fertile loose, black earth, which nourishes and supports a dark grove.... These high forest trees surrounding the bason...so effectively shade the waters, that...we seem at once shut up in darkness and the waters appear black, yet are clear.... But that which is most singular and to me unaccountable, is the infundibuliform cavities, even on the top of these high hills.... In and about the Great Sink are to be seen incredible numbers of crocodiles, some of which are of enormous size...taking up fish, which continually crowd in upon them from the river and creeks, draining from the savanna....[77]

---

[73] *WBT*, 183; *FHBT*, 118.

[74] *WBT*, 187–90; *FHBT*, 119–22.

[75] *WBT*, 120–21.

[76] Ibid., 119–32.

[77] *WBT*, 204–205; *FHBT*, 129–30.

Lakes and ponds occur during rainy seasons in Florida wherever there are basins, which hold water in their centers. The lakes and ponds vary in size, water quality, etc., depending on the surrounding soils and ecosystems (e.g., whether they are connected to streams). There are sand hill lakes, clay-hill lakes, swamp lakes, flatland lakes, and ponds.[78]

A wet "sinkhole," such as observed by Bartram, is a hole in which groundwater is visible because it intersects the water table. The limestone underlying the ground gives way, and an opening is created, which often becomes vegetated. The sinkhole basin is connected to underground channels and caves filled with water.

After exploring the sink, Bartram and the trading party returned to the previous night's camp. The next day, they started back to the Lower Store and "fell into the old trading path" that they had followed during their outward journey.

To the Suwannee River and Talahasochte

Back at the Lower Store, Bartram found the trading company for the Suwannee River (also called Little St. Juan's, Little St. John's, Suannee) preparing for its departure.[79] He journeyed by horseback with the party to the Suwannee River and the village of Talahasochte beginning in the middle of June 1774; the trip lasted for about twenty-five days. Bartram's three descriptions of the course of the trip vary and disagree on the campsites and daily progress.[80]

In the *Travels* account, the trading group followed the same route they had previously taken to the Alachua Savanna. From there, they probably visited Blue Sink, near present-day Newberry, and then traveled on to Talahasochte (its presumed site is on the banks of the Suwannee at the current Ross Landing within the Andrews Wildlife Management Area). Their mission was to reestablish active trade with the Creeks and Seminole Indians at the Spalding store.

Arriving at "the town of Talahasochte, on the banks of Little St. Juan," Bartram proclaimed,

---

[78] Whitney, Means, and Rudloe, *Priceless Florida*, 197–213.
[79] Sanders, *Guide to William Bartram's Travels*, 130–34.
[80] *FHBT*, 358.

The river Little St. Juan may, with singular propriety, be termed the pellucid river. The waters are the clearest and purest of any river I ever saw, transmitting distinctly the natural form and appearance of the objects moving in the transparent floods, or reposing on the silvery bed, with the finny inhabitants sporting in its generally flowing stream.[81]

After settling in at Talahasochte, the traders conducted business with the chiefs who waited for their leader, White King, to return from a hunting trip. When Bartram's interpreter companion suggested "another little voyage down the river," Bartram was very amenable. They set off and "descended pleasantly, riding on the crystal flood." Several hours later, they "approached the admirable Manate[e] Spring.... This charming nympheum is the product of primitive nature, not to be imitated much less equaled by the united effort of human power and ingenuity!" Bartram recorded the "vegetable productions which cover and ornament" the area around the springs, a winter refuge for manatees. He examined the remains of a manatee skeleton and teeth from an earlier Indian food kill and made observations about the manatee's diet and the ivory quality of the bones.[82]

The following day, they explored the area along "the ancient Spanish high road to Pensacola"; in the evening, they returned to Talahasochte at about the same time that White King and his successful bear-hunting party arrived. Seizing the opportunity, Bartram made notes and drawings of the feast, ceremonies, and festivities that followed. White King admired Bartram's drawings and invited him to travel around the leader's whole country at pleasure, collecting "physic plants and flowers, and every other production."[83]

"Next day early in the morning we left the town and the river," and the leader of the trading group led Bartram to a "very curious place, called the Alligator-Hole, which was lately formed by an extraordinary eruption or jet

---

[81] *WBT,* 224; *FHBT,* 141–42.

[82] *WBT,* 230–32; *FHBT,* 373. Manatees were first described during Columbus's first voyage and later called *manati* by the Spanish. Their immense numbers were diminished by hunters who used the flesh, bones, and skin for food and other products. Manatees have no natural predators but are sensitive to cold and spend the winter in Florida springs with connections to the Gulf of Mexico and ocean streams. Manatee Springs is now a Florida State Park. Today, the manatee, Florida's official marine mammal, is an endangered species.

[83] *WBT,* 238; *FHBT,* 150.

of water; it is one of those vast circular sinks, which we behold almost every-where about us as we traversed these forests."[84]

Bartram made drawings and copious notes here and at many familiar places along their return route to the Lower Store, which he added to his report. He also included new drawings after brief encounters with Indian groups along the way, "collecting a variety of specimens and seeds of vegetables, some of which appeared new to me, particularly Sophora, Cistus, Tradescantia...Echium, &c."[85]

Back at the Lower Store

When Bartram arrived back at the Lower Store, "As a loading could not be procured until late in the autumn...I resolved upon another little voyage up the river." His "little voyage" included stopovers—"where I passed the night, but not without frequent attacks from the musquitoes"—and days "increasing my collections of specimens, seeds and roots."[86] Bartram traveled once again to Mt. Royal, to the Great Springs (Salt Springs), and to several half-abandoned plantations, where he lamented the destruction of ancient fruitful orange groves, which had been replaced with indigo, cotton, and other crops. One deserted plantation was that of Dr. Stork, whose *Description of East-Florida* contained an account of John Bartram's 1765–1766 journey. With a final call at Mt. Royal, William returned to the Lower Store, "bringing with me valuable collections."[87]

At the Lower Store, he found a large party of Lower Creeks, "a predatory band of the Siminoles" encamped in the grove. Led by Long Warrior, whose portrait Bartram later painted and published as the frontispiece of *Travels*, the Indians had just arrived from trading in St. Augustine and had stopped both for festivities and to negotiate trade with the Lower Store manager, Charles McLatchie, before setting out to fight their traditional enemies, the Choctaws. A dispute, which Bartram witnessed, arose when McLatchie refused to offer a line of credit to Long Warrior for goods he wished the party to take with them. Later, some young braves frightened Bartram by forcefully entreating "Puc-Puggy (see pg. 36) [cross ref]" to go to their camp to rid it of a rattlesnake, which was taboo for them to kill. After Bartram slew the rattlesnake and secured its head and fangs for future art and collections, with

---

[84] Ibid.
[85] *WBT*, 248; *FHBT*, 156.
[86] *WBT*, 252; *FHBT*, 159, ch. 8.
[87] *WBT*, 160.

"shouting and proclaiming," the Lower Creeks declared "Puc-Puggy was their friend…a sincere friend to the Siminoles."[88]

Rattlesnakes, Birds, and Other Animals

At this point in *Travels*, in chapter 10 in part 2, Bartram elaborates on his recent rattlesnake experience.[89] Although snakes (and the rattlesnake in particular) were taboo for the Seminoles, for Bartram they were "serpents in the garden" and a source of fascination; many colonists were convinced of the "attractive power" of rattlesnakes.[90] Bartram recounted in great detail his other experiences with rattlesnakes, including the time he "killed a monstrous rattlesnake" with his father (page 15.[91] Bartram's depiction of the rattlesnake and his writing about other snakes—moccasins, rattlesnakes, water, green, pine, etc.—preceded, in many cases, their description and technical naming by others. Bartram's published descriptions of frogs and toads in *Travels* are the best account up to 1791.[92] He is credited with the original discovery and description of several species, including the Southern bullfrog, Southern tree frog, Southern cricket frog, and little tree frog although he did not give them technical names.[93] His brief accounts of half a dozen lizards led to technical descriptions and later to their scientific names. In some cases Bartram was credited; he did scientifically name and describe the gopher turtle or tortoise and many mammals that had not previously been validly described. In his summary, Bartram included animals from the later West Florida portion of his travels.

Bartram commented on "some observations on birds," pointing out that the ancients and recent zoologists "have done very little towards elucidating the subject of the migration of birds, or accounting for annual appearance and disappearance, and vanishing of these beautiful and entertaining beings who visit us at certain stated seasons." He used his observations to cite examples that discount or support many popular hypotheses and concluded that

---

[88] *WBT*, 255–63; *FHBT*, 161–66, see ch. 7.

[89] Bartram's drawings are collected in Ewan, *William Bartram, Botanical and Zoological Drawings*, and in Magee, *The Art and Science of William Bartram*.

[90] Irmscher, *The Poetics of Natural History*.

[91] *WBT*, 264–73; *FHBT*, 167–70.

[92] *WBT*, 276–80; *FHBT*, 173–76.

[93] *FHBT*, 377.

"future observation" was needed. In the meantime, he was willing "to contribute my mite towards illustrating the subject."[94] Bartram listed the birds of North America and his observations of their travel patterns, identifying five categories, including those that migrate to Florida from the south, breed, and then return south, and those that are natives of Florida, where they breed and remain year round.

Harper noted, "These pages deserve attention as containing the first serious American contribution to the fascinating subject of bird migration."[95] Bartram's annotated lists of birds that follow, along with miscellaneous observations here and elsewhere in *Travels*, established him as America's foremost ornithologist of the time.[96] Many of the bird names first appeared in *Travels* and then became the subject of nomenclatural discussions in subsequent years.[97]

Completing what Bartram called "these historical observations," he resumed "the subject of our journey." He joined Lower Store manager McLatchie on a short trip "to regal ourselves at a feast of Water Melons and Oranges" at an Indian settlement. Subsequently (in either September or November 1774, depending on the source), "with the vessel being loaded and ready to depart, I got all my collections on board." Bartram returned to Charleston by way of Georgia in March 1775 "to plan my future travels, agreeable to Dr. Fothergill's instructions, and the council and advice of Dr. Chalmers of Charleston, with other gentlemen of that city, eminent for the promotions of science and encouraging merit and industry."[98]

To West Florida

Bartram's plans for further exploration (see map below) included traveling through the Cherokee Nation in the southern Appalachians to Mobile in West Florida and then to the Mississippi River, returning by way of the Cherokee Nation to Charleston and, finally, home to Philadelphia over land.[99] However, while in West Florida, William Bartram became ill. He was severely weakened and was bedridden at times. Poor health notwithstanding, Bartram

---

[94] *WBT*, 288; *FHBT*, 180.

[95] *FHBT*, 377.

[96] Coues, "Fasti ornithologiae redivivi,"—No. 1, Bartram's "Travels," 338–58; Stone, "The Work of William, Son of John Bartram," 20–23.

[97] *FHBT*, 378–79.

[98] *FHBT*, 192–94, 307, ch. 11.

[99] See Sanders, *Guide to William Bartram's Travels*, 250–97.

continued his Gulf Coast travels by boat, eventually reaching the Mississippi River and traveling a short distance up the river. So debilitating was his illness that sometimes Bartram was "incapable of making any observations for my eyes could not bear the light," but he continued collecting and sketching.

As Harper has pointed out, "Bartram does not succeed in recording a single date correctly. The year dates are advanced from one to three years, and even the months are not invariably correct."[100] Possible reasons for these discrepancies include Bartram's fevers and illness, his isolation from others while on the trail, and sloppiness. For example, Bartram visited many towns in the Cherokee Nation during the spring and summer 1775, not 1776 as indicated in the opening of part 3, chapter 1 of *Travels*. By 26 July 1775, Bartram had arrived in Mobile, which was in West Florida at that time.[101]

In September 1775, after suffering symptoms of a fever, "which in a few days laid me up and became dangerous," Bartram made brief excursions around Mobile. He was waiting for a vessel to take him west from Mobile to the Pearl River and "sought opportunities to fill up this time to the best advantage possible."[102] He found a captain who offered passage around Mobile Bay and along the coast "in a light sailing-boat" to "secur[e] the remains of a wreck." Finding the wreck after it had been scavenged of its sails, etc., the captain decided to sail on to Pensacola. As Bartram noted in *Travels*, "My arrival at this capital…was merely accidental and undersigned; and having left at Mobile all my papers and testimonials, I designed to conceal my avocations." However, Dr. John Lorimer, the garrison physician, naturalist, and member of the American Philosophical Society, recognized Bartram, and he was subsequently introduced to Governor Peter Chester of West Florida. The governor entertained Bartram, who noted that Chester "commended my pursuits, and invited me to continue in West Florida in researches after subjects of natural history."[103] Governor Chester offered to pay for Bartram's expenses

---

[100] *FHBT*, 380.

[101] At the time, Mobile was part of British West Florida, as were other areas of modern day Alabama and Louisiana where Bartram traveled. As mentioned in the preface, the focus of the current work is on the natural history areas of the southeast that became the Florida territory of the United States in 1821 and then a state in 1845. The British colonial government was based in Pensacola, and the West Florida colony included the part of formerly Spanish Florida west of the Apalachicola River, plus the parts of French Louisiana that had previously been taken by the British. West Florida thus comprised all territory between the Mississippi and Apalachicola rivers, with a northern boundary arbitrarily set at the 31st parallel north. This northern boundary shifted several times.

[102] *WBT*, 413; *FHBT*, 260–61.

[103] *WBT*, 415; *FHBT*, 262.

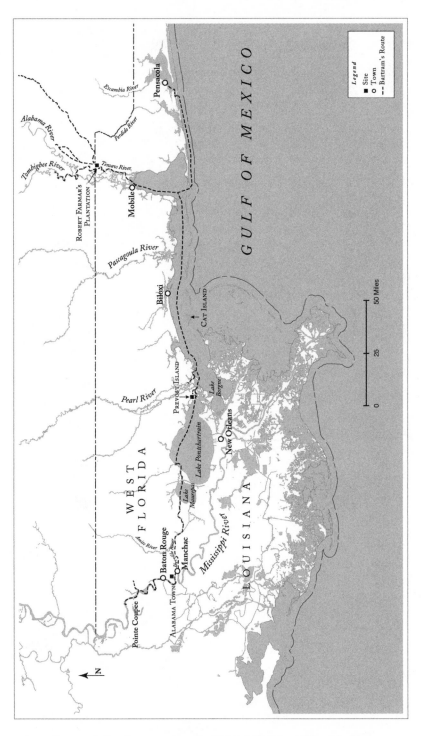

Bartram's Southwestern travels (1773–1776) into West Florida.
Courtesy of Brad Sanders.

and put him up with his own family for as long as Bartram chose to remain. Already committed to collecting specimens for Dr. Fothergill, Bartram declined the governor's offer to survey West Florida's natural history. The governor, however, was pleased to endorse Bartram's missions and wrote a flowery testimonial for Bartram and his efforts. Although Bartram's visit to Pensacola lasted less than twenty-four hours, he described the city in great detail:

> This city is beautifully situated (and commands some natural advantages, superior to any other in this province....There are several hundred habitations in Pensacola: the governor's palace is a large stone building ornamented with a tower built by the Spaniards.... There were growing on the sand hills, environing Pensacola, several curious non-described plants; particularly on of the verticilate order, about eighteen inches in height, the flowers which formed loose spikes, were large and of a fine scarlet colour.[104]

Bartram's description of "a new and very elegant species of Saracinia," a hooded pitcher-plant, characterizes one of his finds during his brief stopover.[105] However, in what Harper calls "a misplaced observation," the discovery was not made at this Pensacola location.[106]

Back to Philadelphia

After returning to Mobile, Bartram became ill and traveled with great difficulty to the Pearl River en route to the Mississippi River.[107] His illness delayed him for a month. He eventually continued to the Mississippi River and then returned to Mobile to ship his specimens and other items to Charleston before traveling back himself in spring 1776 through the Creek territory to Georgia, where he lingered around the Savannah coast.

William reached Philadelphia in January 1777—arriving only months before his father's death in September. Days after John passed, the British occupied Philadelphia and remained there until June 1788. The American Revolution, which William had first heard about during his last days in Georgia, was now underway.[108]

John Bartram left William £200 (the remainder of his inheritance),

---

[104] *WBT*, 415; *FHBT*, 263.

[105] *WBT*, 417; *FHBT*, 264.

[106] *FHBT*, 407.

[107] Sanders, *Guide to William Bartram's Travels*, 298–334.

[108] Cashin, *William Bartram and the American Revolution on the Southern Frontier*.

while his brother John received their father's house and gardens in Kings-essing, where William would live and work for the next thirty-six years. Perhaps because of his health, William never again left Philadelphia and instead spent his time helping restore the gardens, working on the plant side of the horticultural business at Bartram's Garden, analyzing data and specimens from his Southern travels, writing, and mentoring younger naturalists.

CHAPTER 3

FLOWERING OF BARTRAM'S GARDEN

"Bartram was a source of reference to many naturalists of his day, and there was scarcely an American or foreign writer who attempted the natural history of this country but applied to him for information on their relative treatise...."[1]

—George Ord

Following his expedition to the Floridas in 1777, William Bartram returned to his father's home and garden in Kingsessing at the age of thirty-eight. For the next forty-six years, William continued studying and writing about American botanicals. Until his death in 1823, he and his father's famous Bartram's Garden were visited by many distinguished naturalists from Europe, as well as countless aspiring American naturalists who sought William's insights into the natural history of America's Southern frontier. In 1791, William completed and published his famous *Travels*.

Under William Bartram's care, the seeds that were planted in Bartram's Garden sprouted and grew into the flowers of American natural history. Through the efforts of individuals who were intellectually nurtured and influenced by Bartram, the scientific natural history of American plants and animals was first written "in Philadelphia." They created the Academy of Natural Sciences of Philadelphia, and Bartram was its godfather. These early Academy founders were the first generation of American Florida explorers who followed—*in Bartram's tracks*.

William at Work

Soon after William's return from the Floridas, the Bartram family was preoccupied with John's failing health and subsequent death in September 1777. Following his father's passing, William assisted in the family farm and horticulture enterprises. His older brother, John Jr., inherited the family

---

[1] Ord, "Biographical Sketch of William Bartram," in Doughty, *Cabinet of Natural History and Rural Sports*, 67.

property and ran the business. Most of William's inheritance had already been spent on his unsuccessful Florida plantation venture and other debt obligations. While John Jr. continued annual plant-gathering trips in nearby states to renew their supplies, William tended to the written and academic side of the enterprise: writing bills, making plant lists, creating catalogues, and developing plant descriptions. Together, the brothers cultivated the garden and packed seeds and plants for sale and shipment abroad.

William also catalogued the natural history treasures he had gathered during his travels, making inventories and classifying specimens using his and his father's books, or those provided by his correspondents.[2] Although William was named to a professorship at the University of Pennsylvania (1782) and elected a member of the American Philosophical Society (1786), he declined the former, citing ill health, and accepted the latter but seldom ventured into Philadelphia for meetings. During the first several years after returning from Florida, William corresponded with his father's network of colonial colleagues, who were often helpful in his research and studies since the Revolutionary War made it difficult or even impossible to communicate with Europeans. William also published several essays about his findings and continued writing the *Travels* chapters that he had begun in Florida.[3]

Through his work, William Bartram identified 358 plants, 150 of which were unknown to science at the time. Receiving credit for the first discovery of these species, however, was complicated. Numerous species he had discovered while in Florida had since been described and published by others between the time Bartram had collected and recorded them in his journal (1774–1776) and when he published *Travels* in 1791. Although this gave others priority of authorship, in many instances, later revisions of the taxonomic research reassigned credit to Bartram.[4]

The Bartrams' garden business and European trade were interrupted between the end of American-British hostilities in 1781 and the signing of the Treaty of Paris in spring 1783. That year, John Jr. and William issued a printed garden catalogue.[5] The *Catalogue of American Trees, Shrubs and Herbaceous Plants* was a simple, single large-sheet list, a "broadside" of plants and

---

[2] The ANSP possesses at least three works of Linnaeus that Bartram owned and used in the technical naming of plants: *Species plantarum*, 2nd ed., *Systema vegetabilium* (1774), and *Systema naturae* (1758).

[3] HH, 282–94.

[4] Rembert, "The Botanical Explorations of William Bartram in the Southeast"; Volmer, "Planting a New World," 230–36.

[5] Fry, "An International Catalogue of North American Trees and Shrubs," 3–66.

seeds available for sale from their garden. To help his friends and the American cause, Benjamin Franklin arranged for the catalogue to be translated into French and published in Paris. The Bartrams' *Catalogue* was the first printed list of North American plants and one of the earliest known U.S. nursery catalogues. Written by William in Linnaean botanic style, the catalogue described the native plant collection unique to Bartram's Garden.

The Bartrams' 1783 *Catalogue* listed 218 species of plants, most of which had been collected and planted by the senior John Bartram.[6] The scientific nomenclature of American plants listed in this catalogue was one of William's first significant contributions to the field of botany. Although many of the plants are common in Florida and other parts of the Southeast (for example, "Cornus Florida," the flowering dogwood), some were found only in Florida. Indeed, the entry "Dwarf Laurel from Florida" is distinct from another "Dwarf Laurel" entry. So, too, the "Scarlet Oak of Florida" is a unique Florida listing suggesting a different indigenous species. At the end of the list is a note: "Three Undescript Shrubs, lately from Florida." These were probably among William's contribution to the family garden from his travels in the Floridas.

As William wrote about and drew plants and animals that were new to science, many were first described in *Arbustrum Americanum* (1785) by Humphry Marshall (1722–1801). Marshall, a neighboring farmer and relative of the Bartrams, was a botanist, plant dealer, and member of the American Philosophical Society. *Arbustrum* is recognized as the first true American botanical treatise because, as stated on the title page, it was "Compiled from Actual Knowledge and Observations, and the Assistance of Botanical Authors by Humphrey Marshall" about American plants. As indicated by the extended title, *The American Grove, or an Alphabetical Catalogue of Forest Trees and Shrubs, Natives of the American United States, Arranged According to the Linnaean System. Containing, The Particular distinguishing Characters of each Genus, with plain, simple and familiar Descriptions of the Manner of Growth, Appearance, etc. of their several Species and Varieties*, the text targeted a general audience. The book contained "Also, Some Hints of Their Uses in Medicine, Dyes and Domestic Oeconomy." It included an exhaustive list of the tree and shrub "Natives of our United States," as well as a catalogue for botanical clients—a work that implicitly asserted the value of both American flora and science. Although couched in terms of the utility of plants for medicine,

---

[6] Ibid., 3–66; Fry, "John Bartram and His Garden," 155–83.

agriculture, and horticulture, and arranged alphabetically to that end, the *Arbustrum* is a work of advanced science that used the then newest Linnaean taxonomic nomenclature. Marshall referenced Bartram's *Catalogue* and Florida observations, including descriptions of Florida plants with their habitat information. One example of such a description is, "White Poplar, or Cotton-Tree of Carolina (Bartram's Catalog). It grows naturally upon rich lowlands, on the banks of large rivers in Carolina and Florida."[7] Although fewer than a hundred copies of *Arbustrum* sold in the U.S., it attracted great interest in European scientific circles and by 1788 had been translated into French and German.[8]

Bartram, however, made slow progress in publishing his major findings about Florida and the Southeast. After the deaths of Dr. Fothergill in 1780 and Dr. Solander in 1782, Bartram remained uncertain about the fate of the specimens, journal notes, and correspondence that he had sent to London following his travels. In 1788, he wrote an inquiry to Mr. Robert Barclay, Esq., of Buryhill, a friend of the late Dr. Fothergill and patron of British botany, in London and included some specimens:

> I collected these specimens amongst many hundreds others...when on Botanical researches...which I sent to Doctor Fothergill; very few of which I find have entered the Systema Vegetabilium, not even in the last Edition. The number of specimens that I sent were submitted to the examination of Doctor Solander which by returns I received from the Doctor...appear'd most of them to be either New Genera or Species; soon after Doctor Solander deceas'd & Doctor Fothergill soon after followed him. I have never learn'd what became of the specimens.[9]

Bartram's specimens and inquiries to Barclay did not receive detailed replies.[10] However, more than thirty of the plant specimens that Bartram sent are in the British Museum (Natural History) today, along with over two hundred Bartram specimens that came from Fothergill, Solander, and Barclay

---

[7] Marshall, *Arbustrum Americanum*, 19. Refers to the ironwood tree from "Bartram's Catalog," 36–37, dogwood as *Cornus Florida*, 84; "Magnolia Grandiflora. Ever-Green Laurel-Leaved Tulip Tree. This grows naturally in Florida...," 98–99; Olea Americanum, American olive tree, "...grows naturally in Florida," 106; Populus deltoide, White Poplar, or Cotton-Tree of Carolina (Bartram's Catalog) "It grows naturally upon rich lowlands, on the banks of large rivers in Carolina and Florida."

[8] Darlington, *Memorials of John Bartram & Humphry Marshall.*

[9] WB to Robert Barclay, 1788, in HH, 142–49.

[10] HH, 393.

through intermediaries.

A year later, in 1789, William Aiton, gardener to His Majesty at Kew Gardens, described 5,500 species in *Hortus Kewensis*. Among the plants described were specimens from Bartram's expedition that had ended up at Kew Gardens by way of Collinson and Fothergill.[11]

Although many naturalists who visited and talked with Bartram focused on his unique Florida discoveries of unknown plants and animals, many were also interested in the location of his findings, the season of observation, and the association with other known plants and animals. In particular, unique and exotic species were of great interest. While his sensational alligator and bear stories often delighted listeners, they frequently raised questions in the minds of naturalists about the accuracy of his accounts. Many of those who listened to Bartram's stories, saw his drawings, or read *Travels* were inspired to see the unique Florida plants, animals, and landscapes that Bartram described in his words and pictures firsthand. Additionally, some naturalists wanted to verify and expand upon Bartram's observations for scientific purposes.

Bartram's work aroused interest in America's unique natural wonders, particularly among those who were engaged in building Philadelphia's early institutions of education and learning. One individual who was particularly stimulated by Bartram's work was Charles Willson Peale.

Peale's Museum

Charles Willson Peale (1741–1827) was a native of Maryland and a painter of portraits for wealthy patrons throughout Maryland. Peale was a revolutionist and army enlistee, and his enthusiasm for the emerging revolutionary government brought him and his large family to Philadelphia in 1776, where he painted portraits of American notables. Later, through contacts he had made while serving as a captain in the Continental Army, Peale painted a remarkable assemblage of Revolutionary War figures, most importantly, George Washington. After the end of the war, Peale returned to painting full-time and completed the most comprehensive portrait series of Washington ever painted. Peale displayed the paintings in his portrait gallery/studio, which he opened to the public on 18 July 1786.[12]

In 1783, while illustrating mastodon fossils belonging to a portrait client, Peale was inspired by the public's growing interest in natural history and

---

[11] London, 1789.

[12] Richardson, Hindle, and Miller, *Charles Willson Peale and His World*, 193; Sellers, *Mr. Peale's Museum*; Bennett, "The Peales and Science in Philadelphia."

opened an expanded public museum. Visitors to his art gallery, Peale's Museum at the American Philosophical Society, marveled over the various fossils, birds, and insects that he and his family collected and displayed alongside the art. Peale imagined an even greater public undertaking, a "Repository for Natural Curiosities—The Public he hopes will thereby be gratified in the sight of many of the Wonderful Works of Nature which are now closeted but seldom seen."[13] Peale's Museum, which began as a mixture of his portraits of Revolutionary War heroes and an assortment of nature specimens, became a fusion of American heroes and American nature. This amalgam resonated with a citizenry eager to establish a new national identity that would proclaim all American treasures and differentiate the young country from Britain. Similarly, this was Bartram's dream for *Travels*, which he planned to publish in Philadelphia.

As the zoological and archeological collections in the museum grew through Charles Willson Peale's efforts, the members of Peale's large family, including his sons Rubens, Rembrandt, and Titian Peale II (named after Charles's deceased son), followed in their father's trade as curators and museum managers.[14] Bartram's Garden was the Peales' haunt, and William Bartram was their tutor. In 1808, Charles Willson Peale painted the first and only original portrait of Bartram. The artist added it to his gallery of distinguished men.[15]

Bartram's Visitors

In 1777, after William Bartram returned from Florida, his reputation blossomed in the growing scientific community in Philadelphia and among the British. Everyone was interested in and intrigued by Bartram's discoveries, specimens, drawings, and tales about his travels. The publication of *Travels* in 1791 solidified his growing reputation, and William Bartram's scientific legacy began.

After returning from the Floridas, Bartram did not venture far from the garden; instead, everyone came to him. President Washington was interested

---

[13] Sellers, *Mr. Peale's Museum*, 23.

[14] Rubens (1784–1865) was a botanist, mineralogist, and museum administrator. Elected to the Academy in 1813, he managed Peale's Philadelphia Museum from 1810–1822. Later he managed his brother Rembrandt's Baltimore museum and his own in New York. Rembrandt was interested in chemistry and mechanics and in 1814 established his museum in Baltimore and later helped found what is now the Baltimore Gas and Electric Company.

[15] Richardson, Hindle, and Miller, *Charles Willson Peale and His World*, 193.

William Bartram (1739–1823) by Charles Willson Peale, 1808.
Courtesy of Independence National Historical Park.

in plants for his Mount Vernon gardens, and President Jefferson tried to persuade Bartram to join the Lewis and Clark expedition to no avail. William's garden bloomed with dignitaries and distinguished European naturalists. Many enthusiastic and talented young Philadelphia naturalists were interested in William's travels and the specimens he had accumulated. With William's encouragement, his colleagues and students sought answers to many of the scientific questions that his travels had raised about plants and animals, and they continued his work of locating, collecting, naming, and writing about American plants, animals, and geology.

All were impressed by the hard work of William and his brother, John Jr., on behalf of the garden. However, visitors from out of town were often surprised at the Bartrams' disheveled physical appearance. Because William was more knowledgeable about plants and worked in his father's office, he was often mistaken for the proprietor of the garden. However, despite the prestige of the garden, the Bartrams' business, like many in the Philadelphia area, suffered financially because of embargoes and disruptions in shipping during the Revolutionary War period through 1783 and then intermittently during the war with Britain from 1812 through 1815.

André and François Michaux. In 1785, André Michaux (1746–1802), botanist to King Louis XVI of France, arrived in America with his son, François André Michaux (1770–1855), to explore North America for timber resources suitable for the French Navy.[16] At the first of many meetings, Bartram provided André and his sixteen-year-old son with guidance and letters of recommendation. The two men set off, following in his scientific and geographical footsteps, on their botanical explorations in the Southeast and East Florida.[17]

André Michaux established two gardens to propagate and export plants: one near Hackensack, New Jersey, and the other in Charleston, South Carolina. François assisted André during his exploration and later became the keeper of his father's garden in Charleston.[18] His ever-critical father did not suspect that François would surpass him in his achievements in botany and

---

[16] François André Michaux was elected Academy correspondent in 1818. See Ewan, *A Short History of Botany in the United States,* 38–39; Kastner, *A Species of Eternity,* 114–19; Savage and Savage, *André and François André;* Fishman, *Journeys through Paradise;* Taylor and Norman, *André Michaux in Florida,* x–7, 15–7.

[17] For an excellent discussion of Michaux's and Bartram's "tracks" in Florida, see Taylor and Norman, *André Michaux in Florida,* 24–31.

[18] Ibid., 18.

his descriptions of American trees.

Between 1811 and 1819, François André Michaux published his monumental three-volume work, *The North American Sylva*, first in French and then in English. *Sylva* became a classic in American literature and the scientific foundation of American forestry, and it included illustrations by two masters of botanical art: Pierre-Joseph Redouté and Pancrace Bessa.

The Michauxs explored Spanish East Florida from February to May 1788, fourteen years after Bartram's travels. This trip was their southernmost venture in their eleven years (1785–1796) of North American exploration. Walter Kingsley Taylor and Eliane M. Norman have provided a detailed account of the Michauxs' Florida exploration, combining André's original journal with writings about him by later authors.[19] Included in full documentary form are all the plants that the father and son collected and observed in Florida, fully collated with the findings of John and William Bartram.[20] Details about the plants indicated by André Michaux as part of Florida's flora are also summarized.[21] Today, the name Michaux often appears in Florida plant names, from the scientific name of endangered yellow violets that grow wild in the Florida panhandle to the Florida rosemary of the east Florida scrub to southern Florida's Michaux's orchid (*Habenaria quinqueseta*).

The French Revolution (1789–1799) created financial difficulties for André's commercial ventures in the U.S. To escape the financial worries that plagued him, he often took his son to visit William Bartram for a few days of recovery from the exertions of traveling and to engage in discussions about specimens and their observations. In 1790, François returned to England to continue his studies, which had been interrupted, and he returned to the U.S. in 1801. André Michaux remained in America, adding to his collections and garden and shipping young plants and seeds back to France. André returned to France in 1796 and died there in 1802.

Johann David Schöpf. Another traveler to Florida who sought Bartram's guidance was German botanist Johann David Schöpf (1752–1800). Schöpf came to the U.S. in 1777 as a physician to a regiment of German "mercenaries" in the pay of the British Army. After the war ended, he traveled for two years in the U.S., British East Florida, and the Bahamas to study the Americas' natural history. Based on his travels, he produced a two-volume *Travels*

---

[19] Ibid., 64–120.
[20] Ibid., 133–49.
[21] Ibid., 150–84.

in the Confederation (1783–1784) and a treatise on American *materia medica* that recounted his observations.[22] In a chapter titled "East Florida," Schöpf describes his travels along the coast to St. Augustine and mentions plants, fishes, birds, and alligators without providing details. In the following chapter, "St Augustin to Bahama Islands," Schöpf was more technical, particularly in discussing the Gulf Stream, plants, fishes, turtles, and creatures of scientific and economic interest.

During a 1783 visit with Bartram, Schöpf was very impressed by Bartram's growing manuscript about his travels in the Southeast and Florida. Speaking with scientific authority, he encouraged Bartram to publish his work.[23]

Benjamin Smith Barton. A frequent local visitor to Bartram's Garden was Benjamin Smith Barton (1766–1815), an aspiring physician with botanical interests and the nephew of eminent Philadelphia astronomer David Rittenhouse (1732–1796). Barton frequented the garden during his early studies at the College of Philadelphia and immediately became one of William Bartram's disciples.[24] After completing his American studies, Barton studied medicine at the University of Edinburgh, combining his interest in botany and other areas of natural science with medicine. He left Edinburgh under a dark cloud related to his failure to return funds borrowed from the Royal Medical Society and did not complete his degree.

While in Scotland, Barton tried to convince William Bartram to seek an English publisher for his book about his natural history travels and attempted to establish himself as a coauthor to enhance his minor reputation. Since Bartram wanted to encourage Barton's interest in botany, he often acceded to Barton's many requests for information and illustrations for his publications. However, Bartram wanted his book published in America by Americans. Although Bartram began his work as a British citizen and was sponsored by British patrons, he developed an intense American pride after the American Revolution. He also managed to avoid co-authorship with Barton.

---

[22] Schoepf, *Travels in the Confederation (1783–1784)*, 224–51. See also the original German citation in the bibliography.

[23] *FHBT*, xxi.

[24] Ewan and Ewan, *Benjamin Smith Barton*. The College of Philadelphia was a colonial college founded in 1744 that became, along with Franklin's Academy and his vision, part of the University of Pennsylvania. Technically, the College joined with the University of the State of Pennsylvania in 1791 and thus became the University of Pennsylvania (see www.archives.upenn.edu/histy/features/1700s/penn1700s.html).

In 1789, after returning to Philadelphia, Barton practiced medicine. He was also elected professor of natural history and botany at the College of Philadelphia in 1790. When the college and its medical school became a part of the University of Pennsylvania in 1791, Barton became professor of *materia medica*. At the time, the scientific study of medicinal drugs and their botanical sources were integrated into medical studies. Through his publications, Barton preserved many observations and illustrations that Bartram himself did not take the time and effort to publish. At the same time, Barton, much to his credit, persisted in encouraging Bartram to publish his explorations in the South.

Travels, *1791*

Thomas Hallock, Nancy Hoffman, Joel Fry, and others have thoughtfully detailed Bartram's long and arduous path of authorship after returning to Bartram's Garden in 1777 and before publishing *Travels* in Philadelphia in 1791.[25] The British blockade of the port of Philadelphia curtailed Bartram's correspondence, and the Revolutionary War and the deaths of Dr. Fothergill and Daniel Solander interrupted Bartram's taxonomic work on his plants. As a result, his writing and the recognition of his discoveries were substantially delayed.

Bartram wrote several short articles for various publications and authored unpublished tracts on slavery and Native Americans. He kept journals and also his "Garden Book," in which he recorded the weather, species of birds that visited the garden, and comments about garden visitors.[26] William also maintained a pharmacopoeia, a book describing the medicinal value of plants he had studied. Some of Bartram's drawings were published by Barton in his works, and others were completed for Alexander Wilson and François Michaux.[27] Although Bartram remained interested in the development of the natural sciences, he did so away from the public and academic arenas.

By 1783, Bartram had completed a draft of *Travels* and also shared many of his botanical and zoological findings with correspondents and the public through a plant catalog.[28] Bartram first attempted to publish *Travels* in 1786 through the Philadelphia publisher Enoch Story, Jr., but failed to attract the

---

[25] HH, 118–58, 282–93. See also *FHBT*, xx–xxviii.

[26] Fairhead and Hoffmann, "William Bartram's Garden Calendar," 462–80.

[27] Hallock and Fry, "Preliminary List of Illustrations by William Bartram," 499–514.

[28] HH, 5.

needed subscribers to fund it. Finally, in 1790, with initial interest in subscriptions shown by President George Washington, Vice-President John Adams, and Secretary of State Thomas Jefferson, James and Johnson issued a second proposal to publish *Travels*. Bartram dedicated the book to Pennsylvania governor Thomas Mifflin, and it was published in Philadelphia, as Bartram, true to his devotion to the Revolutionary cause, wanted. However, William expressed dissatisfaction with the first edition of *Travels*, in which he found many errors, specifically in the spelling of scientific names. Bartram's *Travels* was published in London in 1792 and simultaneously in Berlin and Vienna in 1793 in German as *William Bartram's Reisen...*

William Bartram's *Travels*, and its numerous editions and interpretative reprints, is read for many different reasons, including its scientific, ethnographic, and poetic content, and is often quoted in many forms of literature. Scholars of the history of botany, zoology, ethnography, and modern ecology pay tribute to William Bartram for his significant contribution to these various disciplines. His influence is seen in the writings of the great Romantic poets Samuel Coleridge and William Wordsworth. William Bartram is often regarded as a pioneer in ecology; a radical rather than a conservative in his politics, nationalism, and religion; and a Romantic or Spiritualist instead of a man of the Enlightenment. It is difficult to say how aware Bartram was of his influence or whether he intentionally wrote for a specific readership. For commercial reasons, he accepted the Long Warrior, Seminole frontispiece at his publisher's request, rather than a sandhill crane or mockingbird. His statement of purpose in *Travels* speaks to the author's complexity:

> I am continually impelled by a restless spirit of curiosity in pursuit of new productions of nature, my chief happiness consists in tracing and admiring the infinite power, majesty, and perfection of the great almighty Creator, and in the contemplation, that through divine aid and permission, I might be instrumental in discovering, and introducing into my native country, some original productions of nature, which might become useful to society.[29]

Bartram's Influence Grows

Andrew Ellicott. With the successful publication of *Travels*, Bartram influenced many through his Florida exploration and observations. Some, like Andrew Ellicott, studied and used Bartram's work but did not have the same extended access to his company and attention as Benjamin Barton, Thomas

---

[29] Rembert, "The Botanical Explorations of William Bartram in the Southeast," 4.

Say, Alexander Wilson, George Ord, and others.

Andrew Ellicott (1754–1820) was a U.S. surveyor who helped map many territories west of the Appalachians, surveyed the boundaries of the District of Columbia, and completed the plan for Washington, D.C. He also taught survey methods to Meriwether Lewis and studied astronomy and mathematics. In 1796, Ellicott was appointed by President George Washington to head a survey commission to define a boundary line between the U.S. and Spanish possessions in Florida. Ellicott met with Bartram and followed *Travels* in his fieldwork. Like several others, including John James Audubon (see ch. 8), Ellicott took exception to Bartram's "Florida as an Elysium." In a letter from Pensacola to his wife, Ellicott wrote,

> This country is hot both day and night, and cursed with poverty, and muskittoes;—The inhabitants of this town have to import earth to make their gardens with. What Bartram has described as a Paradise appears to me like purgatory, but somewhat worse! A Principality would not induce me to stay in it one hour longer than I can possibly avoid it.—If it had not been for pride I would certainly have ran away from it six months ago. It might do for a place of Banishment.[30]

Nevertheless, Ellicott agreed with Bartram's narrative about Pensacola, describing the place as remarkably healthy and Pensacola Bay as a beautiful body of water replete with various fine fishes, crabs, and oysters. Ellicott concluded his letter that the harbor was "justly considered one of the best on the whole coast."[31]

Ellicott experienced another fifteen months of adventure and another four hundred miles of work on the international boundary before returning to Philadelphia. As conflicts between the Indians and the settlers worsened, Ellicott navigated around the Florida peninsula and north to Savannah. His journals describe the difficulties of transporting his surveying instruments by canoe during his Florida travels.[32]

Benjamin Barton Revisited. Several years later, in 1803, Barton, who had continued a close relationship with William Bartram, published *Elements of Botany, or Outlines of the Natural History of Vegetables.* In preparing the first American textbook on botany, as with all his work in natural history and

---

[30] Mathews, *Andrew Ellicott*, 169–70.

[31] Ibid.

[32] Ibid.; Bedini, "Andrew Ellicott, Surveyor of the Wilderness," 113–35; Ellicott, *The Journal of Andrew Ellicott*. Ellicott was elected an Academy member in 1818.

botany, Barton was often assisted by Bartram, who provided information about North American plants as well as "the greater number of" illustrations for Barton's book. "A species of Convolvulus from Florida" is among the twenty-seven plates of illustrations made by Bartram for Barton's *Elements*.

For this and Bartram's other contributions, Barton paid homage in his acknowledgment:

> The greater number of Plates, by which the work is illustrated, have been engraved from the original drawings* of Mr. William Bartram, of Kingsessing, in the vicinity of Philadelphia. While I thus publicly return my thanks to this ingenious naturalist, for his kind liberality in enriching my work, I sincerely rejoice to have an opportunity of declaring, how much of my happiness, in the study of natural history, has been owing to my acquaintance with him; how often I have availed myself of his knowledge in the investigation of the natural productions of our native country; how sincerely I have loved him for the happiest union of moral integrity, with original genius, and unaspiring science, for which he is eminently distinguished. "Sero in coelom redeat."[33]

Barton's credentials were impressive although controversial. As a member and officer of the American Philosophical Society, Barton became a leader in Philadelphia scientific circles and a confidant of Thomas Jefferson, and he was honored with many awards.[34] Barton had established the trust of Jefferson, to whom he had dedicated a book on Native-American languages and after whom he had named a plant. However, Barton's medical credentials from England were questionable, particularly his lack of a medical degree. Furthermore, he engaged in acquisitive academic pursuits, often not crediting other contributors or even blatantly stealing data, both of which alienated many of his American and Edinburgh colleagues, including Charles Willson Peale and some of the aspiring younger American naturalists, such as Alexander Wilson and Thomas Say. Peale noted that Barton "never scrupled to take the feathers of others to enrich his own plumage."[35] The American Linnaean Society, which Barton founded in Philadelphia in 1803, consequently had a short life. Many who revered Bartram disdained Barton; they believed he took

---

[33] Barton, *Elements of Botany*, x–xi. This line translates as "It is too late to return to heaven."

[34] Graustein, "The Eminent Benjamin Smith Barton," 423–38. His older brother, William Barton, was also a member of the American Philosophical Society. His maternal uncle, David Rittenhouse, served as the Society's second president after the death of founder Benjamin Franklin in 1790.

[35] Miller, *The Selected Papers of Charles Willson Peale*, 5:420–24, 515n.

advantage of their teacher, mentor, and generous supporter.

However, Barton did thank Bartram effusively in *Elements of Botany*. Barton also stimulated and mentored a new generation of American botanists, including G. H. E. Muhlenberg, John Torrey, William Baldwin, William Darlington, and others who later became members of the Academy of Natural Sciences of Philadelphia. Barton's *Elements of Botany* long remained the textbook for American botany. In addition, his forays into archeology and ethnology resulted in other major works.[36]

William Baldwin. Barton often took his medical students to visit William Bartram and the botanical garden as part of their studies. For William Baldwin (1779–1819), the visits to the Bartram garden confirmed his lifelong interest in botany and lasting admiration for Bartram. When Baldwin moved to Georgia as a naval surgeon, he botanized on the Florida-Georgia border, with occasional ventures into Spanish Florida to confirm and extend Bartram's plant findings, as will be discussed in chapter 6.

Bartram's Students.

Although William's international renown grew after the publication of *Travels,* his daily activities in the garden changed very little. He continued to mentor friends, aspiring naturalists, and amateurs interested in natural history. Many of these naturalists would become founders and developers of the Academy and would go on to explore Florida's natural history.

Alexander Wilson. Alexander Wilson (1765–1813), the author of the nine-volume work *American Ornithology,* was born in Scotland and immigrated to America in 1794, where he became a citizen.[37] He was a schoolteacher near Philadelphia until 1802, when he moved to take charge of a school near Bartram's Garden. Wilson and Bartram quickly became close friends, and Wilson's life course changed when William Bartram began to

---

[36] In 1803, he published a comparative study of linguistics, *Etymology of Certain English Words and on Their Affinity to Words in the Languages of Different European, Asiatic and American (Indian) Nations* and a text on the origin of the first American people, *New Views of the Origin of the Tribes and Nations of America* (1797). Barton may have been the first to suggest a significant age to the Indian mounds, speculating that they may have been older than biblical chronology. Barton also correctly suggested that Native Americans were from Asia.

[37] Hunter, *The Life and Letters of Alexander Wilson*; Burtt and Davis, *Alexander Wilson.*

teach him the rudiments of ornithology and natural history illustration.

Wilson's first bird models were Bartram's drawings and specimens, aided by garden observations and reference books from Bartram's library. By 1804, in a stream of correspondence, Wilson had started sending colored drawings of the local birds to Bartram along with an earnest request for criticism. Although Wilson did not know the names of many of the bird species, he began collecting drawings of Pennsylvania birds. He sent Bartram twenty-eight drawings, noting in the accompanying letter, "Criticise these, my dear friend, without fear of offending me—this will instruct, but not discourage me. For there is not among all our naturalists one who knows so well what they are, and how they ought to be represented."[38]

Wilson was aided in his work by Charles Willson Peale's collection of bird specimens, which Wilson often added to with his own collections of field specimens. As Bartram continued to teach him ornithology, Wilson also received lessons in drawing from Alexander Lawson, an engraver and fellow immigrant Scotsman.[39] These lessons led Wilson to consider publishing his work. In 1806, after Wilson had taken a position in Philadelphia as an assistant editor of *Rhee's Cyclopedia*, the publisher became enthusiastic about Wilson's ornithology project and agreed to publish an illustrated prospectus for distribution to acquire subscribers for Wilson's proposed multivolume work about American birds. Wilson canvassed north into New York state and south to Maryland to acquire subscribers. Two hundred copies of the first volume were published in 1808 with an investment by the publisher, his colleague, and the subscriptions acquired by Wilson. The project would continue if Wilson could raise a matching number of subscribers. After consulting with William Bartram in March 1809, Wilson traveled as far south as Savannah, observing and painting birds and collecting subscribers for *American Ornithology*.

In one of many letters written to William Bartram, Wilson devoted several paragraphs to John Abbot, commenting, "There is a Mr. Abbot here, who has resided in Georgia thirty-three years drawing insects and birds. He has published in London one large folio volume of the Lepidopterous Insects of Georgia. It is a very splendid work."[40] Wilson spent a lot of time with

<hr />

[38] Hunter, *The Life and Letters of Alexander Wilson*, 244.

[39] The biographical papers, engravings, manuscripts, etc., of Alexander Lawson and his daughters are in the ANSP Archives. See www.ansp.org/research/library/archives/historical-collections.

[40] Alexander Wilson to WB, 5 March 1809, in Hunter, *The Life and Letters of Alexander Wilson*, 308, 396–98.

Abbot, who had traveled into East Florida. For *American Ornithology*, Wilson pictured several birds that Abbot had discovered, and Abbot continued to supply Wilson with bird specimens after he returned to Philadelphia. Wilson gave Abbot full credit in *Ornithology*, and many mounted specimens and skins became part of the collections in Peale's Museum. The mayor of Savannah, William Bulloch, and thirty-four other citizens also became *Ornithology* subscribers.

For the next four years, Wilson continued his travels in search of subscribers, his fieldwork in search of specimens, and his work on the eight subsequent volumes of *American Ornithology*. Wilson also spent a great deal of time at the Bartram house. His friend and nature enthusiast George Ord later wrote, "Wilson resided the better part of the years 1811–12 at the Botanic Garden of his friend, Mr. Bartram."[41] When he was traveling, Wilson corresponded regularly with Bartram, requesting information and critical judgment. In 1813, the year of his early death at age forty-seven, Wilson wrote to Bartram, asking, "Will it be convenient for the family to accommodate me (as I shall be alone) this summer? Please let me know."[42]

During visits and stays at the garden, Wilson became a close friend and mentor of many of Bartram's students, including François Michaux, George Ord, and Thomas Say. All would become leaders in their specialties in the emerging science of American natural history.

François Michaux Revisited. In 1801, François Michaux returned to the U.S. after completing his botanical studies in France. The following year, his father's last year of life, the younger Michaux had been appointed by the French government to report on the condition of the nursery gardens that André had established in America and to study trees that might be useful for planting in France.

Wilson and François Michaux often met and lived at Bartram's Garden. When Michaux returned to France in 1803, they frequently corresponded: "Mr. Wm. Bartram is still as you left him, and you are frequently the subject of our conversation at table."[43] Correspondence among Wilson, Bartram, and

---

[41] Ord, *Supplement to the American Ornithology of Alexander Wilson.* Ord completed volume 8 after Wilson's death and wrote volume 9, titling it *Supplement to....* His biographical sketch of Wilson first appeared in volume 8 but was added to all volumes of Wilson's *American Ornithology* in later editions.

[42] Alexander Wilson to WB, in Hunter, *The Life and Letters of Alexander Wilson,* 405.

[43] Alexander Wilson to Francois Michaux, 6 June 1812, in ibid., 400.

Michaux continued and included drawings of plants and animals. Some drawings were lost in transport during the Napoleonic Wars, as ships were captured and the cargo never reached its destination. Nevertheless, some drawings that Bartram sent to Michaux are housed at the Musee d'Histoire Naturelle in Paris.

Alexander Wilson's American Ornithology. Wilson's *American Ornithology* was the first systematic natural history book focused solely on American birds.[44] The book contains comprehensive scientific references to birds collected and preserved in Peale's Museum and includes complete literature citations and credit for the discovery of each bird. Each descriptive entry displays the bird's Linnaean name and the specimen number (when available) in Peale's Museum followed by a narrative about the bird's biology. The description is accompanied by Wilson's illustration of the bird, often with its egg or nest. Although Wilson was forced to crowd several images of different birds on one engraving plate, the quality of the scientific detail in each image is remarkable.

For example, in a ten-page summary, Wilson described the common mockingbird, which had been earlier illustrated by Mark Catesby (see page xiv), now the Florida state bird, and cited the Peale Museum reference specimen as No. 5288.[45] The references cite Mark Catesby, several other Linnaean descriptions, and Bartram's observations with citations for Bartram's *Travels* and personal communications—"Mr. Bartram also informs me." To support the narrative, Wilson included information about the mockingbird's geographic range, "Maine to Florida"; behavioral information, such as mockingbird songs and their eating habits involving specific plant seeds and insects; and mating and nesting information, including the building time, number of eggs, brooding time, and enemies of the nest. Wilson's detailed description of a black snake attack and the female mocker's reaction is animated with her triumph after a bloody fight.[46] Field marks for identification

---

[44] Wilson, *American Ornithology; or, The Natural History of the Birds of the United States: illustrated with plates, engraved and colored from original drawings taken from nature.* 9 vols. (Philadelphia: Bradford and Inskeep, 1808–1814); Ord, "Biographical sketch of Alexander Wilson," 9:xiii–xlviii.

[45] Wilson, *American Ornithology*, 2:94–105.

[46] Audubon's later drawings and text were often strongly influenced by (or copied from) Wilson. As Ord often pointed out, Wilson's illustrations were frequently published without appropriate credits.

are detailed. Wilson describes the practice of "caging" a young mockingbird for singing purposes in detail and expressed concern about conserving the species. Wilson, a conservationist like Bartram, sounded the first alarms for protecting different birds from extinction in his *American Ornithology*.[47]

After Wilson's early death, his friend George Ord enlisted Bartram's help to add the finishing touches to complete volume 8. Ord also prepared the entire ninth volume of *American Ornithology* for publication. William Bartram is profusely referenced and acknowledged in all volumes of *American Ornithology*. Ord included a biography of Wilson in volume 9 and also in later editions of *American Ornithology*.[48]

George Ord

George Ord (1781–1866) was born and grew up in Philadelphia, where he joined his father's ship chandler business and continued the enterprise after his father's death. Ord retired early to live a comfortable life devoted to pursuing his scholarly interests in philology and natural history.

At a young age, Ord became interested in studying natural history and literature. He frequently visited Bartram's Garden and became well acquainted with William Bartram, who encouraged and guided the development of Ord's natural history pursuits. Around 1804, Ord met Alexander Wilson at the garden, and the two men became close friends, often making local field trips together. Wilson was beginning his bird project and Ord, the philologist, critiqued and edited Wilson's natural history writings.[49] Ord started visiting Bartram more frequently and described and also scientifically named the bird specimens returned by the Lewis and Clark expedition, in addition to preparing a major article on systematic North American zoology, which was published in 1808 in William Guthrie's *New Geographical and Commercial Grammar*.[50] It was the first comprehensive American zoology

---

[47] See the scarlet tanager reference and others in Wilson, *American Ornithology*. Although Wilson expressed concern when he first met Rubens Peale in the woods shooting birds, he soon discovered the importance of a bird specimen in the museum for art and science.

[48] George Ord, "Life of Alexander Wilson," in vol. 9 of *American Ornithology*.

[49] He assisted in enlarging Samuel Johnson's dictionary and the first edition of Noah Webster's dictionary.

[50] Guthrie's *Geography* with Ord's article was published in 1809 and reprinted without Ord's systematic list in 1815. All editions disappeared until a copy of the original was found by Samuel Rhoads in the 1850s. He secured permissions and published a reprint in 1858. He also discovered a separate copy of George Ord's article in the library

treatise.

Ord set new scientific standards and used Linnaean binomial scientific names for the first time for many species of American birds, mammals, amphibians, and reptiles. In addition to scientific lists, Ord's detailed narratives about each organism clarified previous observations and writings about the creature and its habitat. In the introduction to a reprinting of George Ord's classic work (the original version appeared in Guthrie's book, which was on the verge of extinction in the 1850s), Samuel Nicholson Rhoads wrote,

> The name of George Ord was long ago immortally associated with that of Alexander Wilson. If the latter is the Father of North American Ornithology, Mr. Ord, in a humbler sense, may be characterized Father of North American Zoology, his contributions to Guthrie's Geography being the first systematic Zoology of America by an American. The limited and concise nature of this production gives only a casual glimpse at the personality of its author: when, however, it does reveal itself, the same lofty and sacred animals which inspired the noblest writings of Wilson and Audubon is unmistakable.[51]

Ord noted the scientific name and description of many animals that "inhabit Florida," including the panther, many birds, snakes, and lizards. He made several references that "Mr. William Bartram was the first naturalist who indicated this bird as a distinct species from the preceding; notwithstanding which, all the Ornithologists of Europe have confounded it with the Turkey-buzzard in the Atlantic States."[52] The references to Wilson are frequent, with adulation, such as Ord's quoting Wilson's bald eagle as a hunter: "If Mr. Wilson had never written a line except the above, he would have deserved the highest eulogy for a description which is perhaps unrivalled by the whole tribe of naturalists, from the age of Pliny to the present day."[53] In addition to completing Wilson's work after his early death, Ord became the executor of Wilson's legacy.

---

of the ANSP, as he recounted in the introduction to the 1858 edition (Rhoads, *A Reprint of the North American Zoology*). The appendix in Rhoads's book includes critical notes by Witmer Stone and Elliott Coues. Throughout, Ord is praised for the scientific quality and his modesty.

[51] Rhoads, *A Reprint of the North American Zoology*, 283.

[52] Ibid., 320.

[53] Ibid., 321.

Thomas Say

Several years earlier, at Bartram's Garden, Wilson and Ord met William Bartram's grandnephew, the younger Thomas Say (1787–1834). Say's mother was the granddaughter of John Bartram, and his father was a successful Philadelphia physician, apothecary, and legislator. As a boy, Thomas Say passionately collected insects and other creatures around his father's country estate and nearby at Bartram's Garden under the watchful eye of his great uncle, William Bartram.

In 1801, Say left his exclusive boarding school with his parents' permission at the age of fifteen. Bored with schooling, he read extensively, became increasingly interested in natural history, and assisted his father in running his Philadelphia shop, Benjamin Say & Son, druggists and apothecaries. In addition to his country and botanical garden excursions, Say collected beetles and butterflies in Philadelphia with Rubens and Titian Peale, the sons of Charles Willson Peale, and frequented Peale's Museum. Say's youthful interest became a mania for collecting and naming insects. His only other competing interest was amassing and classifying shells. William Bartram encouraged and tutored Say; just as Bartram had influenced Wilson's focus and passion for American birds, he fostered Say's concentration on American insects and mollusks.

Thomas Nuttall

Thomas Nuttall (1786–1859) first arrived in 1808 from England during a period of peace, but politics, personal reasons, and scientific events often resulted in his journeying back and forth to England.[54] His interest in botany and natural history immediately put him into contact with Benjamin Smith Barton, who gave Nuttall lessons and sponsored his plant-collecting trips in America. It was not long before Nuttall was introduced to William Bartram and soon was making regular visits to Bartram's Garden, often in the company of Thomas Say. Say, Wilson, and Ord stimulated Nuttall's interest in North American birds while François Michaux piqued Nuttall's interest in trees and shrubs.

When Wilson was working on his *American Ornithology*, François Michaux was writing his grand opus about American trees and forests, *Histoire des Arhres forestiers de l'Amerique septentrionale*, first in French and then

---

[54] Graustein, *Thomas Nuttall*. Nuttall was in America from 1808–1811, 1815–1841, and for three-month periods often thereafter, as permitted by his estate holdings, until his death in 1859.

in an English translation, *The North American Sylva* in 1817–1819. With illustrations by Pierre-Joseph Redouté and Pancrace Bessa, two masters of botanical art, Michaux's opus rapidly became a landmark in American literature and the foundation of American forestry. In the introduction, he paid tribute to William Bartram, "known equally for his travels and various knowledge in natural history, for the amiability of his character and the obliging readiness with which he communicates to others the result of his studies and observations."[55] Throughout the book, Michaux described and included plates of many trees "we met with in East Florida."

Michaux's *American Sylva* and Wilson's volumes on birds inspired other naturalists. The followers of Wilson's birds included George Ord, Charles Lucien Bonaparte, Titian Peale, and John James Audubon. Thomas Nuttall continued Michaux's search for new and unidentified trees.

Nuttall stayed at the Bartram house so often that one of the rooms has been unofficially named after him. Because of the imminent War of 1812, Nuttall interrupted his exploration of the American Northwest and southern areas to return to England, where he worked on his collections and notes until he arrived back in the U.S. in 1815.

The Academy of Natural Sciences of Philadelphia. By 1812, Thomas Say's father had established a partnership for Thomas to join John Speakman (1783–1854) in Speakman's apothecary store in the heart of Philadelphia.[56] Young Say, however, was seriously committed to his study of insects and shells and destined to become one of America's first professional naturalists and museum curators. Speakman managed the apothecary shop while Say expanded his interest in natural history and continued his studies with William Bartram and, at his father's behest, at the University of Pennsylvania. Natural history occupied Say's interest, and his circle of friends expanded to include many in the business community—amateurs with similar interests in natural history.

Many of these young men also frequently visited Bartram's Garden. Jacob Gilliams (1783–1868), a Philadelphia dentist, was an avid herpetologist—influenced by Bartram—as was later noted: "Jacob Gilliams became a regular visitor with Say to the Bartram Garden…and attributed his love of nature mainly to the influence of those visits."[57]

---

[55] Michaux, *The North American Sylva*, 1:7–8.

[56] England, *The First Century of the Philadelphia College of Pharmacy*, 13, 30–31.

[57] Ruschenberger, *A Notice of the Origin, Progress, and Present Condition of the Academy of Natural Sciences of Philadelphia.*

Say continued to visit Bartram frequently and attended science evenings with John Speakman, Jacob Gilliams, Alexander Wilson, and others at Bartram's Garden or other locations. There were few opportunities for Jacob Gilliams and many others—who were by day tradesmen, artisans or mechanics, physicians, merchants, apprentices, and the like—who wished to occupy their leisure hours with natural history inquiry and discussion. For them, there were few available libraries, collections, or cabinets of specimens open for study and examination and not many appropriate locations for group meetings and prolonged discourse. Peale's Museum had become a popular entertainment center and no longer fully met their needs.

At one of their informal Philadelphia gatherings, Speakman suggested a regular weekly meeting, at stated times, to exchange ideas, while Jacob Gilliams proposed they form an association. Speakman and Gilliams invited various friends they thought would be interested in forming a society for studying natural history. With these ideas in mind, six friends of science (Bartram's apostles) met above Speakman and Say's Apothecary Shop on Market Street on Saturday night, 25 January 1812.[58] It was the founder's meeting of the Academy of Natural Sciences of Philadelphia.

---

[58] Phillips and Phillips, *Guide to the Microfilm Publication of the Minutes and Correspondence*; Peck and Stroud, *A Glorious Enterprise*, 2–90. Cited hereafter as Peck & Stroud.

CHAPTER 4

A GLORIOUS ENTERPRISE BEGINS

"To the Academy of Natural Sciences of Philadelphia, to whose founders is due the first effective impulse given to the study of natural science of North America, and whose labors have been mainly instrumental in developing the natural history of this country."[1]

—Dr. Amos Binney

On the evening of Saturday, 25 January 1812, six friends of science accepted John Speakman and Jacob Gilliams's invitation to gather above Speakman's and Thomas Say's apothecary.[2] Speakman acted as chairman of the group, which also included Dr. Gerard Troost, Dr. Camillus McMahon Mann, John Shinn, Jr., and Nicholas S. Parmentier. Although Say was away on military service related to the War of 1812 during this initial meeting, he was an enthusiastic attendee of the subsequent evening science meetings and regarded as a founder of the society.

Say and several others were either friends or students of William Bartram. Others, including Troost, Mann, Shinn, and Parmentier, were immigrants who had recently arrived in Philadelphia. These were men of various religious and political persuasions, with university and academic training, who had already or would later become American citizens.

The most prominent scientist to inaugurate the new society was Gerard Troost.[3] Troost held degrees in pharmacy and medicine from the University

---

[1] Binney, *The Terrestrial Air-breathing Mollusks of the United States*, n.p. [dedication page].

[2] See Peck and Stroud, *A Glorious Enterprise*; Bennett, "The History of the Academy of Natural Sciences of Philadelphia."

[3] Prior to arriving in America, Troost was a scholar in residence at the Natural History Museum in Paris. In the 1820s, Troost published his pioneering geological mapping of the Philadelphia area and began exploring the American frontier. He later moved to New Harmony with Maclure and others from the Academy and eventually settled in Tennessee, where he became a pioneer in Southern geological studies (Corgan, "Early American Geological Surveys," 41–49).

of Leiden and received advanced training in mineralogy and geology in Paris before becoming the mineralogist to the King of Holland. During a King's mission in 1810, Troost was stranded in Philadelphia due to political upheaval in Europe. With the abdication of the king, Troost decided to stay in Philadelphia and become an American citizen. He ran an alum manufacturing business while continuing to explore his natural history interests in mineralogy, geology, and herpetology. Troost is generally credited as America's first crystallographer.

At the meeting, the founders agreed that the exclusive mission of the new society should be

> to form, constitute and become a Society for the purpose of occupying their leisure...on subjects of NATURAL SCIENCE, interesting and useful to the country and the world, and in model conducive to the general and individual satisfaction of the members, as well as to the primary object the advancement and diffusion of useful liberal human knowledge...[4]

According to the meeting minutes, on 21 March 1812, the founders adopted the name "Academy of Natural Sciences of Philadelphia." Although Dr. Samuel Jackson of the University of Pennsylvania suggested the name, Jackson, a young physician, did not join the group meetings. He feared that, however unjustly, the society would be considered lacking in proper respect for religion because its members had banned religious discussion during meetings and believed his involvement could be detrimental to his career.

In their earlier deliberations, the founders had cited examples of prominent religious controversies, such as "[Francis] Bacon being immured ten years in a dungeon, and Galileo condemned to be burnt alive for promulgating laws of Nature and theories of Nature's phenomena." To ensure that religious fears would not inhibit scientific discovery, the founders decided, "All party-cant-words, polemics and controversy, religious, national and political, are by consequence excluded [from] our conversation in the Society."[5]

At the same meeting where they chose the institutional name, the founders also decided that the Academy's founding date should be 21 March 1812. The six founders included Thomas Say in absentia; he later signed the founding act. They also approved a constitution that listed the Academy's purposes as the formation of a natural history museum, a library of works of science, a chemical laboratory, and a collection of experimental philosophical apparatus for the illustration and advancement of knowledge to "the common benefit

---

[4] ANSP Archive, Minutes, coll. 527.
[5] ANSP Archives, Meetings, coll. 502; Peck & Stroud, 6.

of all individuals who may be admitted members of our institution."

Membership

The Academy founders created two specific residence-based categories of membership: *members* were Philadelphia residents, and *correspondents* were nonresidents.[6] The distinction between members and correspondents was made clear in the bylaws and adhered to until 1924: "The Society shall consist of members and correspondents" exclusively, and those who belong to it "cannot lawfully assume in this connection any other title, such as 'life member,' or 'corresponding member' or 'non-resident member.'" Correspondents had the privilege of attending and presenting scientific papers at monthly meetings and using the museum's facilities and resources. In addition to the correspondents' privileges, members also possessed the right to vote, hold office, and conduct business. Election to the Academy was a rigorous process that was the same for both members and correspondents. To join, two active members of the society were required to sponsor the new member, and a majority of members had to vote by secret ballot in favor of the election of the new member. Members and correspondents communicated and also exchanged and deposited specimens, collections, books, instruments, and other items at the museum. They presented papers at meetings; when the journal was established in 1817, they also published articles.

At the April 1812 business meeting, Dr. John Barnes was nominated and elected the first new member. The meeting occurred in a newly rented meeting room near the first meeting location with the beginnings of a museum and library.

On 7 May 1812, officers were elected for the first time: Dr. Troost as president, Nicholas S. Parmentier and John Shinn, Jr., as vice-presidents, John Speakman as treasurer, Jacob Gilliams as controller, Thomas Say as conservator, and Dr. C. M. Mann as secretary. Dr. Troost was chosen as president because he was the only founding member who could lay claim to sound

---

[6] By the end of 1812, six members and twenty-seven correspondents had been elected. There were three thousand members by 1900. One hundred and forty were resident members; the others were correspondents living in forty-eight countries, including the U.S. At least ten lists of members and correspondents have been printed by the Academy. The most complete were in 1836, 1848, 1868, and 1893; many have been reprinted, including one by BiblioLife, LLC, 2010, *Members and Correspondents of the Academy of Natural Sciences of Philadelphia, 1877* (Philadelphia: Academy, 1877).

scientific credentials.[7] All the members, with the exception of Dr. John Barnes, held an official position in the inaugural Academy.

After John Barnes became the first member in April, Andrew Ellicott, surveyor of Florida (page 55), was elected as the first correspondent in May. In July, William Maclure was elected to membership and William Bartram became a correspondent.[8]

The growing library and museum prompted the Academy to relocate to the upper floor of a three-story house in September; the apartments were named the "Hall of the Academy of Natural Sciences." The Hall included a "conversation hall," a reading room, and a place to deposit scientific specimens, all for the benefit of the growing membership.

By the end of 1812, six new members and twenty-seven correspondents had been elected. In 1813, an additional ten members and seven correspondents joined. Several correspondents who were elected in 1812 illustrate the geographic diversity of the growing society, including Daniel Drake, M.D., from Cincinnati, L'Abbé Haüy from Paris, and Augustus Oemler from Savannah. Members and correspondents shared scientific information via conversations, letters, meetings, and publications. These activities were made possible because the Academy generated common resources for its members, such as a museum where meetings were held weekly; collections were deposited, curated, and displayed; and equipment and a library were available. The creation and publication of a journal in 1817 enabled the membership to disseminate original scientific information to nonmembers, including individual subscribers and other societies and libraries.

In brief, the Academy provided its members with the democratic infrastructure to engender research, discovery, data preservation, and dissemination of new knowledge about natural history. At the time, no other institution in America was a natural history research institute. Peale's Museum was pri-

---

[7] Gerard Troost (1776–1850) immigrated to Philadelphia in 1810. His geological background had enabled him to develop the royal cabinet of minerals for King Louis Napoleon of the Netherlands and serve as a protégé of Haüy in residence at the Paris Natural History Museum. He worked with Maclure on geological projects in Pennsylvania and mapped Philadelphia. Later he joined the "Boat Load of Knowledge" in New Harmony (page 147) and subsequently became state geologist of Tennessee (Corgan, "Early American Geological Surveys," 41–49).

[8] William Bartram was proposed by Thomas Say and chemist Dr. John Manners and elected 3 December 1812 (ANSP Archives, Publicity, Papers 1880–1957, coll. 417, p. 6). As with many notices, the membership certificate was sent later due to engraving delays.

vately run and followed a public display, education, and increasingly entertainment approach to natural history. The Charleston Library museum was expanding its collection of South Carolina natural history specimens. Columbia College and its College of Physicians, along with the University of Pennsylvania, were leaders in teaching botany, but they provided no support for natural science research; instead, faculty had to utilize their own limited natural history collections.

William Bartram's Influence

William Bartram was de facto the Academy's godfather. His seminal influence on many of the Academy's founders and growing membership continued to drive the Academy and its mission. Many individuals whom Bartram influenced were elected to membership. Alexander Wilson, the "Father of American Ornithology," was elected in June 1813 for his fieldwork, study, and *American Ornithology.* Wilson was an example to other Academy members and correspondents who wrote about American plants and animals. Thomas Say (1812), George Ord (1815), Titian Peale II (1817), and Thomas Nuttall (1817) had major roles in Florida exploration. Reverend Henry Muhlenberg (1812), a botanist, and geographer Andrew Ellicott (1812) from Lancaster, Pennsylvania, also contributed to tracing Florida's natural history.

Several early Academy members were Southern naturalists who collected specimens from and wrote about Georgia and Florida's natural history. Through their specimen collections, presentations, and publications, these men played key roles in the development of the Academy and the exploration of Florida. They also knew and assisted northern and European members of the Academy who were also interested in exploring Florida by following Bartram's *Travels.*

The first Southerner elected as a nonresident member (correspondent) was Augustus Oemler, a German immigrant to Savannah who was a pharmacist, botanist, and entomologist. His neighbor, Louis Le Conte of the Woodmanston Plantation, and his brother, John Eaton Le Conte, a New Yorker who wintered at Woodmanston along the Fort Barrington Road that led to the Altamaha River, were elected to membership in 1815. The Le Contes' botany mentor, Dr. David Hosack of New York, was also elected in 1815, as was Stephen Elliott (1815), their colleague and botanical competitor. Elliott became known as "the Southern botanist" because he was an intellectual leader in Charleston and a plantation owner in Savannah who was active in business and politics; he had also authored *Sketch of the Botany of South Car-*

olina and Georgia. William Baldwin (1817), a Delaware transplant to Georgia, botanized (page 99) and made trips into Florida while stationed in Georgia during the War of 1812. These and other Southern members of the Academy were essential in furthering Bartram's seminal exploration of the Southern states and the unknown territory of Spanish Florida.

William Maclure

William Maclure, a colleague of William Bartram and other founders of the Academy, was elected to membership in 1812.[9] However, when the organizing meetings were held in 1812, Maclure was in Europe conducting extensive geological studies. Further, even though he was one of the first resident members elected, he traveled frequently and was often absent from Philadelphia until 1816. Upon his return, he assumed a very active scientific role, with his leadership and wealth serving the development of the Academy for twenty-five years and his contributions to geology earning him the title "father of American geology."

A Scotsman, William Maclure experienced early success in the mercantile business and began pursuing European rock collecting as a hobby. His interests in geology became increasingly serious, and he devoted all of his leisure time to the new science. In 1796, he moved to Philadelphia, became a U.S. citizen, and continued his business enterprises in several American cities as he wound down his European interests. Having amassed a large fortune, Maclure retired in 1799 at age thirty-six to pursue his geological studies full-time and to become an American patron of science and education. He extended his European geological studies to America, became active in the scientific community of Philadelphia, and was elected to the American Philosophical Society in 1799.

Maclure traveled back and forth between various European cities and Philadelphia as he transferred his geological studies from Europe to America.[10] He mapped the geology of northern Europe, the West Indies, and the U.S. His geological surveys of the eastern U.S. from Maine to Georgia and from the Atlantic Ocean to the Mississippi River were reported in his paper, "Observations on the Geology of the United States," which he read in 1809 at a meeting of the American Philosophical Society and published in its *Transactions.*[11] A French translation was issued in 1817, and enlarged and revised book editions were printed in 1817 and 1818. Each was accompanied

---

[9] See Warren, *Maclure of New Harmony*, 126–36.

[10] Warren, *Maclure of New Harmony*, 21–23.

[11] Maclure, "Observations on the Geology of the United States," 411–28.

by a colored map, which exists in several variations, copied and recopied. One or another served as the basis for a description of American geology for several decades. Maclure's work was the first widely read work on the geology of the U.S. It established his international reputation and legacy.[12] Similar to Bartram, Wilson, and Say, Maclure was an outspoken advocate of American science being conducted by Americans and published in America.

Bartram and Maclure were both enthusiastic in their expeditionary and collection efforts, but their styles differed. Bartram was a patron-supported independent explorer who became a natural history teacher and mentor. Maclure was also an independent explorer; however, he used his scientific and business acumen and financial resources to attract talented companions from diverse fields in his scientific and expeditionary enterprises and often became their patron. Maclure admired Bartram's extensive Southern travels, collections, recollections and, of course, *Travels*. Without success, he often entreated Bartram to join him and others on excursions to western Pennsylvania. Maclure was particularly intrigued by Bartram's travels in East and West Florida, areas he had not explored in his mapping of the U.S. because they were in Spanish Florida. For Maclure, it was imperative to expand Bartram's Florida observations, which were very limited in geology, and to include key Bartram plant and animal specimen data in the Academy's growing collections.[13]

Collections

From the beginning, the Academy's founders agreed that the principal areas for future development would be the formation of scientific collections and a library based on their programs of exploration. The natural history collections initially encompassed a few insects and shells, several stuffed birds, and several herbaria.[14]

During spring 1812, John Speakman purchased a collection of minerals from Philadelphian Adam Seybert. Seybert received his medical degree from the University of Pennsylvania before moving to Paris to study under eminent crystallographer L'Abbé René Haüy.[15] Before returning to America, Seybert

---

[12] White, "William Maclure's maps of the geology of the United States," 266–69.

[13] HH, 183. Maclure's letter to Bartram mentions their conversations and sending a carriage for him.

[14] Peck and Stroud, *A Glorious Enterprise*, 6–9.

[15] Haüy was one of the first correspondents from France elected to membership in 1812, shortly after Bartram.

acquired a substantial study collection of minerals in Göttingen, which he expanded through field collecting once back in Philadelphia in the early 1800s. Speakman purchased Seybert's collection with the intent of installing it as the Academy's first collection. Gerard Troost, who had also studied crystallography under Haüy and began collecting minerals in 1811, was enthusiastic about the Seybert mineral collection becoming the core around which the Academy's collections could develop.[16] The deposition of the Seybert mineral collection at the Academy was followed by Parmentier's herbarium.

Over time, the Academy expanded its facilities, hired staff, and became a museum of research, exhibition, and education. This expansion was driven by the Academy's collections, which grew through the donation or purchase of existing collections or individual specimens and the collection of new ones during expeditions sponsored by the Academy or conducted by individual scientists. In certain instances, the Academy also housed and cared for collections from other institutions. For example, some of the natural history collections of Peale's Museum and the American Philosophical Society have been permanently relocated to the Academy.

Collections of specimens as databases became the foundation of nineteenth-century scientific inquiry in natural history. Academy members engaged in taxonomy, the science of discovering, describing, naming, and classifying species. The goal was to catalog America's plants and animals. The first collected specimens, the *types*, became the reference material for future taxonomic studies on an organism.[17] The study of old collections can engender new interpretations through changing and evolving technologies and novel scientific questions. For instance, the introduction of the microscope allowed new visual analysis and data to be produced using old curated specimens. Over time, new methods of physical, chemical and biological analyses—microscopy, spectroscopy, DNA sequences—have been used to examine specimens and were complemented by new methods for data analysis and interpretation.

---

[16] See website of *The Mineralogical Record*, http://www.minrec.org. Philadelphia's Academy of Natural Sciences (1812–). The Mineralogical Record Biographical Archive.

[17] According to a precise set of rules first laid down by Linnaeus and later the International Commissions on Nomenclature, a *type* is one particular specimen (or in some cases a group of specimens) of an organism to which the scientific name of that organism is formally attached. Other specimens that are not the same unique type specimen are called voucher specimens. Types are usually physical specimens kept in a specially designated *type collection* in a museum research collection or are a particular plant sample in a herbarium. Usually types are a physical specimen, but failing that, an image of a specimen can be used.

In the setting of the Academy, the collection's type and voucher specimens were linked with collateral natural history information and literature citations through the library. Together, this information became the first American natural history database, including information on species taxonomy, nomenclature, and pertinent literature. The Academy began communicating this database information via public lectures in 1813 and through its publications programs in 1817.

The library began with contributions from members who brought their personal donations of books, articles, and manuscripts. These gifts and deposits created a highly prized, workable library; when the Academy began its own publication program, exchanges of its periodicals with those of international scientific societies also expanded its offerings.

New Building

By 1814, as the Academy's membership grew, a committee of members planned to move the burgeoning collection of specimens and books and the overcrowded lecture room to larger quarters. Jacob Gilliams offered to build a facility behind his father's dwelling on Arch Street, between Front and Second Streets in Gilliams' Court, a short distance from Speakman's apothecary shop. At a meeting in April 1815, the Academy's first building committee proposed that the three-story facility recommended by Mr. Gilliams be constructed and that the land be rented by the Academy for $200 per annum. The second and third floors would be used by the library and museum, while the ground floor would serve as laboratory and lecture space.

Fortunately, William Maclure arrived back in Philadelphia during fall 1816 to assist in funding and to manage the leasing and final construction of the Academy's new building. Maclure had returned from an extensive geological and natural history survey of the West Indies that skirted Spanish Florida. He was assisted by Charles-Alexandre Lesueur, a distinguished French naturalist, artist, and engraver who joined the Academy. With Maclure's assistance, the Academy moved into its first permanent home in 1817.

1817—A Banner Year

In his 17 January 1817 report on behalf of the curators, Thomas Say stated the condition of the Academy:

The present collection of the Academy of Natural Sciences of Philadelphia amounts to from four to five hundred volumes of Books four to five thousand specimens of minerals native and foreign numerous preparations of quadrupeds, birds, reptiles and dried plants a large collection of native Insects and some foreign ones a collection of several thousand shells native and foreign. The above articles are scientifically arranged.[18]

The growth and development of the Academy during 1817 under the aegis of William Maclure set the stage for the Academy's future governance, publishing activities, library, collections management, and expeditions.[19] Maclure, who had been intimately involved with the new building, as well its geological and library collections, chaired Academy committees and assumed a strong leadership role at the Academy. One of his responsibilities involved governance issues related to incorporation as an institution in the Commonwealth of Pennsylvania. This would affect the Academy's finances, property development, and aspirations for national and international membership. On 24 March 1817, the Academy was legally incorporated by the Commonwealth of Pennsylvania.

Maclure purchased and installed a printing facility to support the Academy's first publication, *A Circular to Captains and Voyagers,* which provided directions for collecting, preserving, and transporting specimens.[20] The methods developed by the Bartrams and other Academy members were the basis for the publication, which was prepared for new correspondents, members, and sea or land carriers. On 20 May 1817, under Maclure's direction with Say as editor, the *Journal of the Academy of Natural Sciences of Philadelphia* was founded to publish original works of science.[21]

With the inaugural publication of the Academy's *Journal,* Thomas Say's listing of collections, as he presented for the minutes in such general terms as "numerous preparations," "a large collection," or "a collection of several thousand," was transformed into detailed lists of individual items of "Donations to the Museum," which appeared in the end matter of each issue.

In his usual spontaneous manner, Maclure organized a week-long collecting expedition to New Jersey for himself, Lesueur, Say, and Troost in spring 1817. Although Bartram declined to join them, Maclure often met with Bartram to discuss expeditions and seek his advice. Bartram's conversations and observations about Florida continued to spark Maclure's interest,

---

[18] Thomas Say, "Report of the Curators" in the ANSP Archives, Meetings, 17 January 1817.

[19] For further reading, see Bennett, "The 1817 Florida Expedition of the Academy of Natural Sciences," 1–21.

[20] Published in Philadelphia by the Academy of Natural Sciences in 1817.

[21] Stroud, "The Founding of the Academy of Natural Sciences of Philadelphia," 227–36.

and he began planning an Academy expedition to Florida, one of his goals since his recent return to the U.S. by way of the West Indies.

Academy correspondent William Baldwin arrived in Philadelphia after completing extended military duty in Savannah and St. Mary's during the War of 1812. During his personal time, he followed Bartram's *Travels* as he made botanical collecting trips into Spanish East Florida, traveling to St. Augustine, Fort George Island, and the lower St. Johns up to Picolata. Upon his return to Pennsylvania, Baldwin met with Bartram to discuss his collections and Florida experiences. Baldwin's conversations with Bartram stimulated further interest in Florida, as did Philadelphian John Melish's 1816 map of a *Southern Section of the United States including Florida &c.* George Ord had just completed Wilson's unfinished *Ornithology,* with its many references to Bartram's Florida travel and animals, and he was also intrigued with Florida. Thomas Say was eager to collect in Florida after being primed for years by both Bartram and Savannah correspondent Augustus Oemler.

Also eager for a Florida adventure was Titian Peale II, a young colleague of Ord and Say and a new Academy member. Peale, the youngest son of Charles Willson Peale, was a promising natural history illustrator and preparator at Peale's Museum when he was elected to membership in the Academy in 1817. At eighteen years of age, Titian was also the youngest member of the Academy. He had been named after his older brother, who died of yellow fever at the age of eighteen. Titian II grew up in the halls of his father's museum. Titian also collected shells, butterflies, and other insects with his older friends, including Thomas Say, for study with William Bartram. Titian's considerable artistic talents were developed through tutoring by his older brothers, his father, and Bartram. Combining his talents and interests, Titian worked with Thomas Say and completed six colored illustrations for the prospectus of Say's *American Entomology.* This act qualified Titian for election to Academy membership. A Florida expedition in Bartram's tracks along with Maclure, Ord, and Say was an exciting prospect for Titian.

Florida Expedition

By December 1817, with this positive and enthusiastic feedback in addition to Bartram's consultation, Maclure, Ord, Say, and Peale completed plans for an expedition to Spanish Florida. Financed and primarily organized by Maclure, it was the first major Academy expedition to a foreign land. The four planned to follow in Bartram's tracks, and Bartram served as their mentor for the expedition.

In December, as the four Academy members embarked on the 1817–

THE FLORIDA FOUR

Above, William Maclure, 44. Portrait by Charles Willson Peale, ca. 1818.
Below, George Ord, 36. Portrait by John Neagle.

Proceedings of the Academy of Natural Sciences of Philadelphia, *ANSP Library, Collection 286.*
Courtesy of the Academy of Natural Sciences of Drexel University.

Above, Thomas Say, 30. Portrait by Charles Willson Peale, ca. 1818;
Below, Titian Peale. Portrait by Charles Willson Peale, ca. 1818.

Courtesy of the Academy of Natural Sciences of Drexel University.

1818 expedition to Florida, Maclure was elected president of the Academy. George Ord was named vice-president, and Thomas Say was elected curator. Their respective years of age in 1817 were 44, 36, 30, and 18. Along with Titian Peale II, they would have lifelong roles at the Academy and scientific research links to Florida.

Their intention was to confirm and elaborate on William Bartram's earlier natural and cultural observations while gathering new information and collections of specimens for the Academy. Maclure was interested in Florida's geology for a manuscript he was preparing. Ord wanted to expand Wilson's bird work and Bartram's studies on birds and mammals. Say was interested in insects, mollusks, and crustaceans. Peale's task was to help collect and preserve their specimens. The specimens would be deposited for identification, study, and long-term preservation (curation) at the Academy,[22] and original presentations about them would be made at regular Academy meetings. The results for type specimens would be published in the Academy's new *Journal*. This expedition would put the nascent Academy of Natural Sciences of Philadelphia on par with its European counterparts and become a hallmark of Florida exploration.

---

[22] Both duplicates and some individual specimens collected by Peale and Ord ended up at Peale's Museum.

CHAPTER 5

THE FIRST ACADEMY EXPEDITION "IN BARTRAM'S TRACKS" WITH MACLURE, ORD, SAY, AND PEALE

"Our plan now is to ascend as far as convenient the river St. Johns, pursuing pretty much the track of Bartram my excellent & ingenious relative: but whether or not we shall go further than he did will entirely depend on circumstances...."[1]

—Thomas Say

In late 1817, a notable year for the young Academy of Natural Sciences of Philadelphia, four of its newly elected officers departed Philadelphia on the first major natural history expedition undertaken by Americans from an American museum to a foreign land, Spanish Florida. The Florida Four included Academy president William Maclure, vice-president George Ord, and curators Thomas Say and Titian Peale II.[2] Privately funded and outfitted by Maclure, their mission was to explore Spanish East Florida and collect specimens.[3] These new plant and animal discoveries would enrich the Academy's growing scientific collections in the new Gilliam's Court Hall. Members of the Academy, including the Florida Four, would conduct a systematic study of these new specimens. Their findings would be presented, refereed, and published in the Academy's new *Journal of the Academy of Natural Sciences of Philadelphia*. They also hoped to confirm and include, if possible, some of Bartram's original Florida findings of plants and animals in publications and collections.

---

[1] Thomas Say to Jacob Gilliams, from St. Marys, Georgia, 30 January 1818, in Weiss and Ziegler, *Thomas Say*, 55.

[2] The reason for Charles-Alexandre Lesueur's (fish and reptiles) absence from the expedition is unknown; François Michaux (botanist), a likely member, had returned to Paris.

[3] Maclure oversaw the business of the expedition. He sold his horses and carriage, chartered a thirty-ton sloop, acquired supplies, and outfitted it with three hired sailors.

By December 1817, the Florida Four had completed plans for their expedition to "the promised land" in the "track of Bartram."[4] As Say wrote to his colleague, they were determined "to ascend the St. Juan" and "seek...for all those subjects of Nat. Hist. of which the acquisition was the sole object of our undertaking."[5] As the Florida Four pursued William Bartram's earlier route into Florida, their purposes were to study the geological formation of Florida (Maclure); confirm Bartram's observations on plants and animals (Ord and Say); and collect, preserve, and supply specimens (Say and Peale) for study at the Academy. Members and correspondents with specific scientific interests could also study the specimens collected during the expedition.

William Maclure and Thomas Say left Philadelphia on 17 December 1817, and traveled overland by way of Washington to Charleston. Maclure sent a carriage ahead to Savannah, and he and Say then took a steamboat to Savannah from Charleston. On 25 December, they met George Ord and Titian Peale, who had sailed directly from Philadelphia.

Savannah through the Sea Islands

As it had been for Bartram, the port of Savannah was also the jumping-off point for this Florida exploration. In Savannah, Augustus Oemler, an Academy correspondent (elected in 1812), served as their host.[6] A pharmacist, botanist, and entomologist, Oemler had previously hosted Alexander Wilson during his successful collecting and subscription visit to Savannah in 1808 (see page 59). Since his time with Wilson, Oemler had begun exchanging botany specimens with Bartram and insects with Say. For his developing *American Entomology*, Say was particularly interested in information derived from Oemler's insect collections. At this meeting, Oemler, John Abbot, and other local collectors gave boxes of insect specimens to Say. Ord and Peale made good use of their time by hunting in the neighborhood and collecting common birds, which Peale preserved and left with Oemler until their return.

---

[4] Thomas Say to John Gilliams, 30 January 1818, in Weiss and Ziegler, *Thomas Say*, 62.

[5] Ibid.

[6] Members of the Florida Four also likely spent time with other Southern Academy members (e.g., Louis and John Eatton Le Conte, whom Say sponsored for membership in 1815, and Stephen Elliott, also elected in 1815). Say and entomologist John Abbot had many interests in common. William Baldwin had left Georgia by this time. Maclure, however, was intent about the mission's time schedule and drove the group along. Say and Peale also explored and met people on their return trip to Savannah. The Georgia members of the Academy led field trips and gave specimens to Say and Peale during their stay in Savannah, both enroute to Florida and on the return trip.

Say's scientific descriptions of various mollusks, published later in the Academy's *Journal*, indicate that he also collected new varieties by exploring the docks and outdoor markets of Savannah.

Maclure, along with his servant and colleagues—with memories of their conversations with Bartram, William Baldwin, Andrew Ellicott, and John Melish, as well as their maps—sailed via the Sea Islands along the coast of Georgia to the village of St. Mary's at the border of Spanish Florida.

The Sea Islanders welcomed the explorers, "Having learned their route, they also sent word to their friends, to offer every facility to the party." But for Maclure, as Peale noted, "This intended kindness, proved a great annoyance, for at every place they approached, invitations were sent them to come and visit: Mr McClure invariably answered that they were on a trip that did not admit of visiting and they were only equipped for what they had to do."[7] Maclure was a taskmaster on the outward voyage. As Say indicated in his letters to Jacob Gilliams, "Maclure insisted that there was no time to visit." Say added that Maclure argued, "They had a program of work to carry out!" However, on the outward journey, Say and Peale did collect at several Sea Islands: Great Warsaw Island, Ossabaw, and Blackbeard Island.

On Ossabaw Island, and later near the entrance to the St. Johns River in February 1818, Ord gathered specimens of a large black bird that would later be deposited as type specimens at the Academy. After his return to Philadelphia, Ord presented specimens and comments about "the large crow blackbird" or "common grackle" to Academy members.[8] Ord followed with an article in the *Journal*, where he noted, "The Purple Jackdaw or Grackle inhabits the Carolinas, Georgia and Florida, where it is known by the name of Jackdaw. My friend, Mr. William Bartram, informed me that it sometimes visits New Jersey."[9] Ord's collection, description, presentation, publication, and preservation of type specimens at an institution for future study characterize the new scientific sophistication resulting from the Florida Expedition.

The specimens that Ord discussed were entered in the 1818 catalog of

---

[7] L. Peale manuscript; Porter, "Following Bartram's 'Track,'" 435. This misspelling in the Peale manuscript of Maclure's name suggests writing or editing of the manuscript by someone who was unaware of Maclure's insistence about the correct spelling of his name, as Peale certainly was.

[8] Ord, "Observations on Two Species of the Genus Gracula of Latham," 19 May 1818, ANSP Archives, Meetings.

[9] Ibid.; See *FHBT*, 123, for one of Bartram's Florida observations of crows and jackdaws.

the Academy Ornithology Department, with the donors listed as "The Four."[10] The *Journal's* list of donations included "Gracula, one species" by Maclure, Ord, Say, and Peale.[11] Ord additionally discussed a scientific dispute between European naturalists and Alexander Wilson—harking back to William Bartram's description—over the jackdaw (common/Florida grackle) and boat-tail grackle, and their confusion with the crow blackbird. He detailed systematic and behavioral descriptions of the grackles and provided references to pertinent publications by Carl Linnaeus, Mark Catesby, and William Bartram. Ord scientifically settled the dispute in favor of Wilson and Bartram. This example demonstrates the model that the Florida Four established during the Academy Expedition, an approach that became the hallmark of this and future expeditions.

As they sailed the Sea Islands, Maclure's eagerness to reach Florida and insistence that they bypass fertile collecting areas did not go without comment. In a letter to Gilliams, Say wrote about the many lost opportunities to visit the plantations of the Sea Islands, although the expedition "landed on almost every one of those truly productive spots on earth."[12] He detailed one exception, "the intelligent Mr. Shaw who resides on the S.E. end of Cumberland Island," whom they called on when their vessel became grounded on a bar within a mile of his mansion. The occasion allowed for socializing, making observations on landscaping, and collecting insects and mollusks from patio and garden plants. The following day, shortly after their arrival across the Sound at the town of St. Mary's, the "Lieut-Governor of East Florida" came aboard their sloop and "offered any service in his power."[13]

St. Mary's

The *American Daily Advertiser* reported on the expedition in its 18 February 1818 edition noted that at St. Mary's the "four traveling Naturalists

---

[10] Mark Robbins reported on 9 February 1984, that the Ornithology Department of the Academy had listed a Gracula specimen for 1818 with the donors noted as "The Four." The specimen could not be located and was believed to have been deaccessioned many years ago.

[11] *The Journal of the Academy of Natural Sciences of Philadelphia* (hereafter cited as *JANS*) 1, pt. 1 (1817–1818): 499–505, includes a listing of donations made by Maclure, Ord, Say, and Peale for June, July, and November. Included are Sponges, Gorgonia, one species of Gracula, three species of Asterias, Echina, Crustacea, several species of Tubularia, a collection of Crustacea, and seven bottles of Reptilia.

[12] Say to Gilliams, 30 January 1818, in Weiss and Ziegler, *Thomas Say*, 55.

[13] St. Mary's was located on the Georgia side of the Spanish Florida/Georgia border, delineated by the St. Mary's River.

from Philadelphia" were heralded "and deserve the greatest praise from the citizens of the United States, for this arduous and difficult enterprise."

Say wrote to Jacob Gilliams in considerable detail about the expedition, the four distinct personalities, and their interests:

> We are now refitting with as much rapidity as possible for our voyage up the river St. Johns—Mr. Ord is purchasing stores at this moment, Mr. Maclure is looking for a pilot, Mr. Peale is sitting by our cabin fire (though it is not so cold as to need one) reading Bartram's *Travels*, I am writing on a table near him to my friend, Captain is mending his sails taking in water &c, we shall be off in about 3 or 4 days for the promised land, a portion which is indeed now in sight. Our plan now is to ascend as far as convenient the River St. Johns pursing pretty much the track of Bartram my excellent & ingenious relative; but whether or not we shall go further than he did will entirely depend on circumstances; we entertain no fears from the hostility of the Indians, we could even repel the attack of a few of them as there are 8 souls of us armed with guns and pistols…— as we return we propose to examine the Sea islands with some attention, as from them we shall be able to collect the great portion of the southern marine animals, we shall then find it necessary or at least convenient to avail ourselves of our numerous means of becoming acquainted with the inhabitants of the country…shall look sharp on the St Johns for the *Ixea caelestina* discovered by Mr. Bartram & which has not been since found, also for the extremely useful Breadroot.[14]

Alas, they would be unsuccessful in their quest for Bartram's Ixia (*Calydorea coelestina*). It blooms only in the morning during late spring and early summer. Endemic to northeast Florida and now endangered, Bartram's Ixia was rediscovered by John Small (see page 319) in 1923.

At the end of the letter, Say wrote about collecting for Lesueur:

> N. B.: We have hitherto (please tell Mr. Lesueur) found but few fishes notwithstanding our constant endeavors to obtain them by the casting net, hook & line, &c they appear to have deserted the waters on which we have hitherto sailed for the season, or to have secluded themselves in the depths, taking little or no nourishment, otherwise our baits would surely have tempted them or our net captured them…we have 2 species of ? Hydragyra which Mr. L has not described, one of which is marine & the other a fine species of the Marsh water. &c, of the mollusca we have found Actinia, Ascidia, ? Holotheria (2 species) Mainaria, Syllea, medusa,

---

[14] Ibid.

neris, these we have preserved.[15]

St. Mary's had been the Florida departure point for the Bartrams in 1765, William Bartram in 1774, and the "four traveling Naturalists from Philadelphia" on 3 February 1818. The four left St. Mary's and followed William Bartram's 1774 water route, stopping at Fernandina on the beautiful and lush Amelia Island. The next day they sailed to the mouth of the St. Johns River, "and on entering St Johns river great numbers of Porpoises were seen. The next day the party sailed thirty miles up the river seeing among various other birds, some Fishing Pelicans and Whooping Cranes."[16]

Thomas Say wrote, "This noble river we ascended as far as Picolata...about 100 miles from its mouth, stopping occasionally at such places as presented an inviting aspect & making short excursions into the country on each side of the river."[17]

Picolata and Then Overland

When William Bartram visited Florida in 1774, Fort Picolata was already in ruins. As he observed and recorded in his *Travels*: "to my disappointment, found the fort dismantled and deserted...its construction of seashells and fine sand, cemented with lime."[18] The surrounding area proved to be excellent for collecting by Say: "A very common shell...in East Florida. We found them numerous under the ruins of old Fort Picolata on the St. Johns river."[19]

At Picolata, the prospect of a twenty-three-mile trek through an area without any accommodations deterred Maclure—an "old man" in his fifties, nursing his "rheumatism"—from accompanying the three younger men on a day's journey over land to St. Augustine. Maclure's arthritic condition, which he chronicled in his 1821 diary, had improved in the Southern climes that winter, but it was undoubtedly a factor in his decision to stay behind.[20] His desire to work on his manuscripts on geology, which would be published in the *Proceedings of the American Philosophical Society* and the Academy's *Journal* upon his return to Philadelphia, may have been another factor.

---

[15] Ibid.

[16] L. Peale manuscript; Porter, "Following Bartram's 'Track,'" 439.

[17] Thomas Say to John F. Melsheimer, 10 June 1818, from Philadelphia, in Weiss and Ziegler, *Thomas Say*, 58.

[18] *FHBT*, 52.

[19] Say, "Account of Two New Genera," 279.

[20] Doskey, *The European Journals of William Maclure*, 667.

From Picolata, the three younger men traveled overland to St. Augustine and Anastasia Island. In a later letter, Say recounted this trek and stated one expedition objective: "From Picolata we crossed the country on foot to St. Augustine in order to present our passports to the Governor of the Province and to obtain from him such information as might direct our further progress with the greatest probability of success."[21] Maclure had secured royal Spanish passports for the party before leaving Philadelphia. Their hope was that the governor would direct them to safe areas where they would have success in collecting specimens.

En route, as Peale noted, "They passed through pine barrens and swamps, frequently up to their middle in water, the whole 23 miles, and saw no vestige of habitation nor a single inhabitant."[22] They were, however, collecting all along the way. One such example, collected by Ord, was William Bartram's "little Jay," or "Florida Jay."

Florida Jay of Bartram

In *Travels,* Bartram recorded details about a non-crested blue jay, which became known as Bartram's "little jay," or "Florida jay": "in such clumps and coverts are to be seen several kinds of birds, particularly a species of jay; they are generally of an azure blue colour, have no crest or tuft of feathers on the head, nor are they so large as the great crested blue jay of Virginia, but are equally clamorous (pica glandaria cerulea noncrestata)."[23]

After Ord returned to Philadelphia, he read at the Academy's meeting on 26 May 1818, "An Account of the Florida Jay of Bartram" and subsequently published his findings in the *Journal.*[24] In his presentation, he noted, "In William Bartram's *Travels* a Jay is mentioned as inhabiting East Florida; but this notice is unaccompanied with a particular description. Hence succeeding naturalists were in doubt whether to regard it as a new species or not." Ord commented, "we had an opportunity of examining several specimens, which we procured in the vicinity of St. Augustine, and near the mouth of the river St. [Saint] Juan, in East Florida, from the most perfect of which the following description was taken." He classified it as *Garrulus caerulescens:* "Head, neck, wings and tail bright azure; back broccili-brown, inclining to

---

[21] Thomas Say to John F. Melsheimer, 10 June 1818, from Philadelphia in Weiss and Ziegler, *Thomas Say,* 58.

[22] L. Peale manuscript; Porter, "Following Bartram's 'Track,'" 440.

[23] William Bartram in *FHBT,* 109.

[24] Ord, "An Account of the Florida Jay of Bartram," 345–47.

hair-brown; lower parts dark yellowish gray; tail subcuneiform. Bill, legs and claws, black; irides hazel-brown; front, and line over the eyes, pale azure." The description was complete, but the scientific naming controversy that started with Bartram's *Corvus floridanus* did not end with Ord's *Garrulus caerulescens* but continued with revised names by later Academy members.[25] Ord's ecological comments about the scrub jay are also interesting since they now live only farther south in Florida: "When we first entered East Florida, which was in the beginning of February, we saw none of these birds...the first we noticed were in the vicinity of St. Augustine.... We afterwards observed them daily in the thickets near the mouth of the St. Juan. Hence we conjectured that the species is partially migratory."[26]

Ord also mentioned other birds "This beautiful and sprightly bird [blue jay] we observed daily, in company with the Mockingbird and the Cardinal Grosbeak" that they watched and collected.[27]

St. Augustine

The party of three "arrived at the gates of the city about sundown, and were obliged to enter in this soiled condition to the governor's house."

Because of their disheveled appearance, Ord, Say, and Peale, without the ministerial Maclure, were at first received with suspicion and concern at the governor's house. However, after the men presented their royal passports, they received a warm welcome and were offered accommodations.

They enjoyed the governor's hospitality, but he provided little encouragement for their up-river expedition. As Say noted, "From him we learned, that on account of the hostility of the Indians, it would be the extreme imprudence to venture any further up the river, but in the present state of things we would be more safe in exploring the southern rivers and coast, such as

---

[25] Coues, "General Notes," 84.

[26] At the time of Bartram's observations in Putnam County, and in 1818, in the area from Picolata to St. Augustine to the mouth of the St. Johns, scrub habitat and patches were plentiful. There were breeding scrub jays in these areas until the 1940s and 1950s. As scrub habitat was removed for housing and citrus groves in Florida, the scrub jay population decreased dramatically. Currently, only occasional strays from more southern habitats are seen. The Florida scrub jay population now lives primarily in the central ridge of Florida with some in the southern Gulf Coast plains. The scrub jay is threatened, with a Florida population of approximately 2,100 (https://www.nasa.gov/content/the-inquisitive-florida-scrub-jay/).

[27] Johnston and Bennett, "A Summary of Birds," 1–7.

mosquito river &c."[28] Although they had little time to spare in St. Augustine because of Maclure's orders to conduct their official business and return, they collected quickly and voraciously. "This curious species [of fresh water and land shells] we found near St. Augustine, East Florida, in a moist situation. They were observed in considerable numbers...."[29]

They spent another day around St. Augustine and on Anastasia Island, collecting geological specimens of Anastasia rocks and coquina rock. During this time, Say began to develop a new concept for linking fossils and geological time.[30] However, with the governor's discouraging advice, the Florida group, "returned disappointed to our little vessel," after retracing their steps back to Picolata.[31]

This was a period of governmental turmoil in Spanish Florida. Under the leadership of Andrew Jackson, America's territorial interest in Spanish West Florida had spread from New Orleans to Pensacola and further eastward. In East Florida, in and around Amelia Island, Anglo adventurers had founded several independent governments. The Creek Indians in the West and the Seminoles in the East were caught up in ongoing Florida conflicts: the First Seminole War from 1816–1819.[32] Spain's Florida problems were growing.

St. Johns River

After reporting the governor's warning to Maclure, the Florida Four agreed to return downriver to the mouth of the St. Johns and follow the Florida coast southward "to Mosquitto River & perhaps to Cape Florida." As they traveled down the St. Johns, they collected at many new locations and sites they had previously visited, such as the New Switzerland Plantation of Francis Phillip Fatio. Here Say collected land snails with: "Animal longer than the breadth of the shell.... This we found in the orange groves of Mr. Fatio, on the river St. John, East Florida."[33] At another landing,

---

[28] Thomas Say to John F. Melsheimer, 10 June 1818, from Philadelphia, in Weiss and Ziegler, *Thomas Say*, 58.

[29] Say, "Account of Two New Genera," 277.

[30] See Say, "Observations on Some Species"; Harris, "A Reprint of the Paleontological Writings of Thomas Say," 271–354.

[31] Thomas Say to John F. Melsheimer, 10 June 1818, from Philadelphia, in Weiss and Ziegler, *Thomas Say*, 58.

[32] Gannon, *Florida: A Short History*, 24–27.

[33] Say, "Account of Two New Genera," 278.

[T]hey then went ashore to dig at an Indian mound in the middle of a neighbouring plain. It was 90 ft in circumference and 9 or 10 ft high. They dug about 7 ft in the centre of it—found three flint spear heads, a stone hatchet, a copper rod sharp at both ends, and a Choch shell that is not found on the coast of America and is probably extinct—also some lumps of red paint.[34]

They continued downriver until "hearing that the Indians were troublesome in the south so that we would be in great jeopardy there, we determined once more to ascend the St. Juan as high as we had been before, & again seek upon the adjacent country for all those subjects of Nat. Hist. of which the acquisition was the sole object of our undertaking."[35] Again, as they went up the St. Johns, they collected at sites Bartram had visited, as well as at new sites.[36]

Again, they almost reached Picolata, but "we heard of parties of Indians...committing depredations, & one person informed us...his plantation was totally destroyed & his son killed, he narrowly escaped with the remained of his family."[37] With this news, the Florida Four collected in the area, turned around, and returned to collect in and around the mouth of the St. Johns near Cowford (present-day Jacksonville).

During their "coasting the St Johns river," the Florida Four "found the nest of an alligator" and "numbers of alligators"; they "shot a fine Buck, and wounded three others, also a large male squirrel"; they, "returned to get dogs to hunt the wounded Deer—Mr Ord having brought his dogs with him."[38] Some of their forays were for the purpose of gathering food rather than for collecting museum specimens.

Return to Philadelphia

In early April, they returned to St. Mary's. From there, Ord departed to

---

[34] L. Peale manuscript; Porter, "Following Bartram's 'Track,'" 441. Some of these artifacts went to Peale's Museum and are mentioned in Peale's inventory. The Academy had not yet become a museum of ethnology or anthropology.

[35] Say to Melsheimer, 10 June 1818, from Philadelphia, in Weiss and Ziegler, *Thomas Say*, 58–59.

[36] Known sites visited included Ft. George Island, Pablo Creek, St. John's Bluffs, Damer's Point, Francis Philip Fatio's Plantation south of Julington Creek, Pottsburg Creek, Cowford (Jacksonville), Remington, Arlington Creek, and other tributary creeks, stopping at Picolata.

[37] Say to Melsheimer, 10 June 1818, from Philadelphia, in Weiss and Ziegler, *Thomas Say*, 59.

[38] L. Peale manuscript; Porter, "Following Bartram's 'Track,'" 442.

Philadelphia. The others continued their voyage to Savannah, stopping to collect on Cumberland Island and other Sea Islands. In Savannah, Maclure quickly departed by steamboat to Charleston for meetings and then traveled overland to Philadelphia. Peale and Say met again with Augustus Oemler and secured more specimens for the Academy's collections. In mid-April, Peale and Say sailed directly from Savannah to Philadelphia.

A flurry of activity at the Academy followed the return of the Florida explorers. Thomas Say and Titian Peale served as curators of the Florida collections, documenting and preparing them for further study and long-term preservation. Say also began organizing and studying insects, which he would include in his *American Entomology*. In addition, mollusks, and crustaceans had become new study interests to him.[39] George Ord focused on presentations and publications about the Florida rat, grackles, and scrub jay and made several sporadic scientific trips to Europe. William Maclure published his last major scientific publications about American geology before leaving for Europe to pursue his interest in new educational and socially progressive movements, such as the pedagogical doctrines of Swiss educator Johann Heinrich Pestalozzi.[40] Maclure continued, in absentia, as president of the Academy with George Ord presiding.

Presentations and Publications

For the next five years, the Florida Four made presentations and published many articles describing the creatures they had collected on the expedition. Their discoveries—as published in the *Journal*—were substantial, given that the Academy *Journal* only issued information on new type specimens and specimens deposited or donated to its collections. In addition, they published articles in the new *American Journal of Science*, which had been founded in 1818 at Yale College by Benjamin Silliman to emphasize geology and the physical sciences.

Florida Rat

Immediately after returning to Philadelphia from Florida, George Ord sent a scientific description and a drawing by Charles-Alexandre Lesueur for naming a new rat from Florida, *Mus floridanus,* to the Philomatique Society

---

[39] Say, "An Account of the Crustacea of the United States," 235–53; Say, "Account of Two New Genera," 276–84.

[40] Maclure, "Essay on the Formation of Rocks," 261–76, 327–45; 385–410; Maclure, "Observations on the Geology of the United States of North America," 1–91.

of Paris.[41] The Bartrams had previously observed this Florida rodent.

John Bartram provided the earliest mention of the Florida wood rat during his first visit to Florida.[42] William later recorded his observations of the Florida rat at Lake Dexter:

> The wood rat is a very curious animal.... They are not half the size of the domestic rat; of a dark brown or black colour; their tail slender and shorter in proportion, and covered thinly with short hair...construction of their habitations, which are conical pyramids about three or four feet high, constructed with dry branches, which they collect with great labour and perseverance.[43]

The French journal's editor raised questions about Ord's hastily written paper—about the dental evidence, the creature's teeth, and whether the find was indeed a new genus or a sub-species of the known *Myoxus floridanus*.

Much later, a paper presented by Ord (8 March 1825) and subsequently published by Say and Ord contained a detailed description of the rodent and an apology for Ord's haste surrounding the earlier French publication in 1818.[44] The article also described the Florida specimen's collection site: "This beautiful animal was discovered in a log granary, situated in a ruined and deserted plantation in East Florida." They cited the year of collection as 1818 and described the specimens as being "in the collections of Messrs. Maclure, Say, Ord and Peale, and deposited in the Philadelphia Museum."[45] Say and Ord concluded that it was neither genus *Myoxus* nor *Mus*, but that it was a close approximation to *Arvicola*, and they assigned it to a new genus, *Neotoma* (*Neotoma floridana*).

However, the controversy continued to swirl since Richard Harlan, another Academy member, was simultaneously publishing his major work *Fauna Americana*, which also described the same rodent. While Harlan's work was in press, the first article by Say and Ord appeared, followed soon afterward by a second article presented at the Academy on 22 March 1825,

---

[41] Ord, "De Blainville, H, Sur une nouvelle espece de rongeur de la Floride par M. Ord de

Philadelphie," 181–82.

[42] Berkeley and Berkeley, *The Life and Travels of John Bartram*, 260.

[43] William Bartram in *FHBT*, 79.

[44] Say and Ord, "A New Genus of Mammal Is Proposed," 345–49.

[45] The Philadelphia Museum refers to Charles Willson Peale's museum where the Florida Four deposited some of their collections because their holdings in birds and mammals were greater than those at the Academy.

The Florida Rat (*Neotoma floridana*), described by Ord on his return from Florida.
A later *Journal of the Academy of Natural Sciences of Philadelphia* article by Say
and Ord ("Description of a New Species of Mammalia," 352–55)
included this drawing by Charles-Alexandre Lesueur.

Collection QHA16. Courtesy Academy of Natural Sciences of Drexel University.

which was subsequently published in the *Journal*.[46] In their second article, Say and Ord described the same animal using additional dental evidence and constructed another new genus, which they named *Sigmodon*. Much of the data between the two Say-Ord papers were identical, and there may have been printing errors in their second publication, leading to Harlan's critical comments about the taxonomy. In reference to Ord's several papers, Harlan wryly and sarcastically noted that, "In order to avoid confusion, it will be necessary for naturalists to remember that the animal under notice, is at present described as pertaining to three or four distinct genera."[47]

John Audubon and Rev. John Bachman provided a comprehensive review of the Florida rat subject in the *Quadrupeds of North America*.[48] They acknowledged Say and Ord's nomenclature (despite Harlan's objections) and name—*Neotoma floridana*—as well as the accuracy of Bartram's descriptions, notwithstanding a possibly erroneous species assignment.

The Florida rat is an example of the scientific transformation of general observations into scientific databases, the importance of type specimens, the necessity of scholarly publication, and the ability of scientists to refer independently to curated specimens.

Say's Insects

By 1817, Thomas Say had published the first part or section of his classic work, *American Entomology*, which included six plates drawn by Titian Peale II.[49] Say's work aligned with the Jeffersonian spirit of American science conducted by American scientists and the Academy tradition of Alexander Wilson's *American Ornithology*, which was published by an American in America, as had been Bartram's *Travels*. The Florida Expedition enabled Say to extend the scope of his entomological studies and enhance his scientific reputation. While en route to Florida, Say noted in a letter to John Frederick Melsheimer that Florida was a land "abounding in insects &c which are unknown, & if

---

[46] Say and Ord, "Description of a New Species of Mammalia," 352–55.

[47] Harlan, *Fauna Americana*, 141–44.

[48] Audubon and Bachman, *The Quadrupeds of North America*, 1:32–37. Audubon was elected to Academy membership in 1831, Bachman in 1832.

[49] The prospectus volume of twenty-eight pages appeared at the end of 1817 with plates by Titian Peale. The first volume of the "real" *American Entomology* came out in 1824 and included plates by Charles-Alexandre Lesueur in addition to Peale and others. It was dedicated to William Maclure.

they remain unknown, I am determined it shall not be my fault."[50] He later wrote enthusiastically to Jacob Gilliams, "we shall be able to collect the great portion of the southern marine animals" and in a brief after-note, "of the Mollusca we have found Actinia, Ascidia, Holothuria (2 species) Mammaria, Sylloea, Medusa, Neris, these we have preserved."[51] Upon returning to Philadelphia, Say recounted, "we stopped at each of the Sea Islands in order to examine their productions and the sea coast for crustacea, Mollusca &c."[52] However, he also noted, "our voyage of discovery was rendered abortive as we were not in Florida at the season we wished, the Spring, we therefore obtained but very few Insects & these few are but little consequence—My discoveries were principally in the Crustacea."[53] In addition to crustaceans, he published extensively about insects and mollusks.

The Florida collections remained of great interest to Say although he joined Major Stephen Harriman Long's government-sponsored military expedition to the Rocky Mountains shortly following his return to Philadelphia from Florida. The Florida specimens were his subject for innumerable presentations and publications throughout the 1820s. In his 1820 descriptions of the Myriapoda (millipedes, centipedes) of the U.S., Say focused on specimens from Georgia and East Florida.[54] He continued to work on and include Florida material in his *American Entomology*, which he once again began publishing as additional sections in 1824.[55]

Say's *American Entomology*, begun in 1817 as sections, was completed in 1824. He "respectfully inscribed," (i.e., dedicated) the finished book to Maclure. It includes many references to Florida specimens and drawings by Peale and others. Referring to *Xylota ejuncida*, Say noted, "The specimen is a male. I caught it on the banks of the St. Johns River, in East Florida, during a short visit to that country, in company with Messrs. Maclure, Ord and T.

[50] Say to Melsheimer, 12 December 1817, from Washington, in Weiss and Ziegler, *Thomas Say*, 54.

[51] Say to Gilliams, 30 January 1818, from St. Mary's, GA, ibid., 55.

[52] Say to Melsheimer, 10 June 1818, from Philadelphia, ibid., 58–59. John Melsheimer (Johan Friedrich Melsheimer) was the son of Valentin Melsheimer, a Lutheran pastor in Pennsylvania and the first person to publish a regional work on the entomology of North America. The work he published in 1806 was *Catalog of Insects of Pennsylvania*. He and Say had exchanged specimens, and his son and Say, who were close in age, corresponded with each other (See ANSP Archives, coll. 13, Say letters).

[53] Ibid., 59.

[54] Say, "Descriptions of the *Myriapodae* of the United States," 102–14.

[55] Say, *American Entomology*.

R. Peale."[56] In reference to *Curculionides argula*, Say recalls, "My kinsman, the late excellent Wm. Bartram, informed me that it also destroys the European Walnut in this country."[57]

Say's Crustacea

Thomas Say's interest in crustaceans was a logical extension of his work in entomology, and his study of Florida specimens helped him develop the science of carcinology, the study of crustaceans and shellfish. In November, before Say left for Florida, he read his first paper on carcinology before the Academy, "An account of the crustacea of the United States."[58] In an 1818 *Journal* publication, he wrote,

> Since these papers were read to the Academy we have found in the southern states, several interesting and apparently new crustaceous animals, descriptions of some of which will now be added, and those of the remaining ones will form a supplementary addition to this essay; this notice is only given to account for the anachronisms that may appear.[59]

Many crustaceans, including the blue land crab, *Cardisoma guanahumi*, originally identified as *Uca laevis*, were collected on the expedition and are in current Academy collections. Say's first crustacean paper included descriptions of eight unique species that he had collected along the Georgia coast, Amelia Island, the East Florida coast, and near the mouth of the St. Johns River. Say's description of *Lepidactylis dytiscus* is characteristic: "This active little animal is one of the many inhabitants of small pools of water left by the recess of the tide on the coast of Georgia and Florida. In those shallow pools its presence may be ascertained by the numerous and irregular tunnels which it forms in the sand, like miniature representations of those of the mole."[60] Say's subsequent papers published throughout 1818, with descriptions of more than forty new crustaceans from the expedition, established him as the "father of American carcinology."[61]

---

[56] Ibid., note 30.

[57] Ibid.

[58] Say, "An Account of the Crustacea of the United States," 57–80, 155–69, 235–53, 313–19, 374–401, 423–41.

[59] Ibid., 235–53.

[60] Ibid., 235–53.

[61] Spamer and Bogan, "Time Capsule of Carcinology," 87–89; Holthius, "Thomas Say as a Carcinologist."

Say's Mollusks

The Florida specimens of mollusks enabled Say to move into another major area of work: American conchology and malacology.[62] On 25 May 1818, he read an account at the Academy of two new genera and several new species of fresh water and land snails.[63] To quote Say,

> *Polygyra auriculate*—inhabits Florida: This curious species we found near St. Augustine, East Florida, in a moist situation. They were observed in considerable numbers...Regarding *P. septemvolva*: A very common shell in many parts of Georgia...and E. Florida. We also found them on the Oystershell Hammocks, near the sea...under decaying Palmetto logs, roots, &c.... For *Succinea campestris*—This shell is extremely common...on Amelia Island...I found them in plenty on the highest sandy ground of the island.[64]

The deposit of these specimens at the Academy is recorded at various times in the list of donations that appeared annually in the *Journal.* Say's collections included many "types": amber snail (*Succinea campestris*) found on Cumberland Island in the garden of planter James Shaw; globular drop snail labeled *Helicina orbiculata*, as published by Say, became *Olygyra orbiculata*. *H. septemvolva*, as labeled and described by Say, is Florida flatcoil snail *Polygyra septemvolva*. He notes, "We found great numbers [*O. orbiculate*] on what are called Oyster Shell hammocks near the mouth of the river, St John, E FL, in company with *Polygyra septemvolva*."[65]

Say resumed his work on malacology among the Florida Expedition collections after his return from the Long Expedition to the Rocky Mountains in 1820. On 24 July 1821, Say began a series of presentations and papers, beginning with this account: "During occasional visits to our sea coast, and particularly on a journey to East Florida, in company with Messrs. Maclure, Ord, and T. Peale, I availed myself of every favorable opportunity to collect marine shells, whilst engaged in the pursuit of other and more favorite objects."[66] He further noted,

---

[62] The terms "conchology" and "malacology" both refer to the study of mollusks, also called shellfish, and scientifically, mollusca. Conchology is the study of their shells; malacology is the study of the entire organism, including its soft body parts and operculum, not just its shell.

[63] Say, "Account of Two New Genera," 276.

[64] Ibid.

[65] Ibid.

[66] Say, "An Account of Some of the Marine Shells of the United States," 221–22.

Several naturalists who now devote a portion of their attention to conchology, and particularly to that of the United States, having recently requested me to publish an account of our marine shells, I have thought it might be useful to communicate to them immediately descriptions of those which I do not find to be distinctly described by attainable authors. Such species or varieties, only, are made known in the following essay.[67]

The next fifty pages of the "essay" are frequently punctuated by references to Florida: "Inhabits East Florida," "I observed them to be very numerous near the mouth of the St. Johns river," and "inhabiting St. Johns river in East Florida, from its mouth to Fort Picolata, a distance of one hundred miles, where the water was potable." Say continued his descriptions in a second article.[68]

The two articles were the beginning of a series, which eventually led to his monographic work, *American Conchology* (1830), and his national recognition as the "father of American conchology."

Gilliams's Salamanders

As a founding member of the Academy, Jacob Gilliams was an ardent supporter of its goals. He was enthusiastic about amphibians, reptiles, and fishes, but he also had a demanding dental practice. Gilliams's efforts were characteristic of the serious amateur: "business by day, natural history at night." Say's letters kept Gilliams informed about the course of the Florida Expedition, and Gilliams seized the opportunity to study specimens returned by the Florida Four.

In "Description of Two New Species of Linnean Lacerta" in the genus *Salamandra*, Gilliams noted, "I am indebted for these specimens to the Florida Party."[69] The description of *S. variolata* from the expedition was illustrated by C. A. Lesueur in Gilliams's Plate 18. The specimen was probably from one of the "seven bottles of *Reptilia*" noted in the *Journal's* November list of donations for 1817–1818.

Lesueur's Fishes

Another Academy member who remained in Philadelphia and contributed to the study of the Florida Expedition collections was Charles-Alexandre

---

[67] Ibid., 223.
[68] Ibid., 257–77.
[69] Gilliams, "Description of Two New Species of Linnaean Lacerta," 460–61.

Lesueur. Lesueur was a well-established French naturalist by the time that Maclure became his patron and brought him to Philadelphia in 1816.[70] Lesueur's intellect, scientific accomplishments, and artistic abilities served him well in the burgeoning study of American natural history. His expertise in fish and invertebrate animals was unequalled. As an artist and an engraver interested in the new processes of lithography and papyrography, Lesueur was instrumental in Maclure's plan to develop the *Journal* and also the field of natural history illustration in America. A systematic work on the fishes of North America became one of Lesueur's goals.

Lesueur's expertise, as well as his interest in the collections, encouraged Say to pepper his correspondence about the Florida Expedition with fishes. Later, the collections of the Florida Four housed at the Academy provided Lesueur with many opportunities for discoveries and publications in the *Journal*. Lesueur's richly illustrated papers reflect his artistic ability. He noted about *Raia desmarestina*, "It inhabits the sandy coasts of Florida, from whence it was brought by Messrs. Maclure, Ord, Say and T. Peale."[71] His curation of the specimens marked the beginnings of a fish department for the Academy.

In reference to the Florida Bass *Cichla floridana*, Lesueur wrote, "We are indebted for this species to the researches of Messrs. Maclure, Ord, Say and Peale who brought it from East Florida."[72] About *Sciaena multifasciata*, Lesueur noted, "This individual was communicated to me, by Messrs. Maclure, Ord, Say and Peale, who brought it among their collections from Florida, in the dried state."[73]

Lesueur's observations and publications about the Florida Four's specimens are linked with his work on North American fishes, just as Say integrated his insect, mollusk, and crustacean observations with broader studies of American natural history. Their collective studies reached much farther than simple descriptions of newly collected specimens from the 1817 expedition. For example, regarding the Florida specimens, Lesueur observed, "Several of them are undescribed, and one of them appears to constitute a new genus, allied to *Cyprinodon*."[74] He noted the provenance through his title, "Description of a new genus…indigenous to the United States."

---

[70] Ord, "Memoir of Charles Alexander Lesueur," 189–216.

[71] Lesueur, "New Genus and Several New Species of Freshwater Fish," 2–13.

[72] Lesueur, "Descriptions of the Five New Species of the Genus Cichla of Cuvier," 214–21.

[73] Lesueur, "Descriptions of Three New Species of the Genus *Sciaena*," 251–56.

[74] Ibid., 254.

Contributions to American Natural History and a Nexus

The Florida Expedition created an institutional paradigm for natural history research in the European tradition and formalized in America: collection, study, presentation, publication, and curation. The Academy made this model possible and paved the way for later American natural history museums.

The Florida Expedition became a nexus between William Bartram and the next several generations of natural history explorers of Florida. In addition to establishing many new genera and species of plants and animals, the Florida Expedition extended Bartram's observations of numerous organisms and established a solid foundation for the new American sciences of entomology, conchology (malacology), and carcinology. This Academy expedition tradition "in Bartram's tracks" would continue exploring Florida for two centuries through the efforts of many, including John Le Conte, John James Audubon, Joseph Leidy, Angelo Heilprin, Clarence Moore, Henry Pilsbry, Francis Harper, Tucker Abbott, and others associated with the Academy of Natural Sciences.

CHAPTER 6

FLORIDA BOTANY...WITH BALDWIN
AND THE LE CONTES

"Such, he [Bartram] informed me, was his partiality for that delightful country [Florida], that he often fancied himself transported thither in his dreams by night."[1]
—William Baldwin

"Mr. Bartram was a man of unimpeached integrity and veracity, of primeval simplicity of manner and honesty unsuited to these times, when such virtues are not appreciated."[2]
—John Eatton Le Conte

At the end of the eighteenth and the beginning of the nineteenth century, William Bartram's *Travels* stimulated European and American interest in Florida's natural history. However, after Florida was returned to Spanish control in 1783, it became difficult for American and most European naturalists to explore East and West Florida. The coastal Atlantic and southern borders of Georgia provided occasional points of entry for the study of natural history but were risky due to unfriendly natives or military events. Prior to William Maclure's procurement of royal passports for the Florida Four for the Academy's 1817 expedition, Florida natural history had only been studied post-Bartram by a handful of individuals during brief collecting forays. For example, during his naval appointment on the Florida and Georgia border, botanist and physician Dr. William Baldwin explored Florida by way of coastal Georgia near the Sea Islands and Amelia Island. The similarity of the southern Georgia flora and fauna to those in northern Florida provided Louis Le Conte and John Eatton Le Conte with study opportunities around their Georgia plantation near the Florida border. When Florida became a U.S. territory in 1821, Captain John Eatton Le Conte (elected to Academy membership in 1818) led a major expeditionary party to Florida.

---

[1] Darlington, *Reliquiae Baldwinianae*, 237. Facsimile of the 1843 edition; WB to William Darlington, 20 August 1817.
[2] Le Conte, "Notice of American Animals," 13.

William Baldwin

William Baldwin (1779–1819) studied alongside Benjamin Barton while earning a medical degree at the University of Pennsylvania (see page 58). Baldwin developed a lifelong interest in botany and often accompanied Barton on visits to William Bartram at Bartram's Garden. During the War of 1812, Baldwin lived in Georgia as a commissioned naval surgeon based along the Florida-Georgia border at St. Mary's for two and a half years and then in Savannah for two years. With *Travels* in hand, Baldwin botanized extensively to confirm and extend Bartram's plant findings. While collecting in coastal Georgia and making forays into Spanish Florida, Baldwin befriended Augustus Oemler, Steven Elliott, Louis and John Eatton Le Conte, and an increasing number of Georgia and Southern naturalists, many of whom were members of the Academy. Baldwin often shared and sent specimens north to his botanist friends, including another Academy correspondent, Rev. Henry Muhlenberg (elected to the Academy in 1812), in Pennsylvania.

After Baldwin returned to Philadelphia in 1817 and was elected to membership in the Academy, he visited Bartram to share his Florida experiences. In early 1819, Baldwin was appointed, along with Thomas Say and Titian Peale, to serve on the U.S.-sponsored scientific expedition—the Yellowstone Expedition to explore the Missouri River—whose leader was fellow Academy member Major Stephen Harriman Long of the U.S. Corps of Topological Engineers. Long's scientific and engineering party, often called the "Long Expedition," had assignments in zoology, botany, and engineering to explore the Missouri River.[3] Alas, Baldwin, the expedition's key botanist, became ill and died in September shortly after the river expedition began.[4] Many years

---

[3] Major Long was appointed to organize a scientific contingent to accompany soldiers of Col. Henry Atkinson's command on the Yellowstone Expedition (sometimes called the Atkinson-Long Expedition) to explore the upper Missouri River on an experimental steamboat that Long designed, the *Western Engineer*. The venture, which began in June 1819 and is often termed the "First Long Expedition," explored the Missouri River to Council Bluffs, Iowa, where the scientific party wintered over. The Yellowstone Expedition became a costly failure; instead of exploring the Missouri River, President Monroe had Major Long lead an expedition up the Platte River to the Rocky Mountains and back along the Spanish colonial border. This is often termed "The Long Expedition" or "The Long Expedition to the Rocky Mountains." Say and Peale were part of both segments of Long's exploration efforts; Baldwin only the early part of the first. Their portraits and dress by Charles Willson Peale are linked to "The Long Expedition."

[4] Baldwin departed Pittsburgh on 5 May 1819 aboard the *Western Engineer*. He

later, his friend and medical school colleague, William Darlington (elected to Academy membership in 1818), published a memorial volume, *Reliquiae Baldwinianae: Selections from the Correspondence of the Late William Baldwin* (originally published 1843) that included Baldwin's correspondence, his Florida experiences, and information about his botanical explorations.[5]

William Baldwin's Florida Letters

The full extent and timetable of Baldwin's East Florida travels from Savannah and St. Mary's remain largely unknown, except for brief comments in his correspondence with colleagues and his medical school friend, William Darlington.[6] Darlington included Baldwin's "*Floridian letteri*" as "Notices of East Florida, and the Sea Coast of the State of Georgia: In a Series of Letters to a Friend in Pennsylvania" in *Reliquiae Baldwinianae*. In an introductory "Biographical Sketch," Darlington noted that Baldwin had moved to Georgia as a surgeon's mate in the U.S. Navy at the outset of the War of 1812 and later became a naval surgeon. Most of Baldwin's Florida letters were written during his military service—from the summer when the War of 1812 began until autumn 1816—and the following year. During this time, Baldwin made trips to East Florida, particularly the northeastern areas around Amelia Island, and also completed an extended exploration on one occasion.

---

rode out daily on collecting missions in spite of ups and downs with regard to his health. By July 22, his failing health led him to resign his position and remain in medical care at Franklin, MO. He died on September 1 and buried on the banks of the Missouri River.

[5] Darlington, *Reliquiae Balwinianae*, i–xxx (Ewan's introduction). Baldwin is known to the history of botany through his friend and biographer, William Darlington. Baldwin's plant collections are located in the William Darlington Herbarium in West Chester, Pennsylvania, and the Herbier Durand at Paris. Baldwin's personal herbarium was sold to Academy member Zaccheus Collins after his death and subsequently purchased by member Lewis von Schweinitz. Although von Schweinitz discarded Baldwin's labels, archived lists of his collections and von Schweinitz's commentaries exist in the Lewis David von Schweinitz collection in the New York Botanical Garden Archives. The von Schweinitz Herbarium is located at the ANSP. Baldwin's contributions to Stephen Elliott's "Sketch of the Botany of South Carolina and Georgia" were acknowledged by Elliott in his book. Many of Baldwin's manuscripts are held at the Archives, the LuEsther T. Mertz Library, the New York Botanical Garden, and in the Papers of William Baldwin, 1803–1844, at the Gray Herbarium at Harvard University.

[6] Darlington was an avid botanist while he practiced as a physician. He served terms in the United States House of Representatives from 1815–1823 and established a natural history society in West Chester County, Pennsylvania, in 1826. He published several works on botany and natural history, most significantly, *Reliquiae Balwinianae*.

In 1812, at the beginning of Baldwin's military service as a physician, another of his mentors, Rev. Henry Muhlenberg, wrote to him, "You are now at St. Mary's,—an excellent situation to elucidate Bartram's *Travels*. If you have a copy, pray let me have your observations on his dubious plants,— especially on such as are without a scientific name."[7] Thus began Baldwin's four-and-a-half-year exploration of Georgia and East Florida botanicals. In addition to visiting patients, he spent this time making observations, collecting for his herbarium, and describing specimens. He botanized on the Georgia and Florida sides of the St. Mary's River, made day trips to Amelia Island, and wrote letters about his botanical interests to Muhlenberg and Stephen Elliott (elected as an Academy correspondent in 1815), who was becoming known as "the Southern botanist," and William Darlington.

Between November 1816 and May 1817, after many brief physician-related visits to Amelia Island and the surrounding northern areas of East Florida, Baldwin explored East Florida. Leaving St. Mary's, he observed, "We are now on the borders of the Land of Flowers; but not in the flowering season. Enough, however, may be seen, even now, to interest a Botanist from Pennsylvania." With his colleague, Dr. Jonas Cutter, and assistants they hired along the journey, Baldwin made his way by water and land—following in Bartram's tracks—into East Florida: "Fernandina stands on a high calcareous bluff, on the west side of Amelia Island" and, south to Fort George Island, "Seated alone on the summit of the highest land on the Island…and commanding an extensive and varied prospect of the Ocean, the mouth of St. Johns."[8] In responding to an inquiry from Darlington, Baldwin romanticized his trip up the St. Johns River: "Could you only come and go up the beautiful St. Johns with me, with what delight would we pursue the steps of Bartram." He also provided details based on his knowledge and experiences.[9]

After exploring the St. Johns River, Baldwin traveled to St. Augustine and south to Bartram's New Smyrna and Mosquito Lagoon; he returned to St. Mary's by way of Tomoko, near present-day Ormond Beach.

With a borrowed copy of *Travels*, Baldwin sought to verify and expand upon Bartram's observations, following the spirit of Muhlenberg's letter in

---

[7] Muhlenberg to Baldwin, 18 June 1812, in Darlington, *Reliquiae Balwinianae*, 63.

[8] Baldwin to Darlington, 30 March 1817, ibid., 211. Baldwin's letter describing this site lists the Latin names of more than twenty plants that he observed in a twenty-foot community around him.

[9] Darlington, *Reliquiae Balwinianae*, xix. Ewan reports about eighty miles, nearly to Picolata, up the St. John's River.

1812, until he departed for the North in 1817. Baldwin's letters were peppered with Bartram notes, such as, "The *Crinum* mentioned in my *Calendarium* of Sept. 23, is the same spoken of by BARTRAM, in page 59."[10] Some included humor about Bartram's spectacular observations: "Could I only see a huge 'magnanimous' (Bartram) rattlesnake, it would help out my story very much. During 5 years...I have seen but one living rattlesnake! But, had not Bartram been here before me, I would astonish you with my account of the Alligators."[11]

Baldwin was generally positive about Bartram's observations: "Could I have extended my excursion a little more westerly, I should in all probability have found many of Bartram's doubtful plants. I am happy to say, that his authority is good in most instances, where I have had it in my power to travel over the same ground."[12] However, in one area he found Bartram unsatisfactory:

> He is most defective in his Geography; and you rarely find his plants in the situations pointed out in his *Travels*. One of the most extraordinary of his geographical blunders is that of the mouth of the St. Mary's—which he says enters the Atlantic between Amelia and Talbot Islands. How he could have made such a blunder is inconceivable: and it has been copied by Morse, and other Geographers. The St. Mary's discharges itself between Cumberland and Amelia, 20 miles north of Talbot.[13]

After Baldwin returned to Wilmington in July 1817, he planned to study his large collection of plants from Georgia and Florida and reluctantly began to prepare his manuscripts for publication. With Darlington's encouragement, Baldwin started working on a botanical study that he tentatively called *Sketches of East Florida*. He was, however, less than enthusiastic; his preference was to be working in the field. On learning of his election to Academy membership, Baldwin traveled to Philadelphia to meet with Academy

---

[10] Baldwin to Muhlenberg, 26 February 1814, ibid., 127. As he explained to Muhlenberg, Baldwin had lost his personal copy and at long last was able to borrow one. Muhlenberg often wrote and made specific requests referencing *WBT*.

[11] Baldwin to Darlington, 30 March 1817, ibid., 210–11.

[12] Baldwin to Darlington, 27 May 1817, ibid., 229. By "westerly," Baldwin generally refers to the St. John's, Alachua, and Suwannee area where Bartram collected extensively. Baldwin was on the alert but did not find Bartram's *Ixia*, although Darlington had written earlier to Muhlenberg: "*Ixia coelestina* is said to be abundant on St. John's. Le Conte thinks it a new genus" (26 February 1814, ibid., 127).

[13] Baldwin to Darlington, 27 May 1817, ibid., 229.

vice-president Zaccheus Collins and attend his first Academy meeting as a new member.[14] Most importantly, Baldwin was "anxious to see the venerable Bartram," and he did:

> After getting through my business in the city, I paid the venerable William Bartram a short visit on my return homewards. Though far advanced in the vale of years, I found him in the possession of good health; and all the faculties of his mind were as brilliant as in the morning of life. So pleased was he with the little details I gave him of East Florida—and so interested was I in the information which he was capable of affording me, that we parted with great reluctance, and mutual wishes for a further and more intimate acquaintance.[15]

During their conversation, Bartram expressed affection for Florida and satisfaction with Baldwin's work. Baldwin noted,

> Such, he informed me, was his partiality for that delightful country, that he often fancied himself transported thither in his dreams by night. My being able to confirm several of his doubtful plants was extremely gratifying to him; and he wished most anxiously that I would return and find others of them, before he descended to the grave. Aware of the suspicions which some entertain of his veracity, it was truly a feast to me to observe how his time-worn countenance brightened up at the vindication of his character, which I informed him I was prepared to offer.[16]

The visit with Bartram inspired Baldwin to action: "By this visit I am prepared to make his *Lantana Camara* a new species, without hesitation. I saw the true West Indian Camara in perfection; and I find it unequivocally distinct from the Florida plant—which I shall describe, and send to him, under the name of *Lantana Bartramii*. It is an elegant plant."[17]

On a later visit, Baldwin confirmed that Bartram had indeed received

---

[14] Zaccheus Collins (1764–1831) was a merchant and botanist to whom Baldwin's personal herbarium was sold after Baldwin's death. The herbarium was later purchased by Lewis David von Schweinitz and is now at the Academy. A plant genus named after Collins has common wildflowers in Florida, e.g., *Collinsia antonina Hardham*. In a letter to Darlington, Baldwin wrote, "Z. Collins wrote to me before I returned; and I received at the same time a notice of my having been elected a corresponding member of the 'Academy of Natural Sciences of Philadelphia'—an institution I had not heard of, before" (18 September 1817, ibid., 242). Collins was elected to Academy membership in 1815.

[15] Baldwin to Darlington, 3 July 1817, ibid., 234.

[16] Ibid.

[17] Baldwin to Darlington, 20 August 1817, ibid., 238.

his gift of "an elegant plant": "I spent several hours yesterday with our worthy old friend Bartram…. He has now the *Lantana Bartramii* (for the first time) in flower in his garden."[18]

Baldwin's work on his *Miscellaneous Sketches of Georgia and East Florida* was halted when he accepted an appointment as a botanist on Major Long's scientific expedition. However, Baldwin continued to write letters about his Florida work. "His strength, however, failed him, ere the expedition was fairly underway; and he died at Franklin on the banks of the Missouri" on 1 September 1819, at the age of forty-one.[19] Recognizing the importance of the descriptive data in Baldwin's correspondence and encouraged by botanist Asa Gray, William Darlington curated Baldwin's letters and botanical information and published *Reliquiae Baldwinianae: Selections from the correspondence of the late William Baldwin, MD…with occasional notes, and a short biographical memoir* in 1843. In the book, Darlington specifically referenced and discussed Baldwin's Florida letters.

Baldwin's major Florida contributions were the hundreds of plant specimens he provided for the herbaria of other botanists—especially Muhlenberg, Elliott, Collins, and Darlington—and the information about plant habitats he shared in his letters. Some of these specimens eventually ended up at the Academy. When Baldwin died, his large personal herbarium was of great value for botanists Lewis David von Schweinitz, John Torrey, and Asa Gray. Through Baldwin's colleagues and various gifts and purchases, many of his plant specimens were curated at the Academy.[20]

Baldwin also served as a Florida linchpin between his Northern and Southern colleagues—Stephen Elliott, John Abbot, Augustus Oemler, and an increasing number of members of the Le Conte family. They all would play significant roles in Florida exploration, the Academy, and American science.

The Le Conte Family

William Baldwin sought out the Le Contes after he arrived at St. Mary's in 1813 when Reverend Muhlenberg wrote to him: "I shall be extremely glad to see the new plants of Mr. Le Conte—who appears to be a very close observer. Indeed, a fine constellation of Botanists has risen in the Southern

---

[18] Baldwin to Darlington, 14 August 1818, ibid., 277.

[19] Darlington, *Reliquiae Balwinianae*, 14, 321.

[20] Nearly six hundred specimens collected by Baldwin are in the Academy's herbarium (Philadelphia Herbarium, hereafter PH); sixty are from Florida.

states. You are warmer, and shine brighter, than those in the north."[21] With this compliment and encouragement, Baldwin was diligent in meeting Louis and John Eatton Le Conte to discuss natural history and share notes and biological specimens.

Later in November 1816, at the beginning of Baldwin's expedition to East Florida, he wrote to Darlington about the Le Contes:

> About four miles south of Riceborough...—the seat of Messrs. John & Lewis Le Conte. They possess, here, a large and valuable Rice Plantation.... From the truly scientific acquirements of these gentlemen, and their zealous attention to every department of Natural History.... I am indebted to them for much valuable information.... There is, on this plantation, a new and beautiful species of *Porcelia* (Anona, L.-)...and was shewn to me in May, last, by Mr. Lewis Le Conte.[22]

John Eatton Le Conte (1739–1822), the father of Louis (1782–1838) and John Eatton Le Conte (1784–1860), established the Le Conte plantation, Woodmanston, in 1760.[23] The senior John Eatton Le Conte was a New York physician, and Woodmanston, a rice plantation on an inland swamp, was the family's winter residence in Georgia.[24]

As the Le Conte boys grew up, the forests and fields of Manhattan and Georgia were sources of both study and pleasure. The brothers attended Columbia College in New York, where their interest in botany caught the attention of their professor, Dr. David Hosack, New York's preeminent botanist, physician, and professor, at Columbia's College of Physicians and Surgeons.[25]

After Louis and John Eatton received AB degrees from Columbia, Louis

---

[21] Muhlenberg to Baldwin, 22 June 1813, ibid., 93.

[22] Baldwin to Darlington, 24 November 1816, ibid., 332. Louis Le Conte always spelled his name "Louis," but many spelled it "Lewis," which was also the spelling of the name of one of Louis's sons. The Le Contes were ready field resources for botanists who sought Bartram's plant observations in the area around Woodmanston and the Altamaha River (e.g., the *Magnolia pyramidata*).

[23] Bennett, *The Le Contes*, 1–4. The Le Conte-Woodmanston Plantation is now on the National Historic Register. The historic home site and botanical gardens are open to visitors. See www.Le Conte-woodmanston.org/index.html.

[24] The "most distinguished scientific family in America," started by John Eatton Le Conte, became and is a "librarian's nightmare" because of the similarity of given names and published (or mispublished) names of six prominent family members. Jr. and Sr. designations were not used at the time, and often a reference is simply to John Le Conte (see Bennett, *The Le Contes*, 3, for further clarification).

[25] Bennett, *The Le Contes*, 4–6.

briefly studied medicine but did not receive a degree. They continued living in New York and spending winters at Woodmanston, studying botany and gardening at both locations. In New York, they befriended young John Torrey (see page 214), an aspiring botanist who collected plant specimens with Louis for John Eatton, who was preparing a plant catalogue. In 1810, John Eatton published the *Catalogue of the Plants of the Island of New York,* his first botanical work. In the same year, Louis moved to Georgia to manage their father's Woodmanston plantation. Louis and his brother continued to collaborate on natural history projects during John Eatton's many visits and extended winter sojourns.

With Louis's help, John Eatton worked on an extensive botanical catalog and book about Georgia's plants and published journal articles about the plants, and he and Louis supplied specimens to others for herbaria and botany projects.[26]

In 1815, Louis and John Eatton were recognized for their scientific achievements by election to membership in the Academy. Thomas Say was their sponsor. That year, their mentor, Dr. David Hosack, and Stephen Elliott, their South Carolinian/Georgian colleague, were also elected to membership. The Academy strongly influenced the future scientific and personal lives of Louis and John Eatton and their families. Louis was elected to the Academy in recognition of the many contributions he had made to botany with his research and discoveries in New York and the South, and to horticulture in the gardens at Woodmanston.[27] With the Academy's publications and member correspondents, Louis kept abreast of scientific developments although he lived in Georgia and never traveled because of a prenuptial agreement.[28]

---

[26] It was similar to the work he had done on Manhattan Island; however, Stephen Elliott, "the father of Southern botany," preempted the Le Conte brothers and established priority when Elliott began publishing his now-classic *A Sketch of the Botany of South-Carolina and Georgia.*

[27] In the garden at Woodmanston, Louis Le Conte grew many unusual native and exotic plants. He was among the first to prove the hybrid nature of *Amaryllis Johnsonii.* Louis was also one of the first to cultivate *Camellia japonica* outdoors in North America. His camellias, which he grew in the open air, became famous. A double white camellia attained a trunk diameter of more than a foot near the ground and a height of nearly twenty feet (Bennett, *The Le Contes,* 10, 15).

[28] On the legal condition that he remain in the area at Woodmanston, Louis was permitted to marry Anne Quarterman, the daughter of a prominent Georgia family in Liberty County, where their sons John and Joseph and other children were born and grew up.

John Eatton's election was the beginning of a lifelong association with the institution.[29] He often journeyed to Philadelphia for Academy meetings, made presentations, and published in the *Journal of the Academy of Natural Sciences of Philadelphia.* He also frequently visited William Bartram at Bartram's Garden nearby.

In 1818, John Eatton entered the U.S. Army as an assistant typological engineer with the rank of captain. His military assignments in North Carolina and Savannah enabled him to continue his natural history publishing.[30]

John Eatton Le Conte in Florida

Between 1818 and 1821, the boundaries of Florida and the adjacent new Southern states changed repeatedly, presenting many opportunities for surveys and exploration in the national interest backed by federal support. In April 1821, a few weeks after Florida became an official U.S. territory, John Eatton, eager to extend his work in natural history, approached John C. Calhoun, secretary of war, and proposed an expedition to explore the Florida Territory. After detailing and negotiating his expenses and goals for the trip and planning the particulars, Le Conte departed Savannah in early February 1822 for the Fernandina military post on Amelia Island in East Florida.[31] Calhoun ordered that Eatton be outfitted with eight men, including one noncommissioned officer and supplies for six to ten weeks. At Fernandina, another officer, Lieutenant Edwin R. Alberti, joined the East Florida expedition, which set out on 22 February 1822 and returned thirty-three days later (14 March).[32]

The goals of the expedition were to explore the quality of the Florida land for various development purposes (e.g., agriculture, navigation, fortifications) and opportunities for natural, commercial, and agricultural enterprises, "[a]nd finally to explore the St. John's River to its source, through a

---

[29] He later moved to Philadelphia from New York where he, his son, and his grandson played important roles in the Academy's history through collections, curation, publications, and service on committees and as officers.

[30] He published a shortened version, "Catalogue of the fauna and flora of the State of Georgia," of the comprehensive work that he and Louis had planned before Stephen Elliott's *Sketch* was published.

[31] President James Madison was authorized on 3 March 1821 to take possession of East Florida and West Florida for the U.S. and provide for initial governance. On 30 March 1822, the U.S. merged East Florida and part of what formerly constituted West Florida into the Florida Territory.

[32] Adicks, *Le Conte's Report*, 13.

country utterly unknown, and it is believed as yet untrodden by the foot of a European."[33] In John Eatton's mind, the final goal was sufficient for furthering his study of Florida's natural history. Equipped with his well-read copy of *Travels,* John Bartram's published journal, tips from Baldwin, and information about the Academy's 1817–1818 expedition, Captain Le Conte was sufficiently prepared to thoroughly explore East Florida. Although collecting biological specimens was not an official expedition goal, it was a personal prerogative for Le Conte; his field notes would supplement his collections and provide entries for his later official "Report on East Florida." William Simmons later cited Le Conte's efforts (see page 122) in his *Notices of East Florida*:

> Captain Le Conte, a United States Officer of Engineers, who under the orders of the government, lately penetrated to the head of the St. John's…. Being a scientific Botanist, he made many botanical acquisitions…. Captain Le Conte testified to the geographical and botanical accuracy of Bartram, which he had frequent opportunities of ascertaining in his voyage up the river.[34]

Captain Le Conte and his corps faced questions and challenges also encountered by earlier mapmakers and naturalists John and William Bartram. Although considerable effort had gone into charting coastal maps of Florida since the seventeenth century, few maps of the state's interior existed. Further, available maps were very rudimentary and controversial on major issues, such as the origin of the St. Johns River and whether the large Lake Mayaco (now Lake Okeechobee) in the southern peninsula actually existed. It was not until an 1886 Academy expedition that Lake Okeechobee was accurately mapped (see ch. 11). However, some early cartographers illustrated it as the source of the St. Johns based on fragmentary reports about the lake.

The Le Conte expedition followed in Bartram's tracks—from Fernandina, up the St. Johns—passing by Picolata to river localities near John Bartram's "source" location for the St. Johns River, fifty miles north (below) of the river's now-accepted source.[35] Along the way, Le Conte collected biological specimens, made observations, and recorded field notes. He documented the temperature each day at sunrise, three o'clock, and at sunset, with daily

---

[33] Ibid., 10.

[34] Simmons, *Notices of East Florida*, 22–23.

[35] The headwaters of the St. Johns River are in an unnavigable, unpopulated area called St. Johns Marsh located in Indian River and Okeechobee Counties, north of Lake Okeechobee.

notes on the weather. These scientific measurements were cutting-edge for the time. However, as Richard Adicks suggests, "because of poor organization, the indifference of government officials, untrained personnel...Le Conte did not succeed in turning out a report that might have made his expedition the landmark that it ought to have been in the story of the exploration of Florida."[36]

Much to his credit, however, Le Conte correctly determined the impossibility of growing certain crops, such as coffee, and difficulties with others, such as cotton, dates, and olives, in the new territory.[37] He also made recommendations that would guide government policy in establishing future U.S. fortifications in Key West and Tampa Bay, which would become support sites for future Florida expeditions led by Titian Peale, James Audubon, Timothy Conrad, and other Academy members.[38] Le Conte's comments about future water routes for navigating in Florida and across the Florida peninsula (a cross-Florida barge canal) would set the stage for conversations and government consideration of a canal into the twentieth century.[39]

In his official report, Le Conte briefly confirmed and expanded upon the Bartrams' earlier biological and geographic findings. During the expedition, Le Conte ameliorated his own biological collections and those of his Academy colleagues—ultimately the Academy's collections—and published many articles, which included his Florida discoveries.[40]

Le Conte's official report on East Florida was a brief forty pages, with an appendix of temperature readings taken between 10 February and 14 March 1822. He titled the report "Observations on the Soil and Climate of East Florida, February & March, 1822."[41]

The first section is about eight pages and covers general observations

---

[36] Adicks, *Le Conte's Report*, 16.

[37] Ibid., 32–34. His comments about sugarcane planting and production, which became a major crop in south Florida, were limited by the scope of his expedition.

[38] Ibid., 35. He suggested closing the military post at Fernandina and called the post "entirely useless," and continuing to use St. Augustine as a decoy, with the new posts "to prevent smuggling" and the "illegal introduction of slaves," as well as "to destroy the horde of pirates, privateers and wreckers...and in time of war these two positions may be of much value."

[39] Ibid., 28.

[40] ANSP Archives, coll. 531, Le Conte Papers; Mears, "Guide to Plant Collectors," 141–65. Le Conte published many articles in the *Annals of the Lyceum of Natural History of New York*.

[41] Adicks, *Le Conte's Report*, ix.

during Le Conte's exploration of the St. Johns from the river's mouth to what Le Conte concluded was the river's origin, with caveats:

> Its extreme source is a small lake about ten mile in circumference that appears to have no name; in some old delineations of the inner parts of Florida, the river beyond Lake George is made to pass through three lakes of modest dimensions, but which of these is the one from which the river arises, cannot be determined, as there is nothing like any of them in its whole course, and it would be wrong to bestow upon a reality, the name that has been given to a fiction.[42]

In the introductory section of a later publication about air plants, Le Conte mentions the river's source location and landscape: "whilst engaged in exploring the river St. Johns, on the borders of the small lake which forms the source of that stream.... The extensive savannahs, the boundless swamps, and the ancient forests, as yet unpolluted by the encroachments of men."[43] Le Conte's detailed botanical descriptions of the surroundings are consistent with several locations in the area, ranging as far south as Lake Monroe, which he mapped and named for President James Monroe. The marsh region near Lake Monroe was Le Conte's presumed source of the St. Johns River. As discussed several years later by Charles Vignoles, "Le Conte...set that question at rest: indeed the elder Bartram...pursued the same route and arrived at the identical head lake, which terminated captain Le Conte's expedition."[44] However, it was not until the nineteenth and twentieth centuries that the river's headwaters were recognized as originating some fifty miles further south in an unnavigable, unpopulated area, accessible only by airboat and often called the St. Johns Marsh, in Indian River and Okeechobee Counties, west of the Atlantic coast cities of Sebastian and Vero Beach and north of

---

[42] Ibid., 21.

[43] Le Conte, "North American Species of Tillandsia," 129. Read August 21, 1826. The best-known air or epiphytic plants include mosses, orchids, and bromeliads, such as Spanish moss (of the genus *Tillandsia*).

[44] Vignoles, *Observations upon the Floridas*, xiv–lxvi, 67. This bicentennial volume includes the map, book, and several articles about Florida by the eminent British "Civil and Topographical Engineer." As a young itinerant engineer, Vignoles arrived briefly in Florida in 1817 before establishing himself in Charleston and returning to St Augustine to found his survey business in 1821. After surveying the northeast coast from the Georgia border, he completed a map of Florida and published it with this handbook for immigrants to the new U.S. territory in 1823. Vignoles later returned to England and found great success as a railroad engineer.

Lake Okeechobee.[45]

Le Conte's narrative about the source of the St. Johns River is augmented by his observations and comments about the river valley soil, crops and their cultivation, and the climate, with concluding comments discussing the future of Florida and the need for military posts.

In the first section of Le Conte's report, after following a small tributary creek to its source at Silver Glen Spring on the west side of the St. Johns, he observed, "We find its origin to be an immense fountain at least twenty yards in diameter, near the center of which is a continual ebullition, the water being thrown up about a foot from the level of the basin.... There must be several tons of water discharged from this spring every minute."[46]

Earlier, in *Travels*, Bartram similarly reported, "Just under my feet was the enchanting and amazing crystal fountain, which incessantly threw up, from dark, rocky caverns below, tons of water every minute...."[47] Influenced by *Travels*, Samuel Coleridge poetically echoed Bartram in "Kubla Khan": "And from this chasm, with ceaseless turmoil seething/ .... A mighty fountain momently was forced."[48] The many springs, which feed tributaries to the St. Johns, continue to astonish and bemuse observers today.[49]

On a less Bartram-inspired note, regarding cultivating coffee, cotton, sugar cane, and other crops, Le Conte commented, "I cannot but consider all the recent speculations on the subject as visionary."[50] He criticized "the false reports of designing and unprincipled men" and counseled, "Florida has always been over valued; it therefore becomes our duty to lay aside the expectations of an El Dorado or a fountain of immortality, and by a diligent scrutiny, by practical experiments...strive to discover the best uses to which our newly acquired territory can be applied."[51]

Like Bartram, Le Conte filled his report with notes expressing wonder and joy at the creatures he observed and Florida's vast landscapes. At the springs, he commented, "One of the most remarkable things in this fountain

---

[45] Belleville, *River of Lakes*, 14–38.

[46] Adicks, *Le Conte's Report*, 24.

[47] *FHBT*, 104–105; Coleridge quote (based on Bartram), see Wright, "From 'Kubla Khan' to Florida," 76–80.

[48] For the Le Conte quote, at Silver Glen Spring, see Adicks, *Le Conte's Report*, 24.

[49] The best known and most visited is Silver Springs near Ocala. Several are available nearby in Ocala National Park.

[50] Adicks, *Le Conte's Report*, 32.

[51] Ibid., 34.

is the immense quality of fish that inhabits it. It is incredible how many are to be seen sporting about in every direction: no comparison can give any definite idea of their number, and they all move about in perfect safety, careless of everything around." He noted the tranquility and peace that existed, with none having the "least apprehension even to those that are their natural enemies, the most ravenous passing in perfect calmness...their daily prey." He observed that some are "species that only inhabit on borders of the ocean...the skate and stingray," and speculated, "How they ever got here and have become accustomed to live in fresh water is inexplicable, unless we suppose that sea in former ages had a communication with the river."[52]

Return from Florida

Following his return from Florida in late March 1822, Captain Le Conte rejoined his wife, Mary Ann Hampton Lawrence, in New York, where he completed his report and maps while pursuing further scientific interests. He attended meetings of the Lyceum of Natural History of New York, corresponded with members of the Academy, and prepared papers for publication.[53] He and his wife traveled back and forth to Savannah many more times as he surveyed Georgia's coastal islands for the military and continued his scientific work with John Abbot and others.[54] During spring 1825, a son, John Lawrence, was born, but on the way to Savannah that November, Mrs. Le Conte became ill and died. Captain Le Conte chose to spend some time at Woodmanston with Louis's growing family while recovering and caring for John Lawrence. In 1828, Captain Le Conte returned to military service and was promoted to major. He served in the topographical engineers until 1831 when he resigned his commission to spend time with his son and pursue his and John Lawrence's interest in natural history.

John Eatton Le Conte's natural history discoveries in Florida are included in his comprehensive articles in the several areas of his natural history expertise, including specific groups of plants, insects, and tortoises.[55] One

---

[52] Ibid., 3–36.

[53] Founded in 1817, the Lyceum of Natural History of New York (now the New York Academy of Sciences) is the third-oldest scientific society in the U.S. Modeled initially after the Academy, it did not develop museum activities.

[54] J. A. Bois-Duval and J. E. Le Conte, *Histoire Generale et Iconographie des Lepidopteres et des Chenilles de l'Amerique Septentrionale* (Paris, 1833), used Abbot's illustrations.

[55] John Eatton Le Conte began publishing Florida-related topics in volume 1 of the

particular paper focused on Florida air plants, specifically the species of the genus *Tillandsia*, which include Spanish moss. In his published articles, Le Conte is a perfectionist who frequently and graciously points out shortcomings in the publications of his colleagues, including Thomas Say.[56] Le Conte, who was classically well educated, also preferred to write the sections of his papers that focused on scientific descriptions in Latin since "the English language, already sufficiently harsh and inharmonious, can ill bear the introduction of words half English and half Latin (*verba privigna*); they only render it more barbarous."[57]

Le Conte reported several biological discoveries while exploring Florida. Chiefly among these are four carnivorous water plants, bladderworts in the genus *Utricularia,* which he described and illustrated.[58] Further, in his "Descriptions of Some New Species of North American Insects," Le Conte focused on beetles and illustrated many for his publications.

Along with the familiar Spanish moss, Le Conte introduced the scientific community to the new air plants that he discovered in Florida: "From among many plants collected by me in Florida, I select the following as the more interesting in as much as but two species of the genus *Tillandsia* have as yet been with certainty known to inhabit our country."[59] In a critical comment following his Latin description of *Tillandsia Bartramii,* which had been named by Stephen Elliott, Le Conte commented, "Mr. Bartram informed me that he never saw this plant, it has therefore rather improperly been named after him."

Le Conte's "Observations on the North American Species of the Genus *Viola*" is characteristic of many of his articles. Although it "does not profess to be a monograph," it is certainly a good beginning; he included several American violets that are "Habitat...*ad Floridam*," which he had collected in Florida.[60]

John Eatton Le Conte also included recommendations in his report

---

Annals in 1823. His articles in volumes 1 and 2 listed authorship as Captain John Le Conte or as John Le Conte; volume 3 and thereafter, as Major John Le Conte or John Le Conte (ibid., 57–60).

[56] "It is again to that accurate naturalist Le Conte that we are indebted for a knowledge of this beautiful reptile" (Holbrook, *North American Herpetology*, 1, 109).

[57] Le Conte, "On the North American Plants of the Genus Tillandsia," fn on 129–30.

[58] Le Conte, "On the North American Utriculariae," 72–79.

[59] Le Conte, "On the North American Plants of the Genus *Tillandsia*," 129.

[60] Le Conte, "Observations on North American species of the Genus *Viola*," 135–58; see, e.g., p. 149 for examples of the genus from Florida.

about fortifications against native and foreign attacks in Florida. His recommendations stimulated the 1823 construction of Fort Brooke in Tampa and the reinforcement of garrisons in Key West. Both settlements (as discussed further in chs. 7 and 8) became destinations for Academy members who explored Florida. Titian Peale and John Audubon visited Key West in their ornithological exploration of Florida for the revision of Wilson's *American Ornithology* and Audubon's *Birds of America*. Later, Key West would serve as a base for the expeditionary studies of Louis Agassiz and Joseph Le Conte (see ch. 9). Tampa would also be a critical location for the paleontological and geological studies of Timothy Conrad and the Joseph Wilcox/Angelo Heilprin expedition to Lake Okeechobee along the west coast of Florida (see chs. 9 and 11).

After John Eatton resigned his military commission, he lived quietly as a retired army officer in New York City for many years, devoting considerable time to his scientific pursuits through involvement with the Academy and the Lyceum of New York. He mainly focused on entomology, which was also an area of interest for his son, John Lawrence. Together, they often made lengthy visits to Louis and his family at the Woodmanston plantation.

Louis's family had also grown: he had two daughters and four sons. Louis's sons, John (1818–1891) and Joseph (1823–1901), were also scientists; neither had a middle name.[61] John Eatton and John Lawrence spent many days pursuing their common interests in natural history with Louis, John, and Joseph. Close bonds formed between the cousins and uncles through their common interests in science, exploration, and Woodmanston.

The Le Contes, Continued

Louis died of blood poisoning in 1838, shortly after his youngest son, Joseph, entered Franklin College (later the University of Georgia); Joseph's brother, John, was also a student there.[62] Both brothers later received medical degrees from the College of Physicians and Surgeons of Columbia in New York. After a brief period practicing medicine, John became a professor of physics and chemistry at the University of Georgia. Joseph practiced medicine briefly in Georgia before studying for an advanced science degree with Louis Agassiz at Harvard's new Natural Science Department and embarking

---

[61] John sometimes used "Q" to refer to his mother's maiden name, Quarterman.

[62] See Gray, "Some North American Botanists," 197–99; Stevenson, "Joseph Le Conte Obituary," 150; Armes, *Autobiography of Joseph Le Conte*; Stephens, *Joseph Le Conte, Gentle Prophet of Evolution*; Joseph Le Conte, "Memoir of John Le Conte, 1818–1891."

on an exploration of Florida's coastal reefs with Agassiz in 1851 (see ch. 7). In 1853, John was elected to Academy membership. Upon completion of his Harvard degree, Joseph returned to Georgia and entered academia. John and Joseph both prospered in their scientific pursuits and became professors at the University of South Carolina until their work was interrupted by the Civil War and they enlisted in the Army of the Confederate States.[63] Following the war, their research (and the university) faced difficulties related to reconstruction; as a result, the brothers moved to Berkeley, California, to help establish a new university. They both became distinguished founding professors, and John served as the first President of the University of California at Berkeley.

From an early age, John and Joseph's cousin, John Lawrence, shared a similar interest as his father, John Eatton Le Conte, in insects, particularly beetles and weevils. While studying medicine with his cousins John and Joseph Le Conte at the College of Physicians and Surgeons in New York, John Lawrence published three papers on beetles. Before he graduated, he was one of the youngest members elected to the Academy. After he received his medical degree in 1846, he joined his father in Philadelphia, serving as curator of entomology and many other offices at the Academy. At the beginning of the Civil War, John Lawrence entered the U.S. Army Medical Corps, where he eventually reached the rank of lieutenant colonel. He returned to the Academy after the war, earned many scientific honors, and was often acclaimed by his scientific colleagues as America's most distinguished entomologist. His beetle collection, which expanded upon his father's, included many Florida specimens and laid the foundation for modern North American beetle research.[64]

In 1852, John Eatton permanently relocated from New York to Philadelphia where he had established temporary residence shortly after John Lawrence became an active member of the Academy.[65] As a resident Academy member, John Eatton worked on his collections in the entomology section and also accepted officer (e.g., vice-president) positions.

---

[63] See Joseph Le Conte, 'Ware Sherman.'

[64] J. L. Le Conte with his student and longtime friend and colleague, Dr. G. H. Horn (member 1866), described about one-fourth of all presently known North American beetle species while working at the ANSP during the nineteenth century. In 1884, following Le Conte's death, the collections were transferred to Harvard's Museum of Comparative Zoology, where they are curated today.

[65] Barnhart, "John Eatton Le Conte," 135–38; Graham, "Reminiscences of Major John E. Le Conte," 303–11.

John Eatton also continued publishing articles related to his Florida expedition, primarily in the *Proceedings of the Academy of Natural Sciences*, which replaced the *Journal of the Academy of Natural Sciences* during 1841–1843.[66] His article "Descriptions…with Remarks upon Other North American Rodents" clarifies some of the issues that arose with George Ord's Florida rat publications from the Academy's 1817–1818 expedition (see page 90) . In particular, Le Conte brings attention to Dr. Richard Harlan's scandalous use of data (i.e., Ord's specimen from Florida) for his own publication:

> When Mr. Ord first brought this animal from Florida, he deposited his specimen in the Philadelphia Museum, in care of Mr. Peale, with a particular injunction against its getting into the hands of anyone else. Dr. Harlan, who had free admission to this institution at all times, went there when he knew no one would be present, took the specimen away, and afterwards described it under the very inappropriate name of *Arvicola hortensis*.[67]

John Eatton had met with Bartram and then frequently visited the Garden after Bartram's death in 1823. Le Conte's Florida publications continued to include many comments and references to Bartram and the species described in *Travels*.[68] At the 24 October 1854 meeting of the Academy, John Eatton reported examining "original locality authentic specimens of *Magnolia pyramidata* mentioned in Bartram's *Travels*, p. 5." Le Conte stated, in support of his conclusions (which contradicted Stephen Elliott's), "that he had been personally informed by Mr. Bartram that his *M. pyramidata* had lanceolate leaves."[69] Le Conte's final and most significant judgment of Bartram came in comments about animals that seemed to be disappearing from Florida's nature, in particular, Florida's "Great soft-shelled tortoise," which is the "*Trionyae*, of Bartram's. *Travels*, p. 177." Le Conte stated,

> I remember when it was very much the custom to ridicule Mr. Bartram, and to doubt the truth of many of his relations. For my own part I must say, that having traveled in his track I have tested his accuracy, and can bear testimony to the absolute correctness of all his statements. I travelled through Florida before it was overrun by its present inhabitants, and

---

[66] Le Conte, "An Enumeration of the Vines of North America," 269–74; Le Conte, "Description of a New Species of the Pacane Nut," 402.

[67] Le Conte, "Descriptions of Three New Species of Arvicola," 415.

[68] *FHBT*, 377. Le Conte technically named the Bartram discoveries.

[69] John Eatton Le Conte, "Remarks on *Magnolia pyramidata* of Bartram," *PANS* 7 (1854): 174–75.

found everything exactly as he reported it to be when he was there, even to the locality of small and insignificant plants. Mr. Bartram was a man of unimpeached integrity and veracity, of primeval simplicity of manner and honesty unsuited to these times, when such virtues are not appreciated.[70]

In 1858, as the presidency of the Academy passed from George Ord to Isaac Lea, John Eatton Le Conte was elected vice-president and continued in this role until his death in 1860. Memorial services were held at the Academy, and commemoratives were published in many scientific journals.[71] John Lawrence continued his stellar contributions at the Academy to entomology and serving in many administrative roles. His son, Robert Grier Le Conte M.D., was elected to Academy membership at the turn of the twentieth century and served on the Academy's Centennial Committee in 1912.

The Le Conte family accounted for more distinguished nineteenth-century American scientists and academics than any other. Louis's and John Eatton's boyhood homestead is now an historic site: the Le Conte-Woodmanston Plantation and Botanical Gardens. Many plants, turtles, birds, and other creatures are named in honor of John Eatton or his son. Le Conte's sparrow, or *Ammospiza Le Conteii*, was named by John James Audubon for John Lawrence; many turtles and tortoises have been named after John Eatton, who described and named twenty-two species of tortoises, including the Florida cooter (*Pseudemys floridana*) as well as William Bartram's gopher.[72] Le Conte's drawings of North American tortoises led some naturalists to call him "the Audubon of turtles."[73] Many of these credits contributed to and stimulated future Academy-related Florida exploration.

---

[70] Le Conte, "Notice of American Animals," 13. This statement was in the context of scientific discussion about Bartram's observations on the Florida giant soft-shelled tortoise, which was documented with two illustrations on p. 177 of *WBT*.

[71] Barnhart, "John Eatton Le Conte," 135–38; Graham, "Reminiscences of Major John E. Le Conte," 303–11.

[72] Le Conte, "Description of North American Tortoises," 91–131. In the beginning of this paper, where Le Conte describes his own observations about Bartram's gopher tortoise, Le Conte is very critical of Bartram's observations.

[73] Anonymous, "The Audubon of Turtles," 15–18.

PART 2

INTRODUCTION TO PART 2

Florida History

An official Florida Territory of the United States was created from Spanish East and West Florida in 1821. At that time, the recently admitted states of Louisiana (1812), Mississippi (1817), and Alabama (1819) had annexed portions of Spanish West Florida.[1] This redistribution of land meant that some of William Bartram's travel sites in West Florida were now located in Mobile, Alabama, and near Lake Pontchartrain in Louisiana. The new Florida Territory had two counties: St. Johns in the east and Escambia in the west. Delegates from the two counties met with the Legislative Council of the territory at both St. Augustine and at Pensacola to conduct business with the territorial governor.

The new territorial government's delegates experienced difficulty traveling for their first two annual meetings, a twenty-day trip each way through four hundred miles of unsettled wilderness. As a result, they proposed a Florida capital in a more central location. John Lee Williams of Pensacola and Dr. William Hayne Simmons of St. Augustine made up a two-person commission selected to explore several new capital locations. Dr. Simmons, a physician graduate of the University of Pennsylvania who had moved to St. Augustine in 1822, recommended the village area of the chief of the Tallahassee Indians as the Florida capital since it was conveniently located midway between St. Augustine and Pensacola.[2]

Dr. Simmons was encouraged to write about his Florida experiences and views; many eager Americans wanted information about the newly acquired southern land. His articles appeared in the *Charleston City Gazette,* and in 1822, he published *Notices of East Florida with an Account of the Seminole Nation of Indians.*[3]

Like other Florida travelers and immigrants, Dr. Simmons used Bartram's *Travels* as a guidebook for his personal exploration. In the quest for a suitable new capital, Dr. Simmons explored the Alachua Savanna (see page

---

[1] For further reading, see Gannon, *The New History of Florida.*

[2] Simmons, *Notices of East Florida* (1822); see Buker's introduction to *Notices of East Florida* (1973), xxvi–xxx.

[3] Ibid., 1822 ed.

36) and studied and wrote about the sandhill cranes (earlier observed by Bartram), stating, "This is no doubt, the species alluded to by Bartram, when he speaks in his strange language, of the 'Seraphic Cranes.'" Simmons notes the Native Americans called the cranes "Wortola-lacha."[4] He discussed the breeding habits of the crane and his unsuccessful search for their nests. Bartram's writing inspired Dr. Simmons's epic poem *Onea: An Indian Tale*, in which he often quoted Bartram's *Travels*.[5]

In *Notices of East Florida*, Dr. Simmons cited others who had recently explored the new "Province," including an Academy member, John Eatton Le Conte:

> Captain Le Conte, a United States Officer of Engineers, who under the orders of the government, lately penetrated to the head of the St. John's…. Being a scientific Botanist, he made many botanical acquisitions…. Captain Le Conte testified to the geographical and botanical accuracy of Bartram, which he had frequent opportunities of ascertaining in his voyage up the river.[6]

In the 1830s, Tallahassee and the surrounding area became centers of growth for both the new territory and botanical studies (see ch. 10), including the discovery of one of the world's rarest trees, the Florida Torreya, by Hardy Croom (elected as a correspondent to the Academy in 1835). Florida's population and plantations, including Croom's, flourished due to Tallahassee's proximity to Georgia's fertile soil for cotton, tobacco, and sugar cane; the travel required to trade these products also helped establish commerce routes. This burgeoning region came to be called Central Florida.

Florida's population primarily grew in the new counties formed as the population increased around Tallahassee and southward near Tampa (now the Interstate 75 corridor). Primitive roads connected Tallahassee to St. Augustine and Amelia Island on the east coast and a new town at the mouth of the St. Johns River. Jacksonville, which was named in honor of Andrew Jackson, the first territorial governor, was platted in 1822 in the Cowford area. Settlements occurred along the St. Johns River; nearer to Tallahassee, ports on the western Gulf Coast also flourished. One exception was Pensacola, where growth was erratic due to population devastation from several yellow

---

[4] Ibid., 39, 1822 ed.

[5] Simmons, *Onea: An Indian Tale*, iii–iv (an expanded version published later had a different title and acknowledgement to Bartram); Simmons, *Alasco, an Indian Tale*, 7–9.

[6] Simmons, *Notices of East Florida*, 23, 1822 ed. Le Conte's 1821 exploration of Florida is described in ch. 6.

fever epidemics in the nineteenth century.

In 1824, Major John Eatton Le Conte (see ch. 6) suggested that the U.S. Army establish Fort Brooke in Tampa as the first southwest Gulf Coast settlement. No major settlements existed south of the headwaters of the St. Johns River until Key West became a U.S. naval station in 1823. A thriving salvage industry based on the sunken cargo of shipwrecks made Key West an important early settlement. These southern forts and establishments facilitated further exploration of Florida, including its flora and fauna.

Florida's total population was approaching the 60,000-person requirement for statehood by 1838. Various constituents of East and West Florida began the legislative process to join the Union. On 3 March 1845, Florida became the twenty-seventh U.S. state.[7]

The 27ʰ State

In the years following statehood, Florida settlements developed outward from Fernandina on Amelia Island and Jacksonville, southward along the St. Johns River to Lake George, with railroads connecting East Florida with inland areas in Alachua County, Tallahassee, and the west coast port of Cedar Key. Earlier colonial and new Southern plantations dominated the economy. However, the discovery of easily mined clay only four to six feet beneath the earth's surface lead to important economic changes in north central Florida. Inland quarries sprang up near Gainesville and Archer; bricks of local clay were produced as early as 1853. These large-scale commercial digs spurred further geological and paleontological exploration in Florida (see chs. 9 and 11). The inland pinelands promoted the development of the timber and turpentine industries. Further south, cattle ranching, based on older Spanish rancheros, expanded to serve Caribbean markets.

Early travel throughout Florida was primitive and slow, but wilderness and frontier opportunities, like those in the American West, attracted pioneers, investors, speculators, and seasonal visitors. However, Florida's summer climate hindered the development of commerce and restricted leisure and exploration to the extended "winter season." The oppressive weather from April through October was a deterrent, particularly farther south. For residents, the mild winters compensated for the harsh summers; the winter warmth also attracted visitors. The mild months from October through April

---

[7] After several variations were considered (for example, the merger of East Florida with Georgia and West Florida with Alabama), both East and West were admitted simply as Florida, a slave state, when Iowa entered the Union as a free state (Doty, "Florida, Iowa, and the National 'Balance of Power,' 1845," 30–59).

appealed to many Northerners for health reasons; others came for the active outdoor experiences of camping, wildlife observation, boating, hunting, and fishing. The landscape and leisure opportunities were enchanting, and the growing travelers amenity industry encouraged the exploration of Florida's history and its natural wonders. However, just as Florida's development was flourishing and spreading outward from the port areas, the Civil War and then Reconstruction negatively affected the region, including natural history exploration.[8]

On 10 January 1861, Florida became the third Southern state to secede from the United States. Jacksonville, an important Confederate supply port, changed hands several times during the Civil War. By mid-1862, most of Florida's east coast was occupied by the Union and remained so for the duration of the war. A major Confederate victory, the Battle of Olustee, arrested General Truman Seymour's advance into central Florida and halted Union attempts to capture Tallahassee. At war's end in 1865, Florida, its capital unscathed, emerged less pillaged and ravaged by Union armies than other Confederate states. It quickly recovered during the 1870s and boomed during the 1880s.

The state was heavily in debt after the Civil War. To clear this debt, Governor William Bloxham sold four million acres of land in the central-southern area along the Kissimmee River in 1881 for 25 cents per acre to Hamilton Disston, a Philadelphia industrialist and real-estate developer.[9] Disston's purchase attracted railroad builders, since the State of Florida offered land deals for railroad development, similar to the growing transconti-

---

[8] The greatest negative impact was on the Le Contes (see ch. 6), who lost everything professionally and relocated to California to begin anew. In Florida, Chapman was less negatively affected (see ch. 11) in his botanical work.

[9] Disston's four million acres was larger than the state of Connecticut; it was reportedly the largest single land purchase by a single person in history. Disston's investment in Florida's infrastructure spurred statewide growth. His related efforts to drain the Everglades triggered the state's first land boom, establishing numerous towns and cities in the area. Disston's land purchase and investments were directly responsible for creating or fostering the towns of Kissimmee, St. Cloud, Gulfport, and Tarpon Springs and indirectly aided the rapid growth of St. Petersburg (Silcox, "Henry Disston's Model Industrial Community," 483–515; see also Grunwald, *The Swamp*). Disston made several important Florida fossil specimen contributions to the ANSP, including a molar tooth of an extinct "Florida Elephant," which was discussed by Joseph Leidy in *The Transactions of the Wagner Free Institute*, 1889.

nental railroad system in the West. Southwest Florida was extensively explored during this period (see ch. 11), including the southwest coastal expedition in 1886 by Academy curators Joseph Willcox and Angelo Heilprin.

During the late nineteenth century, William D. Chipley, Henry B. Plant, and Henry M. Flagler—three wealthy railroad and tourism investors—played major roles in modernizing the state. They constructed rail transportation systems and palatial hotels that enticed visitors and advanced Florida's mining, commercial, and agricultural development. Between 1881 and 1891, there was a fivefold increase in Florida's railroad mileage; the sevenfold increase witnessed by 1900 further expanded the state's economic growth.[10]

This surge in the construction of railroads and roadbeds, dredging of clay quarries for brick production, and excavation of land to obtain pebble phosphate for fertilizer export by rail also exposed geological formations and fossils. While these new developments lead to exploration opportunities for geologists and paleontologists and for botanists and zoologists, the accompanying environmental changes garnered research interest as well as growing concern. As geologists and paleontologists unraveled plant and animal extinctions from the distant past, botanists and zoologists observed similar contemporary changes resulting from population, agricultural, and industrial expansion, which were altering and endangering the current native species and their habitats. These explorers recognized and articulated the need to preserve Florida's wildlife and its habitats, as did prominent writers who visited Florida.[11] As the twentieth century began, rapid development in Florida also created interest, opportunities, and challenges for archeologists and anthropologists to study Florida's vanished native peoples and their environments (see ch. 12).

Natural History Studies

During the first third of the nineteenth century, scientific discussions and publications in institutional settings were characterized by the acts of describing, naming, and classifying American plants and animals through field

---

[10] Gannon, *New History of Florida,* 53–59.

[11] Harriet Beecher Stowe extolled nature in Florida and heralded her concerns in *Palmetto Leaves* (Boston: James R. Osgood Co., 1873). See also Sidney Lanier, *Florida, Its Scenery, Climate and History* (Philadelphia: J. P. Lippincott & Co., 1875); and George M. Barbour, *Florida for Tourists, Invalids and Settlers* (New York: D. Appleton & Co., 1882).

studies and collections.[12] Collectors increasingly considered the organism's field conditions—including climate, geological factors, and biological and ecological relationships—as new geographic areas in Florida were explored (see ch. 7). In America, scientific studies of these collected specimens focused mainly on observations of their gross external morphology while ignoring internal anatomy until some (e.g., John James Audubon) began collaborating with European anatomists (see ch. 8). Academy members and correspondents from medical schools in the U.S. soon followed suit.

Societies for those with a serious interest in natural history began forming in Massachusetts, New York, and some western states based on the model of the Academy of Natural Sciences.[13] For example, in 1818, Dr. Daniel Drake, an early Academy correspondent (elected 1812) in Cincinnati, helped found the Western Museum Society, which later became the Western Museum of Cincinnati. The museum's first taxidermist was a young, unknown artist named John Audubon (see ch. 8).[14] Many of these societies and start-up museums lasted for only a few years or eventually transitioned into other institutions. The Academy of Natural Sciences of Philadelphia was the exception, and it remained at the scientific cutting edge, celebrating its two hundredth anniversary in 2012.[15]

Many new natural history societies began by offering courses in the sciences and mechanics for a general science audience; botany was often the predominant topic. The societies frequently followed the "Lyceum Movement," a European educational movement that spread to America.[16] In 1817, a young botanist, John Torrey (elected as a correspondent to the Academy in 1822), helped found and organize the Lyceum of Natural History in New

---

[12] For further reading, see Daniels, *American Science in the Age of Jackson*, 38–39, 112–15; Oleson and Brown, *The Pursuit of Knowledge in the Early American Republic*.

[13] From 1785–1845, 107 scientific and philosophical societies or academies were founded (van Tassel and Hall, *Science and Society in the United States*, 26–28).

[14] Orosz, *Curators and Culture*, 105–106.

[15] Peck and Stroud, *A Glorious Enterprise*, 20.

[16] The term "lyceum" is ancient and referred to the grove near the temple of Apollo Lyceus in Hellenistic Athens. Prominent intellectuals, such as Socrates, Plato, Isocrates, and Aristotle, taught there, and Aristotle later founded a school in the grove named the Lyceum. This Athenian Lyceum featured daily lectures for private students as well as the general public by the leading thinkers of the day. This model was the modern conception of the "lyceum." In its European precursors and early days in America, a lyceum was associated with mechanics institutes and science education and teaching for the public.

York City.[17] An Academy of Natural Sciences member, John Eatton Le Conte, was involved in the startup and ongoing success of the Lyceum while actively exploring Florida and Georgia. New Yorker John Torrey avidly worked with many Academy members and correspondents; some lived in Florida.[18] Most significantly, Torrey expanded the Columbia University Herbarium as he embarked on publishing *A Flora of North America* with his protégé and collaborator, Asa Gray (elected as a correspondent to the Academy in 1836). Like Torrey, Gray became involved in Florida exploration.

During the early nineteenth century, natural sciences faculty at colleges and universities occasionally taught courses in botany and geology; however, most natural history courses were under the umbrella of medicine, pharmacy, or dentistry. Courses in the basic sciences and departments of natural sciences outside of the medical studies divisions only developed if there was sufficient student interest. Scientific research and collecting were often personal side interests of the faculty, and the scientific collections belonged to those who had amassed them. Occasionally, research specimens or materials specifically fashioned for instruction about minerals, plants, and animals were used to teach classes and therefore maintained by university departments. Some scientific collections later expanded into departmental collections or became the foundations for university natural history museums. Archeology and anthropology collections, representing the cultural interests of faculty in traditional departments of ancient history, biblical, and later social studies, often joined university natural history museums.

A major change in university-level natural science occurred in 1842 with the "endowed" appointment of botanist Asa Gray as a professor of natural history with nonteaching assignments at Harvard University.[19] In his role, Gray would advise several members of the governing Harvard Overseers on

---

[17] The Lyceum of Natural History in New York City was founded in 1817. Although it had no museum, it did begin a journal in 1823 and later evolved into today's New York Academy of Sciences.

[18] Most botanists maintained private herbaria. The Academy's current major early herbaria (Benjamin Barton, Henry Muhlenberg, and Lewis and Clark) were "institution" deposits, after the fact, at the APS and transferred to the Academy early in the twentieth century. These often included specimens from Bartram, Baldwin, Torrey, etc. (see Mears, "Guide to Plant Collectors," 141–65).

[19] A donated capital fund generated income to pay a faculty salary, independent from other sources, such as student fees. They were in perpetuity.

their private botanical collections, further develop the Harvard Botanic Garden as a source of rare plants, and popularize botany nationwide. Most significantly, Gray was provided with time to conduct his own botanical research. By the late 1840s, Gray had established American botany.

Another major change in university programs began in 1846 when Harvard appointed Louis Agassiz professor of zoology/geology to head its new Lawrence Scientific School; he would later found its Museum of Comparative Zoology in 1859. While striving to make Harvard a national scientific center, Agassiz and Gray created a model for other American universities to follow, including curatorial and research time for faculty and museum facilities for scientific collections.[20]

The University of Pennsylvania and other institutions of higher education both in Philadelphia and nationwide were fortunate that the Academy of Natural Sciences effectively served as a burgeoning independent research institute with collections and a library. University faculty who were also Academy members or correspondents could conduct research, make presentations, publish, and deposit their data and collections at the Academy. Later, the Academy would be joined by the independent Wagner Free Institute (1855) and the University of Pennsylvania Museum (1887), which focused on archeology and anthropology, respectively.

Following the Academy's *Journal,* scientific periodicals, such as Benjamin Silliman's *Journal of Science and Art,* which began at Yale in 1818, were created for a broader scientific audience. None, however, insisted on publishing only peer-reviewed original studies in natural science, as did the Academy's *Journal,* which transitioned in 1843 into today's *Proceedings of the Academy of Natural Sciences of Philadelphia.*

Despite the increasing public interest, financial support for natural history institutions remained elusive.[21] Peale's Museum was funded solely by paid admissions during its final years; his attempts to obtain federal, state, or city support for his museum failed. He only received minor federal funding through President Jefferson for the mammoth exhumation expedition in

---

[20] The Boston Brahmins were competing with the Philadelphia Quakers.

[21] Fieldwork was often generally self-financed. Membership dues and personal donations accounted for most operation and facility costs; labor was performed on a volunteer basis. Publication costs were met through subscription fees, volunteer labor, and occasional author fees or contributions. The cost of new periodicals for the library was offset by the exchange of the Academy's *Journal* and other publications for the publications of other institutions and societies.

New York. No other emerging scientific institutions sought or received federal assistance. This lack of funds impeded American scientific organizations from gaining national positions comparable to their European counterparts, which received tax-funded government outlay. Eventually, the creation of a national geological survey by Washington offices, the establishment in 1846 of the Smithsonian Institution, and the formation of new federal agencies associated with land surveys, Indian Affairs, and Civil War military needs marked a change in how these types of institutions were funded.

During the last half of the nineteenth century, American biologists were influenced by European developments in cell biology, physiological chemistry, evolution, and genetics. American scientists used these new methodologies and conceptual frameworks to describe, name, and classify their own living organisms and fossils. Ideas about evolution sparked research interest in the habitats, populations, and geographic distribution of plants and animals as well as their paleontologic origins.

Charles Darwin's election to Academy membership in 1860 was the first for an American scientific society because of Darwin's controversial writings. Darwin was championed by curator and later president Joseph Leidy (see ch. 11; Leidy was elected to Academy membership in 1845). Darwin's controversial evolutionary theory had pitted Leidy and Gray against Louis Agassiz's attacks on Darwin's theory and his election to the Academy. Ironically, Darwin's discovery of the creation of lagoon-islands, atolls, and reefs prompted Agassiz and protégé Joseph Le Conte to explore the Florida Keys.[22] Their popular work led to controversy and doubts regarding earlier paleontological and geological studies about the origins of the Florida peninsula; subsequent investigations by others validated the earlier study. With increased scientific interest in America's prehistoric peoples, Florida expeditions by Clarence B. Moore (elected to Academy membership in 1895) in the late nineteenth and early twentieth century focused on Florida's ancient human inhabitants and their origins. Moore's studies founded Florida anthropology, and his Southeastern discoveries electrified the international scientific community and popular press. As the nineteenth century came to a close, the plethora of new plants, animals, and terra incognita—past and present—meant that there were still many discoveries yet to be made in Florida by Academy curators and members.

---

[22] In "The voyage of the *Beagle*" (December 1831–October 1836), Charles Darwin suggests a single theory for the formation of lagoon-islands, atolls, and reefs. This theory became the subject of Darwin's first long paper and propelled him to the highest circles of British science.

CHAPTER 7

FLORIDA BIRDS…
WITH PEALE AND BONAPARTE

"Mr. Titian Peale's expedition to Florida has enriched the Fauna of the
United States, in several of its departments with many interesting species.
Of the birds, which will be introduced into the pages of my American
Ornithology, the following are more particularly worthy of immediate
notice."[1]

—Charles L. Bonaparte

From 1821–1822, retiring general Andrew Jackson served as military governor of the newly acquired Florida Territory; William Pope Duval, judge of
East Florida, then became the governor. Soon afterward, a territorial capital
was established at a new centrally located city, Tallahassee. Nearby settlements expanded southward into central Florida, and ports were fortified at
St. Marks, Key West, Ft. Brooke (Tampa), Pensacola, and St. Augustine.
Along the St. Johns River, Cowford was renamed Jacksonville in 1822 in
honor of Andrew Jackson and became a designated port of entry into the new
U.S. territory.

In Philadelphia, the scientific community mourned William Bartram,
who died on 22 July 1823 at the age of eighty-four while working in his
garden. George Ord memorialized Bartram: "He was a source of reference to
many naturalists of his day, and there was scarcely an American or foreign
writer who attempted the natural history of this country but applied to him
for Information on their relative treatises."[2] The work of maintaining and
propagating living plant collections from William's travels in the Southeast
and Florida continued after his death through the efforts of Bartram's family
members and other supporters.

With Titian Peale's assistance after he returned from the Long Expedition, Charles Willson Peale continued running Peale's Museum; Titian was

---

[1] On 10 May 1825, Bonaparte read a paper at the Academy, "Additions to the
Ornithology of the United States," *JANS* 5 (pt. 1, 1825): 28–31.
[2] Ord, "Biographical Sketch of William Bartram," 67.

named superintendent of the museum. In 1826, the museum moved to a new city building, and its name changed to the Philadelphia Museum. However, Charles died at the age of eighty-seven in February 1827 before the museum's relocation was complete. Subsequently, the Philadelphia Museum struggled under the vagaries of management and direction by Peale's heirs due to its decreasing scientific importance and popularity. The museum was sold in 1845.[3]

With its growing collections, library, and scientific resources, the Academy continued to prosper due to its ever-increasing number of members and correspondents. The continuing fieldwork of Thomas Say, Titian Peale, and others, as well as some who were less involved in fieldwork and often called "closet naturalists," led to new biological specimen collections and classifications. Many professional clinicians and academics in the field of medicine were also involved in this effort, and they extended the features of external morphology as the basis for the taxonomy and classification of organisms and also used newly developing techniques (e.g., microscopy) to consider internal anatomy and function. Other academics with different backgrounds were interested in taxonomy and nomenclature as it related to geography and biological relationships.

Increasingly, Academy membership included faculty, staff, and graduates of the University of Pennsylvania Medical School, Pennsylvania Hospital, Columbia University, the College of Physicians and Surgeons in New York, and Harvard University. By mid-century, Academy members were strongly linked to emerging schools of science at these and many other newer universities.

To meet the demands for understanding an ever-increasing number of plants and animals collected worldwide and within the new U.S. territories, the study of natural history needed to become more scientific. This new era of field collecting and discoveries raised novel questions and concerns regarding earlier published descriptions, geographic ranges, the uniqueness of organisms, and their relationships to other similar, perhaps identical, creatures. Linnaeus's system for naming and classification was a good starting point for these advancements; as the nineteenth century progressed, nomenclature and taxonomic identification were even further refined. Arguments for reclassification were often based on new knowledge gained from developing scientific tools for observation or the observer's experiences in the medical field as more anatomists, physicians, dentists, and pharmacists began conducting research

---

[3] Sellers, *Mr. Peale's Museum*, 306–35.

in botany, zoology, and the natural sciences.

The Academy of Natural Sciences Grows

During the Academy's first decade, the size of the collections paralleled that of Peale's Museum. However, with the exception of the ornithology collection, the quantity of the Academy's collections surpassed those of Peale's Museum by 1822. Peale's assortment of birds was the largest collection at that time, and it served as the primary resource for Alexander Wilson's work on his *American Ornithology*. Wilson cited the catalogue numbers of specimens in Peale's Museum so that readers would have a reference specimen to associate with the descriptions and drawings in his book. After Wilson became a member of the Academy in 1813, many of the specimens from his personal collection were integrated into the Academy's holdings, including some that are still curated today.[4] Members' and correspondents' donations of specimens and collections swelled the Academy's resources, while presentations and publications made the Academy the national leader in natural history research.

In 1826, due to the need for larger quarters for the storage of its burgeoning collections and increasing research activities, the Academy purchased and renovated a Swedenborgian church at the southeast corner of Twelfth and George streets in Philadelphia (see the frontispiece). The land and building were the first property owned by the Academy. Although President William Maclure incurred the bulk of the expenses associated with converting the building, the institution still suffered serious financial problems due to the large capital investment and regular operational expenses, which increased substantially from those at its former residence.

By 1828, Maclure convinced the Academy to extend its reach into the local Philadelphia and amateur science communities by opening its doors to the public for two and a half days each week. Without an entrance fee, visitors could see the thousands of shells, minerals, birds, fish, insects, mammals, fossils, and plants that members had acquired and were studying. However, many curators and members were not pleased with President Maclure's vision for the Academy to engage in expanded public education because of concerns

---

[4] Burtt and Davis, *Alexander Wilson*, 310–12. Wilson contributed 279 specimens, including 24 type specimens. Several, including the Mississippi kite and broad-winged hawk, are at the Academy; many others from Peale's Museum later ended up at the Museum of Comparative Zoology at Harvard.

over crowds and also potential damage to the collections.[5] The concerned members passed a resolution that required any non-member admitted to the hall to have a visitor's pass signed by a member. An internal struggle over the balance between the Academy's research vision and its education/exhibit mission for space and resources began and would continue.

In 1840, financial considerations tipped the balance in favor of public education when the Commonwealth of Pennsylvania legislature exempted the institution from taxation based on the Academy's educational usefulness to the public. Following this change, members began to react more favorably to public access.

Florida Ornithology

The history of ornithology in Florida began in the sixteenth century when the earliest known reports were made by Spanish and French explorers of birds in La Florida.[6] More than two hundred years after these early accounts, William Bartram traveled through British East and West Florida, identifying many bird species and habitats along the way (pages 34,40) . The Academy's 1817–1818 expedition in north Florida confirmed and extended many of Bartram's findings and observations, including his "little Jay," the Florida scrub jay. Although Alexander Wilson's *American Ornithology* was the premier bird book when it was published, he had not explored Spanish Florida. As new collections were received from the 1817–1818 expeditions, followed by donations of miscellaneous bird specimens after Florida became a U.S. territory, Wilson's *American Ornithology* soon required updating for bird taxonomy and newly found species. South Florida, however, remained unexplored. Charles Lucian Bonaparte, an exiled Frenchman who had recently become a member of the Academy, accepted this birding challenge. Assisted by Titian Peale, Bonaparte undertook a major task in extending Wilson's

---

[5] As historian Nathan Reingold has written, "The development of the cabinets [of specimens], the study of their contents, the use of the contents in classrooms and in popular lectures was the life of science for many Americans for well into the [19th] century. Practicing scientists were quite frequently annoyed, if not outraged, that the cabinets so often provided materials for display, not research" (*Science in Nineteenth-century America*, 30).

[6] Howell, *Florida Bird Life* (1932), 6–12; Johnston, "Additional 16th-Century Bird Reports from Florida," 1–8. With excellent bibliographic information of some 1500 publications about Florida birds, Howell's book was later revised and updated to about 1952.

American Ornithology to birds "not included by Wilson," with Florida species taking priority.

Charles L. Bonaparte

Charles Lucien Bonaparte (1803–1857), second Prince of Canino and Musignano and nephew of Emperor Napoleon, was raised in Italy.[7] During his childhood, he was an avid birder; he discovered a new species of warbler and soon became an established ornithologist. Not long after he married his cousin, Zenaide Bonaparte, the young couple left Europe for Philadelphia to live at the estate of Zenaide's father, Joseph Bonaparte. During their voyage to America, Charles observed and collected many birds, including a new "stormy petrel" or "storm petrel," which he would later name in honor of Alexander Wilson. When they arrived in Philadelphia in 1823, Bonaparte looked forward to the challenge of researching American birds.[8]

Within the growing United States, French communities provided a refuge for thousands of exiles from the waves of French turmoil—Revolutionary, Bonapartist, and Bourbon France—as well as from the strife-torn colony of Saint-Domingue (Haiti). These new French communities flourished, enriched by the influence of the American Revolutionary war hero General Lafayette.[9] In Florida, the U.S. government gifted Lafayette with a land grant, and he selected the Tallahassee area. French immigrants, many of whom were relatives of Napoleon and Charles Lucien Bonaparte, such as Prince Charles Louis Napoleon Achilles Murat, who had settled in St. Augustine with his family and others, flocked to Tallahassee. In 1816, the environs of Philadel-

---

[7] See Stroud, *The Emperor of Nature*; Mearns and Mearns, *Audubon to Xántus*, 95–104.

[8] Stroud, *The Emperor of Nature*, 34–35, 45.

[9] During the American Revolution, Gilbert du Motier, Marquis de Lafayette, loaned money to the U.S. government and supported revolutionary troops in the field. In 1803, to help Lafayette after the French Revolution, the U.S. gave him $24,000 followed by land in what is now Louisiana. In 1824, he was given another $200,000 and his choice of a township's worth of land around the time of his visit to the U.S. circa 1824–1825. He chose land in Tallahassee, which now includes Lake Lafayette. His long-distant efforts to develop the property failed but encouraged French immigrants to the area in Florida. Once on the outskirts of the capital city, the Lafayette tract is now in the city. The home of Hardy Croom (see page 217) occupied a portion of the land later in the nineteenth century and his historic Goodwood Plantation is still there; Frenchtown is nearby.

phia had become another French settlement area; Point Breeze, near Borden-town, New Jersey, the residence of the family of Joseph Bonaparte, Napo-leon's brother and the former king of Spain. His nephew and son-in-law, Charles Lucien Bonaparte, along with his new bride, Zenaide, joined the fam-ily at the Point Breeze estate in 1823.

Because of his interest in the birds that had been deposited at Peale's Museum from the Long Expedition, Charles Bonaparte met with Thomas Say and Titian Peale shortly after arriving in the Philadelphia area. Bonaparte had just begun studying America's birds and was very interested in the species that Say and Peale had brought back from the Western territories. Although Say had already scientifically described and published accounts on about nine of the birds, Bonaparte added descriptions of two more to the Western col-lection. He named one "Say's flycatcher (*Muscicapa saya*)" to honor Say.[10]

On 24 February 1824, a year after arriving in Philadelphia, Bonaparte was elected as a member of the Academy following his nomination by Say and Alexander Lesueur. Several weeks earlier, by invitation, Bonaparte had presented a paper about the new stormy petrel that he had collected en route to America. He named the bird *Procellaria willsonii* after Alexander Wilson and it is now commonly called "Wilson's storm petrel."[11] Later, Bonaparte included Say's flycatcher and Wilson's storm petrel in his major ornithologi-cal work, *American Ornithology; or the Natural History of Birds Inhabiting the United States, not given by Wilson.* Inspired by the ornithological resources at hand, Bonaparte undertook this ambitious project shortly after being elected an Academy member. He wished to follow George Ord in continuing Alex-ander Wilson's legacy. With Ord's blessing, which was needed at the time since Ord was also considering whether to prepare an updated revision of volume 9 of Wilson's *American Ornithology,* Bonaparte confidently proceeded with his projected multivolume sequel of American birds "not given by Wil-son."[12]

---

[10] Stroud, *The Emperor of Nature*, 68.

[11] Bonaparte, "An Account of Four Species of Stormy Petrels," 227–33.

[12] Ord, the legal executor of Wilson's estate, extended his authority to Wilson's ornithological legacy and often took Bonaparte to task about his stated or published scientific corrections of Wilson's work, which Ord often regarded as unwarranted criticism. Ord was more forgiving of Bonaparte than he would later be toward John Audubon. See George Ord, *American ornithology; or, The natural history of the birds of the United States: illustrated with plates, engraved and colored from original drawings taken from nature by Alexander Wilson* (Philadelphia: Samuel F. Bradford, 1824–1825). Vols. 7, 8, 9 only, written by George Ord; Ord, *Supplement to the American Ornithology of Alexander*

Because of his unique knowledge of the changes in bird classification and taxonomy that had occurred since Wilson's publication, Bonaparte's attention and expertise were essential to extending Wilson's work. Unlike Wilson and his American colleagues, Bonaparte had access to European bird collections and libraries in the years after the American Revolution. Once again, Bonaparte departed from the tradition of naturalists (most of whom simultaneously studied many animal groups) by restricting his studies to avian anatomy and detailed descriptions and classifications of birds. Unlike many field naturalists, he worked in the museum as a curator and researcher and relied on others to secure specimens in the field. His personal collection increased rapidly thanks to the efforts of his hired field collectors. In addition, Bonaparte saw a need for adding and integrating new discoveries of and about birds; for example, the many new bird species from the Long Expedition. Bonaparte also realized that Florida birds had seldom been referenced by Wilson, with the exception of Bartram's Florida observations and the Florida Four's specimens and publications. Since Wilson had not explored Florida, Bonaparte engaged Titian Peale for the project on birds "not given by Wilson" to conduct a Florida birding expedition during winter 1824–1825. As Bonaparte explained,

> As the birds of Florida were principally wanting, and it is even supposed that several of those belonging to Cuba, and other West India Islands, may occasionally resort to the southern part of Florida, and thus be entitled to a place in our work, a painter-naturalist was selected to visit that part of the union which Wilson had been so desirous of exploring. A better choice could not have been made than that of Mr. Titian Peale.[13]

Peale to Florida

Titian Peale had married his longtime favorite Eliza Laforgue and he had been working in his father's museum following his return from the Long Expedition.[14] His paid job as superintendent enabled him also to pursue his

---

Wilson; Ord, "Biographical Sketch of Alexander Wilson," 9:xiii–ccx. Later, between 1828 and 1829, Ord produced a three-volume version of *American Ornithology* arranged by bird species. "Sketch of the Life of Wilson" was included, 1:ix–l. At about the same time, Charles Lucien Bonaparte prepared his four-volume *American Ornithology...not given by Wilson*, which was published between 1825 and 1833 and primarily included birds of the Rocky Mountains from the Long Expedition and from Titian Peale's Florida expedition.

[13] Bonaparte, *American Ornithology*, 1:v.

[14] For further reading, see Poesch, *Titian Ramsay Peale: Artist-Naturalist*, 36–65;

artistic interests as well as a profession in natural history. Peale coupled his unique employment with attendance at weekly meetings of the Academy. In addition to serving on its zoological committee, Peale assisted in reviewing manuscripts for publication in the *Journal* and preparing illustrations for papers by Say, Bonaparte, and others. Titian and Eliza now had a son and expected a second child as he developed a unique and successful career in natural history. However, he longed to do more fieldwork, and new areas of Florida came as a challenge.

In addition to his reading of *Travels,* Peale's earlier field experiences in Florida and the West under the tutelage of Bartram, Say, Maclure, and others had given him valuable technical skills and kindled his appetite for more adventures. Peale could handle a gun effectively, prepare specimens, and instantly record his observations in great detail. He also had the necessary artistic ability for field sketches and detailed science-art renderings to supplement his observations at a time when scientific illustration was becoming increasingly important in ornithology.

Peale had developed a close working relationship with Bonaparte and had prepared all but one of the new illustrations for the first volume of Bonaparte's *American Ornithology,* which extended Wilson's work and would be published in 1825.[15] Peale and Bonaparte, who was a "closet naturalist" not a field ornithologist, made a perfect pair for filling in the gaps and adding Florida birds "not given by Wilson."

Peale left Philadelphia for Florida in October 1824. According to a *Charleston Mercury* news account on 20 November, Peale as superintendent of the Museum of Philadelphia was in Charleston inspecting the Museum of South Carolina and making drawings there. On 24 November, he started a journal, presumably when he left Charleston, but it has been lost.[16] He most

---

Stroud, *The Emperor of Nature,* 52–55; 66–67; Johnston and Bennett, "A Summary of Birds," 1–7.

[15] The only plate of volume 1 of Bonaparte's *American Ornithology* not drawn by Peale was prepared by Alexander Rider and John Audubon. Volume 1 was published July 17, 1825; other volumes followed through 1833. All were illustrated by Rider.

[16] Howell, *Florida Bird Life* (1932), 9. Howell noted that Peale kept a diary of his journey, which was found many years later by S. N. Rhoads in a Philadelphia shop. After passing into the possession of Colonel John E. Thayer, the diary was presented to the Museum of Comparative Zoology, but it was then lost. Poesch attempted to find the journal but writes, "It is impossible to trace the details of his journey since the journal has not yet been located" (*Titian Ramsay Peale,* 49). Peale's dates on sketches and specimen locales provide clues. An abbreviated version of Poesch's account is given here.

likely traveled overland to Savannah, just as Maclure and Say had done in 1817. By mid-December, Peale had arrived in St. Augustine, where he stayed with a cousin of Bonaparte, Prince Charles Louis Napoleon Achilles Murat, who had a house in town and a plantation nearby. Peale proceeded by boat to Key West, with stops at various keys along the way. He returned to Philadelphia in April 1825. Some of his stops from St. Augustine to Key West are documented by his collections (see below) and landscape sketches, such as that of Mr. Snyder's house on Key Vaca on 14 March 1825.

The narrative and several milestones of Peale's Florida expedition can be found in the labels of his discoveries, the locations of his sketches, and Bonaparte's publications. These suggest the approximate route for Peale's Florida travels.[17]

Peale's Birds and Florida

After eagerly beginning work on Peale's Florida birds, Bonaparte presented "Additions to the Ornithology of the United States" at the 10 May meeting of Academy members. He noted, "Mr. Titian Peale's expedition to Florida has enriched the Fauna of the United States, in several of its departments with many interesting species. Of the birds, which will be introduced into the pages of my *American Ornithology*, the following are more particularly worthy of immediate notice."[18]

In his "immediate notice" descriptions, Bonaparte recorded and named several new species, including the white-tailed hawk, Zenaida dove, and limpkin, along with several others (white-crowned pigeon, cayenne or royal tern, and palm warbler) among those Peale had brought back from Florida. His descriptions of the white-tailed hawk (kite) and Zenaida dove are the earliest known Florida records of the birds; limpkins had been observed by Bartram but not named by him. All of these new birds later appeared, along with other Peale discoveries, in lengthy articles by Bonaparte with illustrated plates in volumes 2 and 3 of "the pages of my American Ornithology."

Peale's Florida expedition began with his stopover in St. Augustine at Achille Murat's town house and nearby plantation. During his fieldwork near St. Augustine, Peale encountered a white-tailed hawk or white-tailed kite. Bonaparte describes Peale's collecting experience:

The specimen figured in the plate of the natural size, was shot in Decem-

---

[17] Poesch, *Titian Ramsay Peale*, 49.
[18] Bonaparte, "Further Additions to the Ornithology of the United States," 28.

ber, in the neighbourhood of St. Augustine, East Florida.... It was observed by Mr. Peale about the dawn of day...and on his approach, it flew in easy circles at a moderate elevation, and such was its vigilance, that the greater part of a day was spent in attempting to get within gun-shot. At length the cover of interposing bushes enabled him to affect his purpose.[19]

From St. Augustine, Peale took a southern coastal route to areas of the Florida Keys that were being settled, but whose birds were still scientifically unidentified.

At Key Tavernier, south of Key Largo, Peale collected a Florida limpkin, which Bartram (see page 32) had listed as *Tantalus pictus* and pointed out the Indian name equivalent of "crying bird."[20] In his *American Ornithology*, Bonaparte includes an illustration of this bird, "Drawn from nature by A. Rider," and notes, "The specimen figured was a female, killed on the fifth of February by Mr. Titian Peale, at Key Tavernier, on the Florida reef. Mr. Peale took it for the much disputed Crying Bird of Bartram."[21] Bonaparte named Peale's bird *Rallus giganteus*.[22] The reference "Drawn from nature by A. Rider" applied to the illustrations in volumes 2 through 4 of Bonaparte's *American Ornithology*. He selected Alexander Rider as the artist rather than continuing with Peale, who had successfully completed art for volume 1 before his Florida expedition but was unable to deliver the artwork fast enough for Bonaparte.[23] Peale provided Rider with consultation, birds, notes, and

---

[19] Bonaparte, *American Ornithology*, 2:24–25. Poesch, in "Titian Ramsey Peale," unfortunately referred to this illustration as an "eagle." Howell writes about this bird, raising the question of whether it may be a kite or hawk, the first record of such in Florida (*Florida Bird Life*, 1st ed., 9, 163). White-tailed hawks are larger and more robust, have a shorter tail with a dark band near the tip, and lack the black spots on the wings.

[20] *FHBT*, 93, 147–8, 185, 293.

[21] Bonaparte, *American Ornithology*, 1:114 (Plate XXVI, Fig. 2).

[22] Bonaparte, "Further Additions to the Ornithology of the United States," 31.

[23] Bonaparte became concerned about Titian's reliability to deliver artwork with predictability during their work together on volume 1. Bonaparte retained John James Audubon, an artist visiting Philadelphia with an impressive portfolio, and Alexander Rider to collaborate on the drawings in volume 1 that were not done by Peale. Bonaparte was pleased and became a friend and supporter of both artists and regretted that his efforts to get Audubon elected to Academy membership were thwarted by George Ord. Since Audubon was leaving Philadelphia to ultimately find fame in England, Bonaparte retained Rider's services for the artwork for the remaining three volumes of his *American Ornithology*. For Peale, with his domestic responsibilities and those related to his father's well-being and his museum, Titian's consulting arrangement involving Rider, the engraver Alexander Lawson, and Bonaparte worked well.

sketches from Florida.

Around 14 March 1825, Peale was collecting and sketching at and around Marathon Key and nearby Knight's Key and Key Vaca. In this area, or further south in Key West, Peale procured white-crowned pigeons, "specimens from the southern part of Florida, where they resort to breed."[24] As Bonaparte notes, "This well-known species will now have a place amongst the birds inhabiting the United States.... It inhabits Florida.... Great numbers [breeding] on some of the Florida Keys."[25]

The white-crowned pigeon, Bonaparte noted, "resort to breed, in company with an undescribed Dove." This "undescribed Dove" was one of Peale's unique discoveries, an exquisite dove in the Florida Keys that was fully described by Bonaparte and named the "Zenaida dove" after his wife.[26] Bonaparte also grouped and created a new genus *Zenaide* for the Zenaida dove, mourning dove, and their relatives, thus replacing the name *Columba zenaida* with *Zenaida aurita* for Zenaida's dove. An illustration by A. Rider appears in Bonaparte's *American Ornithology* with the comment, "inhabits the Florida Keys" and reference to the location of the type specimen as "My collection," indicating Bonaparte's private collection.[27] The Zenaida dove, taken by Peale and first reported by Bonaparte in his 1825 presentation, was the first Florida record of what is a rare vagrant in Florida today.[28]

Peale's expedition began and ended at the boundaries of the Florida range of the palm warbler. It was "found during winter in Florida, where it is, at that season, one of the most common birds...are very abundant in the neighbourhood of St. Augustine...and at Key West."[29] Peale left Key West for Philadelphia in April 1825.

Peale returned to Philadelphia to his waiting wife, Eliza, and the eager Bonaparte. Bonaparte consulted with Peale and began examining his bird

---

[24] Ibid., 30.

[25] Bonaparte, *American Ornithology*, 2:19 (Plate XVII, Fig. 1).

[26] (*Columba zenaida* = *Zenaida aurita*). Bonaparte, "Further Additions to the Ornithology of the United States," 30; Bonaparte, *American Ornithology*, 3:23–26 (Plate XVII, Fig. 2); Bonaparte, "Supplement to the Genera of North American Birds," 49–53; Mearns and Mearns, *Audubon to Xántus*, 101–104.

[27] Bonaparte, *American Ornithology*, 1:24. Figure 11 is Plate XVII, Fig. 2, page 18 ff.

[28] The range is throughout the Caribbean and on the northern coast of the Yucatán Peninsula, Mexico. Accidental on Florida Keys and mainland of southern Florida.

[29] (*Sylvia palmarum* = *Dendroica palmarum*). Bonaparte, *American Ornithology*, 2:12–13 (Plate X, Fig. 2).

specimens and notes while Peale and Eliza prepared for the arrival of their first child, a daughter, whom they named Mary Florida.[30]

As a gesture of appreciation for Titian Peale's work, Bonaparte later named an egret for him, *Ardea pealii*, Peale's egret heron, which is now known to be the white phase of the reddish egret.[31] Unaware of the maturing changes in the bird's coloration until Audubon's later Florida work, Bonaparte referred to *Ardea pealii* and compared Peale's specimen and Rider's illustration with those of other white herons. Bonaparte wrote, "We have to state that it is dedicated to Mr. Titian Peale, by whom it was first shot for us in Florida.... Drawn from nature by A. Rider based on the specimen now in 'My Collection.'"[32]

Bonaparte's Birds

Bonaparte continued presentations and publishing *Journal* articles on various birds "not given by Wilson," culminating in the publication of the first volume of his *American Ornithology*.

Shortly after Peale's return to Philadelphia, in a paper published about the descriptions of two new Mexican bird species, Bonaparte observed that one of the birds had as its "most closely allied species...the Florida Jay...very perfect specimens of which have just been brought home by Mr. T. Peale amongst other valuable objects of Natural History."[33] At the time, Bonaparte noted, "Mr. T. Peale has drawn on the spot that fine bird, which was not noticed by Wilson; and his drawing will embellish the second volume of my *American Ornithology*." As mentioned earlier (page 139) , Peale did not illustrate this volume, but the specimen and Peale's drawings aided Alexander Rider in later executing the first published illustration of the Florida Jay—Bartram's "little jay of Florida," Ord's "Florida Jay of Bartram," now called the Florida Scrub Jay—for Bonaparte's *American Ornithology*.

In the first volume of *American Ornithology*, published in 1825, Bonaparte referred to the wild turkey "Drawn from nature by Titian R. Peale" and "procured in the month of March, on St. Johns River, Florida."[34] A mounted

---

[30] Poesch, *Titian Ramsey Peale*, 51.

[31] Bonaparte, *American Ornithology*, 4:96.

[32] Peale's egret heron = reddish egret (*Egretta rufescens*). See Bonaparte, "Further Additions to the Ornithology of the United States," 154 (Plate XVI, Fig. 1), in Bonaparte, *American Ornithology*, 4:109.

[33] Bonaparte, "Descriptions of Two New Species of Mexican Birds," 387–90.

[34] Ibid., 1, 101.

wild turkey from Peale's Philadelphia Museum is now at the Museum of Comparative Zoology at Harvard University (ornithology collection MCZ 67842). This is probably the specimen Titian Peale used to create the illustration, which also appears unmounted in the foreground of Charles Willson Peale's 1821 self-portrait, "The Artist in his Museum."[35]

In lengthy descriptions of the biology and behavior of the wild turkey, Bonaparte quoted William Bartram and many times referred to George Ord's growing nemesis, John Audubon:

> We have particular satisfaction in acknowledging the kindness of Mr. JOHN J. AUDUBON, from whom we have received a copious narrative, containing a considerable portion of the valuable notes collected by him, on this bird {Wild Turkey}, during twenty years that he has been engaged in studying Ornithology, in the only book free from error and contradiction, the great book of nature.[36]

Another bird from the 1818 expedition created a controversy between Ord and Bonaparte when it was described in *American Ornithology*.[37] Referring to Ord's 1818 article about the boat-tailed grackle he had collected in Florida, Bonaparte delivered both praise and criticism:

> Mr. Ord has published an excellent paper in the *Journal of the Academy of Natural Sciences*, proving the existence, in the United States, of two allied species of Crow-Blackbird, in which he gives new descriptions, indicates stable characters, and adds an account of their respective habits; but in attempting to correct Wilson, he has unfortunately misapplied the names.

Bonaparte continued his critical comments, adding salt to the wounds by boasting about the achievements of Ord's new adversary, John James Audubon:

> It is therefore solely by a studious attention to nature, that we can extricate these species from the uncertainty involving them, and place them in a distinct and cognisable situation. With these views we now give a faithful representation of both sexes of the Great Crow-Black-bird, drawn by that zealous observer of nature and skillful artist Mr. John J. Audubon, and hope thereby to remove all doubt relative to this interesting species.

---

[35] Poesch, *Titian Ramsey Peale*, 47.
[36] Stroud, *The Emperor of Nature*, 66.
[37] Bonaparte, *American Ornithology*, 1:35–41 (Plate IV, Fig. 1); Bennett, "The 1817 Expedition," 6–8.

Bonaparte was one of the first to meet frontier ornithologist John Audubon when Audubon arrived in Philadelphia in early 1824 to introduce himself to the Philadelphia scientific community. Bonaparte was so taken with Audubon's drawings that he took him to a meeting of the Academy with the intent to have him elected to membership. Some members were impressed, but not George Ord, who took issue with Audubon's artistic representation of birds in exaggerated poses with botanical and historical backgrounds because it was indicative of art but not science. Although nominated, Audubon was rejected by secret ballot at that time for Academy membership.

Other Florida Studies—Not Birds

Although Peale's main efforts in Florida were bird-related, he also spent time drawing and collecting shells and insects of interest to Thomas Say, with whom he continued to collaborate. Say was still working on his *American Entomology: or Descriptions of the Insects of North America (1824–28)* and formulating ideas for another definitive work on American shells. Peale also made observations and collections about plants, mammals, and reptiles.

During 1824–1825, while Peale was away, many studies on Florida's natural history were being completed, presented, or published at the Academy. Some were based on specimens from the Academy's 1817–1818 expedition. Others drew from specimens that members received from travelers who had stopped over at one of Florida's increasing number of ports while en route to or from the West Indies. Immediately upon Peale's return from Florida, Bonaparte studied and cataloged his bird specimens. In most cases, these Florida studies extended William Bartram's earlier observations on various creatures and were new entries in the Academy's portfolio of Florida exploration.

In March 1824, Dr. Richard Harlan presented to the Academy membership a description of "a new species of *Manatus,* or Sea Cow…inhabiting the Coast of East Florida."[38] He noted, "The specimens of this animal from which I have drawn its characters consist of two skulls, two ribs, and a strip

---

[38] Richard Harlan (1796–1843, elected to Academy membership in 1815) was a pioneer in the study of comparative anatomy and vertebrate paleontology in the United States. Having received his medical degree from the University of Pennsylvania in 1818, Harlan was employed as an instructor of anatomy at Joseph Parrish's school and the Philadelphia Museum and was also a practicing physician. He was elected to the ANSP in 1815 and to the APS in 1822.

of skin, seven feet six inches in length, half an inch thick."[39] Although incomplete, the two heads enabled the anatomist Harlan to deduce key information based upon the number of teeth, the jaw structure, etc. This information was critical for determining that the specimen represented a new member of the group of known African and South American lamantins, or manatees. Bartram (page 38) had previously observed the Florida creature's skeletal remains at Manatee Springs.[40] Harlan proposed that the name *Trichecus manatus,* which had been used by Bartram, be "denominated *Mantus latirostris.*" This change correctly indicated that the Florida manatee was a sub-species of the South American group that inhabited the West Indies.[41]

Harlan's studies used Florida manatee specimens, along with several alligator skulls provided by "Dr. Burrows, who collected them…on the Coast of East Florida, in the year 1822."[42] Harlan's scientific relationship with the collector was fortuitously based on friendship or sponsorship. Like Bonaparte, Dr. Harlan was not a field collector. Both relied on others for field collecting; their own forte and work took place primarily in the museum, library, and the laboratory.

In June 1824, Rudolph Dietz reported to Academy members his "Description of a testaceous formation at Anastasia Island, extracted from notes made on a journey to the southern part of the United States, during winter 1822 and 1823."[43] Regrettably, there is no documentation of Dietz's travel, which included observations of coquina rock on "Anastasia Island, opposite St. Augustine, along the coast of East Florida." Earlier observations were made by John and William Bartram in 1765 (see page 14) and Say and Peale in 1818 (page 87). The Florida Four returned to Philadelphia with Anastasia

---

[39] Harlan, "On a Species of Lamantin," 390–424.

[40] *WBT,* 146, 231–32.

[41] Harlan, "On a Species of Lamantin," 394.

[42] "Dr. Burrows" may have been the later Academy member (1830), Dr. Marmaduke Burrough, who resided in Philadelphia, had relatives and land holdings in the West Indies, and was a frequent traveler along the Florida coast. "Dr. Burrows" may have also been Mr. Silas E. Burrows, a New York merchant with holdings in Philadelphia and trade routes to the West Indies along the Florida coast at a time when New York City was surpassing Philadelphia as a trading port. Poesch (*Titian Ramsey Peale,* 53) suggests how the Burrows-Burrough confusion could have arisen (Harlan, "On a Species of Lamantin," 392).

[43] Dietz, "Description of a Testaceous Formation," 73–80. The specimen of rock composed of shells examined by Say and others was in the "List of Donations" (*JANS* 3, pt. 2 [1824]: 471). Dietz was elected to Academy membership in 1821.

Island specimens of the unusual rock used to construct the forts at St. Augustine and Picolata, as well as other buildings.[44] Dietz devoted his paper to describing the island and the quarries where slabs of the shell rock were excavated and donated the rock specimen pieces to the Academy. In completing his article, he relied on Say, who identified the individual shell types—ten in total—that made up the rock. Dietz concluded, "It will be observed that all the species here mentioned are bivalves, not the smallest determinable portion of a univalve was observed: from which circumstance we may conclude that the island is almost exclusively formed of bivalve shells, and chiefly of the genus *Arca*." Dietz's speculation, based on fossil shells, about the origins of the rock are among the first comments about Florida's geological origins that would later preoccupy Timothy Conrad, Louis Agassiz, Joseph Le Conte, and other Academy members.[45]

In an October 1824 presentation, Say reported "On the fresh water and land Tortoises of the United States." He included a detailed description, based on an 1818 collection, of Bartram's gopher tortoise:

> *Testudo polyphemus*. This is a true land tortoise…and is well known in the region which it inhabits, by the name of Gopher…. On the bank of the river St. John, Mr. T. Peale and myself dug about ten feet, guided by one of their burrows, before we arrived at its termination and secured the inhabitant. This species is readily distinguished from any other.[46]

Say cited "*Gopher* Bartram's Travels" in his references. As mentioned earlier (see page 34), when Bartram entered the Great Alachua Savannah, he "Observed as we passed over the sand hills, the dens of the great land tortoise, called gopher: this strange creature remains yet undescribed by historians and travelers."[47] Say's publication provided the scientific description and classification of the Florida gopher. Say commented, "Good specimens are in the Philadelphia Museum, one of which is living," without mention of their origins. In his description of another species, *Testudo serrate*, Say noted, "The largest specimen I have seen we obtained in East Florida; it measures about 17 inches."[48]

---

[44] Bennett, "The 1817 Florida Expedition," 21, fn 51.

[45] Conrad, "Observations on the Tertiary and More Recent Formations of a Portion of the Southern States," 128–29.

[46] Say, "On the Fresh Water and Land Tortoises of the United States," 207–208.

[47] *WBT*, 116–17.

[48] Say, "On the Fresh Water and Land Tortoises of the United States," 207–208.

In March 1825, Say and Ord reported on Florida rodents collected during the 1817–1818 expedition and proposed a new genus to include the creatures that they "found to be very numerous in the deserted plantations, lying on the river St. John, in East Florida, particularly in the gardens."[49] Say and Ord also reported further studies on the "Florida rat," which was first observed by the Bartrams (see page 16), with later reports by William Bartram (see page 30) and Ord (see page 89). Say and Ord examined the anatomical details of specimens "Brought from East Florida, in the year 1818," and one "procured by Mr. Say on the Missouri." In their published work, they made observations about teeth and other structural features not previously considered by Ord.[50] This work led Say and Ord to revise the classification of the "Florida rat" from the genus *Mus* or *Myoxus* by creating a new genus *Neotoma*, resulting in the name *Neotoma floridana*. Their presentation and paper followed a presentation given several weeks earlier by Richard Harlan, who had surreptitiously used an 1818 Florida specimen collected by Ord to describe in detail and rename the Florida rat *Arvicola hortensis*.[51] Although Harlan's work was not approved for publication in the refereed *Journal*, he later self-published the article, along with scathing comments about Say and Ord's publication.[52] Today, Ord is the recognized species authority for *Neotoma floridana*, and because of the rat's known extended range, the animal is commonly called the eastern woodrat rather than the Florida rat. A smaller subspecies that lives in the Florida Keys is the Key Largo woodrat.[53]

In addition to assisting Dietz, Ord, and others in their investigations, Say continued his comprehensive work on American shells that he had begun during the 1817–1818 expedition to Florida. Many of his specimens collected in Florida and additions from Peale's 1824–1825 expedition were used in Say's publications.

---

[49] Say and Ord, "Description of a New Species of Mammalia," 352–55.

[50] Say and Ord, "A New Genus of Mammalia Is Proposed," 345–50.

[51] Harlan, *Medical and Physical Researches*, 49–50.

[52] Ibid.

[53] Linzey, Jordan, and Hammerson, *Neotoma floridana* (2016). IUCN Red List of Threatened Species, 2016, Version 2011.2, http://www.iucnredlist.org/details/42650/0 (accessed 4 August 2018) (F. Cassola ["assessor"] 2016, Neotoma floridana [errata version published in 2017]. The IUCN Red List of Threatened Species 2016: e.T42650A115199202).

Academy in Transition

The period 1824–1830 was unsettling for the Academy and its members. Prominent Academy members and leaders, including Thomas Say, Gerhard Troost, John Speakman, and Charles Lesueur, had also become enthusiastic members of Robert Owen's Owenite Society.[54] These Academy members, along with William Maclure, who had recently returned from Europe (where he had become very interested in and a supporter of Owen's plans for a progressive settlement in Indiana), joined Owen and others in December 1825 in relocating to New Harmony, Indiana. They planned a scientific commune.[55]

Although absent from Philadelphia, Maclure and Say continued to participate in the life of the Academy. Maclure generously funded the new building facility, promoted memberships, and influenced the Academy's educational policies. Say's departure created immediate problems for the *Journal*, which he had effectively edited on his own. Say had also been a constant presence at the institution itself, creating order at the Academy's facilities during all operations and policies at a time when a new real estate venture and the subsequent relocation of the institution were imminent.

In the absence of the New Harmony colonists, vice-president George Ord and members Dr. Richard Harlan and Dr. Samuel Morton assumed leadership roles. Because of differences in fiscal policy, ideology, and personality, they began to marginalize Charles Bonaparte.[56]

From the beginning, the relationship had been cool between the friendly and worldly young "prince" (as Bonaparte wished to be addressed when he first arrived) and the maturing but always prickly Ord, who suggested that Bonaparte use the title "Mr." rather than "Prince."[57] Although the two maintained formal professional respect and support for each other on ornithological matters, they often crossed swords on nomenclature and issues of scientific detail. Ord did not respond well to critical comments about his scientific work or about the work of Alexander Wilson and his legacy. As Bonaparte became the "father of descriptive ornithology" because of his scientific approach in his presentations and papers and after the publication of the first

---

[54] Warren, *Maclure of New Harmony*, 179–86. Owenites were those followers of Robert Owen, a social reformer and one of the founders of socialism and the cooperative movement.

[55] Ibid., 179–86; 229–327

[56] Stroud, *The Emperor of Nature*, 75–78.

[57] Ibid., 50, 63–64; Pitzer, "William Maclure's Boatload of Knowledge," 110–37.

volume of his *American Ornithology* in 1825, Ord and Bonaparte's competitive relationship further exacerbated their personal association.

Bonaparte's criticism of Ord's poor descriptive work on the boat-tailed grackle from the 1817–1818 Florida Expedition and Bonaparte's employment of an upstart naturalist artist named John James Audubon to illustrate the birds in the first volume of his *American Ornithology* fueled Ord's irritation. Most damaging to their relationship, however, was Bonaparte's continuing friendship and support of Audubon's early attempts to publish his book about the birds of America and to become a member of the Academy in 1824. With the departure of Maclure and others for New Harmony, Bonaparte became increasingly concerned about the future of the Academy, the completion of his publications, and the final volumes of *American Ornithology...not given by Wilson*. As a result, he planned his return to Europe.[58]

At the end of 1826, Bonaparte left for Europe to complete a generic survey of birds for his *American Ornithology*. He studied American (including Bartram's and other Florida) collections at the British Museum and met Audubon in London in June 1827, where he renewed his acquaintance and shared ornithological notes. Bonaparte briefly returned to America before relocating his family to Europe in 1828 and permanently settling in Italy, where he joined and initiated several ornithological congresses and also lectured and wrote extensively about American and European birds and other branches of natural history. Bonaparte's *American Ornithology; or the Natural History of Birds inhabiting the United States, not given by Wilson* was published in four volumes from 1825–1833, along with articles in scientific journals about Florida birds.[59]

In spite of Bonaparte's prediction and exclamation, "Do not speak to me of the Academy. I think it is damned...forever," Ord and others managed to bring order to the Academy's finances and nurse it back to health after the many unbudgeted expenses incurred in the purchase, renovation, and occupancy of the Academy's new home (see page 132).[60] With Maclure's continued financial support, the scientific backing of Say and other New Harmonists, along with a growing number of members and correspondents, the Academy, under Ord's new regime, moved forward into the 1830s.

At the same time, the settlement of Florida continued despite interrup-

---

[58] As Stroud (*The Emperor of Nature*, 73–74) points out, financial and father-in-law problems contributed to Bonaparte's wish to return to Europe.

[59] Johnston and Bennett, "A Summary of Birds," 6–7.

[60] Stroud, *The Emperor of Nature*, 80; Baatz, "Philadelphia Patronage," 128–30.

tions in areas where brief conflicts between settlers and the Seminoles occurred. This mostly peaceful period, which began during Florida's early territorial period, continued to encourage Academy exploration of Florida, including that of formerly scorned but soon-to-be-elected Academy member John James Audubon.

CHAPTER 8

FLORIDA BIRDS, MAMMALS, AND PLANTS...
WITH AUDUBON

"Here I am in the Floridas...which from my childhood I have consecrated in my imagination as the Garden of the United States.... Mr. Bartram was the first to call this a garden, but he is to be forgiven; he was an enthusiastic botanist, and rare plants, in the eyes of such a man, convert a wilderness at once into a garden."[1]

—John James Audubon

John James Audubon (1785–1851) dreamed of exploring Florida after it had been popularized by William Bartram's *Travels* and the natural history discoveries of George Ord, Thomas Say, and Titian Peale during Academy expeditions. Following a chance meeting with Alexander Wilson, Audubon was inspired to focus his own creative efforts on his paintings and descriptions of American birds. This epiphany culminated in Audubon's study of ornithology, his later involvement with the Academy, and his exploration of Florida—in Bartram's tracks and even further south to Key West. Through Audubon's paintings and descriptions in his *Ornithological Biography, Viviparous Quadrupeds of North America,* and, preeminently, *The Birds of America,* Audubon's Florida exploration in 1831–1832 significantly contributed to our understanding and appreciation of Florida's natural history.

John James Audubon was born in Santo Domingo (now Haiti). He was the son of a French sea captain and his mistress. After his mother's death, John's father moved John and his sister to France, where he and his French wife raised the children. In 1803, John was sent to Mill Grove, a farm that his family owned outside Philadelphia, to evade Napoleon's military conscription.[2] During the young Audubon's several years there, he was enchanted

---

[1] Audubon, letter to the editor (George William Fetherstonehaugh), 12 January 1832, *Monthly American Journal of Geology and Natural Science* 1/10 (June 1832): 535.

[2] Today, 175 acres of Mill Grove remain largely as Audubon knew them: a haven for birds and wildlife. The property boasts more than seven miles of trails and views of the Perkiomen Creek. The historic three-story stone farmhouse serves as a museum

John James Audubon by John Syme, 1826.
Courtesy of White House Collection/White House Historical Association.

with the American landscape and sketched its native wildlife and flora. In 1805, while pursuing his artistic interest and talent, Audubon developed a method to accurately draw birds. He used wires to mark off a grid on a board and then pinned his recently killed bird specimens to the board, often in an action pose. Audubon then duplicated the grid on paper and drew the life-sized bird, with a detailed and artistic touch. During this time, he became a passionate observer and illustrator of birds.[3]

Young Audubon was fortunate to live near an estate owned by the Bakewell family, who befriended him. A daughter in the family, Lucy Bakewell (1787–1882), became his love and partner for life. Lucy was his business and editorial mate and the devoted mother of their two sons, Victor Gifford and John Woodhouse. Over time, Lucy devoted her energy, time, and money to supporting Audubon and their family.[4] Shortly after the couple married in 1808, they traveled to and lived in Louisville, Kentucky, where Audubon partnered with Ferdinand Rozier to run a small retail supply store.[5]

Audubon Meets Wilson

On 19 March 1810, Alexander Wilson (page 58) entered the Audubon-Rozier store after hearing about Audubon's interest in birds from Lucy's uncle, Benjamin Bakewell, whom he had previously met in Pittsburgh.[6] Wilson was traveling the frontier (see page 60) selling subscriptions for volumes of

---

displaying original Audubon prints, oil paintings, and memorabilia. The John James Audubon Center at Mill Grove is owned and operated through a unique partnership between the Montgomery County Department of Parks and Heritage Services and the National Audubon Society (http://johnjames.audubon.org).

[3] Audubon's early work is collected in Richard Rhodes, ed., *Audubon: Early Drawings* (scientific commentary by Scott V. Edwards and foreword by Leslie A. Morris; Cambridge: Harvard University Press, 2008). Audubon's method of drawing is summarized in a letter to a friend: "My Style of Drawing Birds" was reprinted in Audubon, *John James Audubon: Writings and Drawings*, 753–58 and 759–64.

[4] Proby, *Audubon in Florida*, 1–12.

[5] Audubon and Rozier were executing their fathers' business partnership agreement. The sons were sent as companions on the trip to America and spent time together while Audubon was at Mill Grove. Their business partnership, although often unsuccessful, moved westward on the frontier from Kentucky to Missouri.

[6] Rhodes, *John James Audubon: The Making of an American*, 63, 66; Ford, *John James Audubon*, 77–78; Welker, *Birds & Men*, 48–58; Herrick, *Audubon the Naturalist*, 1:202–32.

his *American Ornithology* and, when possible, collecting new birds. Upon reviewing Wilson's portfolio, Audubon was greatly interested in subscribing but was prevented by Rozier, who pointed to their poor financial state. However, Rozier added a compliment about Audubon's paintings, calling them superior to those of Wilson, who "Examined Mr. A____'s drawings, in crayon—very good. Saw two new birds." Wilson left without a subscription, but several days later, "Went out shooting this afternoon with Mr. A. Saw a number of sandhill cranes."[7] The details of their meetings are unknown; however, fragments of accounts from others agree that the meetings had little influence on Wilson's artistic work while Audubon alternatively gained confidence in his own ability and was competitively stimulated.

Over time, for Audubon, his bird paintings took on a greater significance and offered new opportunities for work. Their meeting at the store became embellished and mythologized over the years as Wilson and Audubon's ornithological works became the subjects of academic and commercial competition following Wilson's death in 1813 and Audubon's quest to publish his own work. An academic controversy grew regarding stolen ideas, priority, and the scientific correctness of Audubon's birds versus those of Wilson, with Academy members on both sides of the debate. The Wilson-Audubon controversy (or more appropriately as fueled by George Ord, the Ord-Audubon controversy) ignited during Audubon's visit to Philadelphia and the Academy in 1824.[8]

1824 in Philadelphia

Audubon arrived in Philadelphia on 5 April 1824 during the first leg of his trip east to seek financial support, an engraver, and a publisher for his growing collection of paintings of the birds of America. Dr. James Mease, a Philadelphia resident and friend of Lucy's brother, introduced Audubon to

---

[7] Ford, *John James Audubon*, 78.

[8] Welker, *Birds & Men*, 48–58; Herrick, *Audubon the Naturalist*, 1:202–32. Audubon's account from *Ornithological Biography*, 1:437, is reprinted in Herrick (*Audubon the Naturalist*, 1:220–21). F. N. Egerton noted, "The challenge is to appreciate both his [Audubon's] achievements and failures" ("A History of the Ecological Sciences," 70). Steiner commented, "It is high time for all combatants, especially those in academia, to declare a truce and accept Wilson and Audubon for what they were. The former was the best American ornithologist of his time and not a bad artist. The latter was a brilliant artist who was an accomplished and gifted naturalist. Peace" (*Audubon Art Prints*, 192). Appropriately, today both the Wilson Ornithological Society and the National Audubon Society exist.

portrait painter Thomas Sully (1783–1882) and Academy ornithologist Charles Lucien Bonaparte.[9] Mease cautioned Audubon to temper his braggadocio and cultivated a woodsman appearance during his visits. Sully and Bonaparte were impressed by Audubon's paintings and became advocates for his proposed "great work" on the birds of America.[10] Audubon and Sully exchanged art lessons while Bonaparte engaged Audubon to complete a bird painting and plate that Titian Peale was slow in preparing for Bonaparte's forthcoming *American Ornithology*. The commissioned plate was an illustration of one of George Ord's Florida Expedition birds, the boat-tailed grackle (see page 81). With high hopes for Audubon's election to Academy membership, Bonaparte arranged for the artist to exhibit works from his portfolio.[11]

However, rather than the accolades Audubon expected when he enthusiastically showed his drawings to the members of the Academy, he was instead showered with approbations about the awkward and unscientific postures of his birds, their poorly detailed feather structure, and the inclusion of extraneous leaves and flowers. Some saw his work as a romantic retrograde that was scientifically inferior to that of Wilson and Titian Peale. Audubon's depictions of colorful, active, often multiple birds of a single species in natural settings were a major departure from the formal stiff renderings of birds of different species, often grouped together by publishers due to space limitations, that characterized Wilson's and Peale's work. The detailed anatomical illustrations of birds commonly featured in scientific publications were often lacking in Audubon's work, which instead contained action poses based on fresh-killed specimens.

In contrast to Bonaparte, who considered both his own efforts and those of Audubon to be an extension of Wilson's, George Ord, who was carrying on Wilson's work through a new edition, considered Audubon an anathema.

---

[9] Thomas Sully was one of Philadelphia's most prominent portrait painters. His 1824 portraits of John Quincy Adams (who became president within the year) and then the Marquis de Lafayette, during his triumphal tour of the U.S., brought Sully to the forefront of the art community. He painted portraits of many famous Americans of the day, including Thomas Say (see page 64) and William Maclure (see page 72). These portraits, as well as those of ANSP members, now hang in the Academy's library.

[10] Ford, *John James Audubon*, 145–47; Hart-Davis, *Audubon's Elephant*, 36–37.

[11] Peck and Stroud note, "Although minutes for all Academy meetings exist for this period, there is no mention of Audubon's visit. This would suggest that either Audubon made his presentation during an informal meeting of the Academy or that George Ord was so upset by what transpired that he excised all references to Audubon from the official records of the Academy" (*A Glorious Enterprise*, 78–80, fn. 6, 87).

In addition to Ord's scientific criticism, he considered some of Audubon's comments to be unscientific criticism of Wilson and Peale, and he disliked Audubon's demeanor. Peale agreed with Ord.[12]Alexander Lawson, who had engraved Wilson's and Bonaparte's ornithological publications, also made derogatory statements upon examining Audubon's depictions and declared that he would not engrave Audubon's proposed work.

Discouraged by the negative criticism and the unfriendly reception he received in Philadelphia, Audubon departed for New York. However, he was buoyed by the support of a new patron and subscriber, Edward Harris, a wealthy amateur naturalist who would commission and purchase many of Audubon's early drawings.[13] Further, Sully and Bonaparte, along with Richard Harlan and Charles Lesueur, two of Audubon's new Academy member allies, were enthusiastic in suggesting that he seek publishing opportunities in Europe and wrote letters of introduction and support to their many contacts across the Atlantic. Audubon's visit to his early home, Mill Grove, with Academy member Ruben Haines was a refreshing last stop in Philadelphia.

Although Audubon's reception was warmer in New York City at the Lyceum of Natural History, he soon recognized that his opportunities lay abroad.[14] Any doubts he had were confirmed when he learned that he had been rejected for Academy membership after his nomination as a correspondent shortly after his visit (27 July 1824).[15] His quest for membership and his disappointment over the rejection would continue for almost a decade while he struggled to realize his "great work."

The Floridas and Audubon's "Episodes"

During the next two years, Audubon focused his time and energy on completing his paintings and journals of notes about the birds of America that he had collected over his lifetime. On 17 May 1826, he sailed from New Orleans on a trade schooner, *Delos,* bound for Liverpool, England. During

---

[12] Poesch, *Titian Ramsay Peale,* 47. Peale also refused to show Audubon a rare specimen. Their relationship was polite during Audubon's 1824 visit.

[13] Morris, "History of the Harris Collections" in Rhodes, *Audubon: Early Drawings,* ix–xi; Dwight, *Audubon, Watercolors and Drawings,* 15. Harris was elected to Academy membership in 1835.

[14] Audubon presented and published his first two brief journal articles in volume 1, *Annals of the Lyceum of Natural History of New York,* 1824.

[15] See ANSP nomination records, ANSP Archives, Memberships, coll. 115; Peck and Stroud, *A Glorious Enterprise,* 76–79.

the voyage through the Gulf of Mexico and into the Atlantic, Audubon's 1826 journal was filled with observations about sea life and his first encounter with "the Floridas."[16] Later, these personal essays and remembrances, which Audubon called "Episodes," were published along with his detailed essays about individual species of birds in his *Ornithological Biography*. Sometimes he reported hearsay or invented stories, but most of the "Episodes" were observations written as essays from his journal notes to entertain and liven up the book with a frontier field flavor.

Onboard the *Delos,* Audubon wrote in his entries and in two "Episodes"—"A Long Calm at Sea" and "Still Becalmed"—about dolphins, petrels, and migrating birds off the "capes of Florida." Frequently, a mate onboard the *Delos* shot and provided Audubon with birds. Audubon made sketches of many of the birds, including the dusky petrel, which he would use in his later paintings: "On the 26th of June 1826, while becalmed…off the western shores of Florida…I drew the figure which has been engraved. The notes made at the time are now before me, and afford me the means of presenting you with a short account of the habits of this bird…The mate of the vessel killed four at one shot, and, at my request, brought them on board."[17]

Audubon's fascination with Florida, which would not be satisfied until five years later when he traveled there, was whetted by his passage experiences on board the *Delos.*

Audubon remembered his vexation with George Ord and his Academy allies when the *Thalia* of Philadelphia came up alongside the *Delos* on 29 June to exchange supplies and cargo: "I sent a Petrel, stuffed some days previously, as the captain asked for it for the Philadelphia Society of Sciences."[18] Ord was a recurrent bad memory, as Audubon humorously wrote later in his voyage.

---

[16] See Audubon, *John James Audubon: Writings and Drawings,* 159–92; Maria R. Audubon, *Audubon and His Journals,* 1:89–90; Audubon, "A Long Calm at Sea," *The Complete Audubon,* 2:301–305; Audubon, "Still Becalmed," *The Complete Audubon,* 2:306–309; Ford, *The 1826 Journal of John James Audubon,* 19–38. Ford's work includes many drawings of fishes and birds (noddy tern) by Audubon around the Cape of Florida.

[17] *Dusky Petrel,* Audubon's Plate CCXCIX, in Proby, *Audubon in Florida,* 184–85.

[18] Audubon, *The Complete Audubon,* 1:90. Later in *Ornithological Biography,* Audubon notes, "I preserved the skins of the four specimens procured. One of them I sent to the Academy of Natural Sciences of Philadelphia, by Capitan John R. Butler, of the ship *Thalia*…"(Proby, *Audubon in Florida,* 184–85). Ship captains often read the Academy's 1817 circular about seeking and preserving specimens for inclusion in the Academy's collections.

He referred to a small unknown "Merganser Bird" that Linnaeus had never described, which "neither have I; nor any of my Precedents: Not Even the very highly, Celebrated and most Conspicuous Mr. Ord of the City of Philadelphia state of Pennsylvania: member of all the societies of &ᶜ &ᶜ &ᶜ—the perfect Academician, that Laughed because a Turkey could swim!"[19]

Audubon's "Great Work"

With his letters of introduction, Audubon traveled through England and Scotland and received acclaim for his paintings at his exhibition at the Royal Academy of Arts in Liverpool and at science academies and libraries in many cities. By December 1826, Audubon first hired William H. Lizars in Edinburgh and then, six months later, Robert Havell and his son, to engrave his paintings and publish them in sets of five for subscribers.[20] Writing to Lucy, Audubon exulted, "I am feted, feasted, elected honorary member of societies, making money by my exhibition and by my painting."[21] As he exhibited his work, he sold subscriptions for his "great work," which he called *The Birds of America,* to King George IV, other royals, patrons of the arts, and wealthy commoners.

In a letter to Lucy shortly after he retained Lizars's services in Edinburgh, Audubon wrote, by way of explanation about *The Birds of America,* "it is to come out in numbers of five prints the size of Life and all in the same size paper of my Largest Drawings called Double Elephant paper. They will be brought up and finished in such superb style as to Eclipse all of the Kind in Existence."[22] As Lizars worked on copper engraving plates and black-ink

---

[19] Audubon, "At Sea July 1826," in *John James Audubon: Writings and Drawings,* 163. Ord often took Audubon to task about his field observations, such as this one about turkeys and about rattlesnakes climbing trees, as shown in Audubon's mockingbirds painting.

[20] Rhodes, *John James Audubon, the Making of an American,* 299. Audubon first contracted with William Lizars of Edinburgh. After completing only ten etchings, Lizars's colorists went on strike, and Audubon was forced to find another publisher, namely, Robert Havell and his son, Robert Havell, Jr., of London, who completed the project. Their engravings were considered superior to Lizars's.

[21] Audubon to Lucy Audubon, 21 December 1826, in Corning, *Letters of John James Audubon, 1826–1840,* 1:7.

[22] Ibid., 1:8; Audubon, *John James Audubon: Writings and Drawings,* 798. The engraver prepared each drawing under Audubon's supervision on etched copper plates for printing onto "double elephant folio" paper measuring 28 x 39 inches. Each printed image was then appropriately "brought up," that is, colored by professional colorists with

prints for the first volume of *The Birds of America,* small armies of colorists followed, making hand-coloring textured renderings of the black-ink images; Audubon checked the various stages. Batches of five colored prints numbered by volume and in numerical order were provided to subscribers. The owners could collect and store, display, or use the prints as they wished until the sequence for the entire volume was complete and ready for binding. Volume I included prints 1–100; II, 101–200; III, 201–300; IV, 301–435. Some subscribers had the prints bound in book volumes; others maintained the prints as portfolio collections. Frequently, numbered sets were broken up, and prints were sold individually. From the first plate number of *the male Wild Turkey* published in 1827 to the last in 1838, an estimated 170 copies were produced, and 120 intact copies are known to exist today.[23]

Charles Lucien Bonaparte, a subscriber to Audubon's *Birds,* brought his packet containing the first five prints with him when he returned from England to Philadelphia. The minutes of the Academy's meeting for 16 October 1827 note, "*M. Bonaparte exhibited the first number of Audubon's Ornithology.*" However, no further comment was reported about Audubon's natural history art or about a subscription, even though other business was transacted before the meeting was adjourned. Bonaparte's report to Audubon about the meeting is unknown.

Shortly after arriving in England, Audubon began serious work on written descriptions of the birds that he depicted in the plates of *The Birds of America.* He envisioned these "biographies" to form a multivolume publication separate from but to accompany the plates in his *Birds of America.* This approach differed from Wilson's and others, whose smaller-scale drawings could be easily bound with descriptive text. In addition, because of copyright regulations and publishing costs in England and the United States, it was to Audubon's advantage to issue separate works. Further, he could begin issuing the volumes of what he would call *Ornithological Biography* independently, as soon as they were complete, since the text publishing process was speedier than the production of *The Birds of America.*

Audubon realized that he faced a serious problem in writing text that

---

Audubon's final approval. A year later, Audubon replaced Lizars with Robert Havell of London because of Lizars's failure to produce after "delays and perplexities" due to staff strikes. When Havell retired in 1830, his son Robert, Jr., took on the project and saw it to completion after his father's death in 1832.

[23] Steiner, *Audubon Art Prints,* 257–58.

was beyond his abilities. He was an artist, not a scientist.[24] Although he prided himself on his art and field observations of birds, his formal knowledge of taxonomy, morphology, and science was lacking. Scientific descriptions of more than four hundred species of birds would require a level of sophistication, knowledge, and superior writing skills that he did not possess. His narrative abilities were considerable, and he often used this talent and fiction to fill in the gaps of fact and events. This ability along with his cultivated exotic woodsman persona served him well in the salons of Europe where he exhibited his art and solicited subscriptions for his "great work." To solve his scientific research/writing problem, Audubon wisely took the advice of Bonaparte and sought a scientist co-author.

As Audubon pursued the collaboration of several potential co-authors, he also planned a return trip to America. He had several goals in mind: to persuade Lucy to accompany him back to England; to collect and paint more birds; and, with his new status, to acquire institutional subscribers, particularly the Academy.[25]

During the months following his return to America in May 1829, Audubon visited Camden, New Jersey, and Philadelphia, where he engaged in painting, exploring, and collecting nearby birds in the New Jersey Pine Barrens and southward and later in the "Great Pine Swamp" of Pennsylvania.[26] During this period, he met and hired George Lehman, a Swiss artist, to help complete the floral backgrounds of several drawings. On many occasions, Audubon entreated Lucy through letters to her and their sons to return to England with him. When she finally agreed, Audubon happily went to meet her in Louisiana. In early January 1830, they returned east by way of Washington, DC. There, President Jackson received Audubon, who acquired a congressional subscription for *The Birds of America.*

---

[24] Some criticism leveled against George Ord regarding the Audubon-Ord controversy often does not consider what Audubon himself realized and frequently stated about his scientific limitations with no questions about his artistic acumen. Ord was undoubtedly an irascible individual who became vindictive when criticized, as did Audubon. Ord's position should, however, be credited with attempting to maintain and pursue scientific standards during difficult years for the ANSP.

[25] Audubon returned as a member of the Royal Society of Edinburgh, Wernerian Society of Natural History, Society of Arts of Scotland, Philosophical and Literary Society of Liverpool, Lyceum of New York, Academy of Sciences of Paris, Linnaean Society, etc. His subscribers included King George IV, among other notables and institutions.

[26] Herrick, *Audubon the Naturalist,* 1:420–26.

In Philadelphia, however, despite Richard Harlan's best efforts, Audubon did not secure an Academy institutional subscription. Harlan had presented the reluctant members with a prospectus for *The Birds of America*. Additionally, eminent French naturalist and Academy correspondent member Baron Georges Cuvier praised Audubon's craft: "The work can be characterized briefly by the statement that it is the most magnificent monument which has yet been raised to ornithology."[27] Later, as Harlan explained to a friend, "I had commenced raising a subscription for the price of the work among my friends at the Acad. of Nat. Sciences of Philadelphia and could have succeeded, but Mr. A. declined it on such terms. He has a great deal of pride on this subject."[28] Audubon wanted an official institutional subscription. He left Philadelphia in 1830 to return to England, accompanied by Lucy, a large portfolio of new paintings, bird specimens, and copious notes. During his time in America, he had accomplished much, but not his Academy subscription goal.

He also still needed assistance in writing the scientific text, biographies of the birds, to accompany *The Birds of America*. Before his trip to America, Audubon had taken Bonaparte's advice and sought a co-author; however, Audubon's unwillingness to share co-authorship and his inability to pay large fees left him without an American co-author. When he returned to England, he was fortunately advised to enlist the aid of William MacGillivray, a very talented young man whom Audubon formally hired. MacGillivray was between jobs, having most recently worked as a special assistant to Professor Robert Jameson (elected as an Academy correspondent in 1822), Audubon's patron at the University of Edinburgh and an eminent ornithologist, editor of a soon-to-be-published edition of Wilson's *American Ornithology*. William MacGillivray was a student of the classics and had studied natural history, with a specific passion for ornithology. His interest was broad, and he pursued ornithology in field study, in the laboratory as an anatomist and illustrator, and in the library while attentive to Linnaeus and other authors. With

---

[27] Fries, *The Double Elephant Folio*, 134, 197. Baron Georges Cuvier (elected to Academy membership in 1818), a prominent French naturalist, was instrumental in establishing the fields of comparative anatomy and paleontology through his work comparing living animals with fossils. His book *The Animal Kingdom* was published in English in 1818. Cuvier presented Audubon and his work to the French Royal Academy of Sciences in September 1828, and his very favorable comments began to be recorded.

[28] Richard Harlan to William Swainson, 29 October 1829, Linnaean Society of London, in Fries, *The Double Elephant Folio*, 225.

MacGillivray's collaboration, Audubon began in 1830 to develop a very productive eight-year work pattern, which was supplemented by Lucy's editorial and office support. The first volume of *Ornithological Biography*, a comprehensive text about the birds and habitat depicted in each plate of *The Birds of America*, was published simultaneously in the United States and England.[29] It was ready for presentation to members of the Academy of Natural Sciences when Audubon stopped over in Philadelphia in October 1831 on his way to paint and study birds in Florida.

Philadelphia, En Route to Florida, 1831

Unlike his previous visits in 1824 and 1829, Audubon returned to Philadelphia in 1831 with honors and the recognition and support of legions of European admirers and subscribers. The accolades for and acceptance of Audubon and his ornithological work overwhelmed the opposition that George Ord and his ally, Charles Waterton, had attempted to generate at home and in Europe.[30] Although there was some truth to a few of Ord's criticisms, his relentless rants about Audubon and his work seemed increasingly petty and found little sympathy among the Academy's membership, which Audubon sought to join. As Audubon wrote to Harlan, "Don't you think that I might without blinking, been [sic] entitled to a seat in your own Academy?"[31] As *The Birds of America* took shape (print after magnificent print, volume after impressive volume), Audubon's stature increased exponentially.

While he and Lucy awaited the arrival of their son, Victor, in Philadelphia, Audubon reported his successes in a letter to Havell: "I have obtained Three Subscribers" (the American Philosophical Society and Academy members Richard Harlan and John Wetherill), and "I have some hopes of a few more—My Enemies are going downhill very fast and fine reviews of the Work coming forth."[32] At the 4 October Academy meeting, Audubon presented a copy of the first volume of *Ornithological Biography* and added the

---

[29] Richard Harlan assisted Audubon in obtaining copyright and in publishing in Philadelphia.

[30] Waterton was an eccentric British naturalist who met George Ord in Philadelphia and was enamored of Wilson's work, jumping into the Ord-Audubon controversies with glee and acerbity. Waterton's attacks began shortly after Audubon arrived in England.

[31] Audubon to Harlan, 10 June 1831, in Ford, *John James Audubon*, 286.

[32] Audubon to Havell, 20 September 1831, in Corning, *Letters of John James Audubon, 1826–1840*, 1:136. Ord would stand for reelection as vice-president in 1834; he was elected president and served from 1851–1858. Audubon was elected a member

inscription: "For the Acad. Nat. Sc. Phila., From the Author, Oct. 1831."[33] In conversations with geologist member G. W. Featherstonhaugh (elected as a correspondent in 1830), Audubon agreed to keep him informed about his Florida exploration. Audubon also authorized the geologist to publish information and letters from Audubon to him, as seemed appropriate, in the new *Monthly American Journal of Geology and Natural Sciences*, which Featherstonhaugh would begin publishing in November. In early October, Audubon and his taxidermist, Henry Ward, and assistant artist, George Lehman, left Philadelphia for Baltimore and Washington on their journey south to Florida.

In Washington, Audubon "was received in the most cordial manner," as Featherstonhaugh reported in the first volume of the *Monthly American*, and

> the distinguished gentlemen in authority there, have given him such letters to the military posts on the frontiers, as will assure him the aid and protection his personal safety may require. We anticipate the most interesting reconnaissance, both geological and zoological, from this enterprising naturalist, who is accompanied by Mr. Lehman, as an assistant draftsman, and by an assistant collector who came with him from Europe.[34]

The government support would be invaluable when the Audubon party found themselves twice in Charleston during their exploration trips en route, first to north Florida and then to the Florida Keys.[35]

Shortly after arriving in Charleston, Audubon was sought out by the Reverend John Bachman, a Lutheran minister and enthusiastic naturalist who

---

15 July 1832, while still en route from Europe.

[33] Peck and Stroud, *A Glorious Enterprise*, ch. 4, 80, 87. The minutes of the 4 October 1831 meeting indicate that the presentation of volume 1 took place on that day. Volume 5 bears the inscription, "Acad. Nat. Sciences from the Author, July 27, 1839." Academy Minutes, 17 July 1832, volumes 3 and 4, have no inscriptions, but the bookplates indicate that these were also gifts from Audubon. Inexplicably, volume 2 appears to have been purchased by subscription and presented to the ANSP's library by several members. Peck and Stroud suggest that the original copy was borrowed, lost, and therefore replaced. Possibly it was never received. All five volumes are heavily (and rather critically) annotated by Audubon's nemesis, George Ord.

[34] Featherstonhaugh, *The Monthly American Journal of Geology and Natural Science*, 358.

[35] Top-ranking military officers, the secretary of the navy, and the secretary for the treasury were among the "distinguished gentlemen" who assisted Audubon in his Florida expedition (Herrick, *Audubon the Naturalist*, 2:4–5).

offered the Audubon party accommodations at his family's home. The stop-over with Bachman and members of his family was outstanding; Audubon enthusiastically wrote to Lucy that they were "spending another Sunday un-der the hospitable roof of my most excellent Friend."[36] In Audubon's typically lengthy letter—with details about field experiences, the birds he had drawn, and the people he had met—he also wrote excitedly about learning that he had been elected to membership in the Academy of Natural Sciences of Phil-adelphia: "The Papers here have blown me up sky high. The Society of Nat-ural Sciences of Philadelphia has at last elected me one of their members, the Papers say Unanimously. I dare say my Friend Lea was not in the way.—My friend Bachman was well acquainted with Alexr Wilson and Friend Ord and relates some Capital anecdotes."[37]

Audubon's election had occurred shortly after he left Philadelphia. Dur-ing the 25 October 1831, Academy meeting, "Mr. John James Audubon (proposed by Members Vaux, Smith & Morton) was duly elected Corre-spondent."[38] Audubon's collaborator William MacGillivray was also elected a correspondent.[39] His election to the Academy, during Audubon's stopover in Charleston and meeting John Bachman, became memorable.[40] Lifelong ties developed between Bachman and Audubon during the month that they were together before Audubon and his assistants sailed for St. Augustine on the government schooner *Agnes*.[41]

---

[36] Audubon to Lucy, 7 November 1831, in Corning, *Letters of John James Audubon*, 1:147–48.

[37] Ibid., 1:148.

[38] ANSP Minutes, 25 October 1831.

[39] About MacGillivray: "Everyone in Britain who cares much about birds, does in a real sense, know MacGillivray, for he left a lasting mark on ornithology…. MacGillivray—a trained anatomist—got far beneath the surface and showed that a bird is not always, nor altogether, to be known by its feathers" (*A Memorial Tribute to William MacGillivray* [Edinburgh: Privately printed, 1901] 70). He was also honored in the U.S. and elected in 1831 to the Academy in recognition of his own research, publications, and collaboration with Audubon on volumes of *Birds of America* and *Ornithological Biography*. Audubon was indebted to him for the classification and nomenclature of many birds. A broad field naturalist, MacGillivray also authored books in botany and paleontology (see also William MacGillivray, *A Biography of William MacGillivray* [Edinburgh: J. A. Allen, 1910]).

[40] See Sanders and Ripley, *Audubon: The Charleston Connection*.

[41] Bachman had spent time as a young man in Philadelphia at Bartram's Garden and developed a friendship with Wilson. Bachman's daughters later married Audubon's two sons, and Bachman and Audubon collaborated on *The Viviparous Quadrupeds of*

With memories of his 1826 glimpses of "capes of Florida," dolphins, and migrating petrels and other birds, Audubon was "anxious to see what sort of Country the Florida is." His expedition library included a copy of *Travels*; in his observations and writings, Audubon noted and compared his own experiences with Bartram's visions. Bonaparte's writings about Peale's birds of Florida had also provided a good beginning for Audubon; however, Peale's and Rider's drawings were inconsequential. Ord's and Bonaparte's boat-tailed grackle publications (see page 142) were still on Audubon's mind and what he could learn from publications about the Academy's 1817 expedition. Unfortunately, he had no access to the personal accounts and discussion about the Academy's 1817 Florida Expedition or of Peale's in 1825 because of his strained relationship with Peale and Ord. Further, Thomas Say, whom Audubon admired but had met only briefly in Cincinnati, had left Philadelphia for New Harmony with William Maclure, whom Audubon had never met. However, Audubon was prepared, through his observations, writings, and drawings, to extend the commercial success of *The Birds of America* and the *Ornithological Biography* and, with his assistants, to fill many gaps in his ornithological exploration of Florida.

Audubon's expedition was planned to last from late November through the end of May. It included north Florida, which had been explored by Bartram and the Academy's 1817–1818 expedition, and was set to continue along the Atlantic coast to Key West. However, circumstances changed, and Audubon first explored near St. Augustine, slightly southward, and then around the St. Johns River from 20 November 1831 until 5 March 1932. He returned to Charleston, spent a month with Bachman, then traveled directly to the Florida Keys from 15 April through 31 May. For Audubon, his north Florida exploration was less productive and less enjoyable, as reflected in his letters and journal entries, than his exploration of the Florida Keys. From both areas, however, came many lasting paintings and "Episodes" about Florida's natural history.

St. Augustine and the St. Johns River

Audubon arrived in Florida on 20 November and began working immediately: "On the 24th November of that year [1831], in the course of an excursion near the town of St. Augustine, I observed a bird flying at a great elevation."[42] Audubon dramatically tracked the bird for a mile, fired at it, and

---

North America, which includes Florida animals. Bachman was elected ANSP correspondent in 1832.

[42] Audubon, *Ornithological Biography*, 2:350.

missed twice; Henry Ward killed what appeared to be the same bird two days later while it was scavenging a dead animal. The Caracara eagle specimen, which Audubon probably used for his painting, is now in the collection of the Academy.[43] It is one of twenty bird specimens he sent to the Academy after his Florida exploration.[44] Audubon wrote about the caracara eagle in his *Ornithological Biography:* "I was not aware of the existence of the Caracara or Brazilian Eagle in the United States, until my visit to the Floridas in winter 1831."[45]

In each of his weekly letters to Lucy, Audubon dutifully reported his birding activities, descriptions of the countryside, and his displeasure with St. Augustine, which he indicated by using pejoratives, including "is the poorest hole in the Creation."[46] In a report to Featherstonhaugh for his new *American Monthly Journal of Geology and Natural Science,* Audubon sketched in detail the dawn-to-dusk field hunting, evenings of preparation, and drawings of collected specimens, often hundreds, which exhausted their days. As if to reassure himself, Audubon added, "I know I am engaged in an arduous undertaking; but if I live to complete it, I will offer to my country a beautiful monument of the varied splendor of American nature, and of my devotion to American ornithology."[47]

After about three weeks of hunting in the area, Audubon's team had collected many specimens representing various ages, sexes, and locales of individual species for artwork and later anatomical studies by MacGillivray.[48] The team also collected specimens to sell to collectors and museums in Europe in order to defray their expenses; some specimens would be donated to the Academy. The specimens from this area, which gave rise to the descriptions in the *Ornithological Biography* and *The Birds of America,* included the Caracara, yellow red-poll (palm) warbler, Schinz's sandpiper, Wilson's plover, and the herring gull. Although Audubon depicted the "Greenshank" with a view of the Castillo de San Marcos in St. Augustine, some think that

---

[43] ANSP Ornithology Collections: Specimen, NUM, 73 *Polyborus plancus audubonus*, North America, Florida, St. Augustine; St. Se, 18331.

[44] ANSP, Minutes, July 1832.

[45] Proby, *Audubon in Florida*, 91.

[46] Audubon to Lucy Audubon, 5 December 1831 and 23 November 1831, from St. Augustine, in Corning, *Letters of John James Audubon*, 1:163, 152; see also Rhodes's edited Audubon's letters and "Episodes" pertinent to Florida in *John James Audubon: The Audubon Reader*, 321–66.

[47] Proby, *Audubon in Florida*, 19.

[48] Ibid., 20.

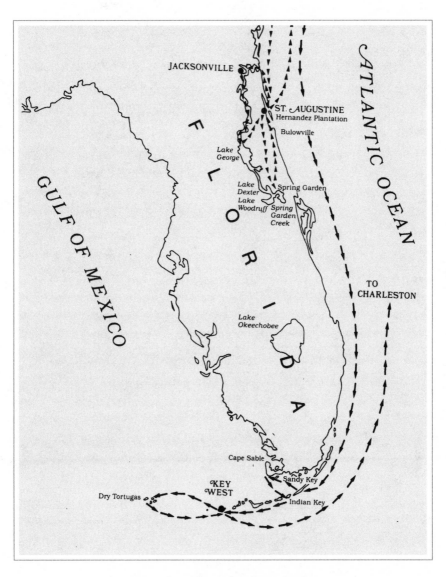

Map of Audubon's travels in Florida.
Courtesy of Brad Sanders.

Audubon saw the bird in the Florida Keys even though it is a European species. The backgrounds that Lehman drew are characteristic of the area, including sand dunes, the ocean, a wild orange tree, and the entrance to St. Augustine Harbor. Audubon's drawing (Plate CCXCI) is a herring gull with view of St. Augustine Harbor "and a young bird…on a bunch of Racoon oysters."[49]

At the invitation of a plantation owner, General Joseph Hernández, the Audubon party left St. Augustine and traveled thirty miles south, where they roamed the wilds while birding and visited several plantation owners, while a guest of Hernández at Mala Compra.[50]

Audubon's American coot, Plate CCXXXIX, from General Hernandez's plantation includes a freshwater pond with cattails and sabal palms. "Mr. Bartram, who no doubt mistook the Common Gallinule for the Coot…The male from which I drew the figure in the plate…was among the best of about thirty shot."[51]

After ten days, they moved on, and at their next stop, fifteen miles further south at John J. Bulow's sugar plantation, Audubon found pleasure while exploring; "with Mr. Bulow there was no abatement of his kindness, or his unremitted efforts to make me comfortable, and to promote my researches."[52] During this stop, Audubon wrote a report for Featherstonhaugh about their wilderness expeditions, including along a winding creek, eastward to the Halifax River, "an inland arm of the sea" where Audubon "was anxious to kill some 25 brown Pelicans…to enable me to make a new drawing of an adult male bird, and to procure the dresses of others."[53] These became models for Audubon's brown pelican, Plate CCLI 423, which "I saw several dozens of these birds perched on the mangroves, and apparently sound asleep."[54] After describing the high adventure and excitement of a successful hunt followed

---

[49] Ibid., 104.

[50] Hernández was Florida's first delegate to the U.S. Congress in 1822 and 1823 and also the first Hispanic to serve in the United States Congress. Audubon collected many American coots at his plantation (Audubon, *Ornithological Biography,* 2:294).

[51] Proby, *Audubon in Florida,* 97.

[52] Proby, *Audubon in Florida,* 22. This is now Bulow Plantation Ruins Historic State Park near Flagler Beach on U.S. A1A.

[53] Audubon, "Letter to the Editor" (no. 2), 407; Herrick, *Audubon the Naturalist,* 2:15–56. Audubon also observed and collected brown pelicans in the Keys (*Ornithological Biography,* 3:376–84, 386). He collected many specimens, which enabled him to paint Plate 424, "Young, first winter."

[54] Proby, *Audubon in Florida,* 107–108.

by a night of heavy winds and running aground in their boat, Audubon concluded, "Good God, what a night!"

Several days later, Audubon traveled alone to Colonel Orlando Rees's plantation at Live Oak Landing. While he was there, he was taken on a several day side-trip to see the "celebrated spring," which he later wrote about, without Bartram's poetic enjoyment (see page 33) , in "Spring Garden."[55]

The party followed Spring Garden Creek through mud flats in Dexter's Lake and Woodruff's Lake "where the Gallinules were seen in great numbers in every bayou leading towards the waters of the St. Johns."[56] At one point, Audubon saw, shot, and lost in the bottomless pit of lake mud "a fine pair of a new species, which if I ever fall in with again, I shall call *Tantalus fuscus*."[57] He later described the borders of Woodruff's Lake "as a perfect Paradise for a poet, but I was not fit to be in Paradise; the loss of my ibis made me as sour as the oranges that hung about me." He continued his Florida diatribe: "A garden where all that is not mud, mud, mud is sand, sand, sand…and where in place of singing birds and golden fishes, you have a species of ibis that you cannot get when you have shot it." He concluded with a complimentary snide remark: "Mr. Bartram was the first to call this a garden, but he is to be forgiven; he was an enthusiastic botanist, and rare plants, in the eyes of such a man, convert a wilderness at once into a garden."[58]

While crediting Bartram for his first observations of the wood ibis (now wood stork), Audubon politely corrects Bartram's behavioral observations as being based on too little data but takes Wilson and Bonaparte to task for repeatedly stating them without verification: "Mr. William Bartram says, 'This solitary bird does not associate in flocks'…. But the habits of this species are entirely at variance with the above quotation, to which I direct your attention not without feeling of pain, being assured that Mr. Bartram could only have made such a statement only because he had few opportunities of studying the bird in question in its proper haunts."[59]

---

[55] Audubon, "Spring Garden," *Ornithological Biography*, 2:263–67. A more caustic version appeared in "Letter to the Editor,"(no. 3), 529–37; Proby, *Audubon in Florida*, 26.

[56] Proby, *Audubon in Florida*, 139; "Common Gallinules," Plate CCXLVI. Audubon confuses the two lakes. Lake Dexter flows into the St. Johns.

[57] Audubon's reference is to birds that William Bartram had earlier termed and illustrated as dusky and white Spanish curlews (*FHBT*, 490), now white ibis.

[58] Proby, *Audubon in Florida*, 26.

[59] Ibid., 152; *Ornithology*, 3:128–30, Plate CCXVI.

After returning to St. Augustine and while awaiting transportation along the Florida coast, Audubon and company explored the St. Johns and the Florida interior from the mouth of the river at Jacksonville, following in Bartram's tracks. When Audubon continued, as planned, to Key West, he excitedly and sarcastically wrote Lucy, "What will my Philadelphia Friends say or think when they read that Audubon is on board of the U.S. Schooner of War the *Spark* going around the Floridas after Birds?"[60] Unfortunately, after traveling about a hundred miles south up the St. Johns to the lakes region, the *Spark* experienced mechanical difficulties and was ordered back to Norfolk, Virginia, for repairs. Undaunted by their loss of the vessel, Audubon and his party abandoned the *Spark*, traveled down river to Picolata, and slogged through rain, following Ord, Say, and Peale's 1818 path back to St. Augustine. Audubon regarded his group's St. Johns return trip as a disaster.[61] The party had been unable to reach Lake George, and the trek back to St. Augustine had been a torturous trip. However, as Kathryn Proby has recounted in her excellent *Audubon in Florida*, Audubon's trip, and the interruption, with time to spend around St. Augustine, served them well.[62] It enabled Audubon to complete the portfolio of birds he hunted, described, or sketched in northeast Florida for the *Ornithological Biography* and *The Birds of America*.

In addition to working on his books, Audubon hunted for several weeks with the "Live Oakers" to pass the time after returning to St. Augustine and again waiting for a boat. These itinerants seasonally traveled to the St. Johns area to harvest live oak trees for naval timber. Audubon wrote two "Episodes"—"The Live-Oakers" and "The Lost One"—based on his encounters.[63] Several of the birds included in his work from this period contributed to twenty or more paintings and references in descriptions of birds from northeast Florida. Most were depicted along with typical vegetation or landscape scenes of the area. For example, a scene by George Lehman includes a glossy ibis, "a bird of superb plumage," that Audubon observed and collected when he was with the Live Oakers at their cabin on the bluffs of the St. Johns. He noted, "The first intimation of the existence of this beautiful species of Ibis...is due to Mr. George Ord...I have given the figure of a male bird...in

---

[60] Audubon to Lucy Audubon, 16 January 1832, quoted in Proby, *Audubon in Florida*, 26.

[61] Audubon, "St. Johns River in Florida," *Ornithological Biography*, 2:291; Herrick, *Audubon the Naturalist*, 2:22–23.

[62] Proby, *Audubon in Florida*, 34–36.

[63] Ibid., 319, 323.

Florida, near a wood-cutter's cabin."[64]

As Audubon waited in St. Augustine, he grew increasingly impatient to get underway to the Florida Keys. He decided that he and his colleagues should return by paid carrier to Charleston, where there would be more opportunities for passage on a government ship along the Florida coast to Key West, as he had been promised. This decision proved to be wise because it enabled the party to spend a productive period during March and early April in Charleston with the Bachmans before returning to Florida for a second time.

Among the nine drawings that Audubon and Lehman made at John Bachman's home between mid-March and mid-April 1832 was a bird that they saw often in Florida, the boat-tail grackle, "…a pair in full spring plumage…on their favorite live-oak tree."[65] Audubon had initially drawn this controversial "Ord" grackle (see page 81) for Bonaparte's *American Ornithology* (see page 142) in 1821.[66]

In his last letter to Lucy written from Charleston before he returned to Florida, Audubon wrote about his success in arranging for a U.S. vessel, which had just arrived in port, to be assigned to convey his party to the Florida Keys. He added, "every facility would be given me to serve my views and Science…I will once more put to sea on board a Man of War and again visit that poor Country the Floridas!!"[67]

Back to Florida

Audubon, Ward, and Lehman left Charleston on 19 April 1832, aboard a U.S. Treasury Department Revenue cutter, the *Marion*.[68] The *Marion* arrived at Indian Key, between upper and lower Matecumbe Keys, on 25 April

---

[64] Ibid., 142–44.

[65] Audubon, *Ornithological Biography,* 2:508 (Plate CLXXXVII).

[66] Dwight, *Audubon, Watercolors and Drawings,* 46. Audubon's drawing as modified by Rider and Lawson is Plate 4 (Great Crow Blackbird) in Bonaparte, *American Ornithology,* 1825; see Steiner, *Audubon Art Prints,* 192–93.

[67] Audubon to Lucy Audubon, 15 April 1832, Charleston in Corning, *Letters of John James Audubon, 1826–1840,* 1:193.

[68] The U.S. Treasury Department created the Revenue Marine to patrol and enforce custom laws. Their small decked ships with one mast, known at the time as "cutters," resulted in the term "Revenue Cutter Service." Many of Audubon's experiences with "wreckers" and other seafarers were the result of the *Marion's* official government revenue cutter duties involved in marine custom inspections.

and anchored there for a week.[69] Later stops included Cape Florida, Key Biscayne, Indian Key, Key West, and the Tortugas with exploration along the way and nearby.[70]

For Audubon, it was a dream come true. "As the 'Marion' neared the inlet called 'Indian Key'...my heart swelled with uncontrollable delight.... The birds which we saw were almost all new to us; their lovely forms appeared to be arrayed in more brilliant apparel that I had ever before seen...we longed to form a more intimate acquaintance with them."[71] Shortly after arriving, Audubon's group was introduced to a guide, Mr. Thurston, who "freely offered his best services, and from that moment until I left Key West he was seldom out of my hearing." Audubon and his assistants began shooting and collecting. He wrote,

> The sailors and other individuals, to whom my name and pursuits had become known, carried our birds to the pilot's house. His good wife had a room ready for me to draw in, and my assistant might have been seen busily engaged in skinning, while George Lehman was making a sketch of this lovely isle. Time is ever precious to the student of nature. I placed several birds in their natural attitudes, and began to outline them.... The birds were skinned, the sketch was on paper.... I went on "grinding"...on paper, to finishing, not merely of my outlines, but of my notes respecting the objects seen this day.[72]

In two "Episodes" about "The Florida Keys," Audubon described the events of his "uncontrollable delight" when birding in the Keys.[73] "On the 26th of April 1832, I and my party visited several small Keys...separated by narrow and tortuous channels...dark mangroves...colonies of Cormorants," wrote Audubon to accompany his plate (CCLII) of a Florida cormorant. *Ap-*

---

[69] Indian Key is now a Florida State Historic Park. At the time of Audubon's visit, Indian Key flourished as a wrecking port for the practice of taking valuables from a shipwreck that foundered close to shore and rivaled Key West as the most prosperous south Florida town. Since Indian Key served as the home island for wreckers, it had a field office with a customs inspector for the U.S. Customs Service. Indian Key reverted to wilderness in the twentieth century.

[70] Proby, *Audubon in Florida*, 2.

[71] Audubon, "The Florida Keys," *Ornithological Biography*, 2:312.

[72] Ibid., 314.

[73] Proby, *Audubon in Florida*, 327–32; 332–37; Audubon, *Ornithological Biography*, 2:312–16, 2:345–49.

pendix: Table 1 summarizes Audubon's birds from the Florida Keys. Audubon's writings and paintings, along with Lehman's landscapes and floral backgrounds, were the first popular comprehensive descriptions of subtropical Florida with its mangrove communities and coral reefs at the interface of the emerald Atlantic and the cerulean Gulf.[74]

On 30 April, the *Marion* sailed for Key West, stopping at Key Vacas and Key Honda (Bahia Honda) before arriving on 4 May. Key West had grown during the previous decade, following Capitan John Eatton Le Conte's recommendation (see page 114) for a fortified army post. It was now one of the most tropical developing ports in the United States. The town, a hundred miles from mainland Florida on a coral island some four by two miles, had become a mecca for adventurers, mariners, pirates, wreckers, turtlers, salvors, marine enterprises, and other businesses. Upon his arrival, Audubon was greeted by Key West's foremost citizen, Dr. Benjamin Strobel, a friend and colleague of Bachman.

Dr. Strobel was the town physician, editor and publisher of the *Key West Gazette*, and town councilman. Formerly from Charleston, Strobel frequently sent natural history specimens to Bachman. Audubon notes, "My first inquires, addressed to Dr. Benjamin Strobel, had reference to Flamingoes, and I felt gratified by learning that he had killed a good number of them, and that he would assist us in securing some."[75] As Audubon had remarked during the voyage from Indian Key when he first saw flamingos flying overhead, "I thought I had now reached the height of all my expectations, for my voyage to the Floridas…studying these lovely birds in their own beautiful islands."[76] His comments about his painting (Plate CCCCXXXI) of an adult male flamingo suggest a departure from his customary field practice: "although I saw a great number of them…I cannot even at this moment boast of having had the satisfaction of shooting a single individual."[77]

As Strobel guided Audubon on birding expeditions in the area around

---

[74] Although Peale sketched and made some plant collections during his 1829 expedition, South Florida and the Keys were a floral incognita and would remain so until the late 1830s–1840s. For this reason, Audubon's botanical work was of great interest and sometimes controversial. For example, the yellow flowered water lily illustrated by Audubon with the great white swan, Plate 384, was disbelieved until it was rediscovered in 1836 by Frederick Leitner and again in 1848 by Ferdinand Rugel.

[75] Audubon, *The Birds of America*, 6:170, American flamingo entry; Audubon, *Birds of America*, 5:255.

[76] Proby, *Audubon in Florida*, 241.

[77] Ibid., 242.

Key West, he also facilitated Audubon's floral work, as in the white crowned pigeon painting (Plate CLXXVII) with a branch from a Geiger tree where it "grew in a yard opposite to that of Dr. Strobel, through whose influence I procured a large bough, from which the drawing was made, with assistance of Mr. Lehman."[78] The yard was at the home of Captain John H. Geiger, a harbor pilot and master "wrecker." His trade was very lucrative when storm winds drove ships onto reefs and wreckers boarded the sinking vessels and salvaged cargo.[79]

In addition to helping with Audubon's collections, Dr. Strobel gave him guidance about writing "Episodes"—"The Wreckers of Florida," "Death of a Pirate," and "The Turtlers"—to include in *Ornithological Biography*. Strobel also published reports about their fieldwork in the *Key West Gazette* and later in the *Charleston Mercury*. While praising "Mr. Audubon's celebrated drawings and plates," Strobel conveyed to readers detailed reports of "the danger and toil…'untried scenes and changes' he [Audubon] has passed in procuring his specimens."[80] [Strobel wrote?]"Mr. Audubon, we understand is highly gratified with his trip to the Florida Keys, having already discovered five new species of Birds…He left here in the Cutter Marion on Tuesday for Tortugas, from whence he will probably return in 4 or 5 days."[81]

After learning so much about "wreckers," Audubon had the good fortune of being hosted aboard a wrecker crew's ship in the Dry Tortugas.[82] He gathered new material for "The Wreckers." He also received their assistance in his birding, which resulted in three plates for *The Birds of America*: sooty tern (Plate CCXXXV), which "I saw a cloud-like mass arise over the 'Bird

---

[78] Audubon, *Ornithological Biography*, 2:443–47, 448.

[79] The home has been restored and, along with a Geiger tree, has become the Audubon House and Tropical Gardens of Key West. See also Audubon's "The Wreckers of Florida," *Ornithological Biography*, 3:158–63.

[80] Strobel, *Charleston Mercury*, 28 June 1833, in Proby, *Audubon in Florida*, 43.

[81] Strobel, *The Key West Gazette*, 9 May 1832; Proby, *Audubon in Florida*, 45. The number of new species is speculative (Stone, "The Work of William, Son of John Bartram," 307). Two are cited from the Keys.

[82] Commonly called "Tortugas," the Dry Tortugas are a small group of islands located in the Gulf of Mexico at the end of the Florida Keys, about 67 miles west of Key West. They are an unincorporated area of Monroe County, Florida. With their surrounding waters, they now constitute the Dry Tortugas National Park. In Audubon's time, there were a dozen small islands, the highest only ten feet in elevation; others were only mud flats. Several, including Bird Key mentioned by Audubon, disappeared in 1875 due to storm action, with another lost in 1935.

Key'"; noddy tern (Plate CCLXXV); and brown booby (Plate CCVII).[83] Later, Lieutenant Day of the *Marion* sent Audubon specimens of the white-tailed tropicbird from the Tortugas, which Audubon noted in *Ornithological Biography*: "not having had an opportunity of studying the habits of this remarkable bird, I am unable to give any information respecting them."[84]

Back in Key West, Audubon and his party continued their work and prepared other specimens and drawings of the area. To honor the local citizens, Audubon wrote, "I have taken it upon myself to name this species the Key West Pigeon, and offer it as a tribute to the generous inhabitants of that island, who favored me with their friendship."[85] In the description of the Key West quail-doves (Key West pigeons), Plate CLXVII, Audubon noted, "The plants represented...a Convolvulus...an Ipomaea.... although ornamental, are destitute of odour."[86]

On 23 May 1832, the *Marion* departed for Charleston with the Audubon party onboard. The next day, a tribute editorial written by Dr. Strobel appeared in the *Key West Gazette*:

> Mr. Audubon. This Gentleman left here...for Charleston, calculating to touch on his way at the Florida Keys, and probably the main land. ...his work on Ornithology, when completed, will be the most splendid production of its kind ever published.... [H]e is frank, free, and generous, always willing to impart information, and to render himself agreeable. The favorable impressions which he has produced upon our minds will not soon be effaced."[87]

As Dr. Strobel mentioned, Audubon intended to continue his Florida work during his trip back to Charleston. The captain of the *Marion* accommodated Audubon's wishes by taking detours before anchoring again at Indian Key. There, Audubon continued his earlier work for several days with Mr. Thurston as his guide. On visits to Cape Sable and Sandy Key, they added several birds to their specimen and drawing portfolios. Audubon is credited with being the first to identify the great white heron as a separate species, and he gave it the name *Ardea occidentalis*. He had pursued the bird first on Indian Key, next in Key West, and again on his return to Indian

---

[83] Proby, *Audubon in Florida*, 281.
[84] Audubon, *Ornithological Biography*, 3:442.
[85] Ibid., 2:382–86.
[86] Proby, *Audubon in Florida*, 271.
[87] Ibid., 46.

Key.[88] In another find, Audubon noted, "On the 26th of May 1832, while sailing along the Florida Keys…A prize ! a prize ! a new bird to the American fauna. And so it was, good reader, for no person before had found the Sandwich tern, (Plate CCLXXIX) on any part of our coast.[89]

Audubon returned to Charleston satisfied with his success in acquiring Florida water birds for *The Birds of America* and the *Ornithological Biography*. As an introduction to his third volume of the latter, he contrasted his more ordinary "Land Bird" experiences with that of "the Water Bird, which sweeps afar over the wide ocean, hovers above the surges, or betakes itself for refuge to the inaccessible rocks on the shore." He noted: "seldom have I experienced greater pleasure than on the Florida Keys."[90]

In Philadelphia

Back in Philadelphia, Audubon wrote to Bachman about his recent meetings with their mutual friends, Harlan, Featherstonhaugh, and Pickering, and added: "The Natives are quite astonished at my Production and Collections, &c—G. Ord has caused a most violent attack on my veracity to be issued in a London Journal—how he will stand mine eye on Tuesday next at the Society is more than I can at present tell."[91] At the Academy meeting on 17 July 1832, the minutes noted with appreciation that Audubon had already presented the Academy with the first volume of his *Ornithological Biography* and "Dr. [Charles] Pickering remarked of the birds presented this evening that they are part of a large collection made by Mr. Audubon in Florida, that several are now added to the catalogue of species of the United States."[92]

---

[88] Ibid., 191–200; Audubon, *Ornithological Biography*, 3:542–50 (Plate CCLXXXI).

[89] Audubon, *Ornithological Biography*, 3:531. See also Florida Keys Best, "A Guide to John Audubon's Visit to the Florida Keys," www.floridakeysbest.com/audubon/sandwich_tern.htm.

[90] Audubon, *Ornithological Biography*, 3:x–xi.

[91] Ord and Waterton specifically accused Audubon of copying several of Wilson's compositions. They also criticized Audubon for errors in scientific accuracy and of using, without attribution, the artistic and scientific work of others.

[92] ANSP Minutes, 17 July 1832. Audubon presented twenty bird skins from Florida to the ANSP at this time. There are various entries in Audubon's Florida journals and writings about specimens gifted to the ANSP from Florida (e.g., dusky petrel, mango hummingbird). He also gifted major collections from other geographic areas. Provenance in the collections may also have come through Edward Harris or members of his family, Gamble, Bachman, or others with whom Audubon collected (Ford, *John James Audubon*,

Audubon is known for collecting bird eggs in Florida. A reddish egret egg specimen with his notations is in the collection at the Academy. The pencil handwriting by Audubon identifies the egg and its Florida source and notes its "smooth shell, of a uniform rather pale sea-green color. They afford excellent eating."[93]

Although Audubon abandoned his plan to include drawings of eggs in his publications as Alexander Wilson had, Audubon still collected and drew many eggs, which were often described in detail (e.g., Louisiana heron, in *Ornithological Biography*[94]). Many specimens from his Florida collections have been identified at other museums; the internal organs of several Florida birds, including a Florida cormorant, were gifted by Audubon to the Museum of the Royal College of Surgeons.[95]

Audubon had hoped to continue his quest for birds in Florida in 1833 with his son John. However, the pressures of completing *The Birds of America* and the *Ornithological Biography* would delay their plans for several years. Audubon published the second volume of the *Ornithological Biography* in 1834, the third in 1835, the fourth in 1838, and the final volume in 1839. He completed *The Birds of America* folios in 1838. Subsequently, Audubon and his sons published combined editions of the two works using conventional sized plates for the illustrations.[96]

Audubon's relationship with the Academy fluctuated during the years following his return from the Florida Territory, intensifying in 1836.[97] He was eager to obtain access to a number of new Academy bird specimens that had been collected by Thomas Nuttall and John Kirk Townsend during their 1834–1836 transcontinental and Oregon expedition. Their discoveries of more than a hundred birds were of enormous interest to Academy members, particularly Audubon, who was eager to include as many as possible in the

---

495–96).

[93] From the collections of the Academy: Specimen 190717. Nate Rice in personal communication noted that the label has been associated with both the bird and the egg since the early 1900s.

[94] Louisiana heron eggs described by Audubon in Proby, *Audubon in Florida*, 74. Over eighty Audubon drawings of eggs are at the Louisiana State Museum; see Dwight, *Audubon, Watercolors and Drawings*, 30, 41.

[95] Ford, *John James Audubon*, 495–96.

[96] Ibid., 490–500. Summary and details about editions of Audubon's book publications.

[97] Peck and Stroud, *A Glorious Enterprise*, 74–89; Ford, *John James Audubon*, 343–45.

Egg specimen of Peale's Egret (reddish egret) from Florida
with Audubon's handwriting.
Courtesy of ANSP Ornithology Department, #190717.

The "Florida" common moorhen (*Gallinula chloropus*) egg, also collected by
Audubon, is #190716.
Courtesy of Nate Rice, Academy of Natural Sciences of Drexel University.

final volume of *The Birds of America*. The competition among ornithologists to publish these birds was keen. Townsend was now traveling to Hawaii, and Nuttall was continuing work on his recently published a popular handbook on birds, *A Manual of the ornithology of the United States and of Canada* (1834).[98] Ultimately, Audubon obtained ninety-three specimens while Townsend received some priority recognition through the efforts of his Academy colleagues.

Thomas Nuttall's *Manual*, with its easy-to-read format and illustrations, was published by Messrs. Andrews & Co. of Boston and became popular among the growing number of amateur and professional ornithologists. Among the listed water birds, for example, there are many references and descriptions of Florida birds and their discovery by Bartram, Peale, Audubon, and others. For the roseate tern, "according to Mr. Audubon, that they even abound on the shores of the Tortugas, at the extremity of East Florida where he likewise saw their nests and eggs."[99] Nuttall acknowledges Audubon's favoring him with information about new species of tern and naming the *Sterna Nuttalii* from the Tortugas after him.

Audubon and Bachman

Other post-Florida events and intrigue surrounding the "American Woodsman (Audubon)" and the Academy are narrated in detail by Peck and Stroud in *A Glorious Enterprise*.[100] Most notable is Audubon's collaboration with John Bachman on *The Viviparous Quadrupeds of North America*.[101]

Like MacGillivray before him, Bachman was an excellent collaborator for Audubon.[102] Bachman was five years younger than Audubon yet already

---

[98] Nuttall, as detailed in ch. 10, 206-208, had become associated with the Academy as a naturalist botanist in early trips to America from England and was curator of the Academy herbarium until moving to Harvard in charge of its Botanical Gardens where his interest turned to birds as he continued his Academy roles in botany and the herbarium. His was a dual role on this expedition.

[99] Ibid., 279.

[100] Peck and Stroud, *A Glorious Enterprise*, 84–85.

[101] Audubon and Bachman, *The Imperial Collection of Audubon Animals*, ix–xvi.

[102] Bachman (1790–1874) was born in New York state, ordained in 1814 as a Lutheran minister and obtained a parish in Charleston, SC, the following year. He became an avid naturalist during his youth and continued throughout life in SC, with many publications, including "On the Migration of the Birds of North America." He visited the German naturalist and explorer Alexander von Humboldt at the University of Berlin in 1838. He helped Audubon write the text of works on North American birds

established in the Southern scientific community. A scholar with a broad interest in nature, he wrote all of the scientific descriptions, compiled the synonymy of species' names, worked out geographic distributions from scanty records, and contributed personal observations on the habits of the animals. As he told Audubon, "You cannot do without me in this business...."[103]

As Bachman and Audubon prepared *Quadrupeds* for publication, they corresponded extensively with other Academy members and gathered information from the Academy's library, collections, and publications. Their work relied on many Academy institutional resources (e.g., staff, volunteers, books, collections, etc.) and Bachman's earlier published articles and those in the Academy's new *Proceedings of the Academy of Natural Sciences of Philadelphia*. In marked contrast to the cold reception with which *The Birds of America* had been received fourteen years earlier, *Quadrupeds* was enthusiastically reviewed by Academy members. At the March 1843 meeting of the Academy, the chairman "called the attention of the Society to the first number of Mr. Audubon's 'Quadrupeds,' which is placed in the Hall for inspection, and for the subscription of such members and others as may desire to possess this truly splendid and invaluable work."[104] The Academy's own subscription copy of that "splendid and invaluable work" still resides in the library, along with *The Birds of North America*, while the Academy's research facilities house for study more than one hundred skins of the birds and mammals that Audubon, Bachman, and their colleagues collected, described, and illustrated in Audubon's books.[105]

The three volumes of the *Quadrupeds* include many plates and descriptions of Florida mammals (Appendix: Table 2). The Florida rat was reported by the Bartrams. Audubon and Bachman further noted, "It was brought from East Florida by Mr. Ord, in 1818, but not published until 1825. It was then supposed by him to be peculiar to Florida, and received its specific name from that circumstance." They discussed the biogeography of the Florida rat and

---

and mammals. In his work as a clergyman, Bachman served for fifty-six years as minister of St. John's Lutheran Church in Charleston, SC, and was one of the founders of Newberry College. Bachman founded the Lutheran Synod of South Carolina and served as its first president. In 1850 he wrote *The Unity of the Human Race*. See Stephens, *Science, Race, and Religion in the American South*, and Waddell, *John Bachman: Selected Writings on Science, Race, and Religion*.

[103] Audubon, *Imperial Collection*, xi.

[104] *PANS* 1 (14 March 1843) 252.

[105] Peck and Stroud, *A Glorious Enterprise*, 86.

the taxonomic wars (see pages 89-91) that surrounded its naming by Say and Ord, concluding with, "More recently naturalists have, however, examined the subject calmly and considerately."[106] Many other mammals that are described and illustrated contain early references to Bartram and geographic references to Florida.

In some cases, an animal had recently been discovered by a member of the Academy but had not yet been described. Most, however, were relatively well known over time, and their geographic ranges included areas other than the Florida Territory. *Quadrupeds*, however, was the first comprehensive scientific description by Bachman, with an illustration by Audubon, of an updated compilation of North American mammals.[107]

Florida Contributions

In addition to Audubon's many original contributions to the exploration of Florida's natural history, he extended the knowledge of previously studied birds and mammals, such as "a pair of Florida Jays on a branch of the persimmon tree" and the Florida rat.[108]

Audubon's paintings and his reports at times became controversial: for example, his depiction of rattlesnake behavior. In one painting, he illustrated the tree-climbing creatures attacking a mockingbird nest.

> Different species of snakes ascend to their nests, and generally suck the eggs or swallow the young; but on all such occasions, not only the pair to which the nest belongs, but many other Mocking Birds from the vicinity, fly to the spot, attack the reptiles, and, in some cases, are so fortunate as either to force them to retreat, or deprive them of life...The Florida Jessamine."[109]

---

[106] Audubon and Bachman, *The Viviparous Quadrupeds of North America*, 1:31–37, Plate 4.

[107] George Ord's *North American Zoology*, which was compiled by him for Johnson & Warner and first published by them in their second American edition of *Guthrie's Geography* in 1815, was out of date. Harlan, in *Fauna Americana*, did not include more recent original western discoveries by Audubon, Bachman, and others. Audubon and Bachman often relied on living or recently collected eastern and southern mammals for their more accurate drawings and descriptions.

[108] Proby, *Audubon in Florida*, 150.

[109] Audubon, *Ornithological Biography*, 1:114. The mockingbird, the state bird of Florida, was well known and had been illustrated by Catesby, Wilson, and others. Audubon did this plate early in production of volume one of *The Birds of America* based

For years, Ord and his allies ignorantly criticized Audubon's work because of his report that rattlesnakes climbed trees and swam in creeks.

Audubon's collaboration with MacGillivray contributed to an appreciation of scientific and anatomical details, including the importance of anatomical organs as specimens, in addition to skins and eggs in ornithological research.[110]

One of Audubon's major scientific contributions to bird study was his collection and analysis of large numbers of specimens of a bird species, including males, females, various ages, and color variants. With MacGillivray's collaboration, he was thus able to clarify taxonomic errors related to these variations, while also detailing life cycle and seasonal variations and introducing population studies into ornithology. Audubon's ornithological studies emphasized the synergistic importance of data collection, laboratory studies, and field observations and enabled Audubon to create masterpieces about Florida birds through his detailed plain-spoken narratives and drawings.

In addition to his impact on the development of Florida ornithology, Audubon's works contributed to our understanding and appreciation of Florida habitats and created interest in Florida's plant life. As he explained, the plants were "amongst those in the vicinity where the birds were found, and are not, as some persons have thought, the trees or plants upon which they always feed or perch."[111] Appendix: Table 3 summarizes examples of the Florida flora that are shown in the plates of *The Birds of America* and mentioned in the narrative of *Ornithological Biography*.

Florida Again

Following Audubon's exhaustive 1831–1832 studies, he wished to return to Florida but became preoccupied with his publications. For more than a decade, very little was added to the knowledge of Florida birds except for the work of the young immigrant German physician-naturalist Frederick Leitner.[112] During the period 1833–1838, Leitner, who was supported by

---

on "West" Florida—Louisiana when Audubon painted and wrote the description—observations and specimens. The painting or sketches may have been included in Audubon's first visit in 1824 to the Academy and contributed to Ord's displeasure, to say the least (Audubon, *Ornithological Biography*, 1:108–14).

[110] Ibid., 4:193–97.

[111] Audubon, *Ornithological Biography*, 1:xii–xiii.

[112] Leitner (1812–1838) arrived from Germany on a medical student subsidy in 1831 and traveled in NY and PA before going to Charleston, SC, where he found a

Bachman and others, made many collecting expeditions to Florida. During one excursion, he verified Audubon's discovery of the yellow flowered water lily depicted with the American swan (Plate CCCCXI).[113] On 20 September 1833, Audubon wrote to his son Victor: "A young German, a good Botanist with whom I am well acquainted, has lately, returned to Charleston from the Everglades spent a summer there and discovered about 50 new Birds, a great number of Plants, etc. The new birds John Bachman will secure for me and I will derive some knowledge from Lightner [sic]."[114] Audubon and Bachman credited Leitner in *Quadrupeds* for a specimen of the rice meadow mouse obtained in the Everglades and for other mammals.[115] Later, Audubon recognized Leitner in *Ornithological Biography* for his observations on birds and commented in the section about flamingoes, "Dr. Leitner also procured some in the course of his botanical excursions along the western coast of Florida where he was at last murdered by some party of Seminole Indians at the time of our last disastrous war with those children of the desert."[116]

In 1837, Audubon again hoped to explore Florida and its west coast. Accompanied by his son John and Edward Harris, he intended to proceed as far as possible westward along the Gulf Coast into Texas.[117] Again, he received the support of President Jackson and the government. However, except for a brief visit near Pensacola, the Florida portion of the expedition failed to materialize due to the Seminole War.[118] Florida had become unsafe as skirmishes

---

German community interested in natural history and became an advanced student at the Medical College of South Carolina where he studied under several Academy members. He met and became a natural history collector and correspondent of Audubon and Bachman. Leitner arranged through subscribers and by volunteering for military service to study the natural history of Florida beginning in 1833 (Gifford, "Edward Fredrick Leitner [1812–1838], Physician-Botanist," 19–20).

[113] Proby, *Audubon in Florida*, 35. Although Audubon was given swans in Florida by the captain of the *Spark*, they were not models for the plate. The lilies were discovered by Audubon and named *Namphaea lutea*, the yellow water lily (Long and Lakela, *A Flora of Tropical Florida*, 4).

[114] Corning, *Letters of John James Audubon, 1826–1840*, 1:252.

[115] Gifford, "Edward Fredrick Leitner (1812–1838), Physician-Botanist," 19–20.

[116] Audubon, *Ornithological Biography*, 5:256. Leitner was killed in January 1838, near Jupiter Inlet.

[117] Both of Audubon's sons, John W. and Victor G., followed and supported his scientific tracks and were elected correspondents of the Academy in 1854 and 1844, respectively. Edward Harris was elected to membership in 1835.

[118] Ford, *John James Audubon*, 346–47; Herrick, *Audubon the Naturalist*, 2:157.

between the Seminoles and the settlers with their military protectors developed into the Second Seminole War from 1835–1842.

Audubon, his son John, and Harris met in Charleston on 17 February 1837. After a prolonged wait, they departed overland by way of Augusta, Montgomery, and Mobile for Pensacola, where they hoped to secure a Revenue cutter for their west coast voyage to Texas. Just before their departure from Charleston, they were relieved to learn of the surrender of Chief Osceola and some three hundred Seminoles under his command.[119] By 25 February the Audubon party was in Pensacola.[120] During their several-day stopover, Audubon did little birding but collected some squirrel and rabbit specimens to send to Bachman. From Pensacola, they cruised westward, making many stops for birding. Although Audubon hoped to sail around the Florida peninsula back to Charleston, government passage was not available. In May, Harris returned north from New Orleans, and Audubon and his son left Mobile and traveled overland to Charleston.[121]

By the 1840s, Academy members had resumed birding expeditions in the Florida Territory, which became a state in 1845. Edward Harris, Audubon's colleague and patron, spent spring 1844 in southern Florida, near the head of the Miami River. Later, as reported at the Academy, "Mr. Edward Harris exhibited a specimen (a young male) of *Cymindis hamatus*, Illig. (*Rostrhamus hamatus*, Mus. A. N. S.).[122] This bird was shot by himself on the 29th of April last, on the Miami river, Cape Florida." This Florida Everglades kite was the first specimen of this bird procured in the United States and the first Florida record.[123] Unfortunately, no details of Harris's trip have been uncovered. During 1848, several Academy members were in the new state.[124]

---

[119] Letter, "P.S. of Feby. 16th [1837]," in Corning, *Letters of John James Audubon, 1826–1840*, 2:143.

[120] Audubon to Bachman, 3 March 1837, ibid., 2:148–50. In New Orleans, Audubon met "good M. Le Sueur," whom he first met in 1824 at the Academy (Herrick, *Audubon the Naturalist*, 2:157).

[121] Streshinsky, *Audubon: Life and Art in the American Wilderness*, 311–14.

[122] Harris's many contributions, often in collaboration with Audubon, were studies and collections made in the Western Territories or in the New Jersey area. See Street, "The Edward Harris Collection of Birds," 167–84. E. Harris, 1844 Academy meeting of business: report, 18 May 1844, *PANS* 2:65.

[123] Howell, *Florida Bird Life* (1932), 6.

[124] Their biographies are referenced in ibid., 556; their collections and relationship to the ANSP type collection are in "Type Specimens of Birds in the Academy of Natural Sciences of Philadelphia" manuscript, 2006 (https://www.ansp.org/~/media/Files/

John Krider, an eminent gun maker and taxidermist in Philadelphia, collected near Miami and Key West. William Gambel reported on Adolphus Heermann's collecting activities around the Miami River and Charlotte Harbor.[125] These 1840's explorations were often cited in later editions of Audubon's works and served to initiate, along with his publications, later Academy ornithological studies (see page 125) in Florida.

Afterword

The Ord-Audubon controversy waned, mostly forgotten, except in the minds of Ord and Audubon. In 1851, the Academy, which initially had been reluctant to accept Audubon, passed a unanimous resolution praising his achievements and expressing "profound regret" upon the death of "their esteemed and venerable Colleague."[126] The members resolved,

> That by the demise of this truly great man and gifted naturalist, science has lost one of her most zealous and successful disciples, and the arts a master in the department he cultivated. and, That we recognize in Mr. Audubon, a man who has happily lived to fulfill his destiny as an explorer of the great field of American Zoology; while the splendid volumes which are the fruit of his labours, will diffuse the knowledge and the love of science to the latest generations.[127]

---

ans/research/sys.../ANSP_typelist_v1.ashx).

[125] Gambel, "Contributions to American Ornithology," 127–30. "Dr. Gambel exhibited and made some observations upon several Birds, recently collected in Florida by Dr. Hermann, among them Rosthramus hamatus, Vireo longirostris, and Ardea Pealii": the Everglade Kite, Black-whiskered Vireo, and Reddish Egret, respectively (*PANS* 4 [August 1, 1848]: 74). Hermann, a German immigrant, was a surgeon and naturalist with the Pacific Railroad Company. He met Audubon in the west in 1843 before returning to Philadelphia and being elected to the Academy in 1846. He received an MD, met Gambel, and became involved in Florida exploration with Academy colleagues in 1848. Many of his bird specimens were donated to the ANSP. See Mearns and Mearns, *Audubon to Xántus*, 225–33; Howell, *Florida Bird Life* (1932), 13; first Florida record, *Florida Bird Life*, 509. John Krider was elected to Academy membership in 1859; William Gambel in 1843, and Adolphus Hermann in 1845.

[126] Audubon died at his home in New York City in 1851 after a brief period of declining mental health.

[127] The original resolution, dated 4 February 1851, is in the Audubon papers, Beinecke Rare Book and Manuscript Library, Yale University. It was published in *PANS* 5 (1851): 146.

A hundred and fifty years later, the Ewell Stewart Library of the Academy of Natural Sciences has a daily "page turning" event for the public at 3:15 p.m. (except on weekends and holidays). As John Neagle's portrait of George Ord gazes down, someone turns a single page in Audubon's *The Birds of America*. Visitors look closely at incomparable life-sized images of birds, some of which are from Florida. They may be viewing Audubon's mockingbirds defending their nest from a rattlesnake as Ord looks down.[128]

Table 1. Audubon's Florida Chronology

A general guide for readers. Dates are compilations from several sources. They include Ford, *John James Audubon: A Biography*, 461–64; "Log Book of U.S. Revenue Cutter *Marion*" as reproduced in Proby, *Audubon in Florida*, 363–70; Corning, *Letters of James Audubon*. The references often vary in the chronological dates by a day or so. See Proby, *Audubon in Florida*, 37, re: entries for Cape Sable and Sandy Key.

1826
17 May   Leaves New Orleans for Europe aboard the *Delos*
22 May   Becalmed near Florida for several days in the Gulf of Mexico
26 June Had been becalmed many days
29 June Sends dusky petrel specimen to the Academy aboard the *Thalia*
8 July   At Sea

1831
2 October   Leaves Philadelphia for Charleston via Baltimore, Washington, and Richmond
16 October   Arrival in Charleston, meets Bachman
25 October   Elected to the Academy of Natural Sciences
20 November   Arrival in St. Augustine aboard the *Agnes*
14 December   Visit at the Hernández Plantation south of St. Augustine
25 December   South to the Bulow Plantation for collecting in the area
28 December   Exploration of the Halifax River with Bulow

1832
6 January   Rees Plantation, Spring Garden, muddy lakes to the St. Johns

---

[128] About the now state bird of Florida, Audubon commented, "The Mockingbird, of course, stands first in my opinion, and is unrivaled."

14 January	St. Augustine; passage to South Florida until rough weather
25 January	Back in St. Augustine
5 February	St. Augustine to the mouth and up the St. Johns on the *Spark*
17 February	Returns by boat and on foot to St. Augustine, Live Oakers
5 March	Returns to Charleston aboard the *Agnes*
19 April 19	Leave Charleston for Florida Keys aboard the *Marion*
24 April	Cape Florida, Key Biscayne
25 April	Indian Key as base; visits mangrove islands, Cape Sable, Sandy Key
30 April–4 May	Sailing with stops, Bahia Honda, Key Vacas, Duck Keys, other keys
May 5–May 9	Key West and surrounding waters
10 May	Tortugas, boarding of vessels including wreckers, various islands
14 May	*"–crew principally employed gathering Shells etc for J.J. Audubon Esq."*
16 May	Returns to Key West and surrounding area
21–28 May	Sails to Indian Key, visits various keys, Sandy Key, Cape Sable
31 May	Departs Indian Key for the return to Charleston

1837

17 February	Departs overland from Charleston with son and Edward Harris for Pensacola
25 February	Several days in and around Pensacola; on to New Orleans and western Gulf Coast
May	Returns overland to Charleston from Mobile

CHAPTER 9

FLORIDA FOSSILS...WITH SAY, CONRAD, TUOMEY, AGASSIZ, AND LE CONTE

"America is rich in fossils.... Certainly very little is yet known about the fossils of North America."[1]
—Thomas Say

"Great nature never rests; her features change
Unceasing as the measured flight of time"[2]
—Timothy Conrad

"I have spent...the winter in Florida, with a view of studying the coral reefs...."[3]
—Louis Agassiz

During his many excursions from Philadelphia, John Bartram composed long letters about the relationships of inorganic and organic matter to fossils as well as about fossil locations as early as the 1730s.[4] Bartram thought that what some Americans and Europeans considered "stones" were instead the remains of marine organisms. Although poorly delineated, Bartram's early map (c. 1750) of the Appalachian Mountains is noteworthy for showing areas where he found fossil seashells. The map was presented to the American Philosophical Society by Benjamin Franklin, who wrote on the back, "Mr. Bartram's Map very curious."[5] During John Bartram's later travels with William Bartram to Florida, he noted near Charleston, "but what engaged my notice most

---

[1] Say, "Observations on Some Species," 382.

[2] Quote from Timothy Conrad's poem see Wheeler, "Timothy Abbot Conrad," 84.

[3] Louis Agassiz to Sir Charles Lyell, Cambridge, 26 April 1851, in Agassiz, *Louis Agassiz: His Life and Correspondence*, 485.

[4] Berkeley and Berkeley, *The Life and Travels of John Bartram*, 136–40.

[5] Murphy D. Smith, *Realms of Gold: A Catalogue of Maps in the Library of the American Philosophical Society* (American Philosophical Society, 1991) 34. Franklin wrote his friend Jared Eliot on 16 July 1747, of Bartram's discoveries: "The great Apalachian

was ye great quantities of great rocks wholy composed of sea shels of ye same kinds with those that ye surf heaved up on shore & placed in every direction."[6] In St. Augustine, John Bartram described the construction of the fort: "A very compact yet porous combination of sea shells of as various dimensions...oyster cockle & clam kinds."[7] He and William made several collecting trips to Anastasia Island and observed coquina rock *in situ* and in the structure of buildings, but he recorded very few observations.[8] On the St. Johns River, John Bartram often made notes about rocks, "all of ground or broken seashells,"[9] and his letters and published journal kindled interest in Florida's rocks and "stones."

In St. Augustine, William Bartram spent time with his father on Anastasia Island inspecting and collecting coquina rock formations. When William returned to East Florida in 1774, he observed the old fort at Picolata. In *Travels,* he noted that the construction material came from Anastasia Island, "opposite St. Augustine: it is of a pale reddish brick colour, and a testaceous

---

Mountains, which run from York [Hudson] River back of these Colonies to the Bay of Mexico, show in many Places near the highest Parts of them, Strata Sea Shells, in some Places the marks of them are in the solid Rocks. 'Tis certainly the Wreck of a World we live on! We have Specimens of those Sea shell Rocks broken off near the Tops of those Mountains, brought and deposited in our Library [the Library Company of Philadelphia] as Curiosities. If you have not seen the like, I'll send you a Piece" (*The Papers of Benjamin Franklin,* 169).

[6] Bartram's observations while traveling from Little River to Charleston along ocean beach were confirmed in 1936 as "The fauna from the Pleistocene deposits...from the coquina...have been identified...Arca" (JB, "Diary of a Journey," 19, 61–62).

[7] Ibid., 33–34.

[8] Coquina rock is a mixture of small clam-like seashell, called coquina, or cockleshell, crushed oyster shell, mollusk shell, fragmented fossils, fragmented coral, crinoids, limestone, red sand, white sand, phosphate, calcite, and perhaps a little clay. Relatively soft when quarried, coquina rock hardens over time, after surface exposure. The rock was formed during the Pleistocene Ice Age, approximately from 1.8 million years ago until approximately 12,000 years ago. The end of the Pleistocene Era corresponds with the retreat of the last continental glacier. Florida itself and its landmass was rising from the sea, and coquina rock began forming along a substantial portion of Florida's east coast during the latter part of this era and the global warming period that came with it. The "Anastasia Formation," composed of inter-bedded sands and coquina limestone, was named by E. H. Sellards in 1912. It overlays the Atlantic Coastal Ridge along the Florida coast from current St. Johns County southward to Palm Beach County and extends inland as far as 20 miles.

[9] JB, "Diary of a Journey," 47, 4 February 1766.

composition, consisting of small fragments of sea-shells and fine sand."[10] In his brief description, he mentions that the building material "constitutes the foundation of that island" and "The castle at St. Augustine, and most of the buildings of that town, are of this stone." During William's ascent of the St. Johns River, he made several other fossil observations of bluffs formed by concretions of shells, substructures of rock often intermixed with animal bones, and "fragments of earthenware of the ancient inhabitants,"[11] blending the latter Native refuse deposits or middens into his geological descriptions. Since William had explored the river with John, Swedish botanist Carl Linnaeus had made some scientific progress in naming "stones" and concretions of animal and mineral material. In William's "Report to Fothergill," a summary of his East Florida observations observed, "Of the Stone creation, Here is some variety...Fossilia...Concrega [coquina?]...Concha [mollusk]...Canceri Oculi [concretions of crustaceans]...Echini [sea urchins, echinoderms]...Conchites [mollusks] Cochlites [mollusks or brachiopods] Cornu amomis [ammonite]."[12] Bartram's observations and writings stimulated the interest of a new generation of naturalists in Florida invertebrate paleontology, particularly Thomas Say and other founders of the Academy, who donated fossil shell collections: "In October, 1815, Mr. Jacob Gilliams presented a collection of fossil shells....This is earliest record of a donation to the department of palaeontology."[13]

Thomas Say

Thomas Say's interest in fossil shells developed along with his studies and descriptions of contemporary shells and intensified during his various field expeditions. While briefly exploring Anastasia Island during the Academy's Florida Expedition in 1817, Say collected specimens of coquina rock that contained fossilized mollusks. He deposited some at the Academy and others at Peale's Museum. As preoccupied as Say was with Florida insect specimens for his *American Entomology* and then the Long Expedition, he still found time to contribute his first major paper about fossils for publication in

---

[10] *FHBT,* 52. Coquina is a sedimentary rock that is composed either wholly or almost entirely of sorted and cemented fossil debris, most commonly coarse shells and shell fragments.

[11] Ibid., 1, 60, 73.

[12] WB, "Travels...: A Report," 169, and annotated index, ibid., 194–227.

[13] Ruschenberger, *Origin, Progress and Present Condition,* 36–40, provides a detailed account of the growth of the paleontological collections until 1852.

Benjamin Silliman's new science journal in 1819.[14] Professor Silliman of Yale, a chemist and geologist, became an Academy correspondent in 1815 and founded the *American Journal of Science* in 1818.[15] Say's paper in his colleague's new journal was the first major contribution to the American study of fossil invertebrate animals.

In his article, Say set the stage for future research in invertebrate paleontology by noting in his introduction, "America is rich in fossils."[16] He commented, "Certainly very little is yet known about the fossils of North America." Say added that progress would be achieved only when "we shall have it in our power to compare them with approved detailed descriptions, plates, or specimens of those of Europe." He noted that if the "investigation of our fossils," was to be done correctly, it would be "attended with some difficulty and labour."

Say's insightful comments linked fossil studies and research in geology that "must be in part founded on a knowledge of the different genera and species of *reliquiae*, which the various accessible strata of the earth present." He referred to the scientific research of Academy correspondent Jean-Baptiste de Lamarck and other European naturalists who had shown the value of "this species of knowledge" as "affording the most obvious means of estimating, with the greatest approximation to truth, the comparative antiquity of formations, and of strata, as well as of identifying those with each other which are in their nature similar."[17] After calling attention to the value of fossils in

---

[14] Say, "Observations on Some Species," 382.

[15] Fisher, *Life of Benjamin Silliman, M.D., LL.D.*, 87–121. During the winters 1802–1803 and 1803–1804, Silliman received his early chemical and natural history education at the University of Pennsylvania with Benjamin Barton, through visits to Peale's Museum and by studying with many future members of the Academy. In 1815, Robert Hare (elected to Academy membership in 1813), who had previously taught Silliman chemistry, spent the summer in New Haven studying geology with Silliman. Silliman founded the *American Journal of Science* in 1818. His son, Benjamin Jr. (elected as an Academy correspondent in 1841) was later a professor at Yale and joined in editing the *AJS*.

[16] This discipline is the scientific study of prehistoric invertebrates by analyzing invertebrate fossils in the geologic record. Hard-bodied invertebrates (mollusks, e.g., clams, snails, mussels, and oysters) were the first and are the easiest to study. Chemical and microscopic techniques enabled researchers to study soft-bodied and minute invertebrates such as hydras, slugs, and worms.

[17] Jean-Baptiste de Lamarck first conceptualized and coined the category "Invertebrata" between 1793 and 1801 and the term "Biology" in 1802. He was elected an Academy correspondent in 1818.

the geologic strata, Say pointed out that the identification of invertebrate fossils required some knowledge of similar living animals.[18] Since fossils occurred in geological strata, the time period of the living ancestors and the fossil record could be used as a guide for dating the rock strata as well as in reverse; both would later be critical in understanding evolutionary theory. By naming and classifying shell fossils as he did living mollusks, in this and his subsequent publications, Say led the development of American conchology and invertebrate paleontology.[19]

Say's unpublished observation notes about his research on a shell mass from Anastasia Island collected by Rudolph Dietz several years after Say's 1817–1818 expedition to Florida contributed a major section in Dietz's presentation at the Academy on 8 June 1824.[20] During winter 1822 and 1823, Dietz traveled in "the southern part of the United States."[21] His report about Anastasia Island, "10 or 12 miles from north to south, and about 1½ miles from east to west," discussed "the substratum…composed of an aggregate of fragments of various shells…characteristic of fossil" and its use for building "in the neighborhood of St. Augustine since about the year 1565." Dietz also speculated on the creation of the "stratigraphical arrangement of this shell mass" by tides and winds.[22]

The second part of Dietz's presentation included the names and descriptions of ten fossil species attributed to Say.[23] Dietz prefaced the section with, "By permission of my very esteemed and learned friend Mr. Thomas Say, I add, as a valuable addition to the above paper, his [Say] notes of various shells composing that aggregated mass, viz. fossil shells found in a shell mass from Anastasia Island." Dietz donated the specimen, which was listed as "Rock from Anastasia Island, East Florida, composed entirely of shells" to the Academy collections for future research.[24] He also examined other specimens: "In

---

[18] Weiss and Ziegler, *Thomas Say*, 193, 198.

[19] Harris, "A Reprint of the Paleontological Writings of Thomas Say," 3–84.

[20] Dietz, "Description of a Testaceous Formation," 73–80. In the 1877 list of *Members and Correspondents*, the name is misspelled as "Deitz." He was first elected to Academy membership in 1821.

[21] Ibid.

[22] Ibid.

[23] Dietz, "Description of a Testaceous Formation," 78; Harris, "A Reprint of the Paleontological Writings of Thomas Say," 296. Harris credits Say for the identification and descriptions. It is not clear whether Dietz edited Say's notes.

[24] See *JANS* 3/2 (1824): 471. Another Academy member, who may have journeyed to Florida with Dietz, Nathaniel Ware (elected nonresident member, 1826) is named in

a small mass in the possession of Dr. Hays, I observed a young indeterminable species of the genus NATICA, and two specimens of a small OLIVA.... A mass in the Philadelphia Museum contains a fragment of NASSA."[25] These specimens were undoubtedly collected by Say during the 1817–1818 Academy expedition to Florida.

As the sciences of invertebrate paleontology, conchology/malacology, and geology developed and grew in Europe, Academy members and correspondents kept abreast of them and also made significant advances in American studies. Thomas Say continued to contribute to the Academy collections and was joined in making fossil donations by young Timothy Conrad. At mid-century, the Academy's collections contained some 25,000 shells and other mollusks, as well as more than 20,000 invertebrate fossils.[26]

Timothy Abbott Conrad

Timothy Conrad (1803–1877) grew up in a home filled with natural history specimens and books collected by his father, Solomon White Conrad (1779–1831), who owned a printing and bookselling firm in Philadelphia.[27] Solomon, however, preferred to be out in the field collecting specimens of plants, shells, and minerals and teaching botany and mineralogy at the University of Pennsylvania. A friend and colleague of William Bartram, Solomon was a member of the American Philosophical Society and was elected a member of the Academy in 1826, where he served as librarian, contributed to the mineral and plant collections, and published in the *Journal*.[28] Timothy followed his father into the printing and publishing business and also the study of natural history but focused on shells and their fossil forms. He also shared Say's interest in living and fossil mollusks.

By the age of thirty, Timothy Conrad had completed many studies on

---

the same donor list as donating "Specimens of Clay from Florida."

[25] Dietz, "Description of a Testaceous Formation," 80. Dr. Isaac Hays (ANSP member, 1818) was a financially generous physician and invaluable member of the Publication [*JANS*] Committee. When the *Journal* was suspended in 1819 for "want of money," Hays funded the recovery and took over *JANS* management in 1821 after joining Say's Committee, which formerly had only Say and Ord, who resigned. See Ruschenberger, *A Notice*, 64. Initially a serious mineralogist, Hays later used his anatomy training to emerge as a dedicated vertebrate paleontologist.

[26] Ruschenberger, *A Notice*, 25, 40.

[27] For further reading, see Wheeler, "Timothy Abbott Conrad."

[28] Solomon Conrad published three papers in *JANS* 6 (1829) about new plant species and one about a mineral.

contemporary fresh and saltwater bivalve mollusks and fossil shells.[29] He was well established as an authority on the former group of animals and a leader in the emerging science of invertebrate paleontology. In his paleontology studies, Conrad was the chief investigator of American Tertiary geological strata.[30] He was a pioneer and one of the first Americans to study interregional and intercontinental geology based on a comparison of their fossil content.

At the May and June 1830 Academy meetings, Timothy Conrad was invited to present "On the Geology and Organic Remains of a Part of the peninsula of Maryland"; in October, he read "Description of Fifteen New Species of Recent and Three of Fossil Shells, Chiefly from the Coast of the United States."[31] In January 1831, Conrad was elected to Academy membership. In the same year, he published a small volume, parts one and two of *American Marine Conchology or Descriptions and Coloured Figures of the Shells of the Atlantic Coast of North America*, illustrated with seventeen hand-colored plates. The following year, he self-published part three *of American Marine Conchology and Fossil Shells of the Tertiary Formations of North America,* Nos. 1 and 2. Continuing work on *Fossil Shells,* in 1833 he shifted his focus to the Tertiary Period in the Southern states and spent a scientifically successful year in Alabama.[32] When he returned to Philadelphia, he served as curator of the Geological Society at Jefferson Medical College and then of the Academy from December 1835–December 1836. Conrad's close association with the Academy continued into the 1840s as curator and on committees, including

---

[29] In addition to seventy-four publications in *JANS* and *PANS* and others in the *AJS*, Timothy Conrad published and illustrated many monographic series, which were later republished. In addition, he was a prolific poet of natural history, primarily geology. Representative publications: "Description of a New Genus of Fresh-water Shells," *JANS* 7/1 (1834): 178–80; *Monography of the Family Unionidae, or Naiades of Lamarck (fresh water bivalve shells) of North America* (Philadelphia: J. Dobson, 1835–1840) 1:1–12, plates 1–6 through 13:111–18; *Fossil Shells of the Tertiary Formations of North America* (Philadelphia, 1832–1835), republished by G. D. Harris (Washington, DC, 1893); *Fossils of the Medial Tertiary of the U.S.* (Philadelphia, 1838–1861), republished by W. H. Dall (Philadelphia, 1893).

[30] The Tertiary Period, which is part of the Cenozoic Era, spans that portion of Earth's history from about 65.5–1.8 million years ago. This period essentially represents the time between the mass extinction of the dinosaurs that were prevalent during the preceding Mesozoic Era and the onset of the most recent ice age. In all, life on Earth became much more similar to that of today during the Tertiary Period, particularly by the end of the period.

[31] Conrad, *JANS* 6, pt. 2 (1830): 205; *JANS* 6, pt. 2 (1830): 256.

[32] Wheeler, "Timothy Abbott Conrad."

the publication committee, while completing work as a paleontologist of the New York State Geological Survey.[33] In 1842, he was an independent scholar working on *Fossils of the Medial Tertiary of the United States* when a unique opportunity to extend his paleontological and geological studies into Florida came his way.

Conrad in Florida

In 1842, the Second Seminole war had ended, and the Florida Territory was three years away from being admitted to statehood. Topographical surveys were still being conducted by U.S. military Gulf coastal engineers as more settlers arrived and fortifications were improved in less developed parts of the territory. Most prominent were the coastal surveys under the command of Lieutenant Levin M. Powell, U.S. Navy (USN).[34] When offered a position as conchologist for "Powell's Survey of Tampa Bay, Florida," Conrad seized the opportunity to extend his extensive studies on Tertiary formations into Florida, its Keys, and the unexplored region of the southwest coast: the Tampa Bay area.

As Conrad began studying living and fossil shells in Florida, he noted, "Having devoted some attention to the Tertiary formations of the Atlantic coast, I have endeavored to ascertain their relation to European formations."[35] In his early studies of the middle-Atlantic coast he had demonstrated the validity and importance of ancient and living invertebrates in understanding the age of layers of earth and their geological time period. His exploration of Florida established the early general features of Florida's invertebrate fossil record and correlated it with a living catalog and related geological records. Through his paleontological assessments of fossil marine invertebrates and comparisons, Conrad significantly contributed to understanding the geologic origin and formation of the Florida peninsula.[36]

---

[33] ANSP Archives, Timothy Abbott Conrad (1803–1877) Papers, coll. 327.

[34] Buker, "Lieutenant Levin M. Powell," 253–75. After his appointment as lieutenant in 1826 during the Seminole wars, Powell commanded a joint Army-Navy force, the "Mosquito Fleet," that operated along the coast. Powell commanded several survey missions in Gulf coastal waters, including from Apalachicola to the Mississippi in 1840–1841. Following the so-called Powell Survey of Tampa Bay, he later commanded military blockades during the Civil War and retired as a rear admiral of the U.S. Navy.

[35] Conrad, "Observations of the Geology of a Part of East Florida," 36–45; Conrad, "Catalogue of Shells Inhabiting Tampa Bay," 393–400.

[36] Jones, "The Marine Invertebrate Fossil Record of Florida," 89–116.

At the time, there was considerable European and American interest in geological and paleontological timelines for Earth's history. In England, Charles Lyell had formulated the terminology and guidelines for the major geological timelines for the eras, periods, and events that occurred. He first published his classic work, *Principles of Geology*, in 1830, two years after he was elected a correspondent of the Academy. During the 1840s, Lyell traveled to the U.S. and wrote two popular travel and geology books: *Travels in North America* (1845) and *A Second Visit to the United States* (1849). During his stay in Philadelphia, Lyell visited and met Academy members Isaac Lea and Samuel George Morton, who were actively investigating invertebrate paleontology of the Tertiary Period.[37] He also met young Joseph Leidy, whom Lyell encouraged, "Stick to paleontology. Don't bother with medicine. Stick to paleontology. That is your future."[38] Timothy Conrad was away, exploring Florida; Leidy would later pioneer vertebrate paleontological investigations in Florida.

Conrad explained in the introduction of his first Florida publication that the "expedition to Florida in the winter of 1842, [was] made in reference to new observations on Tertiary formations."[39] He further noted that it "was through the interest of members of the National Institute that I went on behalf of the Society, in order to furnish its cabinet with specimens of the rocks, fossils, and recent shells of Florida."[40] Conrad was aboard the *Poinsett*, which was destined to survey Tampa Bay under the command of Lieutenant Levin

---

[37] Isaac Lea was elected to Academy membership in 1815; Samuel George Morton in 1820.

[38] Thomson, *The Legacy of the Mastodon*, 105. Leidy was elected to Academy membership in 1845.

[39] Conrad, "Observations on the Geology of a Part of East Florida," 37.

[40] Ibid. Reports no access to his Institution collections. The National Institute (1840–1862) was first organized as the National Institution for the Promotion of Science in Washington, DC, as a society to promote the study of natural history and the physical sciences. In 1842, Congress granted the body a federal charter. The National Institute tried to gain control of James Smithson's behest until the Smithsonian Institution was created in 1846. Despite a chronic lack of funds, the Institute pursued an active program of collecting specimens of natural history but soon faced serious problems due to a lack of space and money for their preservation. This made it impossible for Conrad to access his specimens and data from the Florida Keys. In 1862, the Institute transferred its remaining collections to the Smithsonian Institution and quietly expired. (See "SIA RU007058, National Institute, Records, 1839–1863 and undated," siarchives.si.edu/collections/siris_arc_217217#indexlink, accessed 7 August 2018.)

M. Powell, USN. The route of the voyage from Savannah to Tampa Bay as described by Conrad included many opportunities along the way for his on-shore and shallows excursions beginning at the St Johns River, continuing to Fort Lauderdale, Key Biscayne, Indian and other Keys including Key West before reaching the destination of Tampa Bay.[41] His observations and collections were often supplemented by those of officers. The major collections were in the Bay area and southward to the Manatee River. As a Bartram aside, he reported a settler on the river with a soft-shelled turtle, "which verified the accuracy of Bartram, who describes and figures an unknown species with this character..."[42]

Conrad commented, "During a stay of three months upon the Florida coast, those species only were obtained which can be identified with supposed extinct forms of the Miocene period."[43] Based on observations of deposits made while ascending the St. Johns, he noted, "This Post-Pliocene deposit, taken in connexion [sic] with those of similar age on Tampa Bay, prove a considerable elevation of the whole Florida peninsula in the Post-Pliocene, a movement which clearly has raised all the Florida Keys above water." Unfortunately, the precarious operations of the National Institute in handling Conrad's specimens limited his reports: "As I have not yet had access [now November 1846] to the specimens I sent the Institution, my slight sketch of Tampa bay and the Florida Keys is more imperfect than it would otherwise be." Four years later, he still hoped that "Supplementary observations will, however, in future be published, with a list of such fossils as I found on the Keys." However, in his subsequent publications, because of the failures of the National Institute, he mentioned only a handful of Key West specimens and made few observations about them, thus limiting his publications about the Florida Keys.[44]

Conrad's numerous stops resulted in many and various finds. Near the mouth of the St. Johns River, "a short distance from the sea," he noted, "The most abundant shell is *Mactra lateralis*, Say." Conrad listed twenty-three different species and concluded that twenty-one were "found subsequently at Tampa bay." He identified the banks, which were here elevated some feet above the water level, as a post-Pliocene formation. At Fort Lauderdale, he found "a specimen of *Tellina radiata*" at about "the northern limits of this

---

[41] Ibid., 38–41.

[42] Ibid., 46.

[43] Ibid., 37.

[44] Conrad, "Catalogue of Shells inhabiting Tampa Bay," 393–99; Conrad, "Descriptions of new species of Organic Remains," 399–400.

beautiful but common bivalve." Conrad determined that Indian Key was "composed of a Post-Pliocene limestone, which in places seems little more than a cement for myriads of shells of such species as live in the waters of this latitude, and which are generally identical with those of Cuba." He explored a larger nearby island and noted many species that he had observed but deferred to comment on because "I have not the specimens at present to refer to." With almost certainty, he postulated the following (which would soon create controversy with Louis Agassiz): "I have no doubt the islands all rest on coral reefs, and their elevation above the sea is due to the movement which has raised the Post-Pliocene of the peninsula." Conrad's next stop was Key West. He mentioned "that many of the shells of Cuba occur here," and identified three species, noting, "*Strombus gigas* is common here, but is not found so far north as Tampa bay."[45]

After leaving Key West, Conrad "soon arrived at Tampa bay on the western side of the peninsula, and here the surveying duties of the expedition commenced." As Conrad observed, "I watched with interest such specimens from the bottom as the lead brought up, and by this means I obtained a new *Cerbula*, a specimen of *Dentalium coarctatum*, which I believe to be the first living one found this side of the Atlantic."[46] Conrad's wrote, "We visited frequently many of the Keys which stretched across the mouth of Tampa bay, and several points on both sides of the bay, and in every locality I collected all the species of shells I could find, in order to study their geographical distribution."[47]

Conrad briefly describes his collecting and finds on Mullet Key, Egmont Key, North Passage Key, Passage Key, and Palm Key.[48] On the shores of Tampa Bay, he collected most extensively from "Ballast Point near Fort Brooke, at the head of the bay" and "traced this rock to the Falls of Hillsborough River, nine miles above Tampa," where he found "casts and impressions of shells of species unknown to me." He concluded, "They appear to be extinct species, and are, I believe, referrible to the Eocene period; most prob-

---

[45] Conrad, "Observations on the Geology of a Part of East Florida," 40–41.

[46] Ibid., 47.

[47] Ibid., 41.

[48] Mullet Key, located near St. Petersburg, Florida, became Fort DeSoto in 1900; it is now Fort DeSoto State Park. Egmont Key today is Egmont Island. North Passage Key is Anna Maria Island, off Bradenton. Passage Key is Longboat Key. Palm Key is Siesta Key, south of Sarasota, and not the present Palm Island, off Englewood.

ably to an upper division of that formation." New species of "Organic Remains from the Upper Eocene Limestone of Tampa Bay" collected by Conrad included among others, *Bulla perosa, Nummulites flor*anus and *Venus floridana.*[49]

Referring to Ballast Point, Conrad commented on chalcedony, agatized coral, which was named Florida's state stone by the legislature in 1979:

> This point has been much resorted to for procuring chalcedony of unusual beauty, formerly very abundant, but fine specimens are now rare. It coats masses of coral, a species of Astrea; which are derived from a Tertiary limestone, rising on the shore a few feet above high tide, and containing many casts of a bivalve shells and much silicified coral, which when broken exhibits a cavernous interior lined with chalcedony and sometimes with quartz crystals.[50]

At "Stony Point on the east coast of Tampa bay," Conrad observed "some black, water-worn bones of mammalia" and a large megalodon shark's tooth. In addition, he described in detail, "[o]ne of the most remarkable places near Tampa is a large sulphur spring, eight miles up the Hillsborough river."[51]

Conrad's exploration and description of the Manatee River, near the mouth of Tampa Bay, and its surrounding area are among the first American accounts of that area where settlement had just begun. At the entrance to the Manatee River, Conrad saw what he called "Sarasota Point"; this area was later known as "Shaw's Point" until the 1940s, when it was renamed De Soto Point following the creation of De Soto National Memorial Park to commemorate Hernando De Soto's 1535 landing site.[52] At the point, Conrad described two short sections of bluffs, "about fifteen or twenty feet high, and consisting chiefly of beds of shells...in groups of species, in a kind of indistinct stratification." He reported evidence of the river's namesake: "Bones of the Manatus are occasionally found in the bluff, and the living animal is not uncommon in the Manatee River." He also catalogued five bivalve species

---

[49] Conrad, "Descriptions of New Species," 399.

[50] Conrad, "Observations on the Geology of a Part of East Florida," 43.

[51] Ibid., 45–46. Sulphur Spring's "miraculous" healing waters attracted many visitors. In the 1920s, a developer built a Mediterranean-style building, which has been restored.

[52] Bennett, *The Legacy*, 28–39; Conrad, "Observations on the Geology of a Part of East Florida," 43–45.

and ten univalves collected form the Manatee River and discussed their relative abundance in the past and also during his time. "Sarasota Point is very interesting to a geologist, in consequence of the presence of several mounds of shells, much resembling those of artificial construction, and which would deceive any unpracticed eye."[53] These formations as well as Conrad's speculation about how the Indians would have "procured the animal of the large 'conchs'" were of considerable interest to future Academy anthropologists (see pages 243, 293).[54]

"In the fresh water of the Manatee River," Conrad observed that "a large soft-shelled turtle is frequently caught by the settlers who prize it as an article of food." Referring to Bartram's descriptions, he asked a man who had caught one of these turtles and established "there are five claws to each foot, which verifies the accuracy of Bartram, who describes and figures an unknown species with this character."[55]

Conrad concluded his observations about Tampa Bay and the Florida peninsula with the following:

> I propose to term this, Upper Eocene, and very probably the prevalent limestone of Florida will be included in this division. This rock extends throughout the peninsula, as far south at least as Tampa bay; and both the east and west shores of this peninsula are covered with a Pleistocene formation of recent species of shells and remains of mammalia. The elevation of East Florida above the sea level is so inconsiderable, that all or nearly all of it must have been submerged at the time the post-Pliocene species were existing, and therefore its elevation was contemporaneous with that of the Keys, which line its eastern, southern and western coasts.[56]

Conrad provided paleontologic and geologic evidence that the Florida peninsula had been laid down over time by death and fossilization of marine organisms overlaid by more recent marine and land animals. The events he hypothesized occurred during the Eocene (54–34 million years ago) and Pliocene (5–1.8 million years ago) of the Tertiary Period and during the more recent Pleistocene (2.6 million–12 thousand years ago) .

In *The Geology of Florida*, Douglas Jones, in citing Conrad's work, noted, "The general features of Florida's fossil record have been appreciated

---

[53] Conrad, "Observations on the Geology of a Part of East Florida," 43–45.
[54] Ibid.
[55] Ibid., 46.
[56] Ibid., 47–48.

for many years. Paleontology even played a fundamental role in shaping the initial hypotheses concerning the geologic origin and formation of the Florida peninsula. Yet, despite the long history of study, many significant paleontologic questions remain unanswered."[57]

Other Academy Members' Studies

Conrad's papers were the first to place the Florida formations in definite geologic horizons (i.e., bedding surfaces where there is marked change in the physical characteristics of rocks in the bed). He regarded the entire chain of the Keys as a more recent post-Pliocene sheet and the limestone around Tampa Bay as an earlier Eocene bed. His observations were supported and extended by later work of fellow Academy members Jacob W. Bailey and Michael Tuomey.[58] In the early 1850s, Bailey focused his studies on north central Florida and Tampa; Tuomey, on the Florida Keys and the southern coast. "[W]hile on a visit to Tampa (Fort Brooke), Florida," Bailey extended his microscopic examination of rock samples for fossil and living diatoms, algae, and other "infusoria" and concluded that the deposit belonged to "the eocene tertiary."[59] His findings regarding northern Florida areas were published later.

Michael Tuomey was working further south in Florida at the same time as Conrad. The first Alabama state geologist and a professor of geology at the University of Alabama, Tuomey had added exploration of the Florida Keys and the southern coast of Florida to his earlier work in South Carolina and Alabama.[60] He had worked with other Academy members on invertebrate and vertebrate fossils including the Zeuglodon (*Basilosaurus*).[61] He explored south Florida during summer 1850 and recorded his observations in "Notice of the Geology of the Florida Keys and of the Southern Coast of Florida."[62]

---

[57] Jones, "The Marine Invertebrate Fossil Record of Florida," 89.

[58] Bailey was elected a correspondent to the Academy in 1841; Tuomey in 1845.

[59] Bailey, "Discovery of an Infusorial Stratum in Florida," 282. As one of the first native-born American phycologists, Bailey stimulated early work on diatoms that flourished in the latter part of the nineteenth century: R. Patrick, "The history of the science of diatoms in the United States of America," *Proceedings of the International Diatom Symposium* (D. G. Mann, ed.) 7 (1984): 11–20; M. J. Wynne, "'Phycological Trialblazer': No. 18: Jacob W. Bailey," *Phycological Newsletter* 39/1 (2003): 2–5, plates 1–3.

[60] Smith, "Sketch of the Life of Michael Tuomey," 207.

[61] Tuomey, "Notice of the Discovery of a Crania of the Zuglodon," 151.

[62] See Tuomey, "Notice of the Geology," 390–94; "Descriptions of Some Fossil

Tuomey examined the limestone at the mouth of the Miami River and at the falls of the river leading into the Everglades and described it as being the same age as that at Key West. He noted, "There can be no doubt that this great chain of Keys...is due to the elevation of vast uneven coral reef whose prominent points rising above the water, form the foundation of the Keys the sands driven up by the waves having done the rest."[63] Tuomey agreed with Conrad that the Miami limestone differed from the Tampa Bay limestone and suggested that the Everglades rested upon a vast basin of Miami limestone.

Although Conrad's initial observations and views on the fossils, geology, and the origin of Florida were well supported by Bailey and Tuomey, within months Louis Agassiz and his protégé Joseph Le Conte had also explored South Florida areas and the Keys and later published a differing theory about the coastal extensions and buildup of the Florida peninsula.

Louis Agassiz

Louis Agassiz (1807–1873) was a renowned Swiss paleontologist, glaciologist, geologist, and professor of natural history at the University of Neuchâtel when he was elected a correspondent of the Academy in 1834. In 1837, Agassiz was the first to propose that the Earth had been subject to a past ice age. He came to the U.S. in 1846 to investigate the natural history and geology of North America and to deliver a series of lectures titled "The Plan of Creation as shown in the Animal Kingdom" at the Lowell Institute in Boston, Massachusetts. In 1850, Agassiz accepted a professorship at Harvard and a professorial appointment at Harvard's newly formed Lawrence Scientific School to teach courses in geology and zoology.[64] During that summer, he welcomed Joseph Le Conte into his laboratory as one of two advanced students.[65] Le Conte diligently became Agassiz's protégé and "his [Agassiz's] companion in all his excursions...and on the reefs of Florida."[66]

Joseph Le Conte observed,

> The straits of Florida are probably the most dangerous to navigation in the world, owing to the coral reefs of the region. Professor Bache, of the United States Coast Survey, asked Agassiz to investigate the laws of

Shells," 192; "Descriptions of Some New Fossils," 167.

[63] Tuomey, "Notice of the Geology," 392.

[64] Lurie, *Louis Agassiz*, 122–165.

[65] Bennett, *The Le Contes*, 12–15.

[66] Armes and Conte, *The Autobiography of Joseph Le Conte*, 130; Stephens, *Joseph Le Conte*, 33–39.

growth of these reefs. His expenses and those of his assistants were to be paid, and he offered to take us and his son Alexander, then sixteen, as his assistants. Here was a grand opportunity![67]

Alexander Dallas Bache's request of Agassiz had come in a letter of 30 October 1850: "Would it be possible for you to devote six weeks or two months to the examination of the Florida reefs and keys...to ascertain what they are and how formed?"[68] Bache wanted to identify suitable locations for warning signals, foundations for lighthouses, "and many other questions practically of import and of high scientific interest."[69] He firmly believed, as he exclaimed to Agassiz, "What results would flow to science from your visit to that region!" Agassiz couldn't refuse the proposal: "I offer you a vessel the motions of which you will control, and assistance of the officers and crew of which you will have. You shall be at no expense for going and coming, or while there, and shall choose your own time."[70]

On 1 January 1851, Agassiz, Le Conte, and others left Cambridge during a snowstorm, and less than a week later reached Key West where they "swam in the ocean every day and slept without covering and with the windows wide open; the change was delightful."[71]

Agassiz's energetic diligence exceeded all expectations. He was a driving taskmaster for his students, the military support personnel, and himself, as Le Conte's account reveals:

> We were incessantly at work; sometimes visiting the reefs in a Government steamer; sometimes exploring the Everglades in one direction, sometimes the Tortugas in the other; but always observing, noting, and gathering specimens....Sometimes for several days in succession we would be out all day on the reefs collecting, generally waist-deep in the water;

---

[67] Armes and Le Conte, *The Autobiography*, 130–31.

[68] Bache (1806–1867), the great-grandson of Benjamin Franklin, was educated at and served on the faculty of West Point and briefly as lieutenant of engineers until his appointment in 1828 as a professor of natural philosophy and chemistry at the University of Pennsylvania. His presentations and publications in the natural sciences earned him election to the Academy in 1829. He became head of the newly founded Girard College and established the first magnetic observatory in the U.S. before becoming superintendent of the United States Coast Survey in 1843, a position he held until his death in 1867 (Odgers, *Alexander Dallas Bache, Scientist and Educator*, 154.

[69] Alexander Dallas Bache to Louis Agassiz, 30 October 1850, in Agassiz, *Louis Agassiz: His Life and Correspondence*, 480–81.

[70] Ibid.

[71] Armes and Le Conte, *The Autobiography*, 132.

then for several days in our workroom on the wharf at Key West we would study our specimens with microscopes, draw, and pack away. In the evenings we would gather in Agassiz' room, and discuss the day's work and the conclusions to be drawn therefrom. I never saw any one work like Agassiz; for fourteen hours a day he would work under high pressure, smoking furiously all the time. The harder he worked, the faster he consumed cigars.[72]

The expedition members' survey and mapping of the coral reefs and studies on the plant and animal life were quickly incorporated into Agassiz's report to Bache and published as part of the *Annual Report of the Superintendent of the U.S. Coast Survey for 1851*.[73] Agassiz's natural history ideas about the geology and origins of the Florida peninsula began appearing in publication notes and in his popular public, university, and scientific society lectures. His Lowell Institute Lectures, "Methods of Study in Natural History" (1861–1862), which were published in book form in 1863, included his studies on Florida reefs.[74] Chapters 11 and 12 summarize his expedition's findings about coral reefs and their growth and demise. His scientific interpretation, mixed with creationist thoughts, lead to the conclusion that during the past seventy thousand years, "the Coral Reefs already known to exist in Florida began to grow." From the projected growth of the coral reef they studied, Agassiz extrapolates to his peninsular building theory, "the whole peninsula is formed of successive concentric Reefs, we must believe that hundreds of thousands of years have elapsed since its formation began."[75]

After the expedition and upon receiving his science degree from Harvard, Joseph Le Conte returned to Georgia and accepted an academic position. Since he was a junior researcher to Agassiz, Le Conte did not begin publishing about Florida until 1856.[76] In a modification of Agassiz's view of the coral extension of the peninsula, Le Conte emphasized the role of the Gulf Stream in carrying sediments from the Mississippi basin to the coral reefs while questioning Conrad, Bailey, and Tuomey's earlier theory about the formation of the Florida peninsula.

The popularity of Louis Agassiz and the imprimatur of the U.S. government, under which his Florida exploration was conducted, provided a halo effect for his contradictory view and hypothesis that large coastal portions of

---

[72] Ibid., 133.
[73] *Annual Report of the Superintendent of the Coast*, 145–60.
[74] L. Agassiz, *Methods of Study in Natural History*, 148–201.
[75] Ibid., 189–90.
[76] Le Conte, "On the Agency of the Gulf-Stream," 46–60.

the Florida peninsula were of recent coral origin. Agassiz and Le Conte claimed that the peninsula had extended southward into the ocean by successive annexations of consecutive series of coral reefs, an idea that was accepted for several decades. Indeed, ancient and recent reefs actively grew and experienced accretion, "coral extension," solely from materials accumulated as a result of the action of wind and waves.[77]

Alexander Agassiz, who had assisted his father in exploring Florida, became an established scientist and was elected an Academy correspondent in 1869. In 1880, he collated the published and unpublished data and text omitted from his father's 1851 *Report* and sections of his later *Methods of Study* into a *Report on the Florida Reefs*.[78]

The expedition had been of great importance for Louis Agassiz's collections and also for his fledgling museum at Harvard. The expedition laid the foundation of a very complete collection of corals of all varieties and in all stages of growth. All the specimens, from huge coral heads and branching fans down to the minutest single corals, were given to Louis Agassiz by the government survey group. The value of the whole was greatly enhanced by the drawings made on the spot from the living coral animals. International attention as well as that of Charles Darwin and Charles Lyell focused on the Florida reefs and Keys. However, in contrast to the coral and reef discoveries pictured and discussed in Alexander Agassiz's *Report on the Florida Reefs*, Louis Agassiz's ideas about Florida's geology and the origins of the peninsula became more controversial by 1880.[79]

In an 1881 detailed review of the work of Agassiz, Le Conte, Conrad, and Tuomey published in *On the Geology of Florida*, Eugene Allen Smith noted that "the subject is still enveloped in obscurity, partly because of the isolated character of the earlier [Conrad, Tuomey, et al.] observations, and partly because of the failure of the later observers [Agassiz and Le Conte] to give due weight to the statements of those preceding them."[80] Smith's own

---

[77] Smith, "On the Geology of Florida," 292–309; Jones, "The Marine Invertebrate Fossil Record of Florida," 89; Sellards, "Geological Section across the Everglades," 59–62; L. Agassiz, *Florida Reefs, Keys and Coast*, 153.

[78] Agassiz, *Report on the Florida Reefs*.

[79] In 1865, Conrad identified fossil species from Ocala limestone, which was geographically more central and widespread than his earlier work, that placed the Florida limestone in the Eocene era (Conrad, "Observations on American Fossils," 184).

[80] Smith, *On the Geology of Florida*, 297. Smith was a native of Alabama, educated in Germany and returned to study geology as professor and state geologist in Mississippi; following the death of Tuomey, Smith became Alabama's state geologist and professor at

contributions, in collaboration with Angelo Heilprin, the Academy's new bright young curator, were the first published invertebrate paleontological observations about middle and western Florida since Conrad's in 1865.[81]

Regrettably, despite Smith's acceptance of "the older views" of Conrad and Tuomey, in his text, the graphic "Geological Map of Florida" highlighted the Agassiz/Le Conte view.[82] The picture map, which perpetuated the coral coastal extension idea—showing the coastal portions of the peninsula as alluvial—associated with the Agassiz name was reprinted and received more circulation than did Smith's qualifying text and acceptance of Conrad's view. Smith's article, however, prompted Le Conte to partially retract his earlier views, which he did noting, "following L. Agassiz, I had exaggerated the probable amount of land added to Florida by the combined agency of the Gulf Stream and corals."[83] Subsequent Florida studies, conducted by Academy curators Joseph Willcox and Angelo Heilprin, who first investigated Florida while working with Eugene Smith, helped put Agassiz's and Le Conte's ideas in perspective and further supported Conrad, Tuomey, and Bailey's views on the geologic origins of Florida; William H. Dall delivered the coups de grace to Agassiz's coral extension theory.

As part of the discussion of the changing view of Florida's geological origins that followed the work of Louis Agassiz, Joseph Le Conte, and Timothy Conrad through the mid-1890s, Florida invertebrate paleontologist Douglas Jones recently noted,

> The hypotheses of Agassiz and Le Conte prevailed for several decades.... Eventually these ideas succumbed to modification (Le Conte 1883) as the coral-extension theory was limited to the southernmost (youngest) part of the peninsula. Evidence from investigations throughout the state reaffirmed the older opinions espoused by Conrad, Tuomey, and others concerning the geologic age and nature of the rocks that underlie the greater part of the peninsula.... Whereas early workers such as Conrad first drew attention to Florida fossils [invertebrate], it was not until the late nineteenth century that Angelo Heilprin (1887)—and especially William Healey Dall, with his *Contributions to the Tertiary Fauna of Florida* (1890–1903)—finally brought the extraordinary fossil deposits of the

---

the University of Alabama.

[81] Ibid., 302.

[82] Ibid., 303; map, 305.

[83] Le Conte, "The Reefs, Keys, and Peninsula of Florida," 764.

state (particularly the southern part) to the attention of the scientific community. These studies formed the foundation for a growing number of paleontological investigations in the twentieth century that greatly expanded our understanding of Florida's fossil record.[84]

The story of this exploration and understanding of Florida's fossil record and geological history by William Dall and others will be continued in chapter 11. It involves several Academy members as well as those who pioneered Florida's vertebrate paleontological studies in Bartram's tracks.

While Conrad and Tuomey were conducting their pioneering paleontology and geology studies in Florida and Agassiz and Le Conte were exploring the Florida reefs, their Academy colleagues were investigating Florida's plant life in Bartram's tracks, as will be discussed in chapter 10.

---

[84] Jones, "The Marine Invertebrate Fossil Record of Florida," 89–90.

CHAPTER 10

FLORIDA PLANTS AND THE TORREYA LEGACY… WITH NUTTALL, WARE, TORREY, GRAY, CROOM, CHAPMAN, AND OTHERS

"Did I tell you of a beautiful and new Taxoid tree from Middle Florida? It was discovered about three years ago by my esteemed friend H. B. Croom, Esq., of Tallahassee."[1]
—John Torrey

"Your city Botanists with polished Boots rolled to your favorite haunts in Steam Boats & Cars have but a faint idea of the figure a Florida Botanist cuts in these wild woods."[2]
—Alvan Chapman to John Torrey

From 1815 into Florida's territorial period beginning in 1821, William Baldwin, André and François Michaux, and John Le Conte traced William Bartram's botanical tracks in East Florida (see ch. 6). In the years that followed, Thomas Nuttall, an English immigrant and a protégé of Benjamin Barton and William Bartram, became the dominant American botanist and a leader of botany studies at the Academy.[3] Nuttall was an avid field botanist who collected widely and journeyed to Florida, but he also relied heavily on Florida resident botanists, including Nathaniel A. Ware and Hardy B. Croom, for specimens for his botanical studies, his herbarium work, and some of his publications.[4] Nuttall also depended on the Academy's earlier Florida botanical collections of Thomas Say, and William Baldwin (see pages 97, 104). Nuttall's admirer and younger colleague, Dr. John Torrey and Torrey's pro-

---

[1] Torrey to Walker-Arnott, in Walker-Arnott, "On the Genus Torreya," 128.
[2] Alvan W. Chapman to John Torrey, 19 June 1837, in "Chapman, Alvan Wentworth," Series 1, folder 219, Correspondence; incoming and outgoing, Torrey Papers, NYBG Archives.
[3] Ewan, *A Short History of Botany in the United States*, 39–40.
[4] Hardy B. Croom was elected a correspondent to the Academy in 1832.

tégé, Dr. Asa Gray, later led American botany into the late nineteenth century.[5] They were supported in their national efforts by the Southern regional and Florida collections of another early Florida resident, Dr. Alvan Chapman.[6] Membership in the Academy and access to its herbarium facilitated their botanical cooperation and studies. All were influenced by and laced their publications with references to the Florida discoveries and writings of William Bartram.

In the 1830s, Hardy Croom's botanical findings of the unique Florida Torreya tree and the herb-like Croomia, his namesake, that grew in the tree's shade, linked the scientific interests and attention of Nuttall, Torrey, and Chapman and led to pilgrimages by Torrey and Gray to so-called Middle Florida, the region around Tallahassee and the Apalachicola River, to see the unusual Torreya and Croomia.[7]

Thomas Nuttall

Thomas Nuttall (1786–1859) was born in western Yorkshire, England, and worked for several years as an apprentice printer before his interest in natural history—minerals, plants, and birds—spurred him to pursue his dream of exploring unknown North America.[8] He immigrated to Philadelphia in 1808 and would spend most of his professional life in the United

---

[5] Ibid., 41–45. Dr. John Torrey was elected a correspondent to the Academy in 1822, Dr. Asa Gray in 1836.

[6] Dr. Alvan Chapman was elected a correspondent to the Academy in 1861.

[7] Apalachicola is the present day town at the mouth of the Apalachicola River, which flows into Apalachicola Bay and the Gulf of Mexico. The Spaniards used the Indian word "Apalachicola" for both the river and the Native Americans who lived in the vicinity of the forks of the Chattahoochee River and the Flint River, where the Apalachicola River originates. Another town by the name of "Apalachicola" was located in the forks area and was visited by Bartram in his travels (*FHBT*, 399–401; *WBT* 389). The current Apalachicola was first called Cottonton and then West Point before being approved by the State Legislature as Apalachicola in 1831.

[8] For further reading, see Pennell, "Travels and Scientific Collections," 1–51. This critical and scholarly account of Nuttall's life and botanical work in America was written from the perspective of an eminent field and ANSP herbarium botanist. Graustein's book *Thomas Nuttall* is carefully documented with references to Nuttall's correspondence, scientific papers, and biographical notes. For other perspectives, see Hughes, *The American Biologist through Four Centuries*, 69–78; and Wunderlin, Hansen, and Beckner, "Botanical Exploration in Florida," 49.

States as an explorer, botanist, ornithologist, and professor. Shortly after arriving and while working as a printer, he met Benjamin Barton (see pages 53. 56) , who needed an apprentice and field collector. Barton encouraged Nuttall's interests, particularly in botany, and introduced him to William Bartram, who became Nuttall's friend and mentor. Nuttall began his botanical collecting around Philadelphia under Bartram's tutelage and in Barton's employ before embarking on longer collecting expeditions for the latter. Nuttall also started exploring on his own. He returned to England as the War of 1812 approached. By 1815, he was back in Philadelphia and then off on a collecting trip from North Carolina into Georgia. Nuttall had his first close encounter with Florida when he met William Baldwin (see pages 99, 104) in Savannah in 1815. He spent a month collecting with Baldwin, examining Baldwin's herbarium, and learning about Spanish East Florida. Although Nuttall later reported on Florida plants, he did not collect them during this southern trip; instead, he relied on William Baldwin's specimens and records.[9]

Back in Philadelphia in early 1817, Nuttall sought out Bartram and also renewed his acquaintance with several colleagues who had recently been elected members of the fledgling Academy. Nuttall worked in the Academy herbarium as a guest of his member friends. Using the Academy resources and his own observations and specimens, he began writing a book about the genera of indigenous North American plants and a catalogue of the species.[10] At the time, under William Maclure's leadership, the Academy was planning its first scientific expedition to Spanish Florida and also its first major publication, *Journal of the Academy of Natural Sciences of Philadelphia*. Nuttall was soon actively involved in the Committee of Eight, which led the startup of the *Journal*. He joined its editor, Thomas Say, in producing the first volume of the *Journal*; the two are believed to have set most of the type themselves. The pair also authored several articles in the inaugural issue of the *Journal*,

---

[9] Nuttall, *The Genera of North American Plants*; Wunderlin, Hansen, and Becker, "Botanical Exploration in Florida," 49; Pennell, "Travels and Scientific Collections," 21. In a footnote, Pennell expresses the opinion that all of Nuttall's labeled specimens from Florida at this time were collected by Baldwin and that Nuttall did not collect in Florida. See also Pennell, "Historic Botanical Collections," 137–51.

[10] In 1817, he was elected as a correspondent according to his wishes. See Anonymous, "Nuttall, Thomas Sutton, Lancashire, England, 1817," in *Members and Correspondents of the Academy*, 20. His family inheritance related to his residence being in England. This contrast with admitted speculation by Graustein, *Thomas Nuttall*, 114.

along with George Ord, Charles Lesueur, and William Maclure. Nuttall contributed three papers.[11] He then completed his heroic writing effort and published more than 580 pages of *The Genera of North American Plants, and a Catalogue of the Species to the Year 1817* in two volumes. It was the first systematic work on American flora with plant descriptions written in English instead of Latin, the first book of its kind published in America, and the first summary of scientific descriptions and geographic ranges of the flora of Florida.[12]

Nuttall notes in the preface to *Genera* that his English scientific descriptions of plants, their geographic range, etc., are based on "How much he has drawn from every popular source of information...by the labours of others almost every page can testify." The "others" he referenced included many Florida explorers and collectors—John and William Bartram, John Eatton Le Conte, and William Baldwin—whom Nuttall acknowledged. He proposed a new genus be named for Baldwin ("*Balduina*"). However, as Nuttall named and renamed plants, he often used other botanist's specimens without consultation, permission, or reference, which raised some accusations of "plagiarism," especially from William Baldwin.

In fact, Nuttall scooped Baldwin in naming many Florida plants. Insult was added to injury by Nuttall's published misspelling of Baldwin's name as "Baldwyn," or some variation, throughout the two volumes of *Genera*. "*Balduina*," the new genera name, was "Dedicated as a just tribute of respect for the talents and industry of William Baldwyn, MD...a gentleman whose botanical zeal and knowledge has rarely been excelled in America." "*Silene baldwnii*" was acknowledged to be from "In herb. Baldwyn."[13] Baldwin lamented to his friend and colleague Zaccheus Collins, "I should have felt infinitely more obliged to him, had he simply given me credit for the little I had done in the work of Mr. Elliott, and omitted Baldwina, Baldwini, Baldwynii, and everything else relating to me."[14] In an unapologetic letter to Baldwin, Nuttall

---

[11] Nuttall, "Observations on the genus Eriogonum," pt. 1, 24–30; pt. 3, 33–37; "An Account of Two New Genera of Plants," 111–22; "Description of *Collinsia*, a new genus of Plants," 189–93.

[12] One can speculate that Nuttall's involvement in these publishing activities, his British citizenship, and the amount of Florida botanical information he was working on were reasons he was not involved in the forthcoming ANSP expedition to Spanish Florida. In addition, he could rely on Say and Peale to fill any collecting gaps.

[13] Nuttall, *The Genera of North American Plants,* 1:288.

[14] Baldwin to Zaccheus Collins, 8 August 1818, ANSP Archives, Collins correspondence; Graustein, *Thomas Nuttall,* 124.

wrote that he could have described the new species based on specimens from herbaria other than Baldwin's.[15] While this may have been the case in some instances, it was not true for Baldwin's unique Florida specimens that had been used in Nuttall's research for *Genera*.

Putting aside the Baldwin-Nuttall dispute, Nuttall's *Genera* introduced many enthusiasts and botanists to "Florida" flora for the first time since William Bartram's *Travels* through its plant descriptions complete with range and habitat references. Nuttall's comments and allusions to Bartram's *Travels* accompany plant descriptions, such as "*I. calestina,* A very scarce plant, and of a doubtful genus; discovered in Florida by Mr. Bartram."[16] Personal references, such as "The venerable W. Bartram informs me of the existence," are sprinkled throughout the two volumes.[17] Unpublished botanical findings, "Collected in East Florida by my friend Mr. T. Say," from the 1817–1818 Academy expedition also appear.[18]

With *Genera* completed, Nuttall pursued further field exploration in the Arkansas and Mississippi territories then returned to the Academy to write and publish *Journal of Travels into the Arkansas Territory during the year 1819.* While on this journey, Nuttall met Nathaniel A. Ware, an avid naturalist living near Natchez, Mississippi, who soon began supplying Nuttall with Florida plant collections.[19]

Nathaniel A. Ware

According to Wyatt-Brown, "Nathaniel Ware…seemed to have come out of the mists, bearing no traces of the past"; even his date and place of birth are unknown.[20] His dates are usually given as 1789–1854; he was probably born in Massachusetts or South Carolina, where he studied law and was admitted to the bar before moving to Natchez in the Mississippi Territory around 1815. He married and became wealthy through land speculation in

---

[15] Graustein, *Thomas Nuttall,* 124–25.

[16] Nuttall, *The Genera of North American Plants,* 1:22.

[17] Ibid., 1:22.

[18] Ibid., 2:74; see also *The Genera of North American Plants,* 2:104; Graustein, *Thomas Nuttall,* 120–28.

[19] Ibid., 150. Ware was not formally associated with the Academy at the time of this meeting, as stated in this reference.

[20] The time of his move to Mississippi is also unknown (Wyatt-Brown, *The House of Percy,* 9; Wilson and Fiske, *Appleton's Cyclopedia of American Biography,* 6:358; White, *The National Cyclopedia of American Biography,* 5:149; Wunderlin, Hansen, and Becker, "Botanical Exploration in Florida," 87; Barnhart, "Nathaniel Ware," 21).

Mississippi and elsewhere.[21] Ware's professional success enabled him to pursue his interest in botany and other sciences, and he was soon part of Natchez's affluent artistic and scientific scene. In 1819, he relocated his family to Philadelphia but retained their residence in Mississippi; he later acquired a plantation in the new territory of Florida.[22] During Ware's Philadelphia stay, his interest in botany often led to meetings at the Academy with Thomas Nuttall, for whom he had been collecting plants in Spanish Florida.[23] Ware's botanical inclinations and exploration increased as he restlessly traveled during Florida's transition to a U.S. territory:

> Like William Bartram—Ware crossed the wilderness of rivers, forests and swamps of north central Florida, including the "Alachua plains," which he found extraordinarily fertile, "with beautiful little lakes of clear water and savannas," rich timber stands, and abundant wildlife. But these lands he liked best lay along the Apalachicola River on the upper Gulf coast.[24]

In 1821, Ware was appointed by President Madison to serve as one of two commissioners on a committee to adjudicate land title claims in West Florida. During this period, Ware collected plants for Thomas Nuttall around Pensacola, where the West Florida Committee met, and also on his travels to meetings with members of the East Florida Committee in St. Augustine.[25]

Nuttall read a descriptive paper at an Academy meeting in February 1822 based on some of Ware's specimens. However, because the Academy's *Journal* was not issued from 1822–1823, Nuttall published "A Catalogue of a Collection of Plants made in East Florida, during the Months of October

---

[21] In 1814, Ware married Sarah Percy Ellis, a daughter of Captain Charles Percy, the head of a prominent Southern family. Sarah was the young widow of Judge John Ellis of Natchez. The Wares' first daughter was born just as Nathaniel's career soared. He became a major in the militia, secretary of the Territory, and assistant to the governor (Wyatt-Brown, *The House of Percy*, 75 ff).

[22] In 1819, shortly after Ware's second daughter was born, his wife, Sarah, suffered from a mental illness. Ware quickly relocated the family to Philadelphia so Sarah could receive treatment and care at the premier Pennsylvania Hospital. For the next decade during her hospitalization, Ware maintained an apartment for himself and his two daughters in Philadelphia while keeping their residence in Mississippi. He later acquired a plantation in the new territory of Florida.

[23] Graustein, *Thomas Nuttall*, 150.

[24] Wyatt-Brown, *The House of Percy*, 96.

[25] Ibid., 167.

and November, 1821 by N. A. Ware, Esq." in the *American Journal of Science*.[26] Nuttall listed the known species in Ware's collection and then provided scientific descriptions of twenty-two species and one variety that he considered new to science. Nuttall also linked findings by Ware and Bartram:

> The fruit according to Mr. Ware is about the size of a pea, somewhat oblong, and, as usual, red when ripe. This species commonly used in Florida as a condiment by the inhabitants, is in common with the Cayenne pepper of Jamaica, called "Bird Pepper." It is the pepper spoken of by my friend Wm. Bartram, in his Book of Travels, page 71.[27]

Nuttall completed his article just as he was transitioning to his new position as lecturer in natural history and also the curator of the botanical gardens at Harvard College.

After assuming his positions at Harvard, Nuttall frequently visited the Academy to continue his botanical research. He attended meetings and continued his work with Ware.[28] Ware's relationship with the Academy was formalized in October 1826 by his election to membership during a stay in Philadelphia. Like several other members who maintained a residence in Philadelphia but spent much of their time away, Ware's membership was designated nonresident "(N. R.)" on the lists of members and correspondents of the Academy. During winter 1827–1828, Ware frequently met Nuttall at the Academy during Nuttall's brief visits or leaves from Harvard. Ware contributed a substantial portion of his collections to the Academy herbarium, and Nuttall continued his Florida studies.[29]

Nuttall on Leave...

At Harvard College, Nuttall was hampered by a lack of botanical specimens for comparison and also a shortage of botany books for reference and soon realized he was doing little to advance botanical science. Restless, he requested academic leave, and spent December 1829 and January 1830 at the Academy in Philadelphia before heading south to Charleston. From there, Nuttall started his "pedestrian tour of twelve hundred miles through the states

---

[26] Nuttall, "A Catalogue of a Collection of Plants," 286–304.

[27] Ibid., 289.

[28] Nuttall was frequently on leave or visiting the Academy from his position at Harvard College from 1823–1834 to use the Library or collections and meet with Ware and other colleagues.

[29] Pennell, "Travels and Scientific Collections," 34, fn. 76. Ware collected thirty-seven specimens that are in today's type collection herbarium (in the PH).

of South Carolina, Georgia, Alabama and Florida."[30] In March 1830, he traveled through western Florida near Pensacola, collecting along the Escambia River. Next, Nuttall tramped eastward into what was called Middle Florida; at Chipola, just west of the Apalachicola River, he collected endemic plants, including Florida hedgehyssop (*Gratiola floridana*); at Tallahassee, he gathered Florida chinkapin (*Castanea alnifolia*). He returned to Savannah through lower Georgia and then proceeded on to Philadelphia, arriving in Cambridge by the end of May 1830.[31]

Nuttall again took academic leave to journey to the southern states from February through April 1832. He visited Dr. H. Loomis in New Bern, North Carolina, where he met Loomis's botanizing colleague, Hardy Croom, and learned that they were working on a catalog of plants of the area.[32] Croom was also actively collecting in Middle Florida near the Apalachicola River. After the meeting, Loomis and Croom often sent specimens to Nuttall and Charles Pickering, curator of the Academy's herbarium.

With a lifelong interest in ornithology, Nuttall also birded during his explorations and was stimulated by the works of Wilson, Bonaparte, and Audubon. While in Cambridge, Nuttall wrote the first volume of his *Manual of the Ornithology of the United States and of Canada*, which was published in 1832. It was the first work of moderate size and price about American birds.[33]

With growing concern that he was "vegetating" like the garden plants at Harvard, Nuttall requested a leave of absence to accompany Nathaniel J. Wyeth's transcontinental expedition, which would eventually lead to Hawaii. The trip was partially sponsored by the Academy and scheduled to depart in late 1834. When Harvard rejected Nuttall's request for leave, he resigned. He returned to Philadelphia, attended Academy meetings, and worked in the herbarium while waiting for the expedition to begin. While Nuttall's time at the Academy was brief, "In six or eight weeks he accomplished an amazing amount of botanical work." Three major articles resulted from his efforts. One "was a paper, for which descriptions may well have been accumulating from the visits early and late in 1829, on the new and interesting specimens

---

[30] Pennell, "Travels and Scientific Collections," 32.

[31] Ibid., 32–33.

[32] Graustein, *Thomas Nuttall*, 260–62.

[33] The earlier portfolios and volumes of bird books by Wilson, Audubon, and Bonaparte were sizable and costly, usually purchased by wealthy individuals or by institutions.

in the Academy's collections."[34]

Nuttall's 1834 paper highlighted some of the rarer species in the collections. Nuttall named a new plant species after Loomis, "*Pycnanthemum *Loomisii.*"[35] He included the footnote: "I have dedicated this very distinct species to Dr. H. Loomis, of Newbern, in North Carolina, a gentleman who has devoted much attention to botany, and who in concert with Mr. Croom, published a catalogue of the plants of his neighborhood."[36]

He included many new identifications, descriptions, and comments about Florida specimens forwarded to the Academy by Croom and other Florida collectors. Nuttall also studied Florida plants that Ware had contributed to the Academy herbarium.

Nuttall began the paper: "In a collection of plants made in East Florida, by my friend Mr. Ware…. On obtaining sight of flowering specimens of this curious plant in the herbarium of the Academy of Natural Sciences of this place, I discovered that it constituted a new genus…I propose to call APTERIA."[37] Nuttall continued with a description of the geographical location and variation of species in the new genera based on the herbarium specimens.[38] He also created *Warea*, a new genus, to honor Ware. The type species, *Warea amplexifolia*, was "Discovered by my friend N. A. Ware, Esq., to whom, as a just tribute for his varied and unwearied exertions in the cause of natural science, and particularly in Botany, I beg leave to dedicate this curious plant."[39] Nuttall described in detail other specimens Ware had collected in

---

[34] Ibid., 33–34.

[35] Nuttall, "A Description of Some of the Rarer or Little Known Plants," 100.

[36] Ibid. The reference is to *A Catalogue of Plants, Native or Naturalized, in the Vicinity of New Bern* printed in a limited edition in 1834 with H. Loomis and H. B. Croom as authors. In his article, Nuttall cites many specimens in the PH from Loomis and/or Croom and Nuttall's longer working relationship with Loomis.

[37] Nuttall, "A Description of Some of the Rarer or Little Known Plants," 61–62.

[38] Ibid., 65–67.

[39] Ibid., 84. This species and other *Warea* were collected in northern Florida and were once common in most of Florida but are now endangered and restricted to the central highlands area (Ward, *Plants*, 5). *Warea amplexifolia* is also known as "clasping warea" or "wide-leaf warea." Clasping warea is an erect annual herb in the mustard family (*Warea amplexifolia [Nutt.] Nutt. Earlier: Stanleya amplexifolia Nuttall 1822.* Plate X from Nuttall, "A Description of Some of the Rarer or Little Known Plants," 83).

Florida.[40] Nuttall's article was a botanical end mark for Ware's Florida studies.[41]

In the same article, Nuttall announced earlier Florida specimens collected by Titian Peale and based on his study of the Academy's herbarium specimens.[42] Curiously, Nuttall left the most intriguing Florida botanical story dangling for future botanists by including only a brief description and identification of a Florida specimen from Hardy Croom.

After examining the specimen, Nuttall reported, "From Mr. Croom I have at the same time received a branch of a species of *Toxus*, probably the *T. montana* of Mexico, which according to Mr. C. attains to the magnitude of a considerable tree. Its leaves are apiculated as described by Willdenow, but there is no obvious inequality at their base."[43] Nuttall's passing description—perhaps because he had only vegetative material but no seeds, flowers, or fruit—included the word "probably" in his identification, which left Croom questioning the proof of identity of his commonly called "stinking cedar" branches. In 1834, shortly after the article appeared, Nuttall departed on the Wyeth expedition; Croom decided to consult John Torrey, a New York botanist colleague. Croom's action sparked a series of subsequent events that involved John Torrey and other botanists in a Florida botanical saga and linked America's most prominent nineteenth-century botanists with ties to both the Academy and Florida botany. A background about these key players follows, starting with John Torrey.

John Torrey

John Torrey (1796–1873) was born and grew up in New York City. He pursued his early interest in botany by field collecting in the unsettled areas north of Fourteenth Street on Manhattan Island. One of Torrey's earliest recollections was the sight of two young men coming into the city covered

---

[40] Nuttall, "A Description of Some of the Rarer or Little Known Plants," 82, 96.

[41] After Ware's wife died in 1836, he abandoned botany and devoted his time and attention to his daughters, his business interests, and his new passion for economics (Wyatt-Brown, *The House of Percy*, 101–102; 104–36). See also Diamond, "Nathaniel A. Ware, National Economist," 501–26; Ware, *Notes on Political Economy*. Ware also wrote fiction; see Ware, *Harvey Belden*.

[42] Nuttall, "A Description of Some of the Rarer or Little Known Plants," reference to specimens from Titian Peale's expedition for Bonaparte in 1824–1825; "To the Florida Keys," 82, 90–1; "From Other Florida Collector," 61–115.

[43] Nuttall, "A Description of Some of the Rarer or Little Known Plants," 96.

with dust and loaded with plant collections. He was told that one was "the Le Conte boy."[44] Torrey reportedly later collected plant specimens for John Eaton Le Conte's (see page 106) *Catalogue of the Plants of the Island of New York.* Torrey's boyhood meeting with and botanical tutoring by Amos Eaton further developed Torrey's interest in botany, and Eaton's influence continued.[45]

During Torrey's medical studies (1815–1818) at the College of Physicians and Surgeons, he furthered his botanical training with Professor David Hosack, who had founded Elgin Botanic Gardens, the first botanical garden in New York, taught botany, and was an admirable tutor and role model for young Torrey.[46] As their friendship grew, Torrey continued actively collecting and supplied Hosack with many plant specimens. In 1817, Torrey assisted Dr. Benjamin Silliman and several others in founding the Lyceum of Natural History of New York (see pages 112) .[47] Shortly thereafter, the Lyceum appointed Torrey to a curatorial committee to prepare a catalogue of plants near New York City. Torrey completed the *Catalogue of the Plants growing within thirty miles of the city of New York* and presented it to the Lyceum on 22 December 1817; the catalogue was published in 1819 and earned him notice from other botanists, including Stephen Elliott, Lewis von Schweinitz, and Nuttall.[48]

After receiving his medical degree in 1818, Torrey opened a physician's office but chose to pursue plants rather than patients, often botanizing outside of the city and giving little time to his medical practice. He began a series

---

[44] Burgess, "The Work of the Torrey Botanical Club," 552–58.

[45] The Le Conte boys were likely Louis and John (Major) Eatton, sons of Dr. John E. Le Conte, a friend of John Torrey's father. Major Le Conte published his first botanical efforts, *Catalogue of the plants on the island of New York*, in 1810 (Rodgers, *John Torrey*, 11; Letters to Amos Eaton, John Torrey papers, folder 310, NYBG Archives. Later in life, the student Torrey became the teacher. See Rodgers, *John Torrey*, 13–17, for the Eaton and Torrey relationship. Amos Eaton was elected an Academy correspondent in 1819.

[46] Robbins, *David Hosack: Citizen of New York*, 62; Robbins, "David Hosack's Herbarium and its Linnaean Specimens," 293–313. Hosack was elected ANSP correspondent in 1815. Torrey was a medical doctor, as were many botanists at that time. Since medicine was based on herbalism, doctors had to study botany to learn their craft.

[47] Silliman was a professor at Yale, founder of the *AJS*, and elected an ANSP correspondent in 1815.

[48] Rodgers, *John Torrey*, 34. John Eatton Le Conte published an earlier, more geographically local list in 1810. Stephen Elliott was elected an Academy correspondent in 1815), Lewis von Schweinitz in 1822.

of botanical explorations leading to Philadelphia, where he met with botanists of the Academy, including Zaccheus Collins, who had received a letter of introduction from John Eatton Le Conte:

> Dr. Torrey the bearer of this letter, intends making a botanical tour through the pine barrens of New Jersey...he will stay some days in Philadelphia.... I have taken the liberty of introducing him to you, and of begging you to show him some attention...a well-informed botanist and one whose disposition to communicate any discoveries to his friends is only equaled by his zeal for the advancement of our favorite science.[49]

This visit began Torrey's friendship and association with Collins, Nuttall, and others linked with the Academy.[50]

Torrey was elected an Academy correspondent in 1822 and followed Nuttall's lead by developing his talents as a "closet botanist," publishing on new species and the geographic distribution of known plants collected by field collaborators, many from Florida. In 1823, Torrey hosted Nuttall, "this celebrated naturalist," with a place "to stay altogether at my office" when Nuttall was giving lectures and pursuing job opportunities.[51] Torrey became an increasingly important contact for botanical collectors during Nuttall's transition to and appointment at Harvard College. When Nuttall's interest at Harvard shifted to ornithology, with botanical interludes in the field and herbarium work at the Academy, John Torrey established himself and New York City as an active center for botanical studies while maintaining field contacts in Florida and an interest in Florida's flora.

Asa Gray

In 1830, Asa Gray (1810–1888), a young medical student from upstate New York who avidly read Torrey's publications, sent him some plant specimens. Gray received a cordial reply from Torrey along with a request for more plants. Thereafter, Torrey and the aspiring botanist maintained an active correspondence about botany.[52] After receiving his medical degree in January 1831, Gray began his residency but soon decided to teach science nearby at the Utica Gymnasium. During summer leave, Gray traveled south to Bethlehem, Pennsylvania, collecting fossilized ferns, botanizing, and visiting the elderly Lewis von Schweinitz. Gray returned through New York City, where

---

[49] Ibid., 38.
[50] Ibid., 38–39.
[51] Ibid., 62; Graustein, *Thomas Nuttall*, 167.
[52] Dupree, *Asa Gray*; Rodgers, *John Torrey*, 90–93.

he met Torrey for the first time. They went on a collecting trip nearby; it gave Torrey a chance to assess Gray's field knowledge, which impressed him. In 1833, Torrey engaged Gray to spend the summer collecting plants and to live at Torrey's home for several months while working on the herbarium specimens and editing manuscripts. In 1834, Gray returned to New York as Torrey's teaching assistant at the Medical College and as a resident guest in John Torrey's family household.

In a letter to his father, Asa Gray mentioned, "Dr. Torrey, and myself went last month to Philadelphia, where we stayed a week. We spent our time almost entirely in the rooms of the American Philosophical Society, and of the Academy of Sciences. We met most of the scientific and other learned men, and spent our time very pleasantly."[53] Torrey and Gray later acknowledged their Academy visit, its herbarium, and the people they met as instrumental in what would become their collaborative work on Torrey's *A Flora of North America*.

Gray assisted Torrey in processing and analyzing more specimens from Southern collectors and helped Torrey extend his studies into new areas of geographic interest, such as Middle and South Florida and territories west of the Allegany Mountains. After 1834, Torrey and Gray, rather than Nuttall, played key roles in developing Southern and Florida botany through Torrey's earlier contacts and their collaboration with Hardy Croom and Alvan Chapman, new Florida residents.[54]

Hardy Croom

Hardy Bryan Croom (1797–1837) was born and grew up in Lenoir County, North Carolina, where his prominent father, William Croom, owned several plantations. Hardy received a bachelor's and an honorary master's degree from the University of North Carolina at Chapel Hill and became a successful attorney. While helping manage his father's plantations, Hardy pursued his primary interests (botany and the classics), served in the state senate, and practiced law.

Following his marriage in 1821 to the daughter of a wealthy citizen of nearby coastal New Bern, the couple made their residence there.[55] New Bern

---

[53] Dupree, *Asa Gray*, 41–42; Asa Gray to Moses Gray, 21 November 1834.

[54] In 1834, Nuttall departed the ANSP to explore the West and did not return until 1836. From then until he left for England in 1841, Nuttall worked at the ANSP and contributed to Torrey and Gray's *Flora of North America*.

[55] Croom married Frances Henrietta Smith, the daughter of Nathan Smith, and the

was the perfect location for Hardy to pursue his business interests and his studies as an amateur botanist. His many trips from New Bern to Raleigh, where he served in the state senate, gave him botanizing opportunities for a "Memoranda of a Journey from Newbern to Raleigh by an Amateur Botanist," which he published in the *Harbinger*, a Chapel Hill newspaper.[56] In his botany pursuits, Hardy later collaborated with his New Bern mentor, Dr. H. Loomis, on a floral survey of the region.

Hardy's field interest in Florida's flora began when his father purchased property there in 1826 and again in 1828. On visits, Hardy pursued his botanical interests while he and his brother, Bryan, helped their father develop and manage his plantations in Middle Florida territory, near the Apalachicola River town of Aspalaga.[57] After their father's sudden death in 1829, Hardy and Bryan each inherited some of his estate's fortune and property. Bryan retained and continued to operate their father's plantation. Hardy leased a Florida plantation on the west bank of the Apalachicola River, an area he had come to favor across from the settlement of Aspalaga.

In the early 1830s, Hardy Croom purchased and began developing a 2400-acre plantation further east "on account of its desirable location for a family residence." He hoped it would become attractive to his wife, "being but three miles distant from the City of Tallahassee, the capital of the Territory, in the centre of good society, pleasantly situated on the border of Lake Lafayette, and combining many advantages for a permanent family seat."[58] By 1834, Hardy was living on the plantation in one of several dwellings that he built along the western edge of "Lake Lafayette, near Tallahassee."[59] He planned to lure his wife and family by building on his plantation, later named

---

Crooms had three children, Henrietta Mary, William Henry, and Justina Rosa.

[56] Hardy Croom, "Memoranda of a Journey from New Bern to Raleigh by an Amateur Botanist," 1833, in the *Harbinger*, a Chapel Hill newspaper, cited by Rogers and Clark, *Croom Family*, 234, fn. 29.

[57] Their father's plantation was south of where Interstate 10 now crosses the Apalachicola River. Hardy leased a plantation on the west side of the river near the Aspalaga Bluffs. The small town of Aspalaga faded away in the early twentieth century; an Aspalaga Road remains today.

[58] Redfearn, "The Steamboat Home," 405–24. Croom hoped to convince his wife to relocate with their children from New Bern to Tallahassee.

[59] Indicated as a publication address and also the address on Croom's membership record at the ANSP in 1835.

Goodwood.[60] He was elected to the Academy in 1835 and continued to botanize in shaded ravines and Apalachicola River embankments near Aspalaga and on his frequent trips back and forth to Tallahassee.

Croom had discovered his botanical paradise, "where the flowers ever blossom, the beams ever shine" in Middle Florida, which he enthusiastically described, referencing and rivaling Bartram's passionate comments about Florida.[61] In one of Croom's many articles that appeared in the *Farmers' Register*, he wrote about agricultural issues and included botanical descriptions that extolled Middle Florida. He described the area around Lake Lafayette in Tallahassee in a manner reminiscent of Bartram's effusive poetic style: "The richest uplands are the Hammocks or Hummocks...greets you like an oasis in a desert...and the beauty of its numerous evergreens...the stately Magnolia Grandiflora...the showy Hydrangea, and the gay Azalea.... Such is a Florida hammock—the pride of Flora and the paradise of botanists."[62]

In addition to writing for the *Farmers Register*, Croom focused on collecting Florida specimens and studying their flowering characteristics and environmental distribution. His knowledge and experience with plants and the geographic conditions in Florida and North Carolina allowed him to publish comparisons about these and taxonomic descriptions in a series of "Botanical Communications" in the *American Journal of Science* from 1834–1835.[63] In each article, he devoted several sections to new plant species and their locations and discussed his unique botanical discoveries.

In the cool, shaded ravines along the Apalachicola River near Croom's leased plantation, he collected and then published ten new species that ended

---

[60] The name Goodwood came into use in the 1840s and has been in common use since the 1850s. Goodwood Plantation, the mansion and gardens just outside Tallahassee, were completed by Hardy's younger brother, Bryan, and under his management grew to some eight thousand acres to become one of Florida's most profitable and prestigious plantations. The mansion and gardens are now restored. See www.goodwoodmuseum.org and Wallace Harper Beall, *The Seasons of Goodwood* (Tallahassee: Goodwood Museum and Gardens, Inc., 2015).

[61] Croom, "Some Account of the Agricultural Soil," 1–3.

[62] Ibid., 3. From "Lake Lafayette, near Tallahassee, March, 1834." Croom published five other notes in this volume of *Farmers' Register* about various agricultural topics, including cotton and coffee. One article about fossils was later reprinted in H. B. Croom, "Miscellanies: Some Account of the Organic Remains found in the Marl Pits of Lucas Benner, Esq. in Craven County, N.C.," *AJS and Arts* 27/2 (1835): 168–71.

[63] H. B. Croom, "Botanical Communications," *AJS and Arts* 25/1 (1834): 69–77; *AJS and Arts* 26/2 (1834): 313–20; *AJS and Arts* 28 (1835): 165–67.

up in the Academy's herbarium, some as type specimens.[64] One of these is *Baptisia simplicifolia Croom* (Croom scareweed).[65] Among the plant species ultimately credited to Croom are the *Baptisia simplicifolia, Taxus floridania, Croomia pauciflora,* and *Torreya taxifloria.* The final scientific naming of these plants after Croom first discovered or collected them and then described them was often a long process and involved Nuttall, Torrey, and others.

Florida Torreya

Sometime during the early 1830s, Croom sent cuttings of his unusual Florida discovery to Nuttall or Pickering at the Academy in Philadelphia. One particular branch specimen was from a tree commonly called the "stinking cedar" because its needles gave off a pungent odor when crushed. In 1834, when Croom visited the Academy, he likely had captivating conversations about this and other Florida specimens with Nuttall, curator Pickering, and others.[66] They also may have discussed Nuttall's paper, which was in press, about the rarities in the herbarium collections.[67] While Nuttall dismissed Croom's tree as "a branch of a species...probably the *T. montana* of Mexico," Croom believed it was a new discovery. Later, he either sent or hand-delivered flowering specimens and the fruit of this "stinking cedar" to John Torrey. Croom wanted Torrey's thoughts about Nuttall's recent assessment.

In the intervening period, Croom was elected to membership in the Academy in 1835 while he and his family summered in New York.[68] However, he did not meet with either Gray or Torrey at that time. John Torrey had moved his family to Princeton, where he was teaching. Without Torrey's

---

[64] These can be viewed in the ANSP digital herbarium catalogue (http://ph.ansp.org/).

[65] PH Type Collection. Courtesy ANSP, code [specimen no.]: 7372. H. B. Croom, ""Botanical Communications," *AJS* 25/1 (1834): 74; first reported by Croom "near Quincy, in Middle Florida...Flowers, June, July." Also reported by Nuttall, "A Description of Some of the Rarer or Little Known Plants," 96; named in honor of Croom by Torrey and Gray, "Baptisia," 383; Kral, "*Baptisia simplicifolia Croom,*" 642–45.

[66] Hardy Croom's letters to Frances Croom from Philadelphia during his summer 1834 visit indicate he met Charles Pickering and visited the ANSP. See H. B. Croom to B. Croom, 1 July 1832, in Rogers and Clark, *The Croom Family,* 237 (section C).

[67] Nuttall, "A Description of Some of the Rarer or Little Known Plants," 115.

[68] Hardy Bryan Croom (1798–1837) was elected to ANSP membership on July 28, 1835. Although Croom's membership card lists his name correctly, the published *Members and Correspondents of the Academy of Natural Sciences of Philadelphia,* all editions, list his second initial incorrectly as: "Croom H. P., Tallahassee, Florida, 1835."

support, Asa Gray had returned to his father's home to work on his manuscript for his botany textbook.[69] These moves accounted in part for the delay in response from Torrey about Croom's "stinking cedar" specimens.

To further study Croom's specimens, Torrey sought additional specimens and information from Dr. Alvan Chapman, one of his new collectors who had recently moved to Quincy in Middle Florida.[70] Chapman had previously written to Torrey, explaining that Florida "is most certainly a remarkable field for the Naturalist." Dr. Chapman later enthused, "Mr. Croom, I am happy to state, is now in the Territory. I was favored with a call the other day."[71]

Torrey, Chapman, and Croom soon began three-way communications about the mysterious tree, which Croom later called the Torreya tree, to acknowledge Torrey. In turn, Torrey dubbed the small herbaceous plant that grew in its shade "Croom's herb" or "croomia." Their lifelong friendship and botanical collaboration thus began on "the branch of a species."

When Croom later met with Chapman in fall 1836, the former had recently returned from a New York meeting with John Torrey and Asa Gray to study and discuss Florida plants. Croom had presented "Observations on the genus *Sarracenia*; with an Account of a New Species" at the Lyceum in New York.[72] In this presentation, later called his "Monograph on *Sarracenia*," Croom described *Sarracenia Drummondii*: "from specimens in the herbarium of Dr. Torrey, who received a few leaves, without flowers, from Sir William Jackson Hooker, to whom they had been sent by Drummond, from Apalachicola in 1835. In the spring of the present year (1836), Dr. A. W. Chapman obtained the plant in flower near Apalachicola and gave the specimen to Dr.

---

[69] Dupree, *Asa Gray*, 48.

[70] Trelease, "Alvin Wentworth Chapman," 643–44; Kimball, "Reminiscences of Alvan Wentworth Chapman," 1–12; Fishman, *Journeys through Paradise*, 182–83. Fishman notes, "Personal details about Chapman's life are spotty at best" (184). Quincy is about thirty miles west of Tallahassee. Aspalaga and the region of the Croom plantations are another twenty miles west at the Apalachicola River. Southward some eighty miles, at the mouth of the Apalachicola River, is Apalachicola. Cotton was transported downriver to markets in Apalachicola and for shipment from the Gulf port.

[71] Rodgers, *John Torrey*, 172–73.

[72] Read on 5 September 1836, this paper was published posthumously and became known as Croom's "Monograph on Sarracenia" (Croom, *Annals of the New York Lyceum of Natural History*, 96–104).

Torrey," whom, Croom acknowledged, "by whose kindness I have been permitted to describe it here."[73] Croom's monograph and his earlier contribution to the study of *Sarracenia* led Torrey later to name the whitetop pitcher plant in Croom's honor, *Sarracenia Drummondii Croom*.[74]

In summer 1837, Croom traveled from Florida to New York City to join his family at the graduation of their eldest daughter from finishing school. For his planned meetings with Torrey, Croom brought living plants of his Florida Torreya tree, as he wished to call it, and the small herbaceous plant that Torrey had dubbed "the croomia." Asa Gray, who was working with Torrey, recalled the meeting years later: "I was a pupil and assistant of…Torrey when Mr. Croom brought to him specimens, both of the tree and other herb, both new genera." Gray noted subsequent events: "The former…was named for Dr. Torrey by his correspondent, Arnott. The latter was dedicated to its discoverer by Dr. Torrey."[75] Gray also recalled Croom's reaction to having an herb, "croomia," named in his honor: "I well remember Mr. Croom's remark upon the occasion, that if his name was deemed worthy of botanical honors, it was gratifying to him, and becoming to the circumstance, that it should be borne by the unpretending herb which delighted to shelter itself under the noble Torreya." Croom left the manuscript for his proposed *Catalogue of Plants* for Torrey's editorial and publishing suggestions.

Later, on 7 October 1837, John Torrey and others joined Hardy Croom and his family at the dock as they departed New York Harbor on the steamboat *Home* for Charleston, South Carolina.[76] Tragedy struck two days later

---

[73] William Jackson Hooker was elected an Academy correspondent in 1821. Thomas Drummond (1793–1835) was a prominent Scottish botanical collector. During his second trip to America from 1834–1835, he traveled to Louisiana and Florida, became ill, and died in March 1835 (Wunderlin, Hansen, and Becker, "Botanical Exploration in Florida," 56; Croom, *Annals of the New York Lyceum of Natural History*, 96–97.

[74] "The first part of this Volume (to page 184) was published in July, 1838; the second…the remainder in June 1840." Volume 2 was also issued in parts until completed (Torrey and Gray, *Flora*, xi–xiii; Rodgers, *John Torrey*, 96). For a 2012 *Flora* update, see www.fna.org/Libraries/plib/WWW/Introduction.

[75] Gray, "A Pilgrimage to Torreya," 192, reprinted in Sargent, *Scientific Papers of Asa Gray*, 2:192; Dupree, *Asa Gray*, 408.

[76] Croom had recently purchased a home and relocated his family to Charleston from New Bern. They moved for the cultural and scientific attractions of Charleston; in addition, the city was closer to Florida and had speedy steamboat transportation to New York. His plan was to convince his wife to move even further to Tallahassee. His brother,

when the *Home* sank in a hurricane south of Cape Hatteras. Croom, his wife, and their three children drowned. The bodies of Hardy Croom and his eldest daughter were never recovered. Their deaths shook their family, friends, and the botanical community. Many family members, friends, and business and scientific colleagues became involved in settling issues related to the family's untimely death.[77] John Torrey also willingly gave his time and energy to bringing closure to many open botanical issues.

Hardy Croom had left his unpublished manuscript in Torrey's care. Some work had yet to be done on the *Catalogue of Plants*, the botanical identification of the Torreya tree, and the "little croomia." With grace, Torrey completed the three unfinished commitments for Croom.

Torrey acted swiftly and published Croom's edited manuscript in a new *Catalogue of Plants*.[78] Croom had extended the identifications and descriptions to more plants from the New Bern area and compared the plant's time of blooming and other characteristics with those he had observed in Florida. The front matter in the new *Catalogue* included a preface by Torrey, a biography of Croom by "The Rev. Dr. Hawks of the City," and tribute resolutions and condolences from the Lyceum of New York City. In the preface, Torrey explained his course of action:

> Most of his [Croom] new and rare plants, together with his valuable observations on them, were kindly presented to me, with permission to use them for the benefit of sciences. It is my purpose to describe some of these in a separate paper. He has, however, given us a valuable monograph of

---

Bryan, planned to meet them in Charleston for a trip to Tallahassee after their arrival in Charleston. See Rogers and Clark, *Croom Family*, 45–55, 61.

[77] Hardy died intestate; his final will and testament could not be found, and a legal battle ensued over the Crooms's substantial estate. Torrey, who had spent time with Hardy just before his death, was called for depositions in legal proceedings that lasted for twenty years. The litigation for the estate waged between Bryan in Florida and the mother-in-law/grandmother in North Carolina. The question of which family member died last in the swirling waters became a matter of speculation, debate, and testimony. Florida and North Carolina laws clashed on inheritance rules. In its ruling, the Florida State Supreme Court established case law: "The Steamboat *Home*, Presumptions to the order of death in a common calamity" (Redfearn, "The Steamboat *Home*," 405–24). After a protracted lawsuit, the majority settlement did not favor Bryan, so the well-developed Goodwood Plantation in Tallahassee passed to different owners (Beall, *The Seasons of Goodwood*, 11–16).

[78] Croom, *A Catalogue of Plants*. Torrey's historical account cites Croom's contributions. Honors and biographical information are included.

the genus SARACENIA, which will appear in the forthcoming volume of the New-York Lyceum. Among the new plants discovered by Mr. Croom, and communicated to me, are a beautiful evergreen Andromeda; an arborescent Taxus, allied to *T. Canadensis*, but attaining a height of thirty feet; a noble new genus of *Coniferae* with the foliage of Taxus and a fruit as large as a nutmeg, which Dr. Arnott will shortly publish under the name of *Torreya*; and a very distinct new genus, to which I have given the name of *Croomia*, in honor of my departed friend.[79]

Torrey's preview of "a noble new genus...under the name of *Torreya*... [and] a very distinct new genus, to which I have given the name of *Croomia*" came with his promises about future publications that would take time to fulfill because of his own work overload and that "which Dr. Arnott will shortly publish."

George A. Walker-Arnott (1799–1868), a professor of botany at the University of Glasgow in Scotland, had studied the botany of North America with Sir William Hooker, an English host and collaborator of Torrey and Gray. In an 1838 article, "On the Genus *Torreya*," Arnott recounts,

> Dr. Torrey wrote me as follows: "Did I tell you of a beautiful and new Taxoid tree from Middle Florida? It was discovered about three years ago by my esteemed friend H. B. Croom, Esq., of Tallahassee. Although so abundant about Aspalaga that it is sawed into planks and timber, no description of it has hitherto been published."[80]

In Torrey's letter, which Arnott reprinted as background data, Torrey reported Nuttall's brief preliminary notice of the tree in 1834. Torrey's two pages of detailed descriptions were based on his study of specimens and "fruit preserved in spirits" along with references to several pertinent publications.[81] After further analysis and consideration, Arnott determined, "I feel certain that I express the general wish of all botanists that this name [Torreya] be now appropriated to the Florida tree, of which I proceed to give the following description."[82] Arnott declared a new genus, *"Torreya, Arn."* He ignored various lesser Torreyas, which had already been published, and transferred the name to the Florida tree; he also made Croom's specimen the type species of the new genus *Torreya*. He followed with a full Latin description of Croom's discovery under the name *Torreya taxifolia*.[83]

---

[79] Ibid., iv–v.

[80] Walker-Arnott, "On the Genus Torreya," 126–32.

[81] Ibid., 128–30.

[82] Ibid., 130.

[83] Ibid., 130–32; Chapman, *"Torreya taxifolia,"* 250–54.

Croom, Torrey, and Gray

Torrey's ambitions to meet his many botanical commitments, which included those to Croom, along with his goal for a descriptive flora of North America, suffered as a result of his excessive workload. Fortunately, Asa Gray had matured as Torrey's full collaborator when Gray had left his Utica Gymnasium teaching position and committed himself to botanical research and writing *Elements of Botany*. Gray was also able to devote more time and attention to the *Flora of North America* project. In 1836, *Elements of Botany* was published to excellent reviews, and Gray was elected an Academy correspondent; Torrey soon invited Gray to be a joint author of *A Flora of North America*.[84] They published the two-volume work in parts, completing the first volume in 1840 and the second in 1843. Their collaboration became more difficult when Asa Gray moved to Cambridge in 1842 to accept a position as a professor at Harvard and also to take charge of its botanic garden. They hoped, however, to continue working together after the 1843 completion and publication of volume two of *A Flora of North America*.[85]

While most publications at that time had focused on regional flora of America, *A Flora of North America* comprehensively covered the explored regions north of Mexico. In addition, as the lengthy subtitle boasted, the work was "arranged according to the natural system." *A Flora of North America* effectively ended the Linnaean era in America and became the American benchmark in botany. The work to expand *Flora* would continue through the efforts of Torrey, Gray, and the numerous contributors who sent them "plants of particular districts, accompanied in many instances by valuable notes and observations."

Flora contains many Florida plant entries based on specimens that Torrey began receiving in the 1830s along with descriptions and listings from "numerous correspondents in different parts of the country, who have from time to time furnished us with valuable collections and observations.... to the Botanical Committee of the Academy of Natural Sciences, Philadelphia, who have obligingly afforded us every facility in consulting the large herbarium of

---

[84] Torrey and Gray, *Flora*, 1. "The first part of this Volume (to page 184) was published in July, 1838; the second...the remainder in June, 1840" (Torrey and Gray, *Flora*, xi–xiii; Rodgers, *John Torrey*, 96). For a 2012 *Flora* update, see http://www.fna.org/Libraries/plib/WWW/Introduction.

[85] Sargent, *Scientific Papers of Asa Gray*, 2:864. The three parts of volume 2 were published in 1841, spring 1842, and February 1843, respectively.

that Society."[86] Torrey and Gray also specifically acknowledged several Academy members: "Mr. Elliott, Major Le Conte, and the late Mr. Lewis Le Conte," and

> the late Mr. Croom, who also made very interesting collections in Florida.... From Middle Florida, Dr. A. W. Chapman of Mariana has very fully supplied us with plants of that region. A portion of the plants collected by the late Dr. Baldwin were communicated to us through the late Mr. Schweinitz; but his original herbarium is incorporated in that of the Academy of Natural Sciences, Philadelphia.[87]

"Croom's herb" was formally described in *A Flora of North America* as the type specimen for a new genus, *Croomia,* in honor of its discoverer, Hardy Croom.[88] The section about *Croomia pauciflora* and the site where it was first collected by Croom noted, "Aspalaga, Middle Florida, on the Apalachicola River, under the shade of *Torreya taxifolia,* Mr. Croom!" It continued about *Croomia*: "The genus was established several years since, in a paper read before the Lyceum of Natural History, New York; and named in honor, now alas! In memory, of its discoverer, the late Henry [*sic*] B. Croom, Esq., author of a monograph of *Sarracenia,* and of other papers on the plants of Florida and the Southern States."[89]

The Academy's specimen of *Croomia pauciflora,* which was collected by physician-botanist Alvan Chapman, was in Professor C. W. Short's herbarium when it was donated to the Academy in 1864.[90] Short noted, "collected by Alvan Chapman, locality Cliffs at Aspalaga." The genus *Croomia* has three rare species, one each living in China, Japan, and Florida, which is the type species.

Croom's botanical studies in Middle Florida were continued by his friend and colleague, Alvan Chapman, who was originally based in Quincy before relocating to Apalachicola.

---

[86] Torrey and Gray, *Flora,* 1:xxi, 350. Through the collaborative efforts of over eight hundred botanists today, the online Flora of North America project will contain some 30 volumes.

[87] Ibid., 350.

[88] *Croomia pauciflora* (Nuttall) Torrey in Torrey and Gray, *Flora,* 1:663. Also mentioned by Torrey in the preface to Croom's *A Catalogue*; Croom, "ART," 165. Earlier in the preface of Croom's new *Catalogue,* Torrey had named the herb in honor of Croom.

[89] Torrey and Gray, *Flora,* 1:663.

[90] PH specimen, barcode: 6171Ex Herbarium: Short, C. W.

Alvan Chapman[91]

Though a Florida resident since 1835, Alvan (sometimes "Alvin") Wentworth Chapman (1809–1899) was born and had grown up in Massachusetts. He moved to Georgia to become a teacher and developed a serious interest in botany when he began studying medicine under the tutelage of a local physician. In 1835, Chapman relocated to Quincy, Florida, set up his medical practice, and continued his botanical studies. "At that time I was a mere tyro in botany…and had recently entered upon a friendly and instructive correspondence with Dr. Torrey."

While residing in Quincy (1835–1847) and preparing herbarium specimens, Chapman started a detailed identification list of the local flora with the aid of Torrey and Croom. In 1845, Chapman published "A List of Plants Growing Spontaneously in the Vicinity of Quincy, Florida," in the *Western Journal of Medicine and Surgery*.[92] Because the publication contained new locality information for more than twelve hundred species and held great interest for members of the Academy, member correspondent Professor Charles W. Short of Transylvania College in Kentucky donated a copy of Chapman's twenty-three page article to the Academy Library shortly after the article was published. Professor Short also later gave his personal herbarium of fifteen thousand specimens, many collected by Chapman, to the Academy.[93]

In 1847, Chapman and his family moved to Apalachicola, where he continued his medical practice and was a leading citizen for over fifty years.[94] He extended his botany rambles southward into the Florida wilderness, in-

---

[91] Rodgers, *John Torrey*, 172–73. Note Chapman's gravestone says, "Alvin." Alva, Alvan, and Alvin were used interchangeably by townspeople (Trelease, "Alvin Wentworth Chapman," 643–46; Kimball, "Reminiscences of Alvan Wentworth Chapman," 1–11; Wunderlin, Hansen, and Beckner, "Botanical Exploration in Florida," 59–60; Fishman, *Journeys Through Paradise*, 182–83). Fishman notes, "Personal details about Chapman's life are spotty at best." Some were brought together by Ms. Winifred Kimball and published with notes by John Small (Kimball, "Reminiscences of Alvan Wentworth Chapman," 1–12.

[92] Chapman, "List of Plants Growing Spontaneously in the Vicinity of Quincy, Florida," 461–83. Daniel Drake (elected as a correspondent, 1812) of Cincinnati, Ohio, a professor at the Louisville Institute of Medicine, was also senior editor of the journal. The running title was "Chapman's Florida Plants." It was a "list" of families with genus and species entries but no other information.

[93] Mears, "Guide to Plant Collectors," 162.

[94] Trelease, "Alvin Wentworth Chapman," 643–44.

cluding the often dangerous and unfriendly Indian Territory, and also north-ward into Georgia and the Appalachian mountains. These botanically unex-plored areas yielded new species of plants and allowed Chapman to better document the geographic range of countless others. During this period, Chapman often communicated with Torrey, Gray, and other southern col-lectors.

In his Florida travels, Chapman visited Key West, where he met John Loomis Blodgett (1809–1853), a physician and pharmacist who had settled there in 1838. Regarded as "the most important figure in South Florida's early botanical history," Blodgett collaborated with Nuttall after the latter returned to England in 1841.[95] Many of Blodgett's plants labeled "K. West" were housed in Nuttall's herbarium. Both Torrey and Gray's *Flora* and Chap-man's works contain many Key West records attributed to Blodgett. As Chapman expanded his Florida studies and explored regions of Georgia, he began planning a larger work about Florida and Southern plants based on his observations and collections. Chapman later produced a manuscript when he became a more "closet botanist" and restricted his travels because of his active medical practice and his civic leadership role in Apalachicola.[96]

Chapman split his botanical time between writing and supplying Torrey and Gray with specimens and descriptions. The pair gratefully acknowledged Chapman's contribution of seventy-six species to Torrey and Gray's *Flora*. In naming a genus of mosses *Chapmannia* in his honor, they note, "We dedicate this interesting genus to our friend Dr. A. W. Chapman, an accurate and indefatigable botanist, who has largely contributed to our knowledge of the plants of Middle Florida."[97] "*Chapmannia Floridana*" was described as the

---

[95] Joseph Ewan, "History of Botanical Collecting in Southern Florida," in Long and Lakela, *A Flora of Tropical Florida*, 4; Wunderlin, Hansen, and Beckner, "Botanical Exploration in Florida," 60–61. Nuttall returned to the ANSP from his western exploration in 1836 and worked there, supplying Torrey and Gray with descriptions and collecting specimens for their *Flora*. The death of Nuttall's uncle and the terms of his will required Nuttall to return and remain in England for nine months of each year to inherit the estate. He completed *North American Sylva: Trees not described by F. A. Michaux*, the first book to include all the trees of North America, just before he left the ANSP in December 1841.

[96] Among his friends and colleagues in the fight against yellow fever in Apalachicola was Dr. John Gorrie. Gorrie invented and was the first to patent a mechanical refrigeration system, which he used to manufacture ice in the hot and humid Florida climate to ease Chapman's patients' suffering from yellow fever.

[97] Torrey and Gray, *Flora*, 1:xii, 355.

type species.

Chapman discovered an amazing variety of new plants first encountered by Torrey and Gray; "Middle Florida" was the most frequent locality. They named many plants in honor of Chapman using the species name "*chapmanii*." Among Chapman's numerous finds are the extremely rare Florida evergreen azalea, called Chapman's azalea or Chapman's rhododendron (*Rhododendron chapmanii*), the beautiful Chapman's blazing star (also called Chapman's gayfeather, *Liatris chapmanii*), the Chapman oak (*Quercus chapmanii*), Chapman's fringed orchid (*Habenaria chapmanii* [small]), Chapman's sedge (*Carex chapmanii* [Steud]), Chapman's crownbeard (*Verbesina chapmanii*), and others.[98] Many are endemic and now endangered Florida plants. Specimens of some of these plants, and others collected by Chapman, are located in the Philadelphia Herbarium (PH) of the Academy of Natural Sciences.[99]

Chapman chose to botanize in near isolation in his spare time; by 1859, he had almost completed a draft manuscript based on his work about southern plants. He visited Asa Gray at Harvard University for five months of consultations, for herbarium studies, and to arrange for the publication of his manuscript. As the clouds of the Civil War gathered, Gray guided the book through its final revisions and preserved the printing plates during the war years for later use.[100] The first edition of Chapman's *Flora of the Southern United States* was published in 1860 in New York.[101] However, because of Civil War embargos on the Confederate states, Chapman did not see a copy of his book until 1865. Chapman's *Flora of the Southern United States* went

---

[98] Ibid., 2:502. First mentioned in volume 1 as "interesting variety, or state, sent from Middle Florida by Dr. Chapman" and described on p. 73.

[99] There are 206 specimens listed in the PH at http://ph.ansp.org/. Many were part of the Charles W. Short herbarium of 15,000 species deposited in 1864 (Mears, "Guide to Plant Collectors," 62).

[100] See Fishman, *Journeys through Paradise*, 178–82, for stories about Chapman's wartime activities to aid Union prisoners of war escaping Confederate captors. From April 1862 until the end of the war, Apalachicola was a city "between the lines" of the Union and the Confederacy.

[101] An earlier southern flora book had been published by John T. Darby, MD (nonresident member, 1859), *A Manual of Botany, Adapted to the Production of the Southern States* (Macon: Benjamin F. Griffin, 1841). He was living in Macon, Georgia, at the time, and the flora includes some north Florida plants. Darby's book was panned by Asa Gray, and Darby's specimens were lost during the Civil War; none are at the PH. See Wunderlin, Hansen, and Beckner, "Botanical Exploration in Florida," 58–59.

through two more editions; the third edition, which had been enlarged and revised, appeared in 1897.[102]

Shortly after its publication in 1860, a critical review gave the book the highest praise, "The first thing that strikes our attention...its neat and tasteful typography...a decided advance upon...Gray's Manual for the Northern States...indeed it is the handsomest volume of the kind we know of." The review mentions two unique sections of the book: "An introduction gives a good condensed sketch of the Elements of Botany, and a Glossary of Botanical Terms, so that the book can be used independently." It concludes, "This book is wanted by botanists as well as by students, and we think they will be well pleased....Now that the southern states are provided with a good Flora of their own, we trust that botany will receive a new impulse, both as a scientific pursuit and as a branch of education, in that favored region."[103]

On 26 July 1861, four Academy members nominated Dr. Chapman for Academy membership, and he was elected as a correspondent. Alas, the honor and privileges came three months after the beginning of the Civil War. At war's end, he actively engaged in Academy activities, and "On the completion of the revised edition of the Flora, and under the burden of more than fourscore years, it might be thought that Dr. Chapman would have abandoned active botanical work. Not so, however. Each season saw him eagerly in the field looking for new facts and gathering new species."[104]

Torreya Epilogue

Although John Torrey began identifying and naming Florida plants during the 1830s using specimens sent to him by military personnel as well as by Nuttall, Croom, and Chapman, Torrey did not visit Florida himself until 1872.[105] At the urging of his family, he traveled south to Florida in March of that year and spent four days in Tallahassee. During that time, he "saw the Torreya growing in a garden to the size of a small tree: where it had been planted as I believe by Mr. Croom." Torrey describes visiting the monument "Sacred to the Memory of Hardy Bryan Croom" erected by Hardy's brother:

---

[102] The second edition (1883) had a seventy-page supplement and was reissued (1892) with a second supplement (pp. 655–703). The third edition was completely redone and appeared in 1897.

[103] Anonymous, "Scientific Intelligence," 137.

[104] Trelease, "Alvin Wentworth Chapman," 644.

[105] Wunderlin, Hansen, and Beckner, "Botanical Exploration in Florida," 53; Rodgers, *John Torrey*, 296–97.

"The monument to this endeared friend was visited by me with a sad interest. It stands in front of the Episcopal Church of the City. I copied the inscription—& my thoughts went back to the pleasant days we spent together."[106]

At age seventy-six, John Torrey sat by the obelisk-like monument at the Episcopal Church and took down the Hardy Croom epitaph that visitors to the church may still read, "He was amiable without weakness, learned without arrogance."[107] A year later, Torrey died in New York City. His casket, carried by Asa Gray and other pallbearers, was decorated with fragrant garlands of the Torreya tree. As Gray later wrote, "Sprigs from this tree or its progeny were appropriately borne by the members of the Torrey Botanical Club, at its founder's funeral, two years ago, and laid upon his coffin."[108]

In his reflections on Torrey's funeral in "Pilgrimage to Torreya," Gray recounted his own later Torreya experiences when, for health reasons, he was "ordered to go south until I should meet the tardy spring."[109] He decided to bypass East Florida for the "cures" and instead botanize along the Apalachicola River, visit Chapman, and see Croom's Torreya tree and the croomia growing around it. In March 1875, Gray traveled by train from Savannah through Tallahassee to Chattahoochee, Florida, and by steamboat downriver to Apalachicola. Gray was fortunate, in the remote village of Chattahoochee, to find that the train agent "knew the tree which I was in search of; and it was arranged that his son should conduct me to the locality, not far distant." Residents were delighted by Gray's interest in their "stinking cedar" and search for a small herb growing in its shade.

As he recounts, "My desire for a sight of it was soon gratified. Making our way into the woods north of the railroad track, along the ridges covered with a mixed growth of Pines and deciduous trees, I soon discerned a thrifty young Torreya, and afterwards several of larger size, some of them with male flowers just developed." Gray continues, "As we approached the first one, I

---

[106] Rodgers, *John Torrey*, 296.

[107] Croom is remembered in the Tallahassee area in several ways. The marble obelisk memorializing the tragic loss of the Croom family still stands in the southwest corner of St. John's Church facing a major street. The church was established in 1829, eight years before Croom died, and the current cornerstone was laid in 1838. Goodwood House, since restored, is open to the public. Most importantly, the unique ecosystems of the ravines on the east side of the Apalachicola River, with their rare and endangered plant species, are protected by the Torreya State Park and the Ravine Preserve.

[108] Gray, "A Pilgrimage to Torreya," 262, reprinted in Sargent, *Scientific Papers of Asa Gray*, 2:189–90.

[109] Sargent, *Scientific Papers of Asa Gray*, 2:189.

told my companion that I expected to find under its shade a peculiar low herb.... And there, indeed, it was...the botanically curious little *Croomia pauciflora*, just as it was found by Mr. Croom, when he also discovered the tree."

Gray botanized during his ten-day trip downriver. Arriving in Apalachicola:

> There was the pleasure of renewing our acquaintance with Dr. Chapman, and botanizing with him over some of the ground which he has explored so long and so well, of gathering under his guidance, the stately *Sarracenia Drummondii* in its native habitat, and, not least acquiring from him fuller information respecting the localities where Torreya grows.[110]

On Gray's return up the river, near the bluffs of Aspalaga, he observed areas cleared of Torreya trees, which may have been used for steamboat fuel. Near Chattahoochee, Gray collected thirty or more seedling Torreyas for botanical garden plantings and hoped "that one or more of them may in due time be planted upon the grave of Torrey."

Asa Gray died in 1888, and Alva Chapman, the last in the legacy of Florida Torreya tree discovery, passed away in 1899. He and Mrs. Chapman are buried in Chestnut Cemetery behind his home in Apalachicola, where the Chapman Schools and the Chapman Botanical Garden celebrate his life and legacy.[111] Further north, along the Apalachicola River, in Florida's Torreya State Park and the Ravine Preserve, endangered Torreya trees grow on the bluffs overlooking the river.[112] The park is a designated U.S. National Natural Landmark because of the Torreya tree. Only about 500 specimens of this tree are estimated to remain in the wild. The park's entry sign recognizes that "Hardy Bryan Croom, pioneer Florida planter and botanist, discovered one of the rarest coniferous trees, *Torreya taxifolia*, and named it for Dr. John Torrey."

---

[110] Sargent, *Scientific Papers of Asa Gray*, 2:193–94.

[111] See Merrill, "Unlisted Binomials," 61–70, for a discussion of the various editions of *Flora*. See also an obituary by John G. Ruge, who wrote from close friendship, in *Gulf Fauna and Flora Bulletin* 1/1 (1899): 1–5; Trelease, "Alvin Wentworth Chapman," 643–46, with a portrait; Peattie, "Alvan Wentworth Chapman," 16–17; Kimball, "Reminiscences of Alvan Wentworth Chapman," 1–11.

[112] See Florida's Torreya State Park, www.floridastateparks.org/torreya/.

CHAPTER 11

FLORIDA PALEONTOLOGY AND THE EXPEDITION OF 1886…WITH LEIDY, WILLCOX, HEILPRIN, DALL, AND OTHERS

"Mr. Joseph Willcox…who had spent several successive winters in Florida…suggested…to make an expedition to certain portions of the country, to make the collections and investigations in their geology and fauna."[1]

—Joseph Leidy

"I will prospect around Ocala for a few days, to see if I can find something else with a 'back-bone.'"[2]

—Joseph Willcox

"Since 1886 we find Dr. Leidy once more returned to his early love, and to his pen we owe the elucidation of the remarkable extinct fauna which has recently been discovered in the peninsula of Florida."[3]

—Angelo Heilprin

William Bartram's brief list of *Fossilia* he had observed in East Florida included "Petrificata," which were recognized as objects that received their form from dead animals or plants displaced by a mineral substance: that is, the subjects of vertebrate paleontology or paleobotany.[4] His "*Echini*" included the crust of petrified insects as well as crabs and lobsters, and his "Conchites" were fossil shells: subjects of invertebrate paleontology.

---

[1] Leidy, preface to Heilprin, "Explorations on the West Coast of Florida and to the Okeechobee Wilderness," i–ii.

[2] Joseph Willcox to Joseph Leidy, 28 March 1889, ANSP Archives, Leidy correspondence, coll. 1. This letter also mentions the "tiger tusk" (Smilodon).

[3] Heilprin, "Leidy's Work in Geology and Paleontology," 1891; ANSP Archives, Joseph Leidy, diaries and field notebooks, 1848–1887, coll. 482, 10.

[4] *FHWB*, 169. See also Martin, *Outlines of an Attempt to Establish a Knowledge*, 4.

Following Bartram, Academy explorers —Thomas Say in 1818 and others—focused on Florida's fossil shells and other invertebrate animals. During the post-Civil War period, Joseph Willcox, Academy curator Angelo Heilprin, and William Dall continued these studies on fossil shells and other invertebrates—Florida's invertebrate paleontology. Joseph Willcox also assisted Joseph Leidy, one of the founders of the science of vertebrate paleontology in North America, as Leidy became the first person to study and establish Florida vertebrate paleontology.[5]

Joseph Leidy

The personal and professional life of Dr. Joseph Leidy (1823–1891), from his childhood until his death, centered on the Academy and Philadelphia.[6] Joseph Leidy, "The Last Man Who Knew Everything," as noted by Leonard Warren, was a master of many scientific fields and also a leader. Born in Philadelphia, Leidy was a serious mineralogist and general naturalist as a youth who had considerable artistic talent and active enthusiasm for the Academy. He studied medicine at the University of Pennsylvania where his naturalist interests and medical training were mentored by several physician members of the Academy.

In 1845, at twenty-two years of age, Dr. Joseph Leidy was elected to Academy membership. That year, he presented his first paleontological papers; one was about the ten fossil shell species he had found in a local pond and the other about the vertebrate whale fossil *Zeuglodon*.[7] His major work during this early period was his excavation (1858), preservation, and exhibition (1868) of North America's first dinosaur, *Hadrosaurus foulkii*, from a site in Haddonfield, New Jersey.[8] His skills in anatomy, microscopy, and art

---

[5] See Ray, "An Idiosyncratic History of Florida Vertebrate Paleontology," 143–70. See also Ray, "A list, bibliography, and index of the fossil vertebrates of Florida," for details.

[6] Warren, *Joseph Leidy*; Peck and Stroud, *A Glorious Enterprise*, 161–67; Meyerson and Winegrad, *Gladly Learn and Gladly Teach*, 89–97.

[7] Leidy, "Notes taken on a visit to White Pond," 279–81 (the microscopic examination of a portion of a vertebra of the fossil Zeuglodon shows that it has all the characteristics of recent bone). See ch. 9 for more information on Zeuglodon.

[8] The only known skeleton represented the first dinosaur species known from more than isolated teeth to be identified in North America. In 1868, it became the first mounted dinosaur skeleton. *Hadrosaurus foulkii* is the only species in this genus and has been the official state dinosaur of New Jersey since 1991 and is still exhibited at the Academy in Philadelphia.

Young Joseph Leidy (center) with Edgar Allan Poe (seated)
and member in a top hat, at the Academy. Photo taken by Leidy's
medical mentor and preceptor, Dr. Paul Beck Goddard.

ANSP Archives, Collection 49. Courtesy of the Academy of Natural Sciences of Drexel University.

Joseph Leidy next to the tibia of *Hadrosaurus foulkii*, Philadelphia, Pennsylvania, taken in the museum, ca. 1859.

ANSP Archives, Collection 9. Courtesy of the Academy of Natural Sciences of Drexel University.

put him at the cutting edge of research in several natural history disciplines.

In 1847, Leidy's analysis and interpretation of Academy-curated horse fossils, which had been collected at three different sites, led to his presentation, "On the Fossil Horse of America." His work established the existence of primitive American horses, many of which had since become extinct.[9] Modern horses, which had been reintroduced into the Americas by Europeans, flourished where the earlier American species had failed. Leidy cited Darwin's find of fossil horse molars on the island of Patagonia during the voyage of the *Beagle,* and Darwin later acknowledged Leidy's publications, which supported Darwin's theory.[10]

During the next two decades, Leidy's interest and publications in vertebrate paleontology increased with his fossil finds in the Western territories of the United States. In the 1850s, Leidy made several Western fossil collecting trips. Later, most of the specimens he described in many scientific papers were sent to him by private collectors, government-sponsored natural history surveys of the Western territories, and by Spencer Fullerton Baird, the curator at the recently founded Smithsonian Institution. Leidy's work included descriptions of new species and major studies on fossil horses and extinct ground sloths. He produced more than two hundred paleontology publications, some brief, others monographic, during this period.[11] As fossil mania grew, Leidy opted out of the increasing competition with international teams and several American competitors who had unlimited wealth, including his Academy protégé, Edward Cope. Leidy returned to microscopic research on protozoa,

---

[9] Leidy, "On the Fossil Horse of America," 262, 338.

[10] Darwin's recognition and personal correspondence (Darwin to Leidy, 4 March 1860 and Leidy to Darwin, 10 December 1859, ANSP Archives, Leidy Correspondence, coll. 1) were a personal revelation for Leidy. Darwin was controversial; a fierce battle ensued at Harvard, where Asa Gray and Leidy had become Darwin supporters and engaged the anti-Darwinian Louis Agassiz. Leidy later nominated Darwin for election to membership (1860) in the Academy, the first American institution to honor Darwin after *On the Origin of Species* was published in 1859.

[11] Leidy's publications included descriptions of new species and North American exotics, such as the rhinoceros. He also published four monographs: *The Ancient Fauna of Nebraska* (1853), *Cretaceous Reptiles of the United States* (1865), *On the Extinct Mammalian Fauna of Dakota and Nebraska* (1869), and *Extinct Vertebrate Fauna of the Western Territories* (1873). He described one hundred thirty new genera and more than three hundred species of fossil vertebrates. See multiple authors about Leidy's contributions in many areas, *The Joseph Leidy Commemorative Meeting, Held in Philadelphia, December 6, 1923.*

animal parasites, and Academy-based dinosaur work until he received a collection of fossils from Florida.[12]

Florida Fossils

In 1883, Leidy received a barrel of fossilized bones from Spenser Baird that had been collected in a remote area of Florida, far from the competitive fossil fields in the western states.[13] The Florida fossils ignited Leidy's interest, and he returned to paleontology, giving birth to Florida vertebrate paleontology.[14]

At the 22 April 1884 Academy meeting, Leidy presented "Vertebrate Fossils from Florida" to the twenty-seven members present:

> Prof. Leidy directed attention to some fossils, part of a collection recently referred to him for examination by the Smithsonian Institution. They consist of remains mostly of large terrestrial mammals, especially related with forms which now live in the intertropical portions of the old world. Obtained in Florida, they are of additional interest as evidences of the existence in this region of a formation of tertiary age not previously known.[15]

Leidy observed the "more conspicuous remains" of a young mastodon, several rhinoceros, and fragments of a tapir, a llama, a ruminant, and a small crocodile: "An accompanying letter from Dr. J. C. Neal, of Archer, Florida, informs us that the fossils were discovered in a bed of clay," the "Alachua clay site," which was named after the place of origin.[16] The first major paleontological site discovered in Florida was only miles from the Alachua Savanna

---

[12] Warren, *Joseph Leidy*, 68–70, 166–70. Leidy is generally regarded as the founder of American parasitology.

[13] Dr. J. C. Neal, of Archer, Florida, made the discovery and shipped the fossils to Spencer Fullerton Baird (1823–1887), who sent the fossils to Leidy for identification and descriptions. Baird had been elected to Academy membership (nonresident) in 1842. He was the first curator (1850) at the newly formed Smithsonian and later served as secretary of the Smithsonian from 1878–1887.

[14] Webb, *Pleistocene Mammals of Florida*, 5.

[15] Leidy, "Vertebrate Fossils from Florida," 118–19.

[16] New tourists, settlers, and speculators flooded into the area following the war, including such notables as John Muir and Ulysses S. Grant. The Quakers sent a superintendent and an assistant ahead to purchase acreage in and around Archer. Dr. J. C. Neal, a Quaker, moved to Archer primarily for health reasons. Suffering from consumption, he claimed that his year or two in Archer restored him to a rugged, robust condition. Following the example of other Quakers, Dr. Neal planted oranges; his home

where William Bartram had earlier trekked.

On 10 March 1885, Leidy reported on additional fossil remains: "Rhinoceros and *Hippotherium* [the extinct three-toed ancestor of horses] from Florida," which had been provided by Dr. Neal.[17]

Stimulated by the Florida fossil finds, Major John Wesley Powell, director of the newly created U.S. Geological Survey, dispatched a team to Archer, Florida, in 1885.[18] The team was led by the eminent invertebrate paleontologist William Healey Dall, the Geological Survey's first paleontologist, an honorary curator at the Smithsonian.[19] Dall and his coworkers collected many vertebrates and sent them to Leidy for examination. Leidy proposed the name *Mastodon floridanus* for the new form of mastodon. In addition, he gave three species of llama the names *Auchenia major*, *A. minor*, and *A. minimus*.[20]

At the next Academy meeting, Leidy exhibited a specimen consisting of two fragments of a tooth from an extinct boar from the same collection site. He also reported on "Caries in the Mastodon," an addition to his previous month's report on *Mastodon floridanus*. In his presentations, Leidy used specimens and microscopy to present his data before his findings were published in the proceedings of the meeting for that month.[21]

---

in the middle of Archer was surrounded by a grove of four hundred orange trees, and he pursued his hobby of paleontology (Braley, *Nineteenth Century Archer*, 21).

[17] Leidy, "Rhinoceros and Hippotherium from Florida," 32–33. *Hippotherium* is an extinct genus of horse that lived during the Miocene through Pliocene ~13.65—3.3 Mya.

[18] John Wesley Powell (1834–1902), a soldier, geologist, and explorer of the American West who traversed the Colorado River of the Grand Canyon, was the director of the U.S. Geological Survey (1881–1894) and the Bureau of Ethnology at the Smithsonian Institution. He was elected an Academy correspondent in 1872.

[19] William Healey Dall (1845–1927), a student of Agassiz, was an American naturalist and preeminent authority on living and fossil mollusks. His early work was in the Pacific Northwest and Alaska; he later worked in Florida. Dall was elected Academy correspondent in 1869 in Washington, DC. See Dall, "Notes on the Geology of Florida," 161–70. [20] Leidy, "Mastodon and Llama from Florida," 11–12. After Leidy's death, these preliminary findings were published in detail by Frederic A. Lucas, as described later in this chapter.

[20] Leidy, "Mastodon and Llama from Florida," 11–12. After Leidy's death, these preliminary findings were published in detail by Frederic A. Lucas, as described later in this chapter.

[21] Leidy, "An Extinct Boar from Florida," 36–38; Leidy, "Caries in the Mastodon," 38.

Leidy's vertebrate paleontological research during this period was stimulated by the contributions and support of his longtime friend in mineralogy, other natural history fields, as well as real estate and Academy colleague, Joseph Willcox. Willcox collected in Florida, curated at the Academy, and helped govern the Wagner Free Institute as a trustee. He also influenced and supported Leidy's pioneering research in Florida paleontology, entry into anthropology, and his leadership of the Wagner Free Institute of Science.

Joseph Willcox

Joseph Willcox (1829–1918) was born in the Delaware Valley near Philadelphia and spent most of his life there and in Philadelphia.[22] His family established Ivy Mills, the premier paper mill and later currency printing operation in colonial America, serving the needs of Benjamin Franklin for printing paper and then the young country for producing paper money. Willcox became a serious mineralogist during his youth with interests in geology and paleontology and was elected a member of the Delaware County Institute of Science.[23]

Joseph Willcox and his brothers assisted their father as he expanded Ivy Mills and opened a mercantile house, J. M. Willcox and Company, in Philadelphia. Upon their father's death in 1854, Joseph and his two brothers, Mark and James, inherited and operated the family properties under the firm name of J.M. Willcox & Sons.

Joseph Willcox's management of the company and scientific interests in mineralogy were interrupted in 1862 by his enlisted service in the Union Army and promotion to colonel. After his discharge, Willcox married and settled into business and mineralogical pursuits. In 1866, Willcox's mineralogy pursuits led to his meeting Joseph Leidy and the beginning of both a lasting friendship and Willcox's life in science.

In 1867, Willcox sold his interests in the firm, Ivy Mills, and Glen Mills to his brothers and formed Joseph Willcox & Company for his own holdings and properties. This gave him more time for fieldwork and his collections. The same year, Willcox was elected to the Academy and began winter travel

---

[22] Thomas Peter Bennett, "Joseph Willcox, I: Early Life and Science" (unpublished manuscript, 2014); Thomas Peter Bennett, "Joseph Willcox, II: Florida Exploration" (unpublished manuscript, 2014).

[23] Willcox's work in mineralogy led to his election in 1863 to membership in the Delaware County Institute of Science, which was founded in 1833 and had a roster of Academy members. Willcox added to the Institute's collections, gave presentations and served in several volunteer offices.

to Florida. There his interest in minerals, which were scarce in the field, led him to begin studying fossil shells and collecting assorted specimens for Leidy and others at the Academy.

In Florida

Willcox began seriously exploring Florida in 1875, during the post-Civil War reconstruction period when tourism began, along the St. Johns River where William Bartram had traveled and tried unsuccessfully to farm. Willcox wrote the first of his Florida letters to Leidy from Jacksonville: "I will send to you today by mail a box of moss from a small stream near this town. Please advise me if the animals are still living and if they are specially interesting to you. If they are alive I will send you more from a locality farther south."[24]

At the time, Leidy was actively interested in protozoa associated with many plants and animals; for the next several winters, Willcox shipped various study samples to Leidy. By 1878, Willcox was spending most of his time on the Gulf Coast in and around Cedar Key, the state's largest and busiest port, and also further south in the village of Homosassa on the Homosassa River.[25] His interest in invertebrate paleontology increased. In a letter to Leidy on 5 March 1878, from Homosassa, Willcox wrote,

> I like this place so much that I will remain here a couple of weeks longer. It is on the Gulf Coast about 40 miles south of Cedar Key, which is our nearest Post Office. I have already been here more than 3 weeks.... All of the West Coast of Fla that I have seen is rocky, the soil on the coral being only a few inches deep. The rock is filled with fossil shells. When sailing from Cedar Key to this place the water was only a few feet deep and very clear. I could see thousands of large sponges and echinoderms on the bottom.... I would like to pass all my winters in Florida, and I have taken a great fancy to the Gulf coast.[26]

---

[24] J. Willcox to J. Leidy, 1 February 1875, ANSP Archives, Leidy correspondence, coll. 1B.

[25] Homosassa, established during the 1840s in a sugar plantation area on the Homosassa River near the Gulf, became a port of call for coastal steamers. During the post-Civil War period, Homosassa was developed as a fishing village and vacation spot with railroad access and a resort hotel. Located four miles downriver from Homosassa Springs.

[26] J. Willcox to J. Leidy, 5 March 1878, College of Physicians of Philadelphia (CPP), Joseph Leidy Papers, coll. Mss 2/170-01. The travel routes to Homosassa and the

From this time on, Willcox made Homosassa his Florida base camp, "my favorite place, on the west coast of Florida."[27]

During the next several years, Willcox supplied Leidy with "parasitic worms" from the stomachs of various birds and reptiles for his parasitology work and skins of "birds which I have shot and skinned" for Leidy's new museum at Swarthmore College. Willcox made coastal collecting trips for shells—living and fossil—and sponges.[28] In addition, he explored inland throughout Levy, Hernando, and Alachua counties.[29] Willcox explored the area around Cedar Key and traveled inland around Ocala and Archer, including Gainesville and nearby Payne's Prairie, as Bartram's "Great Alachua Savanna" was called.[30] Willcox's publication included narrative descriptions of the area—in the style of Bartram—such as his details about the Alachua Sink; he shipped specimens to the Academy for curatorial study and publication when appropriate.

When Willcox returned to Philadelphia, he continued his work at the Academy as curator of invertebrates and enjoyed the company of his Academy colleagues and those at the Wagner Free Institute of Science. He began collaborating with the Academy's new curator of invertebrates, Angelo Heilprin, who took great interest in Willcox's Florida collections.

Angelo Heilprin

Angelo Heilprin (1853–1907) was born in Hungary and reared in America. He returned to Europe for three years to study at the Royal School

---

amenities afforded sportsmen and settlers in the town and surroundings made Homosassa and the southwest Florida coast of popular interest. See C. Hallock, *Camp Life in Florida*, 259–343.

[27] J. Willcox to J. Leidy, 22 March 1880 from St. Augustine, ANSP Archives, Leidy correspondence, coll. 1.

[28] J. Willcox to J. Leidy, 8 March 1881, from Homosassa; 18 March 1882; 23 March 1884, detailing collecting, ANSP Archives, Leidy correspondence, coll. 1; seen also Carter, "Catalogue of Marine Sponges," 202–209. Typically, Willcox provided specimens to other Academy colleagues who had expertise to interpret and publish his finds.

[29] Willcox, "Notes on the Geology and Natural History of the West Coast of Florida," 188–92.

[30] The prairie was the stronghold of the Alachua band of the Seminoles tribe under Chief Cowkeeper, whom Bartram met in 1774. The prairie was named for Cowkeeper's eldest surviving son, Payne.

of Mines in London to become a geologist and explorer.[31] In 1879, he settled in Philadelphia and became affiliated with the Academy. Heilprin began studying the Academy collections and Willcox's Florida shipments. He published two papers in *PANS* that year about southeastern Eocene invertebrate fossils.[32] The following year, he was appointed to a professorship of invertebrate paleontology and geology at the Academy. By 1882, Heilprin was publishing about Willcox's recent discovery of nummulite deposits in Florida.[33]

Heilprin reported his examination of the rock samples that Willcox found near the Chasawiska and Homosassa Rivers. Heilprin was convinced of "the occurrence of North American Nummulites" and "would propose, from the name of its discoverer, the specific designation of *N. willcoxi*."[34] The Willcox nummulite was illustrated by Heilprin, an artist, who included detailed drawings in all his publications.[35]

Willcox and Heilprin's cooperative studies were covered in the 20 April 1882, *Philadelphia Times*.[36] Lengthy articles about the proceedings of the Academy meetings were frequently published in the newspaper because of wide public interest. Florida was also a popular topic at the time: "At the last

---

[31] Angelo Heilprin (1853–1907) was one of the eminent sons of the distinguished scholar, linguist, and author Michael Heilprin. For further reading, see G. Pollak, *Michael Heilprin and His Sons: A Biography* (New York: Dodd, Mead and Co., 1912) 233–457.

[32] Heilprin compared earlier collections by Conrad, Lea, and others in southeastern states with European mollusks and articulated the importance of individual species and communities in understanding biogeography and geological eras. See Heilprin, "On Some New Eocene Fossils from the Claiborne Marine Formation of Alabama," 189; Heilprin, "A Comparison of the Eocene Mollusca of the Southeastern United States," 217–25.

[33] Heilprin, "On the Occurrence," 189–93. Nummulites are beautiful and very distinctive fossils of marine protozoa. They are relatively easy to recognize in the field, reaching a diameter of about 5 inches and resembling little coins set into the rocks. A nummulite is characterized by its numerous coils, which are subdivided by septa into chambers. Their North American existence was very doubtful until Willcox's findings and Heilprin's examination.

[34] Heilprin, "On the Occurrence," 191, Figure 1.

[35] Heilprin produced scientific illustrations and was a recognized artist. He exhibited *Autumn's First Whisper* at the Pennsylvania Academy of Fine Arts in 1880 and *Forest Exiles* at the Boston Museum of Fine Arts in 1883.

[36] "Natural Sciences: The Geological Formation of the Western Coast of Florida," *Philadelphia Times*, 20 April 1882 (ANSP Archives, Publicity, Papers 1880–1957, coll. 417).

meeting of the Academy of Natural Sciences Mr. Joseph Willcox gave an account of his study of the geological formation of the western coast of Florida, extending from Cedar Keys to a distance of fifty miles south." The news report noted that Heilprin had stated that Florida: "dated back to that period of geological history designated as the Oligocene." In 1883, Heilprin was elected to fill a curator position and shortly thereafter became curator-in-charge of the Academy's Museum. He continued his Florida collaborative studies with Willcox.[37]

In an 1884 series, the *Philadelphia Times* (24 April, 1 May, and 22 May) reported the studies of Leidy, Willcox, and Heilprin on the paleogeology of Florida and topics associated with Willcox's field collections.[38] The first article discussed Leidy, the fossils collected near Gainesville, Florida, and that he was returning to his interest in vertebrate paleontology:

> The remains are mostly of large terrestrial mammals, especially related to forms which now live in intertropical portions of the old world. They are of additional interest as evidences of the existence in Florida of a formation of the tertiary age not previously known…. Professor Heilprin regarded the discovery of importance, as leading to the theory of the former connection of Florida with South America.

In "Further Notes on Florida—Natural History of Sponges, Etc.," "fifty distinct species of sponges [were] collected on the coast of Florida, and presented by Mr. Joseph Willcox."

Many of the details discussed in the *Philadelphia Times* articles were excerpts from Willcox's presentation, "Notes on the Geology and Natural History of the West Coast of Florida," one of his longest articles.[39] His observation about the coastal areas from Cedar Key southward for fifty miles predated our current understanding of the larger land mass of Florida that existed as recently as the last Ice Age some thirteen thousand years ago and

---

[37] Heilprin, "Notes on Some New Foraminifera," 321; Heilprin, "Report of the Professor of Invertebrate Paleontology," 345.

[38] Heilprin reported that "A new locality for *Nummulites Willcoxi* has been found by Mr. Willcox…. The existence of a true nummulitic basement formation in the State of Florida is thus placed beyond question." A new species was also named, *Nummulites floridensis* (A. Heilprin, "Notes on Some New Foraminifera from the nummulitic formation of Florida," *PANS* 36 [1884]: 321; A. Heilprin, "Report of the Professor of Invertebrate Paleontology," *PANS* 36 [1884]: 345).

[39] Willcox, "Notes on the Geology," 188–92. Read at the Academy on June 24, 1884.

suggested that the Florida coastline extended, at some locations, forty or fifty miles further into the Atlantic and Gulf of Mexico than it does today. The article discussed Willcox's collections for Heilprin "five miles northeast of Mount Lee," where he "discovered a second locality of *Nummulites Willcoxi*, at an altitude of nearly 200 feet above the sea. They are associated with *Orbitoides* and *Heterosstegina* and *Pecten*, as determined by Prof. Heilprin."[40] Willcox also recorded many archeological discoveries related to the "shell mounds of the west coast," including "a half bushel of stone implements, in various stages of manufacture...shell implements of several patterns, made from the shells of *Busycon pyrum*."[41]

The spirit of collaboration among Heilprin, Willcox, and Leidy permeated their publications, their exchange at Academy meetings, and the *Times'* newspaper series, "Further Notes on Florida." Their cooperation led the three to become involved (1885–1891) in new developments at the Wagner Free Institute of Science following the death of its founder in 1885. With Heilprin as professor of geology, Leidy as president of the Institute's faculty, and Willcox an Institute trustee, their further cooperation set the stage for intensive exploration in Florida and an expanded mission for the Wagner Free Institute of Science.

Wagner Free Institute of Science

The Wagner Free Institute of Science was founded by William Wagner (1796–1885), who grew up in Philadelphia and attended the University of Pennsylvania. Wagner began collecting shells, minerals, and fossils at an early age. His extensive collections and studies led to his election to Academy membership on 13 May 1815. He wanted to study medicine, but his parents had other plans. Instead, Wagner entered the counting room of notable Philadelphia philanthropist Stephen Girard, a banker and mercantile magnate who founded Girard College. In 1817, Wagner was sent as an assistant officer in charge of cargo on a Girard trading voyage that lasted nearly two years. While in Europe, he visited scientific institutions and during layovers, he collected

---

[40] "Mount Lee" is unknown to the author. No reference to "Mount Lee" exists in any collection databases at the FLMNH. At nearly two hundred feet above sea level, "Mount Lee" would have to be on one of the higher ridges toward the interior of the state. The fossils that are mentioned seem to be Eocene invertebrates (larger foraminifera and a scallop) associated with limestone outcrops in Florida (personal communication from Douglas Jones [30 August 2014]).

[41] Willcox, "Notes on the Geology," 188–92.

many natural history specimens that were the beginnings of his private museum. Upon his return, he regularly attended Academy meetings and in 1839 published descriptions of five new invertebrate fossils from Maryland and North Carolina.[42] After engaging successfully in various business enterprises, Wagner retired in 1840.

After their two-year residence abroad (1817–1819), Wagner and his wife, Louisa Binney, returned to Philadelphia, and he devoted himself to arranging his collections. In 1847, he began to deliver scientific lectures at their home, free of charge, using his specimens as teaching aids and displaying them for study. Their rural estate, Elm Grove, stood near the sites of the present day Wagner Free Institute of Science and Temple University in Philadelphia.

In 1852, Wagner's large audiences led him to secure space in a larger public hall, and in 1855 Wagner founded and had incorporated by a legislative act the Wagner Free Institute of Science. With a corps of lecturers, Wagner began the First Annual Collegiate Year of the Wagner Institute in the public hall. Several years later, when the city needed the hall space, he began construction of the present building. It was delayed by the Civil War but was completed and dedicated in 1865. The facilities were superbly designed for free public education programs using Wagner's collections for educational demonstrations and scientific training. In addition to their primary educational purpose, the enlarged collections became resources for scholarly research. William Wagner established a board of trustees and legally designated the Wagner Free Institute of Science to be forever used for free instruction in natural science. He continued as president of the Wagner Institute, which made the collections available for educational demonstrations and scientific training at no cost until he died on 17 January 1885, two days after turning ninety.

That same day, unaware that his friend and colleague had died, Joseph Willcox wrote William Wagner a letter from Jacksonville. The previous year, in consideration of his age, Wagner and Louisa had executed deeds of trust regarding the Wagner Institute so that the powers of trusteeship would be transferred to their son, Samuel Wagner, and the six-member board (including Joseph Willcox) upon William's death. When Willcox returned from Florida later in the spring, the board met and immediately expanded the Wagner Institute's mission by selecting faculty. Willcox prevailed upon Leidy to assume the presidency of the faculty, an invitation Leidy accepted. The

---

[42] Wagner, "Description of Five New Fossils," 151–53.

other faculty members were Henry Leffmann (chemistry) and Benjamin Sharp (biology); Angelo Heilprin became a paid staff member. Under the influence and leadership of Willcox and Leidy, the Wagner Institute improved its museum and focused more broadly on research, collections, and publications related to Florida's natural history.[43] This new focus entailed geological and paleontological studies involving Willcox, Leidy, Heilprin, and later, William Dall. Leidy developed the Wagner Institute's museum and arranged its collections for better public viewing. Willcox and Heilprin led the first research excursion: an expedition to the unexplored areas of the west coast of Florida and the entry to Lake Okeechobee.[44]

1886 Florida Expedition

At the November 1885 meetings of the Wagner Institute trustees, "The Chairman [Samuel Wagner] stated that Mr. Willcox had made the offer to pay one half of the expense of a month's scientific expedition to Florida under the auspices of the Institute and under his own personal direction for the collection of geological + zoological specimens for the Museum." The trustees "resolved that this offer of Mr. Willcox be accepted provided that the expenditure shall not exceed $300," and "Mr. Willcox stated, in connection with the preceding motion that the field of operation proposed was very rich in materials and still remained almost entirely unexplored."[45]

Several days later, in a letter to Chairman Samuel Wagner, Willcox reported that he had met with Leidy and Heilprin, and they had agreed to participate. The other expedition personnel chosen by Willcox included Charles H. Brock, elder son of deceased Academy member John P. Brock; Captain Frank Strobhar, master of the schooner *Rambler*; and Moses Natteal, cook. Willcox handled other details of the expedition, including a visit to Secretary Spencer Baird at the Smithsonian to obtain suggestions about logistics and free loans of items, such as copper cans for transporting specimens in alcohol on the expedition.

The course of the expedition, which began in Cedar Key on 14 February 1886 and followed Willcox's many collecting trips by boat along the Gulf

---

[43] Leidy, preface, i–ii.

[44] Leffmann, Willcox, and Skidmore, "The Wagner Free Institute of Science of Philadelphia," 1–6.

[45] November 1885 meetings (November 20, adjourned; November 24, stated), WFIS Archives, series 2, Board of Trustees Records, 1858–1926, meeting minutes 1885–1889, box 3, folder 3.

Coast from Cedar Key to Key West, deviated from Willcox's southerly track at the mouth of the Caloosahatchee River near Punta Rassa.[46] The party then proceeded eastward upriver into "a veritable *terra incognita* to science," the "Okeechobee Wilderness."[47] The return route through Sarasota Bay included collection stops that revealed more *incognita scientia*. The six-week expedition ended on 31 March 1886.[48]

On 10 April 1886, the *Philadelphia Times* summarized the course of the expedition in "At the Academy of Natural Sciences—Geology of Florida" and noted,

> At Rocky Bluff, on the Big Manatee River, the most southern exposure of the Miocene so far determined was found. This and other determinations made during the trip prove conclusively that Agassiz' and Le Conte's assertions that Florida is simply a modern coral reef has no foundation in fact. On the contrary the peninsula is composed of solid rock of the same geological age as that found along the Atlantic border.... The lines on no map yet examined present the boundaries of the lake correctly, the greatest depth sounded was fifteen feet, although it was said that a depth of twenty-two feet had been determined.

This was one of several refutations of Louis Agassiz's and Joseph Le Conte's conclusions (Le Conte more recently had expressed doubts.[49] The

---

[46] Willcox's trips began in 1878. The west coast expedition's southern route to the Caloosahatchee is detailed in *TWFIS* 1 (1887): 1–21.

[47] *TWFIS* 1 (1887):22–38. Describes the route and observations along the river to Fort Thompson and the beginning of the "Okeechobee Wilderness," through the Everglades canal; exploration of "Lake Okeechobee" follows (Ibid., 39–50). Okeechobee Wilderness at Taylor's Creek was drawn by Angelo Heilprin, an accomplished artist, who made this and other drawings included in the report.

[48] Heilprin is frequently cited as the leader of the expedition because he was the sole author of the published "Explorations on the West Coast of Florida and to the Okeechobee Wilderness," *TWFIS* 1 (1887). The record is clear that Willcox was the organizer and leader. Collecting and recording were done by both men; Leidy was the keystone in the expedition structure. The Wagner Free Institute of Science was the primary institutional supporter, along with the Academy and the Smithsonian with funding by Willcox. The appropriate moniker for the expedition is "Florida West Coast and Okeechobee Wilderness Expedition, 1886."

[49] As noted in *TWFIS* 1 (1887): 56, Agassiz's full report was published, after a twenty-year delay, in 1880, in support of the coral reef idea, after a demur announced by Le Conte and a rejection of the coral reef hypothesis (*Science*, 14 December 1883) still left the scientific waters murky in 1886 and reason for strong statements and added data in refutation.

Philadelphia Times article continued,

> Although important geological results were obtained, the recent forms of animal life collected were not as abundant as had been anticipated, probably in consequence of the severity of the past winter having driven the fishes, &c., to more southern regions.... South of this the vegetation was comparatively uninjured. The orange trees did not seem to be permanently damaged, although the oranges were badly frost-bitten. Bananas and pine-apples were even more seriously injured.

On 24 April 1886, Heilprin gave a detailed expedition report at the Wagner Institute, and Leidy extolled the expedition's value for science. *The Industrial Review* announced the program, and a lengthy journalistic report appeared four days later in the *Public Ledger*.[50]

Publications

Following the presentations at the Academy and the Wagner Institute, Heilprin wrote a report for publication. It became the first in a new Wagner Institute publication program, *Transactions of the Wagner Free Institute of Science*. Leidy wrote the introduction to Heilprin's "Explorations on the West Coast of Florida and to the Okeechobee Wilderness." He covered the history of the Wagner Institute and acknowledged Willcox's efforts, noting that Willcox was first to have "suggested the interest it would be to the Institute and to science to make an expedition to certain portions of the country, to make the collections and investigations in their geology and fauna."[51]

The report, as briefly discussed above and in Table 1, focused on the invertebrate fauna, geology, and origins of the Florida peninsula with one of the first scientific explorations of Lake Okeechobee. Although as Heilprin noted, "We certainly met with no trace of that swarm of venomous serpents which Bartram reported issuing from almost every stump," he describes in detail many other creatures they observed, often collected, and some new, which they named, such as *Aplysia Willcoxi,* plate 19; *Ictalurus Okeechobeensis* (Okeechobee cat), plate 18; *Tropidonotus Taxispilotus,* (var. *Brocki*), plate 17.

In the narrative of the report, Heilprin interpreted the general findings of the exploration and commented on Louis Agassiz's coral formation theory:

---

[50] *Public Ledger*, "Florida Explorations," 28 April 1886, ANSP Archives, Publicity, Papers 1880–1957, coll. 417, pg. 24.

[51] Heilprin, "Explorations on the West Coast of Florida and to the Okeechobee Wilderness," i–ii.

Our observations…clearly demonstrate the erroneousness of the views hypothetically set forth, and establish beyond a question of doubt that the progressive growth of the peninsula, as far, at least, as Lake Okeechobee, and probably considerably further, was the result of successive accessions of organic and inorganic material, brought into place through the normal methods of sedimentation and upheaval.[52]

A series of favorable newspaper reviews followed the publication of the expedition report. The *Philadelphia Inquirer* (7 July 1887) reported, "Most of the report is written in technical language, and will best be understood by a geologist; but the conclusion is that Florida is neither a sand-bank nor, as is commonly supposed, a coral reef."[53]

Informative reviews appeared in the *Philadelphia Record, New York Tribune,* and other newspapers.[54] The 30 January 1888 issue of the *New York Times,* which had the longest, most comprehensive and critical review, concluded, "Mr. Heilprin's 'Exploration in Florida' is exactly that kind of book which is in the highest degree satisfactory to the man of science, but, more than that is pleasantly written as to interest those who are neither paleontologists nor geologists."[55]

Spamer and Forster painstakingly prepared a catalogue of specimens from West Florida as described by Heilprin that are now curated at the Wagner Institute.[56] They have taken Heilprin's sketchy type locality and stratigraphic data and worked with other researchers to establish more precise information. Most of the specimens listed in their catalogue of type specimens are from the expedition to the west coast of Florida, from which Heilprin described one hundred fifty species of fossil mollusks, sixty-eight of them new to science.[57]

In a recent summary of "The Marine Invertebrate Fossil Record of Florida," Jones noted,

---

[52] Ibid.

[53] "Explorations in Florida," *Philadelphia Inquirer,* 7 July 1887, WFIS Archives, coll. 89-040, vol. 1, p. 34.

[54] "Floridian Explorations," *Philadelphia Record,* 3 October 1887, WFIS Archives, coll. 89-040, vol. 1, p. 24.

[55] "New Publications—Geological Florida," *New York Times,* 30 January 1888, WFIS Archives, coll. 89-040, vol. 1, p. 25A1.

[56] Spamer and Forster, *A Catalogue of Type Fossils,* 40–42 and following.

[57] Ibid., 40.

Whereas early workers such as Conrad first drew attention to Florida fossils, it was not until the late nineteenth century that Angelo Heilprin (1887)—and especially William Healey Dall, with his Contributions to the Tertiary Fauna of Florida (1890)—finally brought the extraordinary fossil deposits of the state (particularly the southern part) to the attention of the scientific community.[58]

Dall was aided in his classic work, "Contributions to the Tertiary Fauna of Florida," by Willcox. Spamer and Foster commented, "A good part of Dall's reputation was founded on his Florida work. He was directed toward that field, literally and professionally, by Joseph Willcox."[59]

Dall, Willcox, and Leidy

After a trip to Alachua, William Healey Dall (1845–1927) made two expeditions to the west coast of Florida in 1885 and 1887 under instructions from John Wesley Powell, the director of the U.S. Geological Survey.[60] Dall collected at many of the same sites Willcox and Heilprin had explored, particularly around Tampa Bay and to the south of Sarasota Bay. Some of the collections and the observations of the three parties independently duplicated, confirmed, supplemented, or strengthened their individual findings. Dall observed, "The coral-formation observed by Agassiz in the region in the Keys, must be of very limited scope, as it has not been reported from the mainland of Florida by any modern geologist."[61]

Dall reported his 1885 and 1887 findings before the National Academy

---

[58] Jones, "The Marine Invertebrate Fossil Record of Florida," 90.

[59] Spamer and Forster, *A Catalogue of Type Fossils*, 20.

[60] Dall, an invertebrate paleontologist and dean of Alaskan exploration, was appointed to the U.S. Coast Survey in 1871. Beginning in 1868, he assembled and described many of the mollusks collections held by the United States National Museum; from 1880, he served as honorary curator of the museum's division of mollusks. He became a paleontologist with the U.S. Geological Survey in 1884 and held the position until 1925. After his Florida work began, he was honorary curator of the Wagner Institute from 1888 until his death. Dall published more than five hundred scientific papers. His "Contributions to the Tertiary Fauna of Florida," a six-part report written from 1890 to 1903, is considered the most important American publication on Cenozoic molluscan paleontology. See Harald Paul, Alfred Rehder, and Beulah E. Shields Bartsch, *Bibliography and Short Biographical Sketch of William Haley Dall* (Washington: Smithsonian Institution, 1946); C. H. Merriam, "William Healy Dall," *Science* 65/1684 (1927): 345–47; Woodring, *William Healey Dall*.

[61] Dall, "Notes on the Geology," 170.

of Sciences on 21 April 1887, and they were published in the *American Journal of Science* in September 1887. As he noted about Heilprin's work, "Only a part of his report has yet appeared and this is chiefly devoted to descriptions of new species of fossils.*" Dall's footnote called the reader's attention to Heilprin's 1887 publication, "*The whole has appeared since this was put in type."[62] In contrast to the highly competitive period in the western fossil fields that had caused Leidy to give up paleontology and return to protozoology and parasitology, the scientific competition for Florida discoveries was underway, in a genteel spirit.

In 1888, Willcox contacted Dall about analyzing and interpreting Willcox's material for publication in volume 2 of *Transactions*. This was a standard procedure for Willcox; much of his Florida work had been published by professional academics with his cooperation. In their ensuing presentations and publications, Leidy and others frequently quoted Willcox directly and many used his data, with appropriate acknowledgements. Willcox collaborated with those whom he felt could contribute the most to interpreting the specimens that he had collected. In the case of his recent Florida collections, which Heilprin had not yet studied, Willcox, with Leidy's concurrence, chose Dall because of his previous Florida studies, breadth of publications, and access to the National Museum collections that he curated, which could supplement the work. Dall, however, initially hesitated, asking, "Now would not Prof. Heilprin be glad to do the work you refer to?"[63] After receiving assurances that Heilprin had declined and conferring with his colleague and supervisor John Wesley Powell, Dall agreed.[64]

Heilprin later changed his mind and derailed the publication process of the Dall article and other papers based on Willcox's Florida collections submitted for volume 2 of the *Transactions*, for "his individual disappointment in not having the opportunity to write the paper himself."[65] The second volume of *Transactions* was published in December 1889 without Dall's intended article that would have included Willcox's invertebrate fossils. The

---

[62] Ibid., 161.

[63] W. H. Dall to J. Willcox, 27 April 1888; 31 May 1887–9 August 1890, WFIS Archives, coll. 90–015, folder 23, Robert Chambers Collection, 1887–1890.

[64] W. H. Dall to J. Willcox, 11 May 1888, and W. H. Dall to J. Willcox, 9 May 1888, both in WFIS Archives, coll. 90–015, folder 23, Robert Chambers Collection, 1887–1890.

[65] J. Willcox to J. Leidy, 27 June 1888 and 21 June 1888, from ANSP Archives, Media, coll. 1, folder, MS. 1. 1888.

volume included a paper by Edward Potts about freshwater sponges that Willcox had collected in Florida.[66] Potts described the freshwater sponges using lengthy quotes from Willcox, who had collected them in creeks and estuarine areas into the Gulf. Potts honored one sponge with the "name of the noble institution of which Mr. Willcox is an active manager": *Spongilla Wagneri*. Earlier presentations and brief reports were made by Willcox about sponges and the commercial sponge industry in Florida. The volume of *Transactions* also included major articles by Leidy based on Willcox's collections.

Leidy's Contributions

The significance of Leidy's vertebrate paleontology articles based on Willcox's and others' collections are summarized by David Webb in his "Chronology of Florida Pleistocene Mammals":

> The study of extinct mammals in Florida falls into three distinct periods of activity. The earliest systematic studies were those of Joseph Leidy in the latter part of the nineteenth century. Leidy's principal contributions were faunal studies of a limestone cave near Ocala in central Florida (1889a) and of the fluviatile deposits in Peace Creek and the Caloosahatchee River in south Florida (1889b).[67]

From the Pleistocene limestone of the Ocala area, Leidy reported a "small but interesting collection of quaternary mammalian fossils" collected by Willcox.[68] Leidy examined the fossilized bones of a "Saber-tooth Tiger," the size of "the existing Tiger of Asia," which he called *Machairodus floridanus* (later *Smilodon floridanus, Leidy*). Two fragments of the type skull of the saber-tooth tiger were illustrated by Leidy for publication based on the saber-tooth cat skull collected by Willcox and deposited at the Wagner Institute. Leidy also gave details about the Florida remains of a Zeuglodon, a horse, a llama similar to those from South America, and elephant teeth. Frederick A. Lucas later published an extended version of Leidy's Alachua Clay's studies

---

[66] Potts, "Report upon Some Fresh-Water Sponges," 5–7. Potts was elected a member of the Academy in 1876.

[67] Leidy, "Description of Some Mammalian Remains," 13–17; Leidy, "Descriptions of Vertebrate Remains," 19–31; Leidy, "Notice of Some Fossil Human Bones," 9–12; Webb, "Chronology of Florida Pleistocene Mammals," in *Pleistocene Mammals of Florida*, 5.

[68] Leidy, "Description of Some Mammalian Remains," 13.

of Willcox's fossils.[69]

From Willcox's Peace Creek vertebrate fossils came Leidy's report of a tapir similar to those from South America; an entire specimen and teeth of an American elephant; bison; deer; teeth of horses and a three-toed horse, *Hippotherium ingennum*; and dermal plates from giant armadillo-like Glyptodonts "heretofore known…from South America."[70]

In contrast to the fossil mammals commonly discovered in other Southern states, Leidy's findings—links to South American of a unique population of mammals of the Tertiary period to those in North America—raised scientific questions about earlier land connections between Florida and South America.

Leidy enthusiastically contributed a "Notice of Some Fossil Human Bones" to volume 2 of *Transactions.* He was intrigued by Willcox and Heilprin's find of human fossil bones during the 1886 expedition, and Willcox's subsequent collecting activities around Sarasota Bay along with his observations about Florida's Indian mounds. Popular interest in Native-American ethnography and archeology made "Sarasota Man," as the human fossils were called, very timely.

After an introduction that included a statement supporting Darwinism, Leidy recounted the discovery of a pair of human vertebrates in a Sarasota Bay rock fragment. Leidy then reported,

> The following spring Mr. Willcox visited the locality and obtained several additional specimens of human fossils, of which the best preserved is a calcaneum [heel bone] represented in Figure 2, Plate II [Figure 11]. The bones are well preserved and are actually converted into hard limonite. They do not differ in any respect from corresponding recent human bones.[71]

Needless to say, Leidy's report and the earlier article raised questions—such as the age of the skeleton and whether it was one of many—for future Florida archeologists and anthropologists.[72]

---

[69] Leidy, "Fossil Vertebrates from the Alachua Clays of Florida," vii–viii, 1–61. Leidy's manuscripts in preparation at the time of his death were later published in tribute. Dall also posthumously published Leidy's faunal lists for the Alachua Clays, Peace Creek, and Caloosahatchee River. See Dall and Harris, "Correlation Papers," 85–158.

[70] Leidy, "Descriptions of Vertebrate Remains," 25.

[71] Leidy, "Notice of Some Fossil Human Bones," 10.

[72] Willcox also collected archeological artifacts, as Jeffrey M. Mitchem recently discovered. See Mitchem, "The Willcox Copper Plate from Florida," 5–6.

Leidy's "Remarks on the Nature of Organic Species" linked vertebrates and invertebrates in his third article in volume 2 of *Transactions* based on Willcox's Florida fossil collections.[73] Willcox supplied invertebrate specimens and interpretation in a mailing to Leidy, as he often did, noting, "I submit to you some shells which may interest you, and of which you are at liberty to publish notice if you think it worth the while."[74] Willcox compared Florida's invertebrate fossils with contemporary species, linking them in timed evolution. After writing a brief introduction for the article about organic species of vertebrates and invertebrates that referred to Darwinian evolutionary thought, Leidy quoted Willcox in the paper.[75] Willcox's longstanding disagreement with Leidy about accepting Darwin's theory of evolution seems reconciled in Leidy's favor by Willcox's opening quotation: "The shells are part of a considerable series which appear to illustrate the transformation or evolution of an extinct form into that of a living species."[76] Willcox/Leidy's publication makes this case with illustrative plates and data.

By examining hundreds of specimens from separate geological beds, Willcox concluded, "No species has been found to be constant or permanent during a long period of geological time; and there appear to have been periods of rest and periods of activity in the transmutation of species."[77]

Dall's Contributions

By 1889, Dall, following many discussions with Leidy and Willcox, focused on the scientific challenges and opportunities he saw in studying Florida's malacology, paleontology, and geology. He was recognized as one of the great late-nineteenth-century American naturalists with experience in a broad array of taxa, epochs, and biological thought, including physical and cultural anthropology, oceanography, and paleontology. His U.S. Geological Survey work in Florida in 1885 and 1887 had convinced him of the importance of Florida studies for better understanding the Cenozoic period in North Amer-

---

[73] Leidy, "Remarks on the Nature of Organic Species," 51–57.

[74] Ibid., 51.

[75] Ibid., 51–57.

[76] T. P. Bennett, "Joseph Willcox, III: Darwin, Leidy and Evolution" (manuscript in preparation). Perhaps because of his strong religious background, Willcox had maintained a reserved Darwinian opposition position and dialog with Leidy until this publication.

[77] Ibid., 51.

ica. Leidy and Willcox persuaded Dall of the seriousness of the Wagner Institute's interest in exploring and publishing Florida's natural history, and he accepted an appointment as honorary curator in 1888. Willcox became Dall's on-site Florida guide and absentee collector as Dall undertook his grand project related to Florida geology and paleontology: his work on the Tertiary fauna of Florida and the coastal plain of the southeastern U.S.[78]

Dall began publishing "Contributions" in parts in volume 3 of the Wagner Institute's *Transactions* in 1890.[79] The six-part report, which was released at intervals through 1903, totaled 1,654 quarto pages and sixty plates. As W. P. Woodring noted, "The monumental Contributions to the Tertiary Fauna of Florida is the most important American publication on Cenozoic molluscan paleontology and an indispensable starting point for any work on American Cenozoic molluscan faunas."[80]

Further...

Willcox continued collecting in Florida for Dall and Leidy. Heilprin, who had become curator of the museum of the Wagner Institute in addition to his Academy responsibilities, arranged the Florida collections and completely repositioned other Wagner Institute collections under Leidy's supervision, creating the museum very much as it remains today.[81]

Leidy continued working on his Florida manuscripts and his activities at the Academy, along with many other commitments at the university and other Philadelphia institutions.[82] He died after a brief illness on 30 April 1891.

Two years after Leidy's death, Dall and Willcox contributed to restoring Timothy Conrad's published work to scientific attention. Conrad's precursor study of Florida invertebrate paleontology had been overshadowed by Louis

---

[78] The Tertiary Period marks the start of the Cenozoic Era and began 65 million years ago (mya) and lasted more than 63 million years until 1.8 million years ago (mya). The Tertiary is made up of five epochs: the Paleocene (65–54 mya), Eocene (54–38 mya), Oligocene (38–24 mya), Miocene (24–5 mya), and Pliocene (5–1.8 mya).

[79] W. H. Dall, 1890–1903, "Contributions to the Tertiary fauna of Florida, with special reference to the Miocene silex beds of Tampa and the Pliocene beds of the Caloosahatchee River," *TWFIS of Philadelphia* 3, pt. 1 (August 1890) and vol. 3, pt. 6 (October 1903).

[80] Woodring, *William Healey Dall*, 103.

[81] The Wagner Institute's website, www.wagnerfreeinstitute.org/, provides valuable information about the institute's history and current initiatives.

[82] Warren, *Joseph Leidy*, 220–22.

Agassiz's "coral reef" theory, which was put to rest by Willcox, Heilprin, and Dall's work. By 1893, the demand for Conrad's pioneering studies was so great that the Wagner Institute, influenced by Willcox, and with Dall as the editor, reprinted a large portion of Conrad's work with an introduction, index, and notes.[83] This publication further stimulated interest in Florida paleontology.

Leidy left a legacy in Florida paleontology; he also left unpublished manuscripts. At the time of his death, he was preparing an article about fossils collected in Alachua County, primarily near Archer. Ironically, Leidy's last publication about Florida paleontology was about the same fossil site as his first Florida paper and involved John Wesley Powell of the U.S. Geological Survey. Powell asked Frederic A. Lucas to prepare Leidy's manuscript for publication.[84] After several delays, Willcox arranged for the publication of "Fossil Vertebrates from Alachua Clays of Florida" by Joseph Leidy, edited by Frederic A. Lucas as volume 4 of the *Transactions* in January 1896. The paper includes Leidy's final studies of the fossils of the Alachua clays. He describes *Rhinoceros proterus* (Leidy), *Procamelus major* (Leidy), *Procamelus medius* (Leidy), *Procamelous minor* (Leidy), *Mastodon floridanus* (Leidy), *Hippotherium gratum*, *Hippotherium plicatile*, *Megatherium*, *Equs major*, *Hippotherium princeps* (Leidy), tapir, crocodile or alligator, fragments of shell of Emys, scales of a garfish, and several bones of a teleost. There is a lengthy discussion about the Florida mastodon and irony that Leidy's horse topic in paleontology in 1848 is among his last.

In addition to his collaboration with Leidy, Joseph Willcox made substantial contributions to science.[85] As a member and curator of the Academy

---

[83] W. H. Dall, *Republication of Conrad's Fossils of the Medial Tertiary of the United States. With an Introduction by William Healey Dall* (Philadelphia: Wagner Free Institute of Science, 1893). Dall includes an intriguing biographical and bibliographic section about Conrad that is valuable to researchers relying on Conrad citations.

[84] Frederic Augustus Lucas (1852) was a curator/educator and naturalist at the U.S. National Museum beginning in 1882. An "all-round" naturalist, he met and associated with many similar men whose recognition was based on their writings as explorers rather than as academics. Lucas came to be recognized by his contemporaries as an authority on ancient animals—his work on Leidy's paper ensured this—and he published a popular book on the subject. He later (1911) became the director of the American Museum of Natural History in New York, where he remained until 1923 and then served as the honorary director from 1924–1929.

[85] Spamer and Forster, *A Catalogue of Type Fossils*, 29. Named to honor Willcox, including *Nummulites willcoxi*, Heilpr.; *Aplysia willcoxi*; and Willcoxite, a mineral from NC.

of Natural Sciences and secretary and trustee of the Wagner Free Institute of Science, he enriched both institutions with his Florida field collections and exploration. Through fieldwork and collections, he authored and also contributed to many definitive papers about Florida's natural history. His letters and publications focus on personal and scientific relationships with Leidy from 1866–1891. They document a significant period in Florida natural history and offer a preface to Willcox's 1886 exploration of the west coast of Florida with Angelo Heilprin. Willcox extended the earlier geological and paleontological work of Academy explorers and stimulated archeological studies in Florida.

A century after Bartram's trek, the serious study of Florida vertebrate paleontology began in fossil sites near Bartram's heralded Great Alachua Savanna. The study of invertebrate paleontology that had started at Bartram's sites on Anastasia Island extended southward to the Florida west coast and Lake Okeechobee.

Table 1

Expedition on the West Coast of Florida: 1886[86]

Date	Location	Comments
14-Feb	Cedar Keys	Departure
15-Feb	St. Martin's Reef at the mouth of the Homosassa River.	First overnight. Then, 2–5 miles up River (Miliolite Limestone)
16, 17-Feb	Chassahowitzka Bay/River John's Island	Anchored. Explored up River Loenecker''s site for nummulites, explored by Willcox in 1882 (Aboriginal tools)
	Pithlachascotee River	
18,19-Feb	Anclote Keys Dunedin Clearwater Beach	Sponges collected Mastodon findings

[86] The starting date is correct. Other dates are derived from narrative accounts in Heilprin, "Explorations on the West Coast of Florida" (1887). Descriptions of locations are in the text as well as key collections.

	Sand Key	Grounded 1 1/2 days	
		North of John's Pass	
20, 21-Feb	Point Pinellas	Entrance to Old Tampa Bay	
22-Feb	Ballast Point	Also earlier exploredBby Conrad	
	Newman's Landing	and Willcox	
23-Feb	Lower Hillsboro	Heilprin and Natteal explore,	
		collect	
24-Feb	Up Hillsboro,	Heilprin and Natteal	
	Magbey's Spring	Left Tampa in evening	
25, 26-Feb	Manatee River	Braidentown, up River to	
		Rocky Bluff	
		(Miocene mollusks)	
		Brock killed two alligators	
	Perico Island	Stopped to skin alligators, explore	
	Big Sarasota Bay	fiddler crabs, mangroves	
		with oysters	
	Whittaker's	Miocene reef rock	
	Mrs. Hanson's	Anchored for night	
		Limonite skeleton, Sarasota Man	
27-Feb	Phillipi Creek	Strobhar and Heilprin explore	
	Little Sarasota Bay	Willcox and Heilprin collect	
	White Beach		
	North Creek	Brock and Natteal explore	
	Little Sarasota Inlet	Sundown	
	Casey's Pass		
28 –Feb	Little Gasparilla Inlet	Anchored for night	
		Best collecting ground	
		Heilprin names *Aplysia willcoxi*	
1, 2-Mar	Big Gasparilla		
	Boca Grande		
3-Mar	Charlotte Harbor		
	Useppa Island	Anchored	
4-Mar	Sanibel Island	Dragged northern extremity	
	Blind Pass		
4-Mar	Punta Rassa	Aground before reaching at	
		sundown. Drum-fish.	
5-9-Mar	Caloosahatchie River	*Terra incognita*	
	(Caloosahatchee)		

	Telegraph Station	Sable palms
	Thorpe's	Right bank. Sugar mill
	Daniels'	*S. leidyi,* many new species
		Comments about evolution
	Fort Thompson	Four-day ascent of River
		"Floridian" Pliocene series
10-Mar	Okeechobee wilderness	Aground again
	Canal channel	Descriptive passages
	"Lake Flirt"	
11, 12-Mar	Lake Hikpochee	
	(Lake Hicpochee)	
13-Mar	Lake Okeechobee	Six days of exploration
	(Canal, Moore Haven)	Collections, Soundings
	Observation Island (SE)	
	(Liberty Point) (SW)	
	Fish-eating Creek (NW)	
	Taylor's Creek (N)	(More than two days)
	Eagle Bay (NW)	
19-Mar	Canal (SW)	

CHAPTER 12

FLORIDA'S ANCIENT PEOPLES...WITH MORTON, BRINTON, WYMAN, MOORE, CUSHING, AND OTHERS

"The descriptions left by the elder and younger Bartram of the magnitude and character of the Floridian antiquities...induced large expectations of the light they might throw on the civilization of the aborigines of the peninsula."[1]

—Daniel Garrison Brinton

"We sincerely hope that others may be induced to take up and to publish reports of the mounds of the east coast, of the west coast, and of the interior, that the archeology of Florida may be redeemed from the obscurity that has hitherto characterized it."[2]

—Clarence B. Moore

In Florida, John and William Bartram encountered Seminoles, the "runaway" relatives of the Lower Creek Indians. They found vestiges of extinct indigenous Florida natives whose ancestors had lived around the St. Johns River for centuries. As the Bartrams surveyed the St. Johns, they observed and explored "Indian tumuli," finding "pots scattered" and "arrow points, flint knives and hatchets." Their most memorable visit was to an ancient mound site named "Mount Royal" by John and described fifteen years later by William in *Travels*.[3]

William Bartram's later *Travels* served as a guide and reference for anthropological study in Florida during the nineteenth century.[4] The younger Bartram's archaeological observations began on Amelia Island, where he saw "several very large Indian tumuli, which are called Ogeeche mounts."[5] From

---

[1] Brinton, *Notes on the Floridian Peninsula*, 166.
[2] Moore, "Certain Sand Mounds of the St. John's River," 246.
[3] *FHBT*, 353–54; *WBT*, 99.
[4] *FHBT*, 423–24.
[5] Ibid., 66–67; *FHBT*, 42–43.

that location, Waselkov and Braund traced Bartram's anthropological travels in ethnology and archaeology through Florida and the Southeast and included Bartram's Seminole contacts and observations, such as the Long Warrior, as well as Bartram's discoveries of "remains and traces of ancient human habitations and cultivation."[6]

The study of New World human cultures and their origins was slow to develop in the U.S. Strife and warfare with the native populations and historical perceptions of cultural inferiority slowed progress in this arena.[7] In Europe, archaeology and ethnology were still in their early stages, and they were heavily influenced by science and focused on the Ancient World. In the U.S., Thomas Jefferson paved the way for American anthropology.

Jefferson is often called the "father of American archaeology" and celebrated for many "firsts": his writings in *Notes on Virginia* and his "first scientific excavation in the history of archaeology."[8] As U.S. president, he supported exploration of the Pacific Northwest by Meriwether Lewis and William Clark, who followed Jefferson's many suggestions. They returned with artifacts and some of the first ethnological descriptions of western Native Americans and gave those artifacts to President Jefferson for study and his collections. Although Jefferson and several other members of the Philadelphia intellectual community were enthusiastic about linguistic, archeological, and cultural studies of Native Americans and the development of American anthropology, it would be some time before this field would gain recognition.[9] The young "descriptive" period of anthropology at the Academy involved several members who were trained in anatomy, including Samuel George

---

[6] Waselkov and Braund, *William Bartram*, 43, 55; this work is an outstanding volume of William Bartram's writings and contributions to southeastern Indian archaeology, anthropology, and ethnology. See also *FHBT*, 66, 198.

[7] Kehoe, "Philarivalium," 181–87.

[8] Thomas, *Archaeology*, 26–30; Willey and Sabloff, *A History of American Archaeology*, 28–31; Wheeler, *Archaeology from the Earth*, 58. Jefferson noted the stratigraphy of the soil and rock on a cross-section of a burial mound he excavated in the Mississippi Valley and the age difference between skeletons in the lower sections compared to the remains that were closer to the surface. He concluded that the mound had been revisited over the course of years, with a new layer of sediment and human remains being added each time. While this assumption did not reveal who had created the mounds, it was, however, a breakthrough in how archaeology could be used to examine the question.

[9] Fowler and Wilcox, *Philadelphia and the Development of Americanist Archaeology*, xi–xx.

Morton. The fieldwork and research of other members—Daniel Brinton, Jeffries Wyman of Cambridge, and Joseph Willcox with Joseph Leidy and Clarence B. Moore—led to the birth of Florida anthropology in Bartram's tracks.

During the Academy's 1817–1818 Florida Expedition, Thomas Say and Titian Peale had collected Indian artifacts but did not record any descriptions or comment about the several mounds the explorers may have seen along the St. Johns River. Although their journey up river was cut short by Seminole raids, Say and Peale were able to procure and deposit a few Native-American artifacts at the Academy.[10]

Following the Indian Removal Act of 1830, the forced relocation of most Native Americans to the west, and the end of the Second Seminole War in Florida in 1842, competitive curio and research collectors unearthed skeletal remains and other artifacts of interest from abandoned burial sites and ancient burial mounds.[11] At the Academy, Dr. Samuel George Morton took detailed measurements of the anatomical features of human skulls as part of his anatomical studies related to human origins and racial comparisons.[12] Morton was particularly interested in the skulls of Native Americans.

Samuel George Morton

Samuel George Morton (1799–1851) was born in Philadelphia; he graduated from the University of Pennsylvania Medical School in 1820, the same year he was elected a member of the Academy.[13] In 1824, after earning

---

[10] There are entries of Peale donations in ANSP Ethnographic Ledgers and later transfer records to the Heye Foundation; personal communication, Brandon Zimmerman, 2014.

[11] The national focus on Native Americans increased during the 1830s. Legislative and military actions led to the forced "removal" of many tribes from their traditional areas of residence and their relocation to the "West" during this decade. Many skeletal remains were illegally exhumed from burial grounds, and many more were obtained as a result of the fatalities that occurred during this period. The Indian Removal Act of 1830 made skulls more readily available to collectors because the descendants of those buried were no longer present to defend their ancestral graves.

[12] The human skull, scientifically known as the cranium, consists of twenty-two to twenty-six bones. The skull can be divided into two regions: the cranial section and the facial section. Morton made twelve critical measurements on each skull, including drawings and descriptions of the bone structures and sutures.

[13] For further reading on Samuel George Morton, see James Atkin Meigs, *A Memoir of Samuel G. Morton* (Philadelphia: Collins, 1851); Paul A. Erickson, "Morton, Samuel George (1799–1851)," in *History of Physical Anthropology: An Encyclopedia,* ed. Frank

an advanced degree from Edinburgh University in Scotland, Morton began practicing medicine in Philadelphia. The Academy became his institutional home, and he served as recording secretary (1825–1829), curator (1830–1832), corresponding secretary (1831–1840), vice-president (1840–1849), and president (1849–1851). From 1839–1843, he was professor of anatomy at the University of Pennsylvania. In 1830, after making many contributions to invertebrate paleontology and geology, Morton became interested in human origins and races and turned his anatomical skills and research to physical anthropology and ethnography.[14] He collected human skulls and crania from all over the world and measured the osteological structures and specific anatomical areas of the skull and its volume (i.e., the craniometrics).[15] His attention to ethnographic context and his use of more than twelve cranial measurements to compare geographically circumscribed population groups established Morton as a pioneering scientist in physical anthropology.[16] Following Morton's request that his Academy colleagues and others procure Native-American crania for him: "one man assigned to the U.S. Army in Florida picked over the dead of the Seminole War, sending Morton two 'fine' Seminole skulls left unburied after the battle of Lake Okee-Chobee."[17] Morton wrote, "This remarkably characteristic Indian Head was presented to me by my friend Dr. G. Emerson," who would later (1853) become a member of the ANSP.[18]

Spencer (New York: Garland, 1997): 689–90.

[14] For a complete list of Morton's contributions to ANSP publications, see Nolan, *An Index*, 139–41. His most significant and celebrated contribution to paleontology/geology is *Synopsis of the organic remains of the Cretaceous group of the United States* (Philadelphia: Key & Biddle, 1834).

[15] He defined and measured osteological structures and specific anatomical areas of the skull as well as its volume.

[16] Morton's first book on ethnography, published in 1839, was a heavily illustrated volume: *Crania Americana or a comparative View of the Skulls of Various Aboriginal Nations of North and South America* (Philadelphia: J. Dobson, 1839). See also Hrdlička, "Physical Anthropology in America," 508–52; C. Loring Brace, *"Race" is a Four-Letter Word* (New York: Oxford University Press, 2005).

[17] Renschler and Monge, "The Samuel George Morton Cranial Collection," 32. Morton was also interested in the skulls of other Florida creatures (e.g., the Florida manatee and white ibis). See Morton's *Catalog of Skulls of Man and the Inferior Animals, in the Collection of Samuel George Morton* (Philadelphia: Merrihew & Thompson, 1849).

[18] "Seminole warrior, slain at the battle of St. Joseph's thirty miles below St. Augustine in June 1836" (Morton, *Crania Americana*, 166). The Emerson reference is to *Seminole. Plate XXII.*

Morton used Bartram's writings as a resource for interpreting his own studies of hundreds of crania of southeastern Indian Nation individuals and Seminoles. In his publications, Morton included many references to Bartram's Florida observations.[19] Morton included three plates labeled "Seminole" with a detailed description of the skull's origin and the circumstances of his acquisitions. The three crania were from north Florida; one had been collected after a military engagement; another was procured by an Army surgeon.[20] The third was sent by Morton's recently deceased Academy colleague, "the late lamented Henry [sic] B. Croom, Esq."[21] Morton noted about the latter skull, "It possesses the strong traits of the other crania of this nation." Each plate is accompanied by twelve key measurements and the facial angle.[22]

Morton compared Seminole and Cherokee skulls and found them similar to and little different from (although slightly smaller than) the skulls of Caucasians.[23] Morton pointed out the similarities of Florida skulls to those from South America[24] and formulated questions about the origins of the peoples. He compared mounds in Peru with Bartram's observations of the mounds in Florida.[25] Morton's pioneering work stimulated future research in Florida as well as in global ethnology. It paved the way for Philadelphian Daniel Brinton and Bostonian Jefferies Wyman, who explored Florida after Morton's early death in 1851.[26]

---

[19] Morton, *Crania Americana*, 71.

[20] Morton cites many individuals who were medical staff in the U.S. Army.

[21] This is Hardy B. Croom from chapter 10. The author is trying to determine the variations on his name used at the Academy; "H. P." appears on the membership list. Uncertain authors have referenced Croom as, "—Croom, Esq." Morton's reference is to a plate in *Crania* of a *Seminole Skull* provided by Hardy Croom. In Plate XXIV with measurements.

[22] The tabular list of "Measurements" includes the following: the longitudinal diameter (inches), parietal diameter, frontal diameter, vertical diameter, inter-mastoid arch, inter-mastoid line, occipito-frontal arch, horizontal periphery, internal capacity (cubic inches), capacity of the anterior chamber, capacity of the posterior chamber, capacity of the coronal region, and facial angle (degrees).

[23] Morton, *Crania Americana*, 174.

[24] Ibid., 228.

[25] Ibid., 228–29.

[26] By then, Leidy was a prominent American scientist, and many urged him to continue Morton's crania work because of Leidy's developing interest in ethnology and anatomical expertise. Leidy declined this opportunity "not from a want of interest in ethnographic science, but because other studies occupied my time." Instead, Morton's student and protégé, Dr. James Aitken Meigs (1829–1880), continued to build his

Daniel Garrison Brinton

Daniel Garrison Brinton (1837–1899), an archaeologist and ethnologist, specialized in native cultures and linguistics.[27] Born near West Chester, Pennsylvania, Brinton attended Yale University. During his undergraduate studies, he explored Florida in 1856 and published his first article about the young state.[28] In 1859, while preparing for a medical career at Jefferson Medical College in Philadelphia (where he earned his MD in 1861), Brinton published his first book, *Notes on the Floridian Peninsula, Its Literary History, Indian Tribes and Antiquities.*[29]

Notes on the Floridian Peninsula is in part a treatise on East Florida exploration from the Spanish period until Brinton's exploration in 1856. It includes a historical background, ethnographic chapters about sixteenth-century native tribes, later tribes, including the Seminoles, and Spanish missions. The final chapter, "Antiquities," contains Brinton's personal observations from 1856, as he followed in Bartram's tracks, about "Mounds.—Roads.—Shell Heaps.—Old Fields":

> The descriptions left by the elder and younger Bartram of the magnitude and character of the Floridian antiquities, had impressed me with a high opinion of their perfection, and induced large expectations of the light they might throw on the civilization of the aborigines of the peninsula.... On Amelia island...there is an open field, containing some thirty acres...midway of the base of this triangle, stands a mound...a fine view from the summit...a lookout or watch-tower...but from excavations made by myself or others, it proved, like every similar mound I examined...in Florida...to be, in construction, a vast tomb. Human bones, stone axes, darts, and household utensils. Were disinterred in abundance...rudely marked fragments of pottery, and broken oyster, clam and conch shells, were strewn over the field.[30]

Because of Brinton's limited time and encounters with problematic mosquitos, he records, "I could learn nothing of the two large tumuli on this

---

mentor's collection and contribute to the study of ethnology, which he described as "this youngest, most intricate, and most important of the sciences" (Hrdlička, "Physical Anthropology in America," 508–54; Meigs, *Catalogue of Human Crania,* 11).

[27] Brinton, *A Guide-Book of Florida and the South,* xiii–lviii.

[28] Brinton, "A City Gone to Seed," 261. Brinton was chairman of the board of editors of the *Yale Literary Magazine* at this time.

[29] Philadelphia: John Sabin, 1859.

[30] Ibid., 166–67.

island, known as the 'Ogeechee Mounts,' mentioned by the younger Bartram."[31]

Undeterred, however, in "Antiquities," Brinton eloquently describes his own observations and discoveries as he quotes Bartram, while following his travels to "the great mounts, highways, and artificial lakes up St. Juans." Brinton also correlates his own observations and Bartram's with those of earlier Spanish and French explorers.[32] Brinton follows Bartram's path, making detailed observations along the St. Johns to a "rich hammock half a mile below Lake Harney." His travels on other Bartram trails—"rich lands of Marion and Alachua counties...hammocks of the Suwannee"—provided sketches of Brinton's native mound observations: "On the opposite banks of Silver Springs run...are two tumuli. Pottery, axes, and arrow-heads abound in the vicinity, and every sign goes to show that this remarkable spot was once the site of a populous aboriginal settlement."[33]

Brinton's visit to Silver Springs resulted in a detailed appendix about it and other springs in Florida: "The Silver Spring...I had an opportunity to examine it with the aid of proper instruments, which I did with much care."[34] He describes the flora and assesses the depth and geography at many locations, complementing the data with temperature and water flow measurements of "the average daily quantity...of more than three hundred million gallons!"

Exploring further south than Bartram, Brinton traveled along the Gulf Coast to Tampa and also south and up the Manatee River. Brinton observed mounds, which would later be visited by Willcox and Heilprin (see page 245), on Long Key in Sarasota Bay. Brinton provided detailed answers to the question that he advanced, "What now are the characteristics of this class of Floridian mounds?"[35] He referred to and interpreted his own observations along with those of earlier Academy explorers, including Bartram, Timothy Conrad (see page 191) , and Michael Tuomey (see page 197) .

With *Notes on the Floridian Peninsula* published and his medical studies

---

[31] *FHBT*, 65. Waselkov and Braund, *William Bartram*, 43, note 21, point out that Bartram's Ogeechee mounds were originally at least three shell mounds and one sand mound; the latter was excavated by Brinton.

[32] Brinton, *Notes on the Florida Peninsula*, 169.

[33] Ibid.

[34] Ibid., Appendix 1, The Silver Spring, 183–90.

[35] Brinton, *Notes on the Florida Peninsula*, 172–81; Brinton, "Artificial Shell-deposits," 356–58.

completed in 1861, Brinton traveled throughout Europe and continued his anthropological studies in Paris and Heidelberg. After returning to the U.S. in 1862, Brinton joined the Union Army and advanced to surgeon-in-chief of the Second Division, Eleventh Corps of the Army of the Potomac. He saw battlefield action until the end of the Civil War.[36] Brinton then returned to Pennsylvania and practiced medicine in West Chester while pursuing his interests in archaeology and ethnology and editing the weekly *Medical and Surgical Reporter*. He published *Myths of the New World* in 1868, continued writing about his travels in Florida, and in 1869 published *Guide Book of Florida and the South*.

Brinton "had in mind the excellent European Guide-Books of Karl Baedeker," but as he acknowledged, "Though I have not followed his plan very closely, I have done so to the extent the character of our country seems to allow. I have borrowed from him the use of the asterisk (*) to denote that the object so designated is especially noteworthy." Brinton's intent was that his "unpretending little book is designed to give the visitor to Florida such information as will make his trip more useful and pleasant."[37] His four chapters for "Invalids" and "Health Seekers" include medical advice that is still pertinent.[38] Brinton's growing reputation in anthropology produced considerable interest in his book to the increasing number of Florida tourists.

Brinton's many publications in anthropology foreshadowed his career change from a practicing physician and amateur anthropologist. Brinton retired after practicing medicine for a decade to devote himself to anthropology and linguistics. He achieved two firsts in American anthropology: professor of ethnology and archaeology at the Academy of Natural Sciences in 1884 and professor of American linguistics at the University of Pennsylvania in 1886. Some of his later works include Florida references, and he continued to stimulate and encourage anthropological work in Florida.[39] Along with

---

[36] His service included assignments around St. Mary's and Amelia Island.

[37] Brinton, *Guide-Book*, iii. Because of his antebellum exploration of Florida, Brinton's *Guide-Book* scooped later Florida writers—Harriet Beecher Stowe, Sidney Lanier, Silvia Sunshine [Abbie M. Brooks]—in promoting tourism.

[38] Ibid., 115–36. Selecting the correct climate for pulmonary problems, warm weather for rheumatism during cold winters (as Maclure also discovered in 1818), "equable temperature, moderate moisture and regular winds" (124). Based on his studies of Florida and Texas, he concluded, "the most equable climate is on the south-eastern coast of Florida" (126).

[39] Those works include *Ancient Phonetic Alphabet of Yucatan* (1870), *Religious Sentiment* (1876), *American Hero Myths* (1882), *Ancient Nahuatl Poetry* (1887), *Language*

Joseph Leidy and Joseph Willcox, Brinton played a key role in founding and supporting the University of Pennsylvania's Museum of Archaeology, which would later become a repository for Samuel Morton's crania collections as well as other Florida collections. Later, Brinton also provided resources and support for several of Clarence B. Moore's expeditions and Frederick Cushing's Pepper-Hearst expedition to Florida.[40]

During Brinton's exploration and study of Florida, and while professorships in anthropology were being established at the Academy and at the University of Pennsylvania, Jeffries Wyman and, later, Frederic Ward Putnam were busy establishing a museum and anthropological studies at Harvard.[41]

Jeffries Wyman

Jeffries Wyman (1814–1874) was born in Massachusetts and graduated from Harvard College and then Harvard Medical School in 1837. He used his earnings from lecturing at the new Lowell Institute in Boston to travel to Europe and study under anatomist Richard Owen in London from 1841–1842. Back in Boston, Wyman competed for a Harvard professorship that went to Asa Gray. In 1843, Wyman was elected professor of anatomy and physiology at Hampden-Sydney College in Richmond, Virginia; however, he maintained a mailing address in Boston along with plans to return. In 1844, he was elected Academy correspondent from Boston and published primarily on anatomy and animal physiology during the following years. In 1847, Wyman was called to Harvard College to become the Hersey Professor of Anatomy and began assembling extensive collections related to his new research interests in comparative anatomy and archaeology. In 1860, Wyman started spending the winters in Florida for health reasons and camped outdoors with Bostonian George Peabody, a wealthy, enthusiastic amateur archaeologist. Peabody also assisted Wyman in excavating and studying Indian mounds.

---

of the Palaeolithic Man (1888), American Race (1891), Negroes (1891), Religions of Primitive Peoples (1897), Peoples of the Philippines (1898) and Aboriginal American Authors (1883). Brinton's works are of great current interest: http://www.gutenberg.org. He was also a member of numerous learned societies in the U.S. and Europe and was president at different times of the Numismatic and Antiquarian Society of Philadelphia, the American Folklore Society, the American Philosophical Society, and the American Association for the Advancement of Science.

[40] Brinton, "Report of the Professor of Ethnology and Anthropology," 570.

[41] ANSP Correspondents: Jeffries Wyman, MD, Boston, Massachusetts, 1844; F. W. Putnam, Salem, Massachusetts, 1867.

Peabody's keen interest in anthropology led to his founding and support of Harvard's Peabody Museum of American Archaeology and Ethnology in 1866. Peabody named Wyman one of the seven museum trustees, and Wyman became the new museum's first curator. He continued teaching and researched physical anthropology and archaeology during his health-related trips to Florida.

Wyman focused on the shell mounds of the St. Johns River rather than Florida's coastal mounds. In 1869, he published two papers about his findings.[42] During winter 1860–1861, collections were made at Lake Harney, Black Hammock near Lake Jessup, and at Enterprise. At Old Enterprise, on Lake Monroe, in 1861, he found human bones under peculiar circumstances "while making an excavation near the roots of a large palmetto tree, which had been partially uncovered by the action of the water.[43]

In 1867, the same localities were revisited. Several of these sites had been explored by William Bartram. Wyman also published brief notes in the 1868 *Annual Report of the Peabody Museum of American Archaeology and Ethnology*. The results of these early studies and those from his Florida explorations during the winters of 1871–1874 were being published at the time of Wyman's sudden death. This publication was his largest work and the most significant in Florida archaeology up to that time. Shortly thereafter, *Fresh-water Shell Mounds of the St. John's River, Florida* was published by Wyman's admiring friends and colleagues as a memorial volume, which included his final monograph.[44]

---

[42] Wyman, "On the fresh-water shell heaps," 393–403; 449–63. These papers covered mound names and locations; the general size of the mounds from circular heaps, fifteen to twenty feet in diameter, to long ridges several hundred feet in length, and from four to five, or even in some cases fifteen feet in thickness; and the three predominant species of shells found in the mounds. Wyman mentioned fragments of pottery and broken animal bones and added that Peabody found a crude arrowhead of flint, a material not found *in situ* in that part of Florida.

[43] Wyman, *Fresh-water Shell Mounds*, 55.

[44] Wyman, *Fresh-water Shell Mounds*, foreword quote by M. W., Cambridge, Mass., Nov. 1, 1875: "Professor Jeffries Wyman died suddenly...4th September, 1874. A few pages only of this work were then printed. It has been carried through the press by friendly hands, especially by the valuable aid of Mr. F. W. Putnam, the successor of professor Wyman in the curatorship of the Peabody Museum of American Archaeology and Ethnology at Cambridge, who has bestowed much time and attention in comparing the plates with their originals in the museum, and in verifying, wherever possible, the measurements" (xi). The frontispiece, *Shell Mounds at Old Enterprise, Florida.* was drawn

As a prelude to his archaeological observations and excavations, Wyman began the monograph with an historical, biological, and geological description of the St. Johns River. He refers frequently to Bartram's *Travels* while describing wildlife and changes that may have occurred in the ecosystem since Bartram's travels: "the roseate spoonbill sometimes seen, and the flamingo, once a rare visitor, but no longer found."[45] Wyman comments, "The mounds are, as in Bartram's time, particularly well-suited for camping purposes, and are still the most desirable ones which the river affords."[46] He referred to and discussed his own earlier publication about parasites in birds along the river and the geological surveys of the Smithsonian Institution.

Wyman's descriptions of the archaeological sites and his mound excavations, among many, included Old Enterprise, Huntoon (Hontoon) Island, and Orange Bluff, along with "Bartram's Mound."[47] Wyman noted, "The part of the river in which we are especially interested is comprised between Forrester's Point a few miles below Palatka and the Salt Lakes, for it is between these places that nearly all of the fresh water shell heaps are to be seen."[48]

Wyman reported his excavations, mound by mound, often taking stratigraphic advantage of the river's erosion, which exposed some of the mounds. At Osceola Mound he found, "The most interesting discovery was that of parts of two human skeletons, the bones of which were mingled. These were found in the stratum of consolidated shells and mud…at a depth of nine feet below the surface."[49]

At Bartram's Mound, also known as Little Orange, a short distance from the mouth of Lake Dexter, Wyman complemented his observations with a lengthy footnote from *Travels* about Bartram's encounter with the alligators during his camp at the mound.[50]

Wyman provided a list of the forty-eight mounds, which he excavated, with location notes that supplement the sites.[51] Contradicting Brinton, who

---

by Wyman.

[45] Wyman, *Fresh-water Shell Mounds,* 6. Here and at other locations, Wyman references *WBT* when comparing the range of birds and other animals as observed by Bartram and himself.

[46] Wyman, *Fresh-water Shell Mounds,* 11.

[47] Ibid., 10.

[48] Ibid., 8.

[49] Ibid., 33 (Fig. 1).

[50] Ibid., 35.

[51] Ibid., 44.

had concluded that the river mounds, unlike the coastal mounds, were created by river flow and storms, not by humans, Wyman decided, "The shell heaps are the work of man."[52]

After the historical introduction to part 5, "Primitive Man and Implements," Wyman described many found artifacts and their usage.[53] He included illustrations of his finds and detailed descriptions of a variety of implements: stone (small arrowheads, worked flint), bone (awls, antler, carved), and pottery (cups, vases, vessels). An accompanying table summarizes the pottery items collected at six mound locations.[54] Wyman described shell implements and extensively divided them by function: cutting (chisels, awls), drinking, perforated (unknown usage), and ornamental.[55]

Wyman discussed "The Absence of Pipes and of Metals" in the mounds, noting that he found no gold, silver, or metal implements. Based on the implements, he speculated on the human origins and the relation of human remains in the mounds to living or recent Native Americans.

In part 6, Wyman presented the anatomical analysis of the human remains he found and discusses cannibalism, admitting, "We have entered more into details than we otherwise should because the subject of American cannibalism has not received the attention it deserves."[56]

In part 7, "Remains of Animals in the Shell Mounds," Wyman introduced the science later known as zooarchaeology.[57] He included a table that lists twelve mounds and the representative animal (mammals, fishes, reptiles, birds, etc.) remains that he found.[58] This introduction leads to a detailed discussion of historical records of living creatures compared with their remains. In further discussion of "Remains of Extinct Animals," Wyman reported on the fossilized fragments of bones and teeth from horses, mastodon, elephant, and the ribs of a manatee.[59] These fossils were obtained in four unique loca-

---

[52] Ibid., 86.

[53] Ibid., 45.

[54] Ibid., 55.

[55] Ibid., Plate VI.

[56] Ibid., 71.

[57] Zooarchaeology is the study of faunal remains (i.e., the items left behind when an animal dies, such as bones, shells, hair, chitin, scales, and hides, and, recently, proteins and DNA). Wyman was a pioneer in the field. These finds were a prelude to the more detailed studies by Willcox and Leidy, which are discussed in ch. 11.

[58] Ibid., 78.

[59] No reference is given to Bartram's or other finds of more recent manatee remains;

tions, including one from a trip he made along Florida's west coast to Charlotte Harbor.[60]

Trying to access the age of his finds, Wyman lamented his limitation: "No satisfactory data have been found for determining, with any degree of accuracy, the age of the shell heaps." He questioned the validity of the currently accepted, most decisive measure of the age of mounds: the age of the trees found growing on top of the mounds. However, he presented data on tree sizes—as an indicator of their age—from various mounds and suggested they were "older than the discovery of America." Finally, Wyman speculated on the succession of human habitation in Florida:

> Whether the builders of the mounds were the same people as those found by the Spaniards and the French is uncertain. The absence of pipes in all and of pottery in some of the mounds, and the extreme rarity of ornaments, are consistent with the conclusion that they were a different people. To these may be added the negative fact, that no indications have been found that they practiced agriculture.[61]

Wyman set the stage for the next generation of explorers of Florida's ancient peoples. Foremost was a Harvard College student, Clarence B. Moore, who was mentored by Frederic Ward Putnam, Wyman's successor at Harvard's Peabody Museum.

Clarence Bloomfield Moore

Clarence Bloomfield Moore (1852–1936) was born in Philadelphia, where he later pursued a successful business career and became famous for his extensive anthropological studies in Florida and the Southeastern states.[62] His grandfather, Augustus Edward Jessup, was a prominent geologist, member of the Academy, and veteran of Stephen Long's 1818–1819 expedition (see page 99). Moore earned an AB degree at Harvard in 1873; after he graduated, his family (who owned the Jessup and Moore Paper Company) encouraged and funded their son's wanderlust in Europe, Asia Minor, Egypt, and South America during the summer. He spent the winter in Florida. Moore chartered boats to take him up the St. Johns River on many occasions and focused on hunting, fishing, and poking around some of the river's mounds for artifacts.

---

the manatee was presumed extinct by Wyman (*Fresh-water Shell Mounds*, 81, 86).

[60] Ibid., 81.

[61] Ibid., 87.

[62] Peck and Stroud, *A Glorious Enterprise*, 206–10; see also Aten and Milanich, "Clarence Bloomfield Moore," 113–33.

He and Joseph Willcox (see page 238) stayed at the same resort, Magnolia Hotel in Green Cove Springs. In 1878, Moore began to travel around the world but returned home when his father died. He became president of the family company, led it to further success, and eventually handed over its management to others in the late 1880s to pursue his developing interest in archaeology. He cultivated his amateur pursuits in archaeology and photography to what was then a professional level through friendships with Academy members, including his Harvard mentor, Frederic Ward Putnam, colleagues at the Wagner Institute, and the developing archaeological museum at the University of Pennsylvania. Moore became keenly aware of the developments in Florida exploration. Further, the St. Johns River, which he visited during the winter, was a well-known tourist mecca that offered boating, hotels, and amenities for ready access to unexplored areas. With his personal financial resources, Moore continued his Florida explorations, which had begun casually on the St. Johns River more than a decade before, on a massive scale.[63]

Moore began exploring Florida on the "St. John's."[64] In 1891, he reinvestigated Wyman's freshwater shell heap sites and mounted organized expeditions to Florida, focusing on the St. Johns River drainage until 1895. For easy navigation with his assistants, Moore chartered steam-powered, shallow-water tourist boats; later, he deployed his stern-wheel steamer, the *Gopher of Philadelphia*, which he customized with space for artifact storage and a photography laboratory on the lower deck. A skilled photographer and award-winning portraitist, Moore was a pioneer in using photography as a tool for collecting and preserving data about sites and artifacts.[65]

---

[63] See Fairbanks and Milanich, *Florida Archaeology*, 1–13. In the pioneering chapter, "Archaeology in Florida," Milanich and Fairbanks outline Wyman's and Moore's studies that initiated and started Florida on the track of becoming a microcosm for the development of many sub-disciplines of archaeology, including zooarchaeology and historical archaeology. Beginning in the early twentieth century, the developments were supported and influenced by the interdisciplinary and multidisciplinary programs at the University of Florida based in its Florida State Museum (founded 1917), now the Florida Museum of Natural History (FLMNH).

[64] Moore used the spelling "St. John's" with the apostrophe, which came into more general use during the twentieth century. USGS uses "Johns," as have I, except in quoted material.

[65] Moore chartered the *Osceola* at Palatka for the beginning of his 1891 work. The commercial steamship was a typical "Ocklawaha steamer with a shallower draft and a shorter smokestack" than his later *Gopher*. The *Gopher* was named for Bartram's Florida gopher tortoise, *Gopherus polyphemus*, which also burrowed into mounds and middens

Moore was influenced by William Bartram as well as Jeffries Wyman, as reflected in the extensive references to their Florida work in his series of publications about his East Florida excavations.

An introduction to Moore's gargantuan archaeological research in East Florida has been provided by Jeffrey Mitchem, who has presented reprints and in several ways facilitated access to Moore's excavations and publications.[66] Mitchem lists the sites visited or mentioned by Moore, with their current Florida state site numbers, site names, and a summary of the known cultural and temporal archaeological components of each site. The detailed listing of some 175 sites, which Moore excavated, reflects the magnitude of his efforts. These were only simply suggested in Moore's summary illustration in his "first paper" of five articles published as a "Shell Heaps" series between 1892 and 1894.[67] The St. Johns River series was preceded by two papers about his excavation of the burial mound at Tick Island in 1891 and 1892.[68] Mitchem provides an excellent review of these publications, which cover these river sites.

Mount Royal, which had been described by John Bartram and studied by William Bartram during an overnight camp, was a major focus of Moore's St. Johns River work.[69] Mount Royal was among the first mounds Moore and his crews excavated after he left shell middens and concentrated on mounds.[70]

(*FHBT,* 182–83; *FHBT,* 366–67; Pearson, Birchett, and Weinstein, "An Aptly Named Steamboat," 82–87).

[66] Mitchem, *The East Florida Expeditions of Clarence Bloomfield Moore,* 1–52. Mitchem's scholarly work about Moore's Florida work and editorial presentation of Moore's publications (in their original large format) in a series of volumes are highly commended. Everything Moore published is being reprinted by the University of Alabama Press, and there is so much material on Florida that those papers fill three volumes; two are edited by Mitchem. Moore published twenty-one large volumes, mostly in *PANS.* These monographs are richly illustrated and contain informational photographs made by Moore. They continue to serve as valuable references for archeologists regarding the prehistoric American Southeast.

[67] Ibid., 75–125.

[68] Ibid., 53–74. The Tick Island work was mentored by F. W. Putnam of Harvard's Peabody Museum and W. H. Dall at the WFIS.

[69] Milanich, "The Bartrams, Clarence B. Moore, and Mount Royal," 117–36. There are two parts of this site: the mound where Moore worked and the middens.

[70] The usage of terms "tumuli," "shell heaps," and "mounds" in archeological studies became common in the 19th century. Excavations could often determine whether the accumulation was natural, due to water action, or cultural:, for example, a scrap/kitchen/waste heap or a burial or other ceremonial heap/mound. Sometimes in

Moore produced two reports about his Mount Royal excavations (one for each field season)—spring 1893 and 1894—and published the results in the 1894 *Journal of the Academy of Natural Sciences*. This action brought instant recognition to the Mount Royal site, which was then often cited in reviews of archaeology.[71] Moore had been elected to Academy membership in 1893.

In the first of two 1894 publications, Moore began part one of "Mt. Royal, Putnam County," acknowledging, "For 128 years the existence of Mt. Royal has been a matter of history." He followed with lengthy quotations of John and William Bartram's independent descriptions of the Mount Royal site.[72] Moore quoted from what has become a lost manuscript of William's about Mount Royal: "The vast mounds upon the St. John's...differ from those among the Cherokees, with respect to their adjuncts and appendages.... A remarkable example occurs at Mount Royal."[73] Moore described the "Size and Composition of Mound," "Excavations," "Human Remains," and noted, "that Mt. Royal was erected for purposes of sepulture is beyond a doubt." He described conchs, or "Fulgurs," which were made into "drinking cups," wrought from the *Fulgur perversum*, and "Implements, Weapons, etc."—arrowheads, lance points, polished hatches, chisels, gorgets (neck ornaments), ceremonial implements, miscellaneous objects of stone, the mineral galena, beads, pottery, and pearls.[74] Moore also noted that "[i]n every portion...were various objects wrought from, or coated with, sheet copper." Moore commented, "The discovery of copper in considerable quantity is new to records of mound investigation in Florida." Moore had some of the copper artifacts chemically analyzed in Philadelphia but was unable to conclude whether the copper originated in Europe or North America.[75]

---

usage, "one archaeologist's heap or midden was another's mound."

[71] Milanich, introduction to *Famous Florida Sites*, 2–6, 8–13. This introduction is an excellent essay about Moore's Florida work and contributions.

[72] Moore, *East Florida Expeditions*, 139–40; Moore, "Certain Sand Mounds of the St. Johns River," 17–18.

[73] William Bartram quoted by Moore, "Certain Sand Mounds of the St. Johns River," 18; Moore, *East Florida Expeditions*, 140.

[74] A conch that was also made into tool implements, for example, awls. The current name is *Busycon sinistrum*. The pearls were sent to Moore's colleague, Henry Pilsbry, at the ANSP for examination. Pilsbry replied, "I can state with confidence that true pearls they undoubtedly are" (Moore, *East Florida Expeditions*, 140).

[75] Moore's view that the copper was of native origin rather than European is currently supported (Moore, *East Florida Expeditions*, 39).

After concluding his 1895 season having assembled monumental collections and written many publications, Moore wrote with archaeological foresight: "as the St. John's can never again furnish such material for any extended scientific notice, and as archaeologists coming after us will require the fullest records for their work, everything has been included."[76] Thousands of artifacts, which represented the bulk of Moore's collections, were shipped back to the Academy in Philadelphia, where they were stored, conserved, and exhibited.[77] Moore's Florida legacy in anthropology was well established, yet his work was less than half done.[78]

Moore was interested in exploring other areas in Florida and the surrounding states and made brief forays and excavations to the west coast of Florida before 1892. He was well informed about his Academy colleague's 1887 expedition (ch. 11) west to Lake Okeechobee and the discovery of "Sarasota Man" (see page 251). However, that area was unlike the land-titled, often settled property of east Florida around the St. Johns, where Moore received permission to dig and collect, with easy river and rail transportation and communication. Most of the disconnected Florida interior, west coast, and southern regions were dotted with only a few village stores for homesteaders, ranchers, and former fort settlers.[79] However, in some areas near waterways, such as Cedar Key, Crystal River, and Tampa Bay, entrepreneurs interested in railroad, tourism, and real estate development were attracting northern visitors.[80] Moore began excavating in these areas where the supply lines were relatively short and the *Gopher* could navigate. Although Moore regarded archaeological prospects on the lower Gulf coast as poor, he was

---

[76] Ibid., 241; Moore, "Certain Sand Mounds of the St. Johns River," 129. Moore did further work and published several papers about his expeditions in northeast and east Florida, 1895–1896.

[77] The saga of Moore's collections at the ANSP until the late 1920s, when most were transferred to the Heye Foundation, Museum of the American Indian, in New York City, is covered by Peck and Stroud, *A Glorious Enterprise*, 208–11, up to 2012. Moore also held many artifacts in his "home" and generously dispersed them and other collections at various times to several museums in South America, the WFI, and the University of Pennsylvania. See also Aten and Milanich, "Clarence Bloomfield Moore," 131–32.

[78] Mitchem's introduction to *East Florida Expeditions of Clarence Bloomfield Moore* (1–52) and Milanich's Mount Royal section of *Famous Florida Sites* (29–77) summarize Moore's early efforts in Florida.

[79] Hunt and Bennett, foreword to Gilliland, *Key Marco's Buried Treasure*, xi–xii.

[80] Gannon, *Florida: A Short History*, 53–69.

Southwest coastal map showing Key Marco and other locations.
Courtesy of Brad Sanders.

impressed by the dramatic finds made during 1895–1896 excavations in the wetland muck on Key Marco (Marco Island) located on the Gulf coast south of Fort Myers by Frank Hamilton Cushing.[81]

Frank Hamilton Cushing

As a youngster, Frank Hamilton Cushing (1857–1900) became interested in Native-American cultures; he published his first scientific paper at age seventeen.[82] He became a curator of the Smithsonian Institution's Bureau of Ethnology two years later under the direction of John Wesley Powell. In 1895, Cushing led the Pepper-Hearst Expedition to Key Marco in Florida under the auspices of the University Museum.[83]

Earlier that year, W. D. Collier, a resident store owner, and Colonel C. D. Durnford, a British military visitor on a tarpon fishing vacation, made the first archaeological finds at Key Marco. Durnford, an amateur archaeologist, learned that Collier had discovered fragments of rope and wooden objects when "getting 'muck' for fertilizing purposes."[84] Durnford visited Collier and recovered artifacts from his mangrove muck. Later, while returning to England by way of Philadelphia, Durnford called on the curator of archaeology

---

[81] Cushing, "Exploration of Ancient Key Dwellers' Remains on the Gulf Coast of Florida," 329–448. References in *Florida Explored* (this book) are citations of this article. Reprinted in 1897 with title changes, with super-titles of "Pepper-Hearst Expedition" and "A Preliminary Report On The" *Exploration of Ancient Key-Dweller Remains on the Gulf Coast of Florida.* These two references, 1896 and 1897, with grammatical variations on the title, are generally referenced in the literature before the publication in 2000 of Frank Hamilton Cushing, *Exploration of Ancient Key-Dweller Remains on the Gulf Coast of Florida* (Gainesville: University of Florida Press, 2000). This 2000 edition is a reprint of Cushing's 1897 reprint. It has an excellent foreword by editor Jerald T. Milanich and an introduction by Randolph J. Widmer.

[82] Powell, "In Memoriam: Frank Hamilton Cushing," 354–80; Gilliland, *Key Marco's Buried Treasure,* 25–43; see Widmer's introduction to Cushing, *Exploration of Ancient Key-Dweller Remains on the Gulf Coast of Florida,* ix–xxii. See also Phyllis E. Kolianos and Brent R. Weisman, eds., *The Florida Journals of Frank Hamilton Cushing* (Gainesville: University of Florida Press, 2005); Phyllis E. Kolianos and Brent R. Weisman, eds., *The Lost Florida Manuscript of Frank Hamilton Cushing* (Gainesville: University of Florida Press, 2005); Jeffrey M. Mitchem, "A Flawed Genius of Florida Archaeology," review of Kolianos and Weisman, *The Florida Journals.*

[83] Widmer, in *Exploration of Ancient Key-Dweller,* ix–x, has explained the confusion of names (Marco Island, Key Marco, Marco Village, etc., over time). Here, the term "Key Marco" will generally be used except in quotations.

[84] Durnford, "The Discovery of Aboriginal Rope," 1033.

at the University Museum to discuss his artifacts. In an often-told story, Cushing's ill health had brought him to Philadelphia a day earlier to meet with his physician, Dr. William Pepper, at the University Museum.[85] Colonel Durnford met Cushing by accident at the museum and showed him some of his Marco finds. Durnford later discussed the artifacts with Dr. Pepper and deposited some at the museum.[86] Cushing and Pepper became very interested in the Key Marco artifacts. Several weeks later in April, Pepper met with John Powell at the Smithsonian in Washington, DC, to discuss Cushing's health needs. Powell finished the story:

> His [Cushing's] health gave way...and he was compelled to return to the East for medical advice.... [He] finally consulted Dr Pepper, of Philadel-phia, under whose treatment he partially recovered. Then Dr Pepper came to Washington for a consultation with me about the future course of life which Cushing should pursue. He recommended that he should go to Florida for a few months, at least, and perhaps for a year. Dr Pepper offered to raise the money to defray the expenses of an exploring expedi-tion in the everglades and keys of the extreme southern portion of that peninsula. The expense of the expedition was borne in part by Dr Pepper himself, but chiefly by Mrs Phoebe Hearst.[87]

Powell agreed with Pepper's recommendation about Cushing and the expe-dition to Florida.

By the time Durnford returned to England and published on his Key Marco artifacts in the *American Naturalist* in November 1895, Cushing was preparing to leave Philadelphia for Florida to lead the Pepper-Hearst Expedi-tion to Key Marco in search of artifacts.[88] Cushing had in fact traveled to Florida in late April, completed his "First Reconnaissance" of several sites (including Key Marco), and was back in Philadelphia by July 1895.[89] His

---

[85] Cushing, "Exploration," 329–31, 433–48; Gilliland, *Material Culture,* 3–4; Gilliland, *Key Marco's Buried Treasure,* 44–45; Powell, "In Memoriam: Frank Hamilton Cushing," 354–80.

[86] Milanich notes in Widmer, *Exploration of Ancient Key-Dweller,* vii, that Cushing's artifacts are at the University Museum, the Smithsonian, and the FLMNH.

[87] Powell, "In Memoriam: Frank Hamilton Cushing," 355–56.

[88] Durnford, "The Discovery of Aboriginal Rope"; Gilliland, *Key Marco's Buried Treasure,* 6–7. Mrs. Phoebe Hearst, mother of William Randolph Hearst, the news magnate, was a major financial sponsor of the expedition. Other sponsors, friends, and benefactors of the expedition are listed by Gilliland. Davis has pointed out that Phoebe Hearst was the mother, not the wife, of William Randolph (*The Gulf,* 22).

[89] Cushing mentions Willcox and his artifacts that were given to the University

Florida report and artifacts further stimulated Dr. Pepper and his associates to plan an extended expedition with Cushing as the leader. By the end of November, all letters of agreement had been signed by the university and the Smithsonian. On 6 December, Cushing and his wife departed for Jacksonville, where they met other expedition members and traveled to Tarpon Springs, their departure point for Key Marco.[90] When they arrived in mid-December, they received disappointing news about delays for the *Silver Spray*, which Philadelphian and Florida developer Hamilton Disston (see page 169) had made available for the expedition.

While waiting for the *Silver Spray*, Cushing and his crew lost no time in excavating an ancient burial mound (Safford Mound) with the cooperation of the owners in "this pretty little winter resort...on a picturesque bayou...abounding on every hand in prehistoric remains."[91] In a letter to Pepper, Cushing speculated about the mounds in Tarpon Springs and quoted Bartram's descriptions of "Great pillars of wood...commanded the entrance ways to these great houses."[92] Articles in newspapers by various reporters who visited Cushing's archeological digs in Tarpon Springs kept the public informed about the group's progress.[93] Cushing's letters and manuscripts carefully documented the expedition's delay and the activities in Tarpon Springs.[94]

Museum. On reconnaissance, on the way to Marco at stops at Mound Key or Johnson's Key to examine mounds, which were briefly observed by Willcox, Cushing comments, "I have carefully examined an interesting series of both kinds [shell and coarse pottery] gathered here by...Mr. Joseph Wilcox, which offer even better evidence of this, and I am happy to say preserved in the University museum" (Cushing, "Exploration," 448; see also Gilliland, *Key Marco's Buried Treasure*, 55–59).

[90] Gilliland, *Key Marco's Buried Treasure*, 55–59. Mrs. Cushing (Emily Magill Cushing), preparator; Wells M. Sawyer, an artist in the employ of the U.S. Geological Survey; Irving Sayford of Harrisburg, Pennsylvania, field secretary; Carl F. W. Bergmann, curator trained at the University Museum. They were joined in Tarpon Springs by a ship's captain and crew along with George Gause, chief excavator, and several general workers.

[91] Cushing to Pepper, 26 May 1895, from Tarpon Springs in Gilliland, *Key Marco's Buried Treasure*, 60.

[92] Gilliland, *Key Marco's Buried Treasure*, 61; Cushing, *Exploration*, 100.

[93] The reporters did not accompany the expedition further than Tarpon Springs. The media, with Hearst newspapers well represented, were eager for research "scoops." Cushing, *Exploration*, 100, details the media coverage.

[94] Cushing, *Exploration*, 60–68. Cushing's final unpublished manuscript with his observations was lost after his death and was rediscovered in the early 2000s. Cushing's detailed and comprehensive records are rich with archeological data of southwest Florida.

On 23 February 1896, a poet's toast, "Oh, Captain Cushing's in command/The Silver Spray's afloat," by the expedition's artist, Wells Sawyer, marked the start of the three-day voyage from Tarpon Springs to Marco, with a stop at Pine Island for mail, fuel, and water, and reconnaissance along the way.[95] As soon as he arrived on Key Marco, Cushing arranged with "Captain Collier" that the crews would turn over their muck to him in exchange for the artifacts they collected in a designated triangular area called "Court of the Pile Dwellers." They began working without delay.

Excavating and preparing the collections for transport occupied the expedition members for two months. Many details about the excavations are included in letters and notes written by expedition members—Wells Sawyer, George Gause, and Cushing—that have been researched and edited by Gilliland.[96] By 10 May, the expedition members were back in Tarpon Springs, and Cushing wrote to Pepper that he had shipped eleven barrels and thirty boxes of Tarpon Springs specimens and eleven barrels and fifty-nine boxes of Key Marco specimens to Washington. Cushing expected to arrive there himself on 13 May and hoped that Pepper would join him for a press conference on 14 May.[97] While in Washington, Cushing was beset by ill health as he labored to write up his results and prepare for an invited presentation to the members of the American Philosophical Society in Philadelphia in November. There was also distracting media frenzy over his discoveries, which was sometimes abetted by allegations that several artifacts had been purposely altered after their collection.[98]

On 6 November 1896, at the American Philosophical Society (APS) meeting, Cushing presented mind-boggling and eye-popping details about his two trips to Florida. He gave descriptions of the excavations, the finds, and his ethnographic interpretations, supplemented by sixty-seven lantern slide projections and displayed objects.[99] There was discussion led by two APS

See Kolianos and Weisman, *The Lost Florida Manuscript* and *The Florida Journals*.

[95] Gilliland, *Key Marco's Buried Treasure*, 68. Well Sawyer's thirty-six-line poem is a fascinating ode to the ancient people's culture that they will explore and "Will open to the seer," (i.e., Cushing).

[96] Ibid., 60–95. In chapter 8, "Digging up the Past," Gilliland chronicles the excavation through manuscript fragments of Sawyer, Gause, and Cushing (*Key Marco's Buried Treasure*, 60–95).

[97] Ibid., 94.

[98] Ibid., 96–112; Fowler and Wilcox, *Philadelphia and the Development of Americanist Archaeology*, 88–112.

[99] Barrels and boxes of Cushing's collections, the subject of a dispute between the

members, Daniel Brinton (Academy of Natural Sciences) and Frederic Putnam (Peabody Museum), who had reviewed a copy of Cushing's manuscript. Brinton began with lengthy comments of congratulations: "After the brilliant demonstration of discoveries in an entirely new field of American archaeology...."[100] Putnam followed and said, "It is seldom that an archaeologist has the opportunity of examining a collection of objects of so much scientific importance as those on exhibition here tonight." He stated, "The question we are all asking is, where did these people originate?"[101] After critical comments about differences in interpreting the data, a lively back-and-forth discussion ensued with Brinton and Putnam often congratulating Cushing on his discoveries.[102] A general (unrecorded) discussion followed.

Cushing described "the specimens and illustrations displayed in the Hall of the Society."[103] Included were beautifully carved wooden bowls, mortars and pestles, spears and atlatls (spear throwing-sticks); the detailed wooden art forms were unsurpassed and in excellent condition. Artifacts of fishing technology had been well preserved in the Key Marco muck. The ceremonial wooden tablets and plaques, carved animal heads, and painted masks were incredible to behold. Wells Sawyer commented, "Since the collection is practically unique it is almost impossible to cite a single thing without doing the rest an injustice but amongst the most noteworthy examples are the 'Statuette of the Lion or Panther-God' and 'Crested mythic-bird or bird-god' painted on wooden panel."[104]

William Bartram was referenced as Cushing described a Key Marco artifact, a jewel box lid or bottom with a "horned crocodile."[105] "It is of interest to note that the horned crocodile (or alligator) was seen by William Bartram, painted on the façades of the great sacred houses of the Creek Indians," Cushing wrote, "when he visited their chief towns more than a hundred years

---

Smithsonian and the University Museum for years following Cushing's death, were divided and are now at the two museums with some holdings transferred and more recent finds from Key Marco at the FLMNH in Gainesville (Milanich notes in Widmer, *Exploration of Ancient Key-Dweller*, vii).

[100] Brinton, "Discussion," 433–38.
[101] Putnam, "Discussion," 438–39.
[102] Cushing et al., "Discussion," 439–45.
[103] Ibid., 445.
[104] Ibid., 73.
[105] Ibid., 428.

ago."[106] When speculating during his presentation about the early mound inhabitants, Cushing praised Bartram as a leader in ethnography, "William Bartram...indeed, the source of more definite information regarding the Southern Indians than those of any other one of our earlier authorities on the natives of northerly Florida and contiguous states."[107]

Frank Cushing's discoveries electrified the international anthropological and archaeological community and influenced Clarence Moore's ongoing work in Florida. Unlike Moore's, which was linked directly to the Academy, Cushing's exploration and collections were only indirectly tied to the Academy through members John Wesley Powell of the Smithsonian, along with William Pepper, Daniel Brinton, and Joseph Leidy, who had roles in the University Museum.[108]

Cushing's presentations, publicity, and comments by his colleagues became increasingly of interest to Clarence Moore during his study interlude away from the Florida coast and focus on other Southern states.[109] Cushing's

---

[106] Ibid., 428.

[107] Ibid., 381.

[108] John Wesley Powell (ANSP correspondent, Washington, 1872) was the director of the Bureau of Ethnology and Anthropology of the Smithsonian at this time and had often collaborated with Joseph Willcox and Joseph Leidy on Florida paleontology studies, as discussed in ch. 11. Cushing reported to him. William Pepper, Jr. (August 1843–1898), a physician researcher and a professor and leader in medical education, became a longtime provost of the University of Pennsylvania. (He did not use "Jr." in his name.) He was elected an Academy member (1837), later became vice-president of the American Philosophical Society, and formed the University of Pennsylvania Archaeological Association (1889) together with Joseph Leidy, Joseph Willcox, and others. Pepper was attracted to Indian ethnography and archaeology and also was the head of the Anthropology Department at the university; the association between Leidy and Pepper was the catalyst and foundation for the development of the University Museum in 1887 during a period when Pepper was university provost and Joseph Leidy was president of the ANSP. They had earlier tried to add officially the Academy to the university's portfolio as its research museum.

[109] Moore's interim activities between his northern Florida and west coast of Florida studies are covered in Moore, *The Georgia and South Carolina Coastal Expeditions of Clarence Bloomfield Moore*, ed. Lewis Larson (Tuscaloosa: The University of Alabama Press, 1998); Phyllis A. Morse and Dan F. Morse, eds., and Clarence Bloomfield Moore, *The Lower Mississippi Valley Expeditions of Clarence Bloomfield Moore* (Tuscaloosa: The University of Alabama Press, 1998); Craig T. Sheldon Jr., ed., and Clarence Bloomfield Moore, *The Southern and Central Alabama Expeditions of Clarence Bloomfield Moore* (Tuscaloosa: The University of Alabama Press, 2001).

discoveries and the artifacts that Cushing gave to Moore whetted his appetite for further investigation of Florida's southern Gulf Coast.

Moore Returns to Florida

From 1900 until 1907, Moore's *Gopher* traveled Florida from the Gulf Coast—from the Keys, to the panhandle, northwest coast, to Alabama. He also spent several field seasons at interior locations off Crystal River. Beginning in 1907, Moore's focus switched to other southeastern states, but he returned to Florida in 1918 and continued his archaeological work into the 1920s on Florida's northwest Gulf coast and its rivers and the southwest coast.[110]

In 1900, Moore began reconnaissance of southwestern Gulf Coast sites "to determine whether or not a series of seasons could profitably be spent by us in making a thorough examination of what might prove to be so rich a field."[111] He started north of St. Petersburg and explored the Tampa Bay area and southward to Watson's place on the Chatham River in the Ten Thousand Islands. With his crews, Moore excavated many sites, including Cushing's at Demorey Key, Mound Key, and Key Marco. With W. D. Collier, Moore investigated the area of Marco "explored by Mr. Cushing. Absolutely nothing rewarded our efforts." Their work was rewarded, however, by gifts from others who had collected in Cushing's excavation area. At other locations on Key Marco, Moore and his team had better excavation results, which they supplemented with artifacts collected by the local people.[112] Moore's successful reconnaissance expedition was the beginning of comprehensive and intensive expeditions to Key Marco and the Ten Thousand Islands, as detailed by Mitchem in *The West and Central Florida Expeditions of Clarence Bloomfield Moore*.[113]

By this time, Moore had established a winter residence in St. Petersburg, Florida, on Tampa Bay as the base camp for his explorations in the late fall, winter, and early spring. Back home in Philadelphia, he began to write reports on his research in late spring that were published by the Academy of Natural Sciences in oversized, well-illustrated volumes. In Moore's absence, his steamboat pilot, Captain J. S. Raybon, maintained the *Gopher* in St. Petersburg

---

[110] See also David S. Brose and, Nancy Marie White, eds. *The Northwest Florida Expeditions of Clarence Bloomfield Moore* (Tuscaloosa: University of Alabama Press, 1999).

[111] Mitchem, *West and Central Florida Expeditions,* 161; Moore, "Certain Antiquities of the Florida West Coast," 351.

[112] Moore, "Certain Antiquities of the Florida West Coast," 376, figs. 20, 21.

[113] Mitchem, *The West and Central Florida*, 1–48.

and explored waterways to find sites and identify landowners from whom Moore could secure permission to dig in their shell middens and sand burial mounds the following winter.

During the 1900 season, Moore visited nearby Crystal River and then explored further along the northern Gulf Coast and the Panhandle of Florida. He began at the Bear Point site on Perdido Bay, near Florida's boundary with Alabama. He explored near Pensacola in Escambia County and then traveled eastward to a point just west of St. Andrews Bay, about 115 miles.

At Bear Point, Moore found black Pensacola wares decorated with Southern cult motifs associated with sixteenth-century Spanish materials. Later, at Camp Walton (Fort Walton), he found layered artifacts from different time periods and burial urns with perforated bottoms.

In 1902, Moore returned to St. Andrews Bay and continued exploring eastward around the Apalachicola delta, east to Cedar Key, and southward to St. Petersburg and Tampa Bay. He excavated some sixty-eight mounds in the panhandle area but found far fewer large mounds with grave goods from Cedar Key southward on the coast. Moore's second-year report "was a real pioneering venture, opening new vistas on different and distinctive ceramic traditions for anthropologists to study."[114]

After an absence of almost a decade while exploring other navigable rivers, Moore revisited the coast of northwest Florida—where dredging operations had now made travel possible for the *Gopher*—to fill gaps in his early finds and data.[115] The mounds at Crystal River continued to attract him, and Moore was the first to excavate the Crystal River mounds near the Gulf between Tampa Bay and Cedar Key. Moore's description of "Mound Near the Shell-Heap, Crystal River, Citrus County" begins this way: "In full view of the river, about 4.5 miles from the mouth, on the left-hand side going up, is a great symmetrical shell-heap...."[116]

Although the shell-heap and its immediate surroundings were famous (Spanish Mound), the sand mound and its embankments were unknown to the property owner and inhabitants of the village of Crystal River. The sand mound was an archaeological treasure trove that had never been dug, and it gave no evidence of any European provenance when Moore excavated it. For

---

[114] Mitchem, *The West and Central Florida*, 127–358; Brose and White, *Northeast Expeditions*, 6.

[115] Moore, "The Northwestern Florida Coast Revisited," 514–80; Brose and White, *Northeast Expeditions*, 7.

[116] Moore, "Certain Aboriginal Remains," 379.

three seasons (1903, 1906, and 1918), Moore focused on excavating where there "were about 225 burials."[117] He classified the skeletal remains in five distinct postures, along with lone skulls and infants; "Artifacts were very numerous in the elevation and in the mound, though those from the mound proper were of much higher grade." Earthenware, metal, stone, wood, bone, and shells were fashioned into vessels, pipes, gorgets, beads, arrowheads, lance points, and knives. "The most striking object in earthenware...a cylindrical vessel of excellent ware, bearing an incised design showing part of the human hand...There was also found a part of a vessel, showing a human face." These are representative artifacts among hundreds that were photographed, collected, and included in Moore's publications.

Moore discovered that "There was no general deposit" of the artifacts with burials, and he concluded, "it was evident that we were no longer among the mounds of the northwest Florida coast." "The finding of solid copper...in the Crystal river mound came in the nature of a surprise."[118] Crystal River would forever be a famous site.[119]

Moore continued working along the Gulf Coast with inland expeditions until he died after a short illness in March 1936, near his base of operations in St. Petersburg, Florida.[120] The breadth and depth of Moore's archaeological exploration in Florida can be appreciated because of the work of many scholars and also the University of Alabama Press's *Expeditions of Clarence Bloomfield Moore* publications. From Moore's St. Johns River excavations at the Mount Royal site, where Bartram once camped, to the Crystal River sites: "There is still much to learn."[121]

Moore and others—Brinton, Wyman, Willcox, Heilprin, Leidy, Cushing—provided extensive collections and publications: a legacy for Florida and Americanist anthropology in Bartram's tracks.

---

[117] Ibid., 382.
[118] Ibid., 438.
[119] Milanich, *Famous Florida Sites*, 14.
[120] Aten and Milanich, *"Clarence Bloomfield Moore,"* 132–33.
[121] Milanich, *Famous Florida Sites*, 2.

PART 3

INTRODUCTION TO PART 3

This prologue of Florida history[1] and natural history[2] sets the stage for chapters 13 and 14.

Florida History

In 1900, Florida had the lowest population density of any state east of the Mississippi River. Most Floridians lived within 50 miles of the Georgia border. Despite being a fifty-year-old state, sparsely settled and unexplored, Florida still resembled a frontier territory. Seasonal tourists visited the St. Johns River area and other accessible regions around several ports on the Atlantic and Gulf coasts. The Florida economy was based on agriculture, phosphate mining, timber, and fishing. Ships exported Florida cattle to Cuba and imported tobacco for the Tampa cigar industry. Within a hundred years, Florida would be the nation's fourth-largest state. The population grew from 528,542 in 1900 to more than 15,982,824 by 2000; tourism and the space industry became additional economic engines.[3]

The population boom was sparked when Philadelphia industrialist Hamilton Disston (page 124) purchased four million acres of Florida land from south of Orlando into the Everglades toward Miami in 1881 and opened it up for commercial and residential real estate development. The United States' Panama Canal project in the steaming jungles of Central America provided engineering and medical techniques that aided developers in clearing Florida land and controlling malaria and yellow fever. As the Everglades were "reclaimed" and canals were built to drain water from the wetlands, agriculture and towns quickly followed.

Henry Flagler, an industrialist and a principal of Standard Oil, was a key

---

[1] Gannon, *A Short History of Florida*, 67ff. See for further reading Mormino, Gary R., *Land of Sunshine, State of Dreams: A Social History of Modern Florida* (Gainesville: University Press of Florida, 2006); Charlton W. Tebeau, III, "Historical Writing on Twentieth Century Florida," *The Florida Historical Quarterly* 37/2 (1958): 174–77.

[2] Peck and Stroud, *A Glorious Enterprise*, 200ff; Pauly, *Biologists and the Promise of American Life*, 126–44, 239–44; Benson, "From Museum Research to Laboratory Research," 49–83; see also Benson, *The Expansion of American Biology* (Rutgers University Press, 1991).

[3] Florida Census data, www.bebr.ufl.edu/sites/default/files/Research%20Reports/FloridaPop2005_0.pdf (accessed 1 January 2019).

figure in the development of the Atlantic coast of Florida and founder of what became the Florida East Coast Railway. Flagler extended his railroad south from St. Augustine and reached Miami in 1896. Though its construction was twice interrupted by hurricanes, the railroad eventually reached Key West in 1912. The railroads became key in Florida's economic growth and development through movement of agricultural products to northern markets and bringing northern tourists to Florida. At the end of that decade, World War I created new national interest in Florida as military flight schools took advantage of the flat terrain and consistently good weather. Key West was also the site of a major submarine base. The "great land boom" of the 1920s changed Florida from a mysterious frontier to a land speculator's paradise. Investors designed and sold entire communities, such as Coral Gables and Boca Raton. Waves of tourists, aspiring residents, and investors swarmed into Florida. As the real estate bubble grew, human activity increased and threatened Florida's diverse ecosystems.

In 1926 and 1928, disaster struck Florida. Major hurricanes hit south Florida, killing hundreds of people and leaving thousands homeless near overflowing Lake Okeechobee. The Great Depression of the United States had started in Florida. The speculative real estate boom faltered and went bust as banks failed. As the Depression expanded, Florida, like many states, was sustained by federal relief money under President Franklin D. Roosevelt's administration and programs, including the Federal Writers' Project (FWP); the Florida archeology program under the Civil Works Administration (CWA), supervised by Matthew Sterling of the Smithsonian; and the Civilian Conservation Corps (CCC).[4] Roosevelt's New Deal stabilized Florida's economy and developed programs in Florida history, archeology, and nature conservation.

Tourism, which had taken various guises since Ponce de Leon's landing, had been vital to the state's economy. During the late nineteenth century, Florida became a popular tourist destination as railroad traffic expanded and hotels and entertainment offered desired amenities. The major tourist attractions were natural, including trips on the St. Johns River leading to Silver Springs and its famous glass-bottom boat rides, as well as the "Fountain of

---

[4] Records of the Works Progress Administration (WPA), www.archives.gov/research/guide-fed-records/groups/069.html#69.5.5 (accessed 18 September 2018); Bennett, *The Legacy*, 17–20. The FWP was organized in 1935 to employ writers, editors, historians, researchers, art critics, archaeologists, geologists, and map draftsmen. The CCC provided work camps for young men who did pioneer work in eight Florida parks, including a preserve of the Torreya Tree on the Apalachicola River.

Youth" and other historical attractions in St. Augustine. Artificial attractions incorporated living things, such as the Alligator Farm in St. Augustine and other displays of reptiles and birds. In the 1920s, tourist attractions for "tin-can tourists" and others dotted the new U.S. highways from the north, which converged near Ocala and fanned out southwest toward Tampa and Sarasota and southeast near Lake Okeechobee and Miami. Attractions began to be created by incorporating natural and theatrical or artificial features and many survived or were started after the Depression, for example, Bok Tower, Marineland, Cypress Gardens, Sunken Gardens, and Weeki Wachee Springs.[5]

In 1940, Florida's population of 1,897,414 made it the least populated state in the Southeast. Growth occurred during World War II as military bases flourished and agricultural processing machinery and plants expanded, along with aviation and mining operations. By the 1950s, air conditioning and mosquito control made Florida enjoyable and workable during the long summer season; the interstate highway system encouraged emigration from the north. Key West, which was almost bankrupt in the 1930s, saw its population triple. The Atlantic and Gulf coastal towns, which were transformed during World War II as new military recruits arrived to train (and often were stationed in luxury beach hotels because of the severe housing shortage), began to surge when many veterans returned as residents after the war.

Because of its geography and flat terrain, Florida was chosen as a test site for the country's nascent missile program in 1949. Patrick Air Force Base and the Cape Canaveral launch site were established as the 1950s progressed. By the early 1960s, the Space Race had begun; programs were expanded, and communities around Cape Canaveral boomed. A major center of aerospace industries grew around the renamed Kennedy Space Center, creating Florida's "Space Coast." To date, all manned U.S. orbital spaceflights have been launched from Florida.

In 1971, after years of land purchases and development, Walt Disney opened Disney World in an area first developed by Hamilton Disston (see page 124) near Orlando, Florida. It became Florida's best-known international attraction, drawing millions of visitors a year and spinning off other attractions and large tracts of commercial and residential developments. The annual visitor count often exceeds the residential population of Florida. In

---

[5] In 1924, Silver Springs opened a major attraction, and the golden age of roadside attractions began. In 1929, Bok Tower opened in Lake Wales; Cypress Gardens followed in Winter Haven in 1936. Marineland opened as a tourist attraction and movie studio in 1938 on U.S. 1 near St. Augustine.

the first theme park, the Magic Kingdom, nature was recreated as imagined by Disney. In 1998, the fourth theme park, the Animal Kingdom, was developed entirely around the natural environment and animal conservation principles.

In contrast, 161 Florida state parks, which encompass more than 700,000 acres, were also created. National parks include the Everglades National Park along with other National Historic Landmark sites and wilderness preserves in Florida.[6] Many were started by the CCC and served as a starting point for restoring and conserving Florida's natural resources. The conservation efforts and writings of Helen Cruickshank, Marjorie Kinnan Rawlings, Stetson Kennedy, Marjory Stoneman Douglas, Archie and Marjorie Carr, among others, along with the parks, wildlife preserves, the Florida Birding Trail, and the Bartram Heritage Trail, contributed to Florida's growth in both history- and eco-tourism.

Florida evolved from the poorest and most isolated part of the South to a multicultural society, a winter playground for millions, and a tourist mecca for the world. In 2010, the population was 18.84 million and still increasing. During this period of growth, the natural environment was explored and detailed as the challenges of ecology and conservation in Florida came into focus. The race to understand and mitigate the negative impacts of growth on Florida's natural ecosystems began.

Natural History

During the last half of the nineteenth century, American biology was influenced by European developments in cell biology, physiological chemistry, and Darwinian evolution. New methodologies in microscopy and chemistry and novel conceptual frameworks affected the description, naming, and classification of living things and fossils. Ideas about evolution stimulated research interest in the habitats, populations, and geographic distribution of plants and animals and their paleontologic origins. Because of the plethora of new plants and animals and terra incognita in Florida, as well as their accessibility, natural history discoveries flourished during the twentieth century.

Explorers from Philadelphia continued to follow in William Bartram's

---

[6] See www.floridastateparks.org. National parks include Everglades National Park (est. 1947), Biscayne National Park (1980), Dry Tortugas National Park (1992, but Fort Jefferson was recognized as a national monument in 1935), Big Cypress National Preserve (1974), Canaveral National Seashore (1975), and the Timucuan Historic and Archeological Preserve (1988; expanded 1999).

tracks with interest in Florida natural history, often studying how it was affected by the growth of the state. The development of Florida institutions with professionals involved in natural history education and research began late in the nineteenth century and continued as the state's population and economy grew. Several state-supported institutions—the Florida Geological Survey (1907),[7] the Florida State College for Women in Tallahassee (1905),[8] and the University of Florida for Men in Gainesville (1905)—supported staff and faculty who researched and published on Florida geology, botany, and zoology. As the collections of specimens for teaching and research grew, the Florida State Museum was founded at the University of Florida (1917) to accommodate them.[9] Key figures at the Geological Survey included Elias

---

[7] The FGS began in 1907, when legislation created an autonomous permanent geological survey and an office of State Geologist. The law remained unchanged until 1933, when the FGS was placed under the newly formed State Board of Conservation. A major reorganization of the state's government in 1971 placed the FGS in the new Department of Natural Resources. In 1993, the FGS became a bureau of the Department of Environmental Protection, which was created by combining the Departments of Natural Resources and Environmental Regulation. During its first fifty years, two individuals dominated the agency and contributed to its success: state geologists Dr. Elias Sellards (1907–1919) and Dr. Herman Gunter (1919–1958).

[8] Two state-funded seminaries were established in 1851 by the Florida Legislature: the West Florida Seminary in Tallahassee and the East Florida Seminary in Ocala, which were at that time the largest population centers for the young state. Over time, other state-supported institutions were established. In 1905, the Florida Legislators passed a law that reorganized higher education and created the University of Florida for men in Gainesville and the Florida State College for Women in Tallahassee. Both became co-educational in 1947 as the University of Florida and Florida State University.

[9] The FLMNH, formerly known as the Florida State Museum, began in 1891 in Lake City when a professor of natural science at Florida Agriculture College (later the University of Florida) purchased research collections of minerals, fossils, and human anatomy models as aids for teaching biology and agricultural sciences. The initial collections grew steadily with donations from other professors. When the Florida Agriculture College was abolished in 1905, the museum became a part of the newly created University of Florida and was moved to Gainesville in 1906. The collections expanded in size and scope and were put on display. In 1914, Thompson H. Van Hyning was appointed the museum's first director and remained until the late 1940s; the legislature designated the facility as the Florida State Museum at the University of Florida in 1917. Museum research and education experienced explosive growth that continues today; curators, staff, collections, and new facilities were added. In 1987, the name was changed to the Florida Museum of Natural History. It is the largest natural history museum in the Southeast and one of the leading university and independent natural

Sellards, chief geologist, and associate Roland Harper. Thompson van Hyning, museum director, worked with curators and staff at many regional and national museums on Florida-related projects. Major research and collections related to Florida increased at Florida State University (formerly the Florida State College for Women) and the Florida State Museum (associated with the University of Florida) in 1947 during major post-World War II expansions. Several independent colleges also developed significant programs in the natural sciences; Rollins College became the home of Florida's first major shell museum.[10]

Clarence Moore and Henry Pilsbry

Chapter 12 detailed Clarence Moore's Florida studies in the 1890s, which prompted heightened interest in anthropology and a boom in the Academy's growth of collections. At the Academy of Natural Sciences in Philadelphia, many changes occurred following the institution's celebration of its centennial year in 1912.[11] From the late 1930s into the 1950s, the Academy's managing director, Charles Cadwalader, and its staff led the institution into new ventures in worldwide exploration and exhibition while maintaining a continuing interest in Florida exploration, which continued as will be described in the last two chapters of this book.[12]

Chapter 13 chronicles America's foremost conchologist/malacologist, Henry Pilsbry, who extended Clarence Moore's interests and research to include many areas in Florida that had been earlier explored by William Bartram, Thomas Say, and Titian Peale.[13] Pilsbry became a winter resident of Florida in the 1930s and continued his Florida work until his death in 1957. During that period, he influenced the science of Florida malacology through his own publications and by mentoring a generation of Florida malacologists, including Tucker Abbott. As a Florida resident and former Academy curator,

---

history museums in the United States (www.flmnh.ufl.edu).

[10] Founded in 1883, Southern College in Orlando was eventually relocated to Lakeland and was renamed Florida Southern College in 1935. Rollins College first opened in 1885 and ended up in Winter Park. They were institutional survivors among many religious denominational colleges founded during this time in various locations. See Hunt and Carper, *Religious Higher Education in the United States*.

[11] Peck and Stroud, *A Glorious Enterprise*, ch. 10, "Early Man at the Academy."

[12] Peck and Stroud, *A Glorious Enterprise*, ch. 13, "Dioramas Defy the Great Depression;" ch. 14, "Science and Celebrity: The Academy Goes Hollywood."

[13] "Conchology," the study of mollusk shells, was in early general usage. "Malacology" was later used and is the more general science of mollusks, some which do not have shells, e.g., slugs, octopus, etc.

Abbott took a leadership role in rescuing "orphaned" (unwanted, un-curated, and abandoned) shell collections of research and education quality for future generations and was the founding director of the Bailey-Mathews Shell Museum in Sanibel, Florida. Abbott also ensured the continuation at the Shell Museum of *The Nautilus,* which was first nourished by Pilsbry at the Academy of Natural Sciences. Chapter 13 also recounts the study of Florida fishes, which was initiated by William Bartram and continued into the twentieth century by Henry Fowler, Ernest Hemingway, Charles Chaplin, and others associated with the Academy.

Chapter 14 tells the story of the historical quest by Francis Harper and others at the Academy to detail Bartram's natural history tracks in Florida. Their pioneering and comprehensive study about William Bartram in Georgia and Florida began with botanical research at the Academy by Arthur Leeds and Francis Harper, with the later involvement of Francis's brother, Roland. Francis Harper's classic works were the beginning points for many future studies and quests in Bartram's historical tracks leading to the involvement of the Academy's Robert Peck in development of the Bartram Heritage Trail in states traveled by William Bartram.

CHAPTER 13

INTO THE TWENTIETH CENTURY...WITH PILSBRY, FOWLER, AND OTHERS

"A fine example for young men is that of our former librarian, H. A. Pilsbry. Working at his trade of printer he put in his spare moments in the study and classification of shells, and is now professor of conchology in the Philadelphia Academy of Science. He thirsted for knowledge, searched for the spring, and drank deep."[1]
—President James Thompson, Davenport Academy of Natural Sciences

"For Ernest Hemingway, author and angler of great game fishes, in appreciation of his assistance in my work on Gulf Stream fishes."[2]
—Henry W. Fowler

While exploring Florida, Clarence Moore collaborated with many curators at the Academy of Natural Sciences, including Henry Pilsbry and Henry Fowler. Moore provided encouragement and field support for their Florida studies, and these versatile young men assisted in his anthropological and zoological research. Pilsbry's expertise in malacology and Fowler's multifaceted talents and skills in ornithology, herpetology, and ichthyology were invaluable to Moore, whose publications are replete with acknowledgments of Fowler and Pilsbry's Florida fieldwork and for their curatorial contributions to his zoological collections. Pilsbry and Fowler went on to develop premier departments of malacology and ichthyology, respectively, at the Academy and attracted talented friends and curators who also explored Florida.[3]

---

[1] *Proceedings of the Davenport Academy of Sciences* 6 (1891): 298–99. After appropriate graceful tributes, President Thompson began his inaugural address with the following: "And let me say a word to the young men of the city, many of whom are drifting into idleness and crime, just for want of a purpose: Remember we do not live by bread alone. The mind needs food as well as the body. What a chance is yours to come here and learn of Nature and her ways. Here are books and specimens and every inducement to go out and investigate for yourselves the wonders of the world we live in." He then cited Pilsbry as a model to follow.

[2] Fowler, "Description of a New *Scorpaenoid* Fish," 41–43. The fish was named in honor of Ernest Hemingway.

[3] Peck and Stroud, *A Glorious Enterprise*, 392, 400. The malacology department is

Conchology and Malacology

While following Bartram's path in Florida from 1817–1819, Thomas Say led the way for a generation of collectors of Florida's land, freshwater, and coastal mollusks. His early studies and publications, including *American Conchology*, blazed the trail for American conchologists, who primarily studied and collected shells.[4] Conchology further evolved during the late nineteenth century into malacology, the more general science of mollusks, which includes the study of the soft body parts of shelled mollusks like conchs, snails, and clams, as well as other mollusks without shells, including slugs, octopus, and squid.

Say's successors at the Academy were Isaac Lea and Timothy Abbott Conrad.[5] Lea's pioneer work was the basis for the subsequent systematic examination of freshwater mussels. Through his studies on fossil shells, Conrad established the foundation of American tertiary geology and invertebrate paleontology and opened many new avenues for mollusk research. Interest in contemporary mollusks was rekindled through the efforts of Academy correspondent Dr. Amos Binney and young Dr. Joseph Leidy's unique contribution to Binney's *Terrestrial Air-breathing Mollusks of the United States*, which was published in 1851.[6] It was the first American work to include the mor-

---

the oldest in the country and the second largest catalogued one in the world. The department currently has more than 430,000 catalogued lots containing about 10 million specimens, including 30,000–35,000 lots preserved in ethanol. Type specimens of more than four hundred authors are represented in over 12,000 type lots; specimens exist from all over the world. Its greatest strengths are in shallow-water marine mollusks from the tropical Indo-Pacific and the Western Atlantic and worldwide freshwater and land mollusks. The ichthyology department currently houses 1.2 million cataloged specimens representing an estimated 11,000 species and 2,797 primary types. The collection is taxonomically diverse and especially strong among eels, characiforms, and catfish. Its geographic scope is worldwide. Strengths include freshwater species of North and South America and marine species of the Bahamas, Western Atlantic, and Indian Oceans.

[4] "Conchology," the study of mollusk shells, was in early general usage. "Malacology" was later used and is the more general science of mollusks.

[5] Isaac Lea was a partner in a large publishing house in Philadelphia. A gentleman scholar and dedicated malacologist, he was elected to ANSP membership in 1815 and served in many offices, including president of the ANSP (1858–1863). His hundreds of publications included 13 volumes of *Observations on the Genus Unio* (1827–1874).

[6] Dr. Amos Binney (1803–1847) graduated from Brown University in 1821 and Harvard Medical School in 1826. He was a founder of the Boston Society of Natural

phology of the soft body parts of mollusks along with Leidy's pioneering anatomical observations and superb illustrations.[7] Subsequently, Binney and his son, Dr. William G. Binney, who worked at the Academy in Philadelphia, became leading authorities on molluscan species and subspecies; William Binney published many additional volumes of *Terrestrial Air-breathing Mollusks*.[8] In 1878, Academy curator George W. Tryon, Jr. conceived and published the first volume of the *Manual of Conchology*, which led to many reforms in classifying mollusks.[9] The *Manual's* influence increased as Tryon published subsequent volumes about specific groups of mollusks, including various Florida mollusks beginning with Say's work. Tryon's *Manual* was continued and expanded after his death in 1888 by his young successor from Iowa, Henry Augustus Pilsbry.

Iowa and Florida Beginnings: Henry Pilsbry and Charles Simpson

Henry Augustus Pilsbry (1862–1957) grew up on a farm in Iowa where he developed a fascination with collecting and examining both land and aquatic mollusks.[10] Pilsbry studied both zoology and geology while earning a bachelor of science degree at the University of Iowa. After graduation, he

---

History.

[7] Binney, *The Terrestrial Air-breathing Mollusks of the United States*, 1:198–243. The shells and soft-bodied parts of mollusks were presented following European standards, which began emphasizing microscopic studies on soft tissues of mollusks; Leidy's specialty was microscopy.

[8] William Greene Binney (1833–1909, elected to Academy membership in 1856) followed his father and was responsible for volumes 4 and 5 of *The Terrestrial Air-Breathing Mollusks of the United States* and *The Land and Fresh Water Shells of America*. Pilsbry wrote, "Thanks to the Binneys, father and son, we American malacologists rarely have anything but comparatively fair sailing when we have occasion to work with the land mollusks of our Country" (Pilsbry, "On the Orthalicus in Florida," 1).

[9] George Washington Tryon, Jr. (1838–1888) was elected an Academy member in 1859 and became the conservator of the malacology section in 1869. Along with a group of American malacologists, he financed and helped found the *American Journal of Conchology* in 1865, which continued until 1872. Tryon's sister, Adeline S. Tryon, was a conchologist and became an Academy member in 1874. He named a *Limnaea* after her.

[10] Memorial issue to Pilsbry, *The Nautilus* 71/8 (1958): 73–112; in Peck and Stroud, *A Glorious Enterprise*, see index for references to Pilsbry's role in ANSP expeditions through 1957. Pilsbry organized many, participated in some, and used others' efforts to receive, describe, and curate the mollusks they collected.

worked as a proofreader in Davenport, Iowa. In 1884, he was elected to membership in the Davenport Academy of Natural Sciences.[11] At their regular meetings, Pilsbry often "made a verbal report of the discovery of some species of aquatic mollusks new to this locality" and read papers, including "Notes on the Loess of Davenport and Vicinity" and "Remarks on the Anatomy of Certain Fresh-water Snails."[12] He also published his first malacology articles in the *Proceedings of the Davenport Academy of Natural Sciences.*[13] In his role as librarian and curator of conchology, Pilsbry became acquainted with Charles Torrey Simpson and Florida's mollusk treasures while identifying shells for Simpson's "Contributions to Mollusca of Florida" for inclusion in the *Proceedings.*[14]

Charles Torrey Simpson (1846–1932), a farm boy from the region east of Davenport and also a Civil War veteran, became a serious amateur conchologist during a fishing trip to Florida in 1881.[15] Simpson was enamored with the southwest Gulf Coast and the thousands of mollusks on its beaches, rivers, and trees, as well as the innumerable fossil shells. Delighting in the Florida climate, Simpson purchased property there and in April 1882, he and his family settled in Braidentown (now Bradenton) south of Tampa. Simpson collected along the Florida Gulf Coast into the Keys and the Tortugas. In "Collecting Sea Shells," he later commented, "These were the golden days and I look back upon them as the happiest in my life."[16] He sought guidance in identifying and classifying his specimens from contacts at the Davenport Academy of Natural Sciences, the Academy of Natural Sciences of Philadelphia, and the Smithsonian Institution.

Simpson's first published Florida contribution was a catalogue of his

---

[11] Founded in 1867, the Davenport organization had a mission, like the ANSP, to promote discovery in the natural sciences and to disseminate the information among members and corresponding members. Pilsbry became a member on 26 October 1883.

[12] Pilsbry made presentations about his local Iowa studies and was elected librarian and curator of conchology on the Collections Committee (*Proceedings of the Davenport Academy of Natural Sciences* [PDANS] 4 [1882–1884]: 249; 26 September 1884; p. 250, 26 December 1884).

[13] Pilsbry, "Descriptions of a new Hydrobia," 33–34.

[14] *PDANS* 5 [1886]: 45–72. It is not clear from the note on p. 228 from the Report of the Publication Committee whether all or only part of his report was published because of the Davenport Academy's financial difficulties. No other sections were published.

[15] Rothra, *Florida's Pioneer Naturalist*, 21–44; La Plante, "The Sage of Biscayne Bay," 61 ff.

[16] Simpson, *Florida Wild Life*, 31.

collections, with notes and observations made in the field. It was his intention, while residing in Florida, to publish a complete catalogue of all the species of mollusca belonging to the State.[17] His catalogue and its taxonomic work were shepherded through publication by Pilsbry, the elected librarian of the Davenport Academy of Sciences. Simpson's work was based on his discoveries and collections during his 1881 trip and later residency (1882–1886) in Florida.[18]

Simpson's "Contributions to the Mollusca of Florida" lists more than 600 specimens, including many new species of mollusks, along with descriptions, location information, and extended acknowledgments.[19] He thanked William Dall, who named and described *"Pleurotoma (Mangilia?) Simpsoni, n. s.,"* and also quoted Dall, who referenced his work: "Two specimens of this extremely pretty little shell were obtained at Tampa Bay by Mr. Simpson. It differs from any known form from that region heretofore."[20] About one new species, Simpson took "great pleasure in naming it in honor of my friend, Mr. John Ford, of the Academy of Natural Sciences, of Philadelphia, who compared the shells of this type with the *Naticas* of the Academy's collection, and determined it to be new...*Natica (semisulcata* Gray, var.?) *Flordiana,* n. s'...taken alive on sand-flats in Sarasota Bay."[21] He also thanked "Mr. Henry A. Pilsbry, of Davenport, Iowa, for assistance in identifying the *Unios.*"[22] Simpson's work stimulated further interest in Florida mollusks, and his catalogue remains a valuable listing of the species and their locations for ecologic comparisons of collections made today and during earlier periods in Florida.

Simpson also collaborated with Pilsbry, especially on *Unionidae,* the bivalve mollusks that were of great interest to both men.[23] During this period, Pilsbry traveled east to seek job opportunities and visit museums. He met

[17] Simpson, "Contributions to Mollusca of Florida," 45.

[18] Rothra, *Florida's Pioneer Naturalist,* 21–44.

[19] Pratt, "Curators Report," 235. The report lists 600 Florida specimens deposited at the Davenport Academy.

[20] Simpson, "Contributions to Mollusca of Florida," 55.

[21] Ibid., 72.

[22] Ibid., 48.

[23] Pilsbry's papers were on *Unionidae (Unios),* a family of freshwater mussels, the largest in the order *Unionoida.* These bivalve mollusks are sometimes known as river mussels, naiads, or simply as unionids or unios. This group is currently under extensive biodiversity and evolutionary studies (see Erik Stokstad, "Nearly Buried, Mussels Get a Helping Hand," *Science* 33 (2012): 876–77). Pilsbry and Simpson pioneered only the tip of a proverbial "iceberg" of *Unionidae.*

George Washington Tryon, Jr., the Academy's expert on mollusks and author of the ongoing multi-volume *Manual of Conchology*.[24] Tryon was impressed by young Pilsbry's experience in publishing and his substantial knowledge of and enthusiasm for the study of mollusks. Much to the surprise of many, Tryon hired the relatively unknown Pilsbry as his Academy assistant in 1888.

The next year, Simpson also moved east to join William Dall at the Smithsonian and returned to collecting in Florida. From 1899–1902, Simpson continued as a curator at the Smithsonian's National Museum of Natural History. He studied the *Unionidae* until he retired and moved permanently to Florida.[25] The friendship and scientific partnership that began in Davenport between Simpson and Pilsbry persisted as they both relocated to and resided in Florida, with a mutual interest in the *Unionidae* and later in Florida's land snails.

Pilsbry in Philadelphia

In 1888, only three months after Pilsbry began his appointment at the Academy in Philadelphia, George Tryon died suddenly at 50 years of age, and Pilsbry, only 25 years old, inherited the titles of conservator of the conchology section and editor of the *Manual of Conchology*. In 1889, Pilsbry added the founding of a new journal, *The Nautilus,* to his full plate of responsibilities. Pilsbry was prodigious in both the field and laboratory; his scientific output was remarkable. During the next five years, he produced hundreds of detailed pages of the *Manual of Conchology* and prepared many of the plates himself. In addition, as editor of *The Nautilus,* he developed the publication

---

[24] *Manual of Conchology; structural and systematic; with illustrations of the species* was started by G. W. Tryon as an ANSP publication to present in detail the systematic features of species of a large group—genera, family—of mollusks and to depict their characteristic features using illustrated plates. These comprehensive monographs incorporated all the known information about species in the groups and served as reference guides for future research. The purpose of this monograph series was mainly identification. Few data on the ecology or specific habitats remain because not much information was available with the specimens used for the studies.

[25] Among Charles T. Simpson's many publications about *Unios* are "On a revision of the American Unionidae," *The Nautilus* 6/7 (1892): 78–80; "Notes on the Unionidae of Florida and the southeastern states," *Proceedings of the United States National Museum* 15 (1911): 405–36; "New and unfigured Unionidae," *PANS* 52 (1900): 74–86; "On the evidence of the Unionidae regarding the former courses of the Tennessee and other southern rivers," *Science* 12/291 (1900): 133–36.

into an influential malacology journal.[26]

Pilsbry's masterful fieldwork provided a steady supply of new specimens for him and his colleagues to study, dissect, and illustrate, as well as new species to name. In a Florida article, an Academy colleague of Pilsbry's noted, "He was a master of incisive description. His appreciation of the historic development of malacology, and his interest in geography and its influences, were always reflected in his studies."[27] Pilsbry studied mollusks from all over the world and presented comprehensive works that considered all known species of a phylogenetic group or a geographic region. He often included paleontological or other evidence to suggest the origins of the species in a specific area. These skills characterized his long-term studies in Florida from 1894 until 1957.[28]

Pilsbry in Florida

Shortly after arriving at the Academy in 1888, Pilsbry began identifying mollusks sent to him by Clarence Moore, who was excavating shell mounds along the St. Johns River (ch. 12).[29] Moore continued to send specimens and eventually provided enough support for Pilsbry to join Moore and Philadelphian Charles W. Johnson in Florida in 1894.[30]

Pilsbry and Johnson collected diverse mollusk species in the surrounding rivers and lakes and in the middle basin of the St. Johns River, including

---

[26] As editor of the *Manual of Conchology* and *The Nautilus*, a malacology publication, Pilsbry was a major transition figure for studies with the two different research approaches.

[27] Wurtz, "Dr. Pilsbry and fresh-water Mollusca," 85. Wurtz was an editor of *The Nautilus* and a member of the ANSP limnology team that explored Gulf Coast rivers, including the Escambia River in northern Florida. See also Charles B. Wurtz and Selwyn S. Roback, "Invertebrate Fauna of Some Gulf Coast Rivers," *PANS 57* (1956): 167–206.

[28] From a search of the Malacology Department records at the ANSP. "Collected in Florida by Pilsbry" or "Collected by others and named by Pilsbry." Locality: Florida; Collector: Pilsbry: Page 1 of 31 (3,048 records).

[29] Moore, "Certain Shell Heaps of the St. John's River, Florida," 921, 932 *Paludina georgiana*.

[30] Pilsbry, "Report of the Conchological Section," 473–75. Charles W. Johnson, curator at the Wagner Institute, Philadelphia, 1888–1903, and curator of Eocene and Oligocene collections at the ANSP (member since 1892). Johnson moved to St. Augustine, Florida, in 1880. Johnson was co-editor of *The Nautilus* during this period (Pilsbry and Johnson, "A New Floridian *Viviparus*," 48).

Juniper Creek and other tributaries in east central Florida.[31] The two gathered thousands of river mussel specimens from numerous localities. The collections proved to be important in the study of the variable and ill-defined species of Florida *Unionidae*, a family of freshwater mussels first examined by Charles Simpson. Also, while collecting peculiar river snails of the genus *Vivipara*, Pilsbry and Johnson procured many varieties new to science and identified the most divergent forms of a genus that had not yet been discovered, which added an entirely new phase to studies on the series of known variations in the family *Viviparidae*.[32] The pair also established the importance of the study of river mollusks in Florida in understanding genus variety. During their field work, Pilsbry and Johnson also identified many mollusks from the mounds Moore was excavating; Moore became a strong supporter of Pilsbry's further malacological studies in Florida.

In 1899, Pilsbry returned to Florida, explored the islands and the environs of Biscayne Bay (near present-day Miami), and became interested in the colorful air-breathing tree snails of the genus *Liguus*.[33] These tropical tree snails, which were confined to the extreme southern mainland of Florida and the Keys, became Pilsbry's favorites after he reviewed them for publication in the *Manual of Conchology* in 1899. He was convinced that much remained to be learned about the geographic distribution and origins of these exquisite creatures, and he traveled to Florida in 1903 to collect and study them further.

Moore's continued support of the exploration of Florida by Pilsbry and other Academy curators from 1903–1904 further fueled Pilsbry's interest in tree snails.[34] With the assistance of young Henry Fowler, a new Academy hire, Moore collected hundreds of tree snails from the Keys and also the adjacent mainland and deposited them at the Academy. In reporting about Moore's collection, Pilsbry noted, "This is by far the most extensive series of mollusks

---

[31] The St. Johns River is divided into three basins: upper, middle, and lower. The middle basin begins in east-central Florida where the river starts to widen after it is joined by the Econlockhatchee River. The middle basin runs through Ocala National Forest. Lake George, the largest lake found on the St. Johns River, is located in the middle basin.

[32] Specimen included in Academy Malacology Department collection; *Viviparidae* from the 1894 Florida expedition, H. A. Pilsbry and Charles W. Johnson. *Viviparus walkeri*, Pilsbry & Johnson, 1912 (ANSP, 70053) Lecotype.

[33] Pilsbry, "Conservators Report," 541–42.

[34] E.g., Samuel G. Dixon, "Report of the Curators," *PANS* 56 (1904): 845; H. A. Pilsbry, "Report of the Special Curator of the Department of Mollusca," *PANS* 56 (1899): 816–17.

ever obtained on the Florida Keys."[35]

In 1907, Pilsbry again explored the lower Florida Keys, this time collaborating with Charles Torrey Simpson. Simpson had recently retired from the Smithsonian and resided in undeveloped Lemon City, which is now in Miami on Biscayne Bay.[36] He had spent 13 years at the Smithsonian, traveling frequently to Florida, the Bahamas, and the West Indies, and classified 2,000 freshwater snail and mussel species during that time. Simpson now focused on Florida's tropical plants and conservation issues while extending his interest to tree snails.[37]

Pilsbry and Simpson collected tree snails from Bahia Honda Key to Key West, with Big Pine Key as their base. Pilsbry presented and published the results of these findings and Moore's tree snail collections in "A Study of the Variation and Zoogeography of Liguus in Florida"[38] at the Academy's Centenary Celebration Symposium in March 1912.[39] Pilsbry's presentation was one of the earliest international reports in systematics to discuss the zoogeography of a large group of related organisms in a defined area. Pilsbry also used new and developing genetic concepts of variability and paleontological evidence to interpret the results in his discussion. He quoted Moore's field notes

---

[35] Pilsbry, "Report of the Special Curator of the Department of Mollusca," 816–17.

[36] Rothra, *Florida's Pioneer Naturalist*, 76–87. Simpson, who retired at 56, had a very productive life as Florida's leading naturalist and conservationist. *Unionidae* studies were in his past; land snails and horticultural and botanical vistas lay ahead. He wrote about and advocated for Florida conservation issues, including the establishment of Everglades National Park.

[37] Simpson became "The Sage of Biscayne Bay," as he wrote several books and received honors for his conservation work.

[38] (*JANS* ser. 2 15 [1912]: 429–75). This was one of the earliest publications in systematics about issues of zoogeography and new genetic concepts of variability. An abstract of Pilsbry's paper titled "On the Tropical Element in the Molluscan Fauna of Florida" (*PANS* 64 [1912]: 142) appeared before his presentation at the ANSP Centenary.

[39] The ANSP celebrated its centenary on 19–21 March 1912, with festivities and an international scientific symposium attended by members, correspondents, and dignitaries. A special issue of the *PANS* was published that included a record of all events, sessions, cablegrams, etc.; *Proceedings of the Meeting Held March 19, 20, and 21, 1912, In Commemoration of the One Hundredth Anniversary of the Founding of the Academy* (Philadelphia: Academy of Natural Sciences, 1912): 1–160. Scientific papers were published in the *PANS* 64 (1912): 1–600; abstracts and an early program appeared in the *JANS* ser. 2 15 (1912): 429–75.

extensively and used them as the basis for the distribution maps he published. As a model for studies on other organisms, this outstanding contribution with its superb colored plates added greatly to the knowledge of Florida land snails before many species became extinct as their habitats disappeared due to land development.

Pilsbry went on to incorporate the work of other Florida tree snail enthusiasts with his extensive exploration into one comprehensive volume as part of his *Land Mollusca of North America*.[40] These efforts produced the most complete work on the genus *Liguus*.

After many expeditions to Florida, Pilsbry had become a winter resident in 1937, joining his daughter and son-in-law in Lantana, Florida, near south Palm Beach. Using his own backyard as a base camp, he extended his Florida mollusk studies and made many important contributions to all branches of malacology. The marine section of his *Manual* contained information about many Florida seashells along with his classic studies of chitons.[41] In Florida, Pilsbry continued collecting and also published numerous papers about freshwater mollusks in *The Nautilus* and other periodicals. In later years, he became interested in the Pliocene molluscan fauna of central Florida and made frequent field trips to Clewiston and Ortona Locks near Lake Okeechobee, where he collected many specimens for the Academy. Pilsbry's broad interest in mollusks, like that of William Dall, naturally led him to the study of tertiary forms of mollusks with Florida collaborators Thomas McGinty (page 43) and Axel Olsson.[42] Thus, Pilsbry and his colleagues carried on the Florida paleontological tradition set by earlier members of the Academy.

Pilsbry's Florida studies and contributions over his lifetime—discoveries, publications, influence on students, colleagues, and amateurs—defy summary. A graceful and thoughtful beginning, however, was made by Pilsbry's

---

[40] Pilsbry's *Land Mollusca of North America North of Mexico* contains two volumes, both in two parts: vol. 1, part 1 (Philadelphia: Academy of Natural Sciences, 1939); vol. 1, part 2 (Philadelphia: Academy of Natural Sciences, 1940); vol. 2, part 1 (Philadelphia: Academy of Natural Sciences, 1946) and vol. 2, part 2 (Philadelphia: Academy of Natural Sciences, 1948). Still regarded as the best guide for identifying land mollusks in North America, the purpose of this monograph was mainly identification. Few ecological data were included because little was available.

[41] Pilsbry, *Manual of Conchology*. Seashells appeared as volumes 11 through 17 from 1889–1898; chitons were contained in volumes 14 and 15.

[42] Henry A. Pilsbry and Thomas L. McGinty, "Cyclostrematidae and Vitrinellidae of Florida," parts 1–4 in *Nautilus* 59–60 (1945–1946); part 5, *Nautilus* 63 (1950): 85–87. Also see *The Nautilus* papers with Axel A. Olsson and *PANS* 103 (1951): 197–210.

scientific associate, friend, and Florida neighbor, Thomas McGinty, who wrote a memorial article about "Dr. Henry A. Pilsbry in Florida" that was published in a special issue of *The Nautilus*: "Although Dr. Pilsbry had an unusually long life, one is amazed at the vast amount of work he accomplished. Active to the end, always a prodigious worker, he continued to spend at least a portion of each year at his desk in the Academy doing the work he so greatly enjoyed. His regard and deep loyalty for his beloved Academy always came first."[43]

Pilsbry officially retired from the Academy in 1954, but he continued working at the Academy until he suffered a heart attack in 1957. At first, Pilsbry seemed to be recovering, but he died six weeks later at his Florida home. After Pilsbry's death, his students, who had become leaders in various sub-disciplines of malacology, assumed his many roles as editor of *The Nautilus*, in fieldwork, in curatorial involvement at the Academy, and in malacology in Florida.[44] The most involved in the future of Florida malacological exploration was Robert Tucker Abbott, who had taken over many of Pilsbry's responsibilities at the Academy in 1954.

R. Tucker Abbott

Robert Tucker Abbott (1919–1995) became one of the most well-known malacologists of the twentieth century and brought the study of mollusks to the public through his books, most notably, *American Seashells* (1954), *Seashells of the World* (1962), *The Shell* (1972), and *The Kingdom of the Seashell* (1972). His impact on Florida malacology was great and continues today. Abbott's interest in seashells began early; as a boy on Cape Cod, he collected them and started a shell museum in his basement with a friend. As an undergraduate at Harvard University, Abbott became a protégé of the eminent Harvard malacologist William (Bill) James Clench (1897–1984). In 1941, they started the journal *Johnsonia*, which specialized in western Atlantic mollusks. Abbott received his BA degree in 1942 and enlisted in the U.S.

---

[43] McGinty, "Dr. Henry A. Pilsbry in Florida," 97–100. Thomas McGinty was a research associate in the ANSP's Department of Mollusks. He and his brother, Paul L. McGinty, started collecting with their father, Paul P. McGinty, when he moved the family to Florida in 1923. Their home was five miles from the Pilsbry residence in Lantana.

[44] *The Pilsbry Nautilus* 71/3 (January 1958), includes articles and information about those influenced by Pilsbry. See also Leal, "Celebrating a Long Life," 1–7.

Navy as a pilot; he later worked in the Naval Medical Research Unit investigating schistosomiasis.[45] He documented the life cycle of the parasitic schistosome in a small brown freshwater snail, which he studied in the rice fields of the Yangtze Valley in China.

After World War II, Abbott worked as curator in the Department of Mollusks at the Smithsonian and also earned his doctorate in biology at George Washington University. In 1954, Henry Pilsbry convinced Abbott to join him at the Academy and to guide the department after Pilsbry's retirement. By the time Pilsbry died in 1957, Abbott had transformed malacology at the Academy with his interdisciplinary research, introducing new approaches to curating the collections, hiring young curators, and reaching out to the amateur and popular shell community through education and publication programs. In 1954, Abbott published *American Seashells*, the first blockbuster in his legacy of shell books, education kits, and popular materials. He assumed Pilsbry's role as editor of *The Nautilus* and other Academy publications and spearheaded the founding and development of U.S. and international shell clubs. He also occupied the endowed Pilsbry Chair, which honored his predecessor.

In 1969, Abbott moved to the Delaware Museum of Natural History and the DuPont Chair of Malacology, again heading a department of mollusks, and he served as the assistant director of John DuPont's newly founded museum.[46] In 1973, Abbott established his own publishing company, American Malacologists, and then "retired" three years later to Melbourne, Florida, where he conducted research, published malacology books, and served as editor of *The Nautilus*. He provided leadership and worked with amateurs and professionals alike to found and expand shell clubs and shows in Florida.

Throughout his career, Abbott had directed so-called orphaned collections with specimens of research significance to appropriate curators for study, curation, and safe deposit at the Academy and other natural history

---

[45] Schistosomiasis, also known as snail fever, is a disease caused by parasitic flatworms called schistomes transmitted by water-dwelling snails.

[46] The Delaware Museum of Natural History was founded by John DuPont based on his personal shell collection, for which Abbott had provided guidance. DuPont served as president (chief executive officer) of the museum and chair of the board. In 1996, John DuPont shot and killed wrestler David Schultz, an Olympic gold medalist who was living and training at DuPont's sprawling estate, Foxcatcher Farm. DuPont was found guilty but mentally ill in the shooting death, and he died in prison in 2010.

museums.[47] The most significant Florida "shell orphans" became available when the Beal-Maltbie Shell Museum of Rollins College in Winter Park, Florida, was phased out.[48] For each specimen or collection, Abbott determined the appropriate future museum destination for its curation, research and/or exhibition. The space these orphans vacated would be available for Rollins's new and growing Department of Environmental Sciences. Abbott ensured the scientific legacy of Florida's first major shell museum at Rollins by securing the McGinty research collections for the Florida Museum of Natural History (FLMNH) at the University of Florida in Gainesville. For other research orphans and those appropriate for education and exhibition purposes, Abbott began his next project with zeal, founding a unique world-class shell museum the Bailey-Matthews Shell Museum[49] on Sanibel Island, the

---

[47] "Orphaned" collections were those whose owner—a private individual, a college, a university, or a museum—had abandoned or left them unattended for any number of reasons. Many orphaned collections include valuable historical and scientific data sets and specimens of interest because of new environmental research. Abbott was firm in his guidance that research specimens and collections should go to research museums; shells of value only for display and exhibition should be housed in museums with a public education mission.

[48] They were comprehensive, worldwide collections, with many paratypes with considerable Florida material, including the Walter Webb Collection and the McGinty Collections of Thomas, Paul, and their father. These collections had exchange specimens from C. T. Simpson and Pilsbry; the McGintys had worked with Pilsbry on an earlier date (personal communication/discussions with Kurt Auffenberg, 11 December 2012). Rollins College is a private liberal arts college founded in 1885 in Winter Park, Florida. Dr. James Beal of Cocoa, Florida, presented the original collection of 100,000 worldwide shells to Rollins College in 1940. Beal's friend, Birdsey Maltbie, donated the specially designed building to house the shell collection. Because of the research importance of many Florida specimens, in particular the collections made by the McGintys, that were donated to the Beal-Maltbie Museum and the enthusiasm of the FLMNH's curatorial staff in acquiring the research collections, an agreement was approved by the Rollins Board of Trustees in 1988 for the McGinty collections and their endowment to be transferred to the FLMNH. Tucker Abbott continued to serve as a consultant to Rollins College for the disposition of all the remaining shell collections. Rollins renamed the former museum building the Beal-Maltbie Center, which is now home of the Rollins College Environmental Studies Department. including non-research collections.

[49] In 1990, brothers John, Francis, and Sam Bailey gifted eight acres of land in memory of their parents, Frank P. Bailey and Annie Mead Matthews. In their honor, the museum would be named the Bailey-Matthews Shell Museum as a facility of the Shell Museum and Educational Foundation, Inc. Abbott was appointed founding director in 1991. Construction began in May 1994, and the museum opened in June 1995. See

shell capital of the world.

As the founding director of the Bailey-Matthews Shell Museum, Abbott dedicated his energy, experience, malacological wisdom, and contacts to build a unique museum. Alas, the official grand opening of the Shell Museum took place on 18 November 1995, two weeks after Abbott's death.[50] A new director was chosen, and the museum prospered with its exhibitions and events and also became the new home of *The Nautilus*, which Pilsbry had started at the Academy in 1887 and Abbot and his co-editors had continued and sustained until Abbot's death. Since then, under the auspices of the Bailey-Matthews Shell Museum (which added National to its name in 2014), *The Nautilus* has been edited by the director of the Bailey-Matthews National Shell Museum.[51] The Academy's conchology and malacology connection to Florida, which began with Thomas Say "pursuing pretty much the track of Bartram" and was extended by Pilsbry, Abbott, and others, continues today through the malacology collections at the Academy, the FLMNH, and *The Nautilus* at the Bailey-Matthews National Shell Museum in Sanibel, Florida.

Paralleling Henry Pilsbry's Florida legacy in malacology was Henry Fowler's in ichthyology. Both were bolstered by the work of their predecessors at the Academy, and both were first supported by Clarence Moore in conducting fieldwork in Florida.

Henry Weed Fowler

Henry Fowler (1878–1965) was born in Holmesburg, Pennsylvania, and wrote to the board of curators of the Academy when he was fifteen years old: "Having determined to devote my life to the study of Natural History, I respectfully apply for a studentship at the Academy of Natural Sciences."[52]

William Hallstead, *Idea to Reality: An Informal History of the Bailey-Mathews Shell Museum from Concept to Grand Opening* (Sanibel Island: Bailey-Matthews Shell Museum, 1996).

[50] Abbott's health had been declining for two years prior, and he often carried an oxygen supply with him to meetings and luncheon appointments.

[51] Jóse Leal followed Tucker Abbott as director and editor (Leal, "Celebrating a Long Life," 1–7).

[52] H. W. Fowler to the board of curators, 1894, in ANSP Archives, Fowler Papers, coll. 117. For further reading on Fowler, see Conant, "Henry Weed Fowler 1878–1965," 628–29; Phillips and Phillips, "Writings of Henry Ward Fowler," 173–212; Smith-Vaniz and Peck, "Contributions of Henry Weed Fowler," 173–91; Böhlke, "Catalog of Type Specimens in the Ichthyological Collection," 5–10.

Fowler was accepted, and he observed, "My first acquaintance with the Academy's collection of fishes began in 1894 when I entered the institution, like many of my predecessors, as a Jessup student."[53] Fowler was talented and self-taught in natural history before he began studying as a special student for two years (1901–1902) under David Starr Jordan, an eminent ichthyologist and founding president of Stanford University. Fowler returned to Philadelphia and was given the responsibility of curating a growing collection of "cold-blooded vertebrates"—many from Florida—at the Academy.

The study of "cold-blooded" vertebrates—reptiles, amphibians, and fish—as described by Bartram had continued with the Academy's 1817 expedition and the work of Charles Alexandre Lesueur. Later, John Eatton Le Conte and John Edwards Holbrook deposited collections at the Academy and published some descriptions of specimens in the Academy's *Journal*.[54] Like Bartram's, Le Conte's Florida specimens had been procured during his own Florida explorations. Academy correspondent Holbrook received and deposited specimens from many collectors for his classification studies and his monumental monographs.[55] Edward Drinker Cope's more recent personal herpetology and fish collections, which contained many Florida specimens, were deposited at the Academy in 1898. Henry Fowler's task as the new curator was to sort, label, and catalog the extensive collection; fishes were his favorites.[56]

Fowler's earliest reports were about the Academy's collections of fishes from Jamaica, Zanzibar, Nicaragua, China, and southern Florida. After publishing eight papers, Fowler was named the Academy's curator of fishes in

---

[53] The Jessup Fund was established by the children of ANSP member Augustus Edward Jessup (the maternal grandfather of Clarence Moore). Its endowed goal was to provide "assistance of poor young men desiring to study natural history."

[54] For further reading on Holbook, see Theodore Gill, *Biographical Memoir of John Edwards Holbrook, 1794–1871* (Washington, D.C.: Press of Judd & Detweiler, 1903); Lester D. Stephens, "John Edwards Holbrook (1794–1871) and Lewis Reeve Gibbes (1810–1994): Exemplary Naturalist in the Old South," *American Society of Ichthyology and Herpetology Special Publication* 3 (1997): 447–58.

[55] John Edwards Holbrook, "An Account of Several Species of Fishes Observed in Florida, Georgia, etc. *JANS*, ser. 2, 3, no. 1 (1855): 47–58; Holbrook's *Southern Ichthyology: Or the Description of the Fishes Inhabiting the Waters of South Carolina, Georgia and Florida* was issued in volumes and parts beginning with four volumes published in Philadelphia from 1836–1840, followed by additional volumes through 1848.

[56] These are included in Fowler's publications beginning in *PANS* 10 (1858): 510–28: "Some New and Little-Known Percoid Fishes."

1902 and elected to membership in 1903. The same year, he published "Description of a New Gurnard from Florida, with notes on the colors of some Florida Fishes."[57]

In 1904, Fowler and Stewardson Brown (of the Academy's botany section) assisted Clarence Moore in the Florida Keys "to explore the islands for land snails of the genus *Liguus*."[58] With Key West as their base, they traveled to Florida's Marquesas Islands, stopping at Boca Grande Key. Then, from Key West, they traveled along the southern shoreline beyond Vacas Key and returned around the Keys along the northern shore to Key West. While collecting land snails that were of great interest to Moore and also Henry Pilsbry, Fowler noted, "Incidentally we were enabled to explore the flora and fauna of this most interesting region," which they did.[59]

Back at the Academy, Fowler, an enthusiastic birder, published an article on "Birds Observed in the Florida Keys."[60] In another extended research paper, "Some Cold-blooded Vertebrates of the Florida Keys," Fowler noted, "We availed ourselves of every opportunity to gather information, but only data which I feel to be absolutely reliable is included here."[61] The data were about more than a hundred different kinds of fish, amphibians, and reptiles; there were more fish than the other two categories combined. Since the amphibians and reptiles were common, Fowler provided only brief collection site information about them. Many of the fish were unknown to science, and Fowler published descriptions in varying detail about eighty-six fishes and illustrated thirteen. One fish, *Congrammus moorei, Fowler.* Fowler "Named for Mr. Clarence B. Moore of Philadelphia, well known for his valuable research in Archaeology, and through whose interest in Zoology the expedition to the Florida Keys was realized."[62]

---

[57] Henry W. Fowler, "Description of a New Gurnard from Florida, with notes on the colors of some Florida Fishes," *PANS* 55 (1903): 328–36.

[58] Fowler, "Some Cold–blooded Vertebrates," 77–113. Fowler's journals (1884–1907), pp. 57–93, record the events of 15–26 June 1904. Stewardson Brown was elected to Academy membership in 1891.

[59] Ibid., 77.

[60] Henry W. Fowler, *The Auk* 23/4 (1906): 396–405. While searching for land snails between Cape Sable and the Marqesas Keys for Mr. Clarence B. Moore, Fowler notes, "I incidentally observed a number of birds. As some of them may prove of interest I give an annotated list made during June, 1904" (396). He noted 33 birds.

[61] Fowler, "Some Cold-blooded Vertebrates," 77.

[62] Ibid., 105 (fig. 13.), 107.

Henry Fowler began increasing the Academy's fish collections by soliciting specimens. He distributed instructions about collecting and preparing fish for scientific study to Academy members and correspondents, friends, boat captains, and any interested person who was planning field or fish market trips. Fowler then quickly published the new accessions and included detailed descriptions, geography, his masterful self-drawn illustrations, and credits to the collectors. His bibliography of more than 600 publication entries is a virtual list of Academy acquisitions and contains invaluable ichthyological information for the first half of the twentieth century.[63]

Fowler's publications about Florida fishes, which began in 1903 with "Description of a New Gurnard with Notes on the Colors of Some Florida Fishes," continued with his work in the Florida Keys in 1904; additional Florida fish information followed in "Cold-blooded Vertebrates from Florida, the West Indies, Costa Rica and Eastern Brazil" and "Fishes from Florida, Brazil, Bolivia, Argentina and Chile" in 1926.[64] Drawn by opportunities to study marlin and other big game fishes, Fowler turned his focus on Florida's coastal waters that extended to Cuba and the Gulf Stream in 1934.

Fowler and Ernest Hemingway

Help for Fowler to expand his scientific research on Atlantic game fishes south into the Florida waters came from the Academy's managing director, Charles M. B. Cadwalader.[65] After consulting with his prominent big-game fishermen friends, Cadwalader followed an interesting suggestion to send a letter to Ernest Hemingway via the author's New York publisher. In his 6 March 1934, letter, Cadwalader asked Hemingway if he would be interested in cooperating with Academy scientists in conducting research near his Key West, Florida, home to remedy "the lack of knowledge concerning the classification, life histories…of the sailfish, marlin, tuna and other large game fishes and to secure specimens and information in order that our knowledge of these fish may be advanced." In making his case, Cadwalader wrote about the Academy's comprehensive fish collections but its lack of larger game fish

---

[63] See Phillips and Phillips, "Writings of Henry Weed Fowler."

[64] Henry W. Fowler, "Description of a New Gurnard"; "Cold-blooded Vertebrates from Florida, the West Indies, Costa Rica, and Eastern Brazil," *PANS* 67 (1915): 244–369; "Fishes from Florida, Brazil, Bolivia, Argentina and Chile," *PANS* 78 (1926): 249–85.

[65] Peck and Stroud, *A Glorious Enterprise*, 310–14.

Ernest Hemingway shows off two of his catches in 1934.

ANSP Archives, Collection 707. Courtesy of the Academy of Natural Sciences of Drexel University.

and noted, "According to Mr. Fowler, no museum in the world has a comprehensive collection of these big game fish such as we are anxious to secure."[66]

The publisher forwarded the letter to Hemingway in Paris. He responded eagerly and promptly on 2 April 1934, writing while shipboard returning to New York from Europe.[67] The Academy's request was intriguing because Hemingway had focused on Atlantic game fish after he moved to Key West in 1928.[68] In fact, he had begun learning about game fish and writing articles based on his fishing and cruising observations. In his lengthy reply to Cadwalader, Hemingway wrote that he would be pleased to participate in the Academy's research. He described in depth his need to know what specimens the museum already had, the difficulties of preserving fish in a tropical climate, and the problems of making good photographs under the conditions encountered while at sea. After arriving in New York and later while en route to Key West, Hemingway stopped at the Academy on 9 April 1934 to meet Cadwalader and Fowler. Once he had returned to Florida, Hemingway wrote a follow-up invitation for the pair to join him. Based on weather conditions and his assessment of the influence of the Gulf Stream on game fish activity, Hemingway suggested that they depart from the port in Havana, Cuba. They would cruise and fish from his new *Pilar*.[69] He received a prompt and enthusiastic response from Cadwalader, and they were ready to begin their research.

By 25 July 1934, Cadwalader and Fowler were in Havana with Hemingway. They were fishing together in the Florida Gulf waters at the end of July and in and around Cuba in August. Information about their six-week

---

[66] Charles M. B. Cadwalader to Ernest Hemingway, 6 March 1934, ANSP Archives, Expeditions, coll. 113, box 5, IV, #26.

[67] Ernest Hemingway to Charles Cadwalader, 2 April 1934, ibid.

[68] Hemingway and his new wife, Pauline, moved to Key West in 1928. In 1931, they purchased a home, which is now a national landmark, and lived there together until their marriage broke up in 1939. He retained title to the home until his death (www.hemingwayhome.com). Hemingway made observations about fish and raised questions about their variations due to age, size, color, and species that also perplexed ichthyologists of the time.

[69] Ernest Hemingway to Henry W. Fowler, 9 July 1934, ANSP coll. 220. Hemingway used a cash advance in New York to purchase a 38-foot customized wooden yacht, which was brought to Key West and christened *Pilar*, the heroine in *For Whom the Bell Tolls* and his wife's nickname. He secured permission to dock the boat at the Navy Yard in Key West and, in the 1940s, when he moved to Cuba, Hemingway relocated the boat. It is now displayed at his former home in Cuba (Finca Vigia) as a museum.

expedition is based on several sources: Hemingway's article for *Esquire* magazine; the many enthusiastic letters Hemingway, Fowler, and Cadwalader exchanged; and Fowler's publications following their trip.[70]

Back in Philadelphia at the end of August, Cadwalader wrote, "with Hemingway's excellent knowledge of these fishes [marlin] and their habits," Fowler "was able to secure enough information in order that he may revise the classification of the marlin insofar as the Atlantic Ocean goes."[71] In his report on the "successful stay in Cuba," Cadwalader wrote to the Academy's chief curator Witmer Stone:

> Although our expedition was only successful in landing one marlin, which weighed 420 pounds and was captured by our host, Ernest Hemingway, Fowler learned a great deal from him in regard to these large fishes, and also he was able to examine and study other specimens captured by market fishermen. Fowler tells me that as a result of all this work he will have to revise the classification of this particular fish, and that as much misinformation has been published in the past by various ichthyologists.[72]

Fowler continued his correspondence with Hemingway and asked him to procure specific types of fish: high-finned marlin, striped marlin, tuna, and a large wahoo.

He concluded, "I hope that...you will try to help us out."[73] Within a month, Hemingway had completed the fishing expeditions and sent specimens to Fowler with extensive physical descriptions and measurements.[74]

In letters written during winter 1934–1935, Hemingway kept Fowler

---

[70] See Hemingway, "Genio after Josie," 21–22. The Hemingway-ANSP correspondence can be found in ANSP Archives, Expeditions, coll. 113, box 5, folder IV, and in box 8. There is a discussion of some of these letters in Lawrence H. Martin, "Ernest Hemingway Gulf Stream Marine Scientist: The 1934–1935 Academy of Natural Sciences Correspondence," *The Hemingway Review* 20/2 (2001): 5–15. A comical version of the ANSP expedition was published posthumously by the daughter of the young writer, whom Hemingway was encouraging by allowing him to assist on board (Samuelson, *With Hemingway*, 123–30, 141–42).

[71] Charles Cadwalader to Morgan Hebard, 28 August 1934, ANSP Archives, Expeditions, coll. 113, box 5, folder IV.

[72] Charles Cadwalader to Witmer Stone, 23 August 1934, ANSP Archives, Huber-Stone correspondence, coll. 186.

[73] H. Fowler to E. Hemingway, 22 April 1935, ANSP Archives, Expeditions, coll. 113, box 5, folder IV.

[74] E. Hemingway to H. Fowler, 23 July 1935; H. Fowler to E. Hemingway, 31 July 1935, ibid.

and Cadwalader informed about fishing conditions, and Fowler thanked Hemingway for his photographs and fish specimens.[75] Fowler discussed Hemingway's proposition about variations in the marlin specimens and added that his own recent research had arrived at the same conclusion as Hemingway's observations and intuition: "all of these marlins [are] one and the same species." Their correspondence ended in mid-August 1935. Hemingway was in Key West, working on a draft of "The Snows of Kilimanjaro" and correcting page proofs for *Green Hills of Africa*.[76] Fowler expressed his gratitude by naming a new Atlantic fish species, "For Ernest Hemingway, author and angler of great game fishes, in appreciation of his assistance in my work on Gulf Stream fishes." The fish, *Neomerinthe hemingwayi* was a stout little spiny-cheeked scorpionfish.[77]

In his articles and books, Hemingway expressed his gratitude for their exchange of information about fish and other Gulf Stream topics. In "Genio after Josie: A Havana Letter,"[78] Hemingway positively recalled Fowler's and Cadwalader's time aboard the *Pilar*. The author incorporated the ichthyological and marine knowledge he had acquired from his discussions and correspondence with Fowler in "On the Blue Water: A Gulf Stream Letter."[79] Elements of the essay also resurfaced in *The Old Man and the Sea* and in Hemingway's posthumously published *Islands in the Stream*.[80]

More on Florida Fishes

Henry Fowler continued writing about Florida fishes; his publications contained follow-ups to his work with Hemingway and included "A Collection of Fresh-Water Fishes Obtained in Florida, 1939–1940, By Francis Har-

---

[75] H. Fowler to E. Hemingway, 8 August 1935, ibid.

[76] Reynolds, *Chronology*, 81.

[77] Fowler, "Description of a New Scorpaenoid Fish," 41–43. See also Prosanta Chakrabarty, "Papa's fish: a note on *Neomerinthe hemingwayi*," *Hemingway Review* (Chicago: Ernest Hemingway Foundation, 2005). Drawing by Fowler of the fish he named to honor Hemingway, *Neomerinthe hemingwayi* (ANSP Archives, Fowler Illustrations, coll. 197).

[78] Hemingway, "Genio after Josie," 21–22. The article includes photographs.

[79] *Esquire* 5/4 (April 1936): 31, 184–85.

[80] Ernest Hemingway to Charles Scribner, October 1951, in Hemingway, *Selected Letters*, 738. For further discussion of Hemingway's interest in the sea and its influence on his writing, see Mark P. Ott, *A Sea of Change: Ernest Hemingway and the Gulf Stream, A contextual Biography* (Kent, OH: Kent State University Press, 2008).

per, 1940" and "A Collection of Fishes Obtained on the West Coast of Florida by Mr. and Mrs. C. G. Chaplin, 1940."[81] Harper's Florida exploration is the subject of chapter 14. Charles and Louise Chaplin were among the many recruited by Fowler to join his fish ventures. The Chaplins' outstanding contributions to ichthyology at the Academy continued and took new directions in the mid-1950s.[82]

Fowler continued to blend his worldwide studies with Florida-related publications as he collaborated with scientists working in Florida and at Florida's fledgling institutions. In 1952, Fowler published on Florida fishes collected by Thomas L. and Paul L. McGinty, who had extensively collected and studied Florida mollusks while working with Henry Pilsbry in Florida and also at the Academy.[83] In 1951, the McGintys shipped the fishes they had collected off the coast of Palm Beach and the Florida Keys to Fowler.[84] Fowler determined that of the ninety-one fish specimens, thirty-eight were unique; he described five new ones as he noted, "A number are the first to be received by the Academy; several are rare and others new additions to the fauna of the United States." Fowler's last Florida fish article, "Description of a New Blennioid Fish from Southwest Florida," was published in 1954.[85] However, his final publication, "A Catalog of World Fishes," which began with part 1 in 1964 and was completed posthumously, also contains Florida fishes.[86]

Epilogue

Fowler's 1940 article "A Collection of Fresh-Water Fishes Obtained in Florida, 1939–1940, by Francis Harper" links work discussed in this chapter with other studies under way during the same period that were associated

---

[81] ANSP Archives, ANSP Archives, Expeditions, coll. 113, box 5, folder IV.

[82] See Gordon W. Chaplin, *Full Fathom Five: Ocean Warming and a Father's Legacy* (New York: Arcade Publishing, 2013): 49–83.

[83] Fowler, "Fishes from Deep Water off Southern Florida," 1–16.

[84] Thompson, McGinty, and McGinty, "Dredging from the Cruiser Triton," 37–43.

[85] *Notulae Naturae* 25 (1954): 1–3.

[86] Fowler, "A Catalog of World Fishes," *Quarterly Journal of the Taiwan Museum* (1964–68). In parts. See Smith-Vaniz and Peck, *Contributions*, 183, note 29, 188. Fowler began turning over operation of the ichthyology department to Dr. James Böhlke, who led the development of the department to international preeminence. Louise Chaplin established an endowed Chaplin Chair of Ichthyology at the Academy, a role first occupied by Böhlke from 1959 until his death in 1982. After retiring, Fowler continued working on the fish collection and publishing until his death in 1965.

with the botany department at the Academy and will be discussed in chapter 14.[87] In his article's introduction, Fowler acknowledges that for Francis Harper, "The collecting of fishes was largely incidental," since he was on another mission. But for Fowler, who would have had everyone collecting fish if he could, Harper "was successful in obtaining 125 specimens, belonging to 27 species." Fowler also comments, "It is quite interesting to note that three of these species prove to be new, while almost all the others represent unrecorded localities for Florida." Fowler reveals Harper's mission: "Dr. Harper secured this collection, which he presented to the Academy, during two trips on which he was retracing the routes of John and William Bartram."

---

[87] *PANS* 92 (1940): 227.

CHAPTER 14

BARTRAM REDUX...WITH FRANCIS HARPER
AND OTHERS

"I have been away for two months on the Bartram trail, and have had an extremely interesting and satisfactory time. I should like very much to tell you about some of the details whenever you may come into Philadelphia."[1]

—Francis Harper

"Dr. Harper secured this collection, which he presented to the Academy, during two trips on which he was retracing the routes of John and William Bartram."[2]

—Henry Fowler

William Bartram's discoveries in Florida, which inspired the Academy of Natural Sciences' 1817 expedition, were extended by many nineteenth-century Academy members and correspondents, as recounted in previous chapters. However, by the early 1900s, several plants and animals Bartram had described in his *Travels*, such as the "ixia" or "celestial lily"[3] and the "*vultur sacra*,"[4] could not be located by botanists or zoologists. Had William Bartram

---

[1] Francis Harper to Francis C. Pyle, 17 July 1939, ANSP Archives, JB Papers, coll. 15C, folder 1, 3–14. Pyle of George School, PA, is acknowledged in *FHBT* as "having been particularly helpful in unraveling Bartram's route" (132). Francis Harper's publications led to the mixed use and meaning of the "Bartram trail" and "Bartram's trail" versus "Bartrams' trail." The meaning is now generally taken to mean the William Bartram Trail.

[2] Fowler, "A Collection of Fresh-Water Fishes Obtained in Florida," 227–44.

[3] "behold the fields of the cerulean Ixea!" *Ixea caelestina* [plate 3] opposite p. 155 in *WBT* (*FHBT*, 98–99). See John Small's rediscovery, page 319 in this book. See also Alfred E. Schuyler and Elizabeth P. McLean, "The Versatile Bartrams and Their Enduring Botanical Legacy," in *America's Curious Botanist*, ed. Nancy E. Hoffmann and John C. Van Horne (Philadelphia: The American Philosophical Society, 2004).

[4] "Vultur sacra," or painted vulture (*WBT,* 150–52; *FHBT,* 95–96). Bartram's "Vultur sacra," continues to stimulate ornithological interest since the bird has never been

been dreaming? Speculation continued about *Franklinia*, its natural habitat, and its extinction in the wild. In addition, considerable attention was given to clarifying the scientific nomenclature used by Bartram and keying it to current scientific use. Interest in plant communities in areas explored by Bartram was also increasing. Clarence Moore, Henry Pilsbry, and Henry Fowler continued Bartram's Florida studies into the twentieth century. By the 1930s, the three were joined by many other members and correspondents of the Academy, whose efforts were supported by other Philadelphia and national institutions.

In the late 1890s, two organizations were founded in Philadelphia that advanced scientific research at the Academy—often related to William Bartram's Florida travels—through volunteer efforts and financial support. The Philadelphia Botanical Club (1891), which focused on a general interest in botany in the Philadelphia area, was invaluable in furthering the interest and contributions of amateurs to botany.[5] The John Bartram Association (1893) was formed to preserve John Bartram's garden and house.[6] These groups generated enthusiasm for the Bartrams through the 1931 celebration at the Academy of the "Two Hundredth Anniversary of the Founding of the First Botanic Garden in the American Colonies by John Bartram" and during the Academy's 1939 William Bartram Bicentennial Celebration.[7] Among Academy participants who later pursued a better understanding of William Bartram's botanical findings and his travels were Francis Pennell and Arthur

observed by anyone other than Bartram. See Snyder and Fry, "Validity of Bartram's Painted Vulture (*Aves: Cathartidae*)," 61–82.

[5] The Philadelphia Botanical Club held its first meeting on 1 December 1891 at the ANSP. The objectives of the new club were "to further the interests of Botany and to make a checklist and herbarium of the plants found within the radius of fifty miles from Philadelphia." The club focused on building the collection of local plants at the Academy's herbarium and supporting the botany department, (darwin.ansp.org/hosted/botany_club/history.html [accessed 21 August 2018]).

[6] The John Bartram Association's mission is to protect and enhance the landmark Bartram's Garden and House, advance the Bartram legacy of discovery, gardening, and art, and inspire audiences of all ages to care for the natural world, www.bartramsgarden.org (accessed 1 January 2019).

[7] *Bartonia: Proceeding of the Philadelphia Botanical Club* 12, Supplement (1931); Harper, "William Bartram's Bicentennial," 380–84. To celebrate, papers were read, and events were held at the Academy; a Bartram exhibition opened and included personal Bartram items from his Florida travels. The celebration was jointly sponsored by the Academy and the John Bartram Association.

Leeds, who were associated with the Academy's Botany Department and herbarium, and also Francis Harper and Roland Harper. Their interest and work, followed by Robert McCracken Peck and others, contributed to the founding of the Bartram Heritage Trail through eight southern United States, including Florida, in the late 1970s.

Florida Plants and the Philadelphia Herbarium

During the nineteenth century, many Florida plant specimens joined the ongoing worldwide collection of plants being deposited in the herbarium of the Academy of Natural Sciences. The Florida specimens included those of Academy members and correspondents, such as Henry Muhlenberg and Lewis David von Schweinitz. Later came specimens from the herbaria of William Baldwin, Thomas Nuttall (see page x) , John Eatton Le Conte, Hardy Croom, and Alva Chapman, along with Florida specimens from non-botanists, such as Angelo Heilprin and Joseph Willcox.[8] In addition, many Florida plants collected by individuals associated with other institutions were deposited at the Academy as a resource for curators and members and to vouchsafe reference materials for future research.

During the early twentieth century, the largest number of and most important Southeastern and Florida specimens deposited were those collected by John Small and Roland Harper.[9] Small's interest in botany began in Lancaster County, Pennsylvania, where he grew up, and was nurtured at Franklin and Marshall College before he began his doctoral dissertation on southern botany at Columbia University.[10] During his doctoral studies under Nathaniel Britton, Small collected extensively in Florida. Small then joined Britton's new venture, the New York Botanical Garden, and continued his

---

[8] Mears, "Guide to Plant Collectors," 141–65. During the early twentieth century, herbaria of Florida specimens were also started at the University of Florida and the Florida College for Women (later Florida State University) and expanded at the New York Botanical Garden because of John Small's work.

[9] See, e.g., Earl L. Core, "John Kunkel Small," *Castanea* 3 (1938): 27–28; Daniel F. Austin, et al., *The Florida of John Kunkel Small* (Bronx, NY: The New York Botanical Garden, 1987); Joseph Ewan, "Roland McMillan Harper (1878–1966)," *Bulletin of the Torrey Botanical Club* 95 (1968): 390–93; Elizabeth Findley Shores, *On Harper's Trail: Roland McMillan Harper, Pioneering Botanist of the Southern Coastal Plain* (Athens: University of Georgia Press, 2008).

[10] Small's doctoral dissertation, published as *Flora of the Southeastern United States* in 1903 and revised in 1913 and 1933, remains the best floristic reference for much of the South at that time.

lifelong study of Florida's flora.[11] During his early work, Small deposited more than 4000 plant specimens, many from Florida, in the Academy's herbarium.[12] In 1931, with field assistance from professors Lord and Hume of the University of Florida, John Small rediscovered William Bartram's ixia or celestial lily northeast of Gainesville.[13] The other major contributor of Southern plants, Roland Harper, deposited the type specimen of his first named plant at the Academy in 1897 when he was beginning his undergraduate studies at the University of Georgia. At Columbia, he followed in Small's footsteps and focused his doctoral studies on the flora geography of southern Georgia and northern Florida. He also often sent specimens to the Academy to be deposited.[14]

By the early twentieth century, the Academy's international herbarium held some of the oldest and most important plant collections in the Americas, including 1.4 million dried, pressed specimens. It became known academically and internationally as the Philadelphia Herbarium (PH).

Curating the large number of specimens became increasingly time-consuming and difficult for the volunteer Academy members. A backlog of specimens was always waiting to be accessioned. Labels had to be updated and revised; specimens required protection from insects; loans to other institutions needed to be processed; and other tasks of daily upkeep needed to be performed. In 1902, the Academy formally appointed Stewardson Brown (1867–1921), the president of the Philadelphia Botanical Club, as the first

---

[11] Britton was a professor of botany and geology at Columbia and a founder and the first director-in-chief of the New York Botanical Garden. His herbarium was the initial herbarium of the New York Botanical Garden, and his most distinguished doctoral student was John Small. As the first curator of museums at the New York Botanical Garden, Small served from 1898 until 1906. In 1906, as the staff expanded, Small was named head curator, a position he held until 1934. In this role, he played an active part in building the institution and establishing the herbarium collections and the protocols for their exhibition. During much of this time, Francis Pennell served as associate curator under Small.

[12] Mears, "Guide to Plant Collectors," 162.

[13] Small, "Bartram's *Ixia coelestina* Rediscovered," 155–61.

[14] Roland M. Harper (1945), a president of the Torrey Botanical Club, wrote in his memoirs that he arrived at Columbia University in fall 1899. He remembers that at that time, the main building of the New York Botanical Garden was not complete, but the herbarium and its exhibits were being moved into the building. He added that Drs. Britton and Small and George V. Nash, the head gardener, had already established homes nearby (nynjctbotany.org/tbshist/nybg.html [accessed 7 July 2014]).

curator of the herbarium.[15] In 1904, Brown and Henry Fowler assisted Clarence Moore (see page 308) on a Florida Keys expedition, where Brown collected extensively and deposited plant specimens in the Academy's herbarium.[16] Following Brown's death in 1921, the Academy hired Dr. Francis Pennell, a full-time experienced curator from the New York Botanical Garden, to lead the Botany Department and to continue to develop the PH.[17]

Francis Pennell (1886–1952) had strong ties to the Academy beginning with his student days as a Jessup Fellow and as a member of the Philadelphia Botanical Club. His interest in the Bartrams' travels and discoveries, which began during his Quaker childhood, was stimulated during high school at Westtown School near Philadelphia and continued at the University of Pennsylvania. Pennell became a curator at the New York Botanical Garden, and John Small, his boss and mentor, initiated Pennell's research on Southeastern plants and collecting in Florida. In 1930, while conducting research at the British Museum, Pennell reviewed William Bartram's travel report to Dr. Fothergill and researched the location of the Bartrams' specimens and manuscripts in England. This experience expanded Pennell's historical view of his own contemporary research in southern botany. At the Academy, Pennell's interest in the history of American botany and the Bartrams extended to writing biographies about contemporary botanists, such as Arthur Leeds.[18]

---

[15] Stewardson Brown grew up on a farm near Philadelphia and became a skilled naturalist despite having no formal training. He pursued his interest in botany and became an Academy member on 27 January 1891, where he assisted in the herbarium. Brown was also involved in founding the Philadelphia Botanical Club, serving as its first secretary and later as president (Britton, "Stewardson Brown," 110–12; Stone, "Stewardson Brown," 1–7; ANSP Archives, Stewardson Brown Papers, 1882–1906, coll. 168.

[16] Fowler, "Some Cold-Blooded Vertebrates," 77–113.

[17] Camp, "Francis Whittier Pennell," 83; McCormick, "Francis Whittier Pennell," University of North Carolina Herbarium, www.herbarium.unc.edu/Collectors/pennell.htm (accessed 21 August 2018). Pennell grew up on a farm outside Philadelphia, pursued his botanical interests as a Jessup Student at the ANSP, and received a bachelor of science degree in 1911 and then a doctorate in 1913 from the University of Pennsylvania. He wrote his thesis on the *Scrophulariaceae* (the figwort family), a group on which he became a world authority. From 1914–1921, he was associate curator at the New York Botanical Garden. Pennell focused on the Academy's botanical collections and conducted a series of field studies on the *Scrophulariaceae* throughout eastern North America, including Florida (ANSP Archives, Expeditions, coll. 113, Pennell trip (1st), 1923, box 5, folder 43).

[18] ANSP Archives, Pennell biographies. The material is arranged into two series,

Arthur Newlin Leeds

Arthur Leeds (1871–1939) was born in Philadelphia and became a successful businessman, a serious amateur botanist, and a founder of the Philadelphia Botanical Club.[19] During his decade of service as its treasurer, Leeds was elected a member of the Academy in 1896 as he pursued his interest in ferns in the herbarium and the botany department. In 1928, after selling his business, Leeds was appointed research associate in charge of the herbarium fern collections at the Academy. Working alongside Pennell and his growing team, Leeds devoted himself and his considerable resources to organizing the Academy's herbarium. He personally hired an assistant and provided funds for other departmental needs. His own herbarium followed professional botanical museum standards, as did his field notebooks, which covered several southern states in addition to Florida.

Because of Pennell's involvement in starting *Biological Abstracts*, Leeds and Pennell had frequent conversations with Francis Harper, a staff member of the *Abstracts*, during his visits to the Academy.[20] Like Leeds and Pennell, Francis Harper had a keen interest in William Bartram's explorations.

Francis Harper

Francis Harper (1886–1972) was born in Massachusetts and moved to Georgia shortly thereafter with his family. His father, a science teacher and school superintendent, relocated the family because the eldest son, Roland (1878–1966), had been diagnosed with possible tuberculosis; it was hoped that his health would benefit from the warmer climate of Georgia and fortunately it did. As a youngster in rural southern Georgia, Francis Harper became an avid and well-rounded naturalist, following in Roland's footsteps.[21]

"General Biographies" and "Biographies of Individuals" and includes biographical information about Arthur Leeds.

[19] Harper, "Arthur Newlin Leeds," 282–83; Morris E. Leeds, *Arthur Newlin Leeds: A Brief Biography by Morris E. Leeds* (Philadelphia: privately published, 1940), in ANSP Archives, Pennell biographies, Leeds.

[20] *Biological Abstracts* (begun in 1926) was formed by the union of *Abstracts of Bacteriology* (1917–1925), and *Botanical Abstracts* (1919–1926). The abstracts of journal articles were written by scientists and staff and published in paperback subject sections by Williams and Wilkins of Baltimore. Francis Harper was elected Academy correspondent in 1929.

[21] Shores, *On Harper's Trail*, 112. Roland Harper was eight years older than Francis Harper and encouraged his interests in natural history throughout their lives. Roland was

Francis Harper and the family returned north, first to Massachusetts, when their father accepted a position as a school principal and then to the New York City area. Francis began his undergraduate studies at Cornell University in 1905 but was interrupted after only two years when his father died of pneumonia in 1907.[22] Roland Harper encouraged and tutored Francis, who became active in the American Ornithological Union (AOU) and was later elected a member.

In 1912, Francis Harper resumed his studies at Cornell and joined a faculty team a year later to study wildlife in the Okefenokee Swamp in Georgia and Florida.[23] In early 1917 while continuing his studies in the Floyd's Island Prairie of the Okefenokee, Harper identified and extended the range of the Florida water rat (*Neofiber alleni*) working with colleagues in Gainesville, Florida.[24] In his studies he also extended the range of several other plants and animals thought to be restricted to Florida habitats through trips and studies between Georgia and Florida. These experiences piqued his growing interest in William Bartram's discoveries in Georgia and Florida. Francis Harper also developed a lasting interest in the biota and people of the Okefenokee.

After receiving a bachelor's degree from Cornell, Francis Harper worked for the New York Conservation Commission as a fisheries investigator and then as an assistant biologist for the U.S. Biological Survey. He enlisted in the U.S. Army in 1917 and served until 1919, when he rejoined the Biological Survey. In 1921, he returned to Cornell for graduate study, where he met and later married Jean Sherwood.[25] She shared his passion for the Okefenokee, where Francis Harper was conducting fieldwork for his doctoral degree.

---

always distant from the other members of the family.

[22] Francis attended Cornell University from 1905–1907, interrupted his studies to support his mother and earn money, and then studied there again from 1912–1914. He returned to Cornell for graduate study from 1921–1924.

[23] The Okefenokee Swamp is one of the world's largest intact freshwater ecosystems, covering more than 400,000 acres in three Georgia counties and in Baker County, Florida, between Tallahassee and Jacksonville. The principal outlet of the swamp, the Suwannee River, originates in the heart of the Okefenokee and drains southwest into the Gulf of Mexico. The Cornell studies were the first systematic investigations of the flora and fauna of the region and the beginning of an appreciation of the biological importance of the swamp, leading to its future designation as the Okefenokee National Wildlife Refuge.

[24] Harper, "The Florida Water-Rat," 65–66.

[25] Sherwood was earning a master's degree at the College of Agriculture and enjoyed

In 1925, after receiving his doctorate based on a study of the mammals of the Okefenokee, Francis Harper found employment with the Boston Society of Natural History as secretary, editor, and curator of mammals and fishes.[26] During his appointment, he acquired a reputation for being a talented but temperamental field zoologist with a keen memory and an accessible writing style who was also an outspoken perfectionist. His personality made it difficult for some to work with him; others thrived when they collaborated. Due to personality conflicts, he was forced to give up his staff position with the Boston Society in 1929.[27]

Francis Harper was quickly hired by Witmer Stone, the research director of the Academy, to lead a collecting expedition that was leaving immediately to spend several months in Texas.[28] During Francis Harper's first formal and brief Academy appointment, he met several future colleagues and became more familiar with the Academy's resources. Subsequently, he worked as an independent scholar and field researcher and then took a position as a paid writer for *Biological Abstracts* in Boston, although he maintained frequent

---

her studies and fieldwork with Francis Harper. They married in 1923 and collaborated soon thereafter on a handbook of the animals of the Adirondack Mountains and subsequent works. During her earlier studies at Vassar College and afterward, Jean Sherwood served as a nanny for President Roosevelt's children during the Roosevelts' stays at nearby Hyde Park; Franklin Roosevelt hoped she would return to manage his orchards when her studies were complete, but instead she became an environmentalist who shared Francis's passion for the Okefenokee. When it was threatened by a proposed interstate and intrastate swamp road and canal, she communicated with President Roosevelt to intercede, which he did. In 1937, he signed Executive Order 7593 establishing the Okefenokee as a federal wildlife and nature preserve with limited access. During the Great Depression, when the Harpers' employment was interrupted, the family moved to a cabin in the Okefenokee (Davis, *Southern United States*, 231–32; Harper and Presley, *Okefinokee Album*, 7–8).

[26] Johnson, "The Rise and Fall of the Boston Society of Natural History," 81–108. The Boston Society of Natural History was founded in 1830 and continued until 1948 as an organization dedicated to studying and promoting natural history. The society published a scholarly journal and established a museum. By 1951, most of the society's collections and the library had been transferred to other institutions, and the museum is now the Boston Museum of Science.

[27] Norment, "Francis Harper," 72.

[28] Witmer Stone was director emeritus of the Academy, and Charles Cadwalader was the managing director who hired Harper on a contractual basis. See correspondence of Stone, Cadwalader, and Harper in ANSP Archives, Expeditions, coll. 113, January–October 1929, box #6, folder 12.

contact with Francis Pennell at the Academy. Francis Harper also remained active in the American Society of Mammalogists and served as corresponding secretary, often working with its past president, Witmer Stone. These contacts and Harper's field knowledge about the southern region of Bartram's travels led to Francis Harper's research collaboration with Arthur Leeds.

Arthur Leeds and Francis Harper in Bartram's Tracks

Initially, Leeds and Francis Harper researched Bartram's route and botanical finds through Alexander Wilson's copy of *Travels* in the Academy library using period maps they found at the Academy and other Philadelphia institutions. Mark Van Doren's recent edited edition of Bartram's *Travels* cost less and was smaller and more portable than previous reprint publications; thus it became invaluable in their field research.[29] In 1930, as Arthur Leeds and Francis Harper were planning their first "Bartram reconnaissance trip" to southern Georgia, Pennell was in London at the British Museum (Natural History). He was studying William Bartram's manuscript notes, his report to Dr. Fothergill, and other drawings and specimens, especially those of *Franklinia*. The information Pennell brought back intrigued Leeds and Francis Harper, who then decided that their first Bartram expedition to southern Georgia would focus on *Franklinia*.[30] Fortunately for them, the area near the Altamaha River that they targeted had been extensively studied by Roland Harper, who provided them with additional maps and information for their exploration.[31]

In April 1933, Arthur Leeds and Francis Harper "drove down a narrow tongue of the sand hills to the site of historic Fort Barrington and gazed on the wide, muddy waters of the Altamaha, where Bartram had been ferried over by a Creek Indian 160 years before."[32] Their goal was to identify sites compatible with William Bartram's writings and the observations of several later botanists about the habitat and type locality of *Franklinia*. Leeds and Francis Harper mapped the locations of several plant communities that Bartram had described as occurring near *Franklinia* plants. A year later, in May

---

[29] Mark Van Doren, ed., *William Bartram: The Travels of William Bartram* (New York: Macy-Masius, Dover Publications, 1928).

[30] See Francis Harper and Arthur N. Leeds, "A Supplementary Chapter on *Franklinia alatamaha*," *Bartonia: Proceedings of the Philadelphia Botanical Club* 19 (1937): 1–13.

[31] Roland Harper's dissertation was about the Altamaha Grit region, and he continued his fieldwork in the area and throughout the Gulf Coastal Plain.

[32] Harper and Leeds, "A Supplementary Chapter," 1–13.

1934, Leeds and Francis Harper used a similar method of geographic mapping of plants to locate William Bartram's Buffalo Lick in Oglethorpe County southeast of Athens, Georgia. These two brief expeditions—working out logistics, mapping, and collecting specimens in familiar territory—became models, along with Roland Harper's suggestions, for their future expeditions.

During this period of the Great Depression, Leeds funded expenses and honoraria for their expeditions while Francis Harper was patching together money to support his family through various "jobs." Harper continued in his "paid job" for *Biological Abstracts* in Boston, which he regarded as "drudgery." In early 1936, the American Committee for International Wild Life Protection approached him about working as a research associate on a major project concerning extinct and vanishing mammals.[33] Francis Harper was diffident about the offer until Charles Cadwalader, a member of the organization and managing director of the Academy, offered the Academy as a resource and location for Harper to work on the project. Francis Harper's reservations about the project soon changed to enthusiasm.[34]

As Francis and Jean Harper prepared to move their family to the Philadelphia area from Boston, he returned to the Altamaha River region in March 1936 to continue studying possible *Franklinia* sites. In April, Leeds joined Francis Harper in surveying the area. Although Harper began his new job in May 1936, he continued his work with Leeds and others as a side project.

A year later, Leeds and Francis Harper, accompanied by six other naturalists, including Bartram family descendants, traveled to several sites where the Bartrams may have found *Franklinia*.[35] Later in 1937, Harper and Leeds

---

[33] Barrow, *Nature's Ghosts*, 158–60.

[34] "For six and a half months Mr. Francis Harper, formerly with Biological Abstracts, has been working intensely on the problem of preparing a list of the recently extinct and vanishing mammals of the world, using the valuable library of the Academy of Natural Sciences of Philadelphia. He has prepared over 1200 cards with information on these species. He still has several months more work before the final list of perhaps 350 forms can be completed. The Committee proposes to make wide use of this report in the recommendation of areas which should be set aside as future reserves and national parks throughout the world" (16 December 1936 meeting of the Boone and Crockett Club, Boone and Crockett Club Records [Mss 738], Archives and Special Collections, Maureen and Mike Mansfield Library, University of Montana-Missoula, http://cdm16013.contentdm.oclc.org/cdm/ref/collection/p16013coll13/id/190 [accessed 21 August 2018]).

[35] Ibid., 10.

wrote "A Supplementary Chapter on *Franklinia alatamaha*."[36] They summarized possibilities for *Franklinia*'s type locality and causes of its extinction and concluded, "After all, however, the disappearance of *Franklinia* in a wild state is a mystery still awaiting solution."[37]

Francis Harper later described their progress:

> Within the next year or so we gradually formulated a plan for bringing out annotated editions of John Bartram's manuscript diary of 1765–66 and William Bartram's manuscript report of 1773–74 to his London patron, Dr. John Fothergill. This plan envisaged a considerable amount of field work in the South, for the purpose of retracing the routes of the Bartrams, relocating and photographing the points of particular interest mentioned by them, and collecting for observing as many as possible of their plants and animals in the very localities where they had recorded them. In this way we hoped to succeed in determining the identity of many of their puzzling species.... Other affairs interrupted the progress of these studies during the ensuing three years.[38]

Harper's job as a research associate for the American Committee for International Wild Life Protection had an uneasy course.[39] The organization expected his project about extinct animals to be completed within a year, by 1937. After waiting two more years, they fired Francis Harper, thus delaying for a decade the publication of his contracted book on extinct and vanishing mammals.[40] At the time, Harper was more concerned about Leeds's health, which had been failing during the past several months. Francis Harper was also involved in the William Bartram bicentennial events and was planning an exploration in Bartram's tracks for 1939.

In April 1939, Harper's article, "William Bartram's Bicentennial" appeared in *Scientific Monthly*. He described the 9 February commemorative exercises held at Rollins College in Winter Park, Florida, and the special exhibit of Bartramiana at the Academy. Francis Harper also called attention to informative and informal publications about William Bartram by the John

---

[36] Harper and Leeds, "A Supplementary Chapter." A summary of these trips is included in JB, "Diary of a Journey," 8.

[37] JB, "Diary of a Journey," 13.

[38] Ibid., 8.

[39] Barrow, *Nature's Ghosts*, 158–60.

[40] Ibid., 162–66; Francis Harper, *Extinct and Vanishing Mammals of the Old World* (Special Publication No. 12, American Committee for International Wild Life Protection (Baltimore: The Lord Baltimore Press, 1945).

Bartram Association and the National Park Service. In this article, he briefly discussed the ongoing scientific dialog about Bartram's observations and the need to retrace Bartram's routes. Francis Harper planned to do this and had "in prospect the publication of a lengthy and highly significant manuscript which throws much new light on his published 'Travels'...sponsored by the John Bartram Association."[41]

Sadly, in May 1939, Arthur Leeds died of a kidney infection at age 68, and "the progress of these studies" was interrupted. Francis Harper was determined to continue exploring in Bartram's tracks following the plan that he and Leeds had developed. Based on their Bartram fieldwork, publications, and earlier plans, Harper secured funding for his subsequent (1939–1944) work on Bartram's tracks, including grants from the John Bartram Association in Philadelphia, the Penrose Fund of the American Philosophical Society, and the Guggenheim Foundation. In his role as research director for the John Bartram Association, Francis Harper became an "historical biologist" who employed historical scholarship and on-site scientific exploration to trace the Bartrams' travels in Florida and the South while reviving scientific and popular interest in their work.[42] Harper began fulfilling a friendly exhortation ("I hope you will make Bartram live again"[43]) and a process that he began in the past:

> Intrigued originally, many years ago, by Bartram's legendary account of my beloved Okefinokee Swamp (*Travels*, 24–26), I eventually found it more essential to consult and utilize the *Travels* in my own studies on Georgia and neighboring states. As far back as 1917, while on a biological tour of Florida, I had followed (though perhaps not too consciously) the footsteps and paddle strokes of John and William Bartram along the St. John's from its mouth up to Lake Harney.[44]

Francis Harper sought his brother's field experience and many contacts throughout the Southeast to retrace John and William Bartram's tracks. As in the past, Roland was ready to help, as Francis later acknowledged.[45]

---

[41] Harper, "William Bartram's Bicentennial," 383–84.

[42] "Historical biology" is used, as is "historical archeology," to describe the discipline that combines historical scholarship and biological fieldwork.

[43] William H. Mills to Francis Harper, 1939, *FHBT*, v. Mills was a professor of rural economics at Clemson College. He identified several Bartram sites in South Carolina.

[44] *FHBT*, vi.

[45] "Dr. Roland M. Harper, of the Geological Survey of Alabama, has placed at my

Roland M. Harper and Florida

Roland Harper (1878–1966) had long mentored and supported his younger brother, Francis, beginning with their nature explorations during their childhood in Georgia.[46] At the urging of their father, in 1897 Roland entered the University of Georgia early while the family was living in Georgia. Later that year, Roland Harper made his first original plant discovery along the muddy banks of the Middle Oconee River and proudly deposited a type specimen at the Academy.[47] Botany became Roland Harper's obsession, but he majored in engineering at the behest of his father. After graduation, Harper moved back to Massachusetts with his family and worked in an optical factory while continuing to botanize. He published descriptions of the plants of Worcester County, Massachusetts, in 1899.[48] That year, he also secured a scholarship for graduate study at Columbia University.

For his dissertation topic, Roland Harper chose an interdisciplinary study about the flora and geology of a Southeastern area—the Altamaha Grit Region of southeastern Georgia.[49] It was familiar territory to him and also of interest to Nathaniel Britton, John Small, and other Columbia University faculty. Roland Harper's fieldwork often crossed Bartram's tracks, and he dutifully noted and contemplated Bartram's long lost *Franklinia*.[50] Roland received his doctorate in 1905 and started working as a botanist and geographer for the Geological Survey of Alabama at the University of Alabama in Tusca-

---

disposal his extensive knowledge of the vegetation, geography, and geology of the Southeastern States" (JB, "Diary of a Journey," 12, 133).

[46] Shores, *On Harper's Trail*, 13–23, 113–15.

[47] Barcode: 24543; Date Collected: May 23, 1897; Cyperaceae *Scirpus georgianus* R. M. Harper; Type Specimen. In May 1924, he deposited the type specimen for Aristolochiaceae *Hexastylis speciosa*. R. M. Harper from Alabama; Barcode: 14412.

[48] See R. M. Harper, "A new station for *Potentilla tridentata*," *Rhodora* 1 (1899): 90–91; "Additions to the flora of Worcester County, Massachusetts–II," *Rhodora* 1 (1899): 201–205; "Forests of Worcester County, Massachusetts," *Torreya* 18 (1918): 110–20.

[49] The "Altamaha Grit" was named by W. H. Dall in 1892. Variously called Region or Formation, it is a geological sandstone formation covered in many places by a layer of Pleistocene deposits overgrown with wiregrass and many outcrop plants, which intrigued Roland Harper. See Roland McMillan Harper, "A Phytogeographical Sketch of The Altamaha Grit Region of the Coastal Plain of Georgia," *Annals of the New York Academy of Sciences* 17, part 1 (September 1906).

[50] Shores, *On Harper's Trail*, 31–32.

loosa. In late 1908, he became a botanist and geographer for the Florida Geological Survey based in Tallahassee, Florida, although he still retained his connections with the university and the Alabama Survey.

As land development got under way in Florida, Roland Harper's expertise was in demand for vegetation and soil surveys. He first worked with the Florida Geological Survey staff on surveys of the Apalachicola River region. The area had been explored by Hardy Croom and Alvin Chapman and was the type locality for *Torreya taxifolia* and other endemic Florida plants.[51] Harper spent time in the region and then returned in 1910 to confirm his earlier observation that the range of the Torreya tree extended one mile north of earlier published reports. Technically, the Torreya was a pervasive plant that lived in the southwestern corner of Georgia as well as in Florida.[52] In other studies in this area, Roland Harper's efforts to relocate Chapman's rhododendron proved futile.[53]

Harper followed his exploration of the northern region of Florida with studies in other parts of the state. He completed detailed surveys and analyses of vegetation and its relationship to soil types for publication as Florida Geological Surveys and also for reports commissioned on natural resources.[54] His surveys were syntheses of botanical, geological, and geographic data, foundations for understanding the ecology of Florida. As part of the 1914 annual report, the Florida Survey published Roland Harper's massive phytogeography account on the northern part of the state. Another of his lengthy analyses of Florida vegetation appeared the following year, and in 1921, Harper prepared a paper about central Florida's plant geography for the Survey's Annual Report. He completed his Surveys reports in 1927 and published the results along with fieldwork that he had conducted in 1909, 1924, and 1925 in southern Florida. In 1931, Roland Harper returned to Tuscaloosa and was appointed to a permanent position at the Alabama Geological Survey.

During these years in Florida and Alabama, Roland Harper frequently spent time in the field with Francis Harper, often in the Okefenokee, and

---

[51] Shores provides a comprehensive account of Roland Harper's fieldwork in "In the Footsteps of Croom and Chapman," ibid., 54–72.

[52] Ibid., 69.

[53] Ibid., 68. *Rhododendron chapmanii* occurs naturally only in Florida. It is now found in the wild in only five counties in the central Panhandle around Tallahassee and a single location (possibly introduced) in Clay County.

[54] For more information, see FGS Publications, www.dep.state.fl.us/geology/publications/listofpubs.htm (accessed 21 August 2018).

discussed Francis's and Arthur Leeds's growing interest in the Bartrams' exploration. Roland Harper's Florida mapping fieldwork and publications—photographs and descriptions of the geology, topography, soils, and climate of plant communities—became a model for Francis Harper's studies on the Bartram Trail. Following Leeds's death, Roland quickly offered to guide Francis on his Bartram exploration through Alabama to Tallahassee, Florida.

Francis Harper on William Bartram's Trail in Florida, 1939

In May 1939, Francis Harper left Philadelphia and spent a month exploring Bartram territory in the Carolinas and Georgia by car and also on foot. He collected and identified sites visited by William Bartram. Sponsored by the John Bartram Association and the Penrose Fund of the American Philosophical Society, Francis Harper wrote a series of letter reports to Philadelphian Charles Jenkins ("You may be interested in hearing of some of my adventures on the Bartram trail during the past several weeks"[55]). His usage of the term "Bartram trail" identified the connecting sites along the way. In mid-June, Francis met Roland in Montgomery, Alabama, which had been a part of West Florida during Bartram's time. Roland introduced Francis to several Bartram scholars, and they spent time linking historical maps of the region with Bartram's possible route based on text found in Francis's marked-up copy of Mark Van Doren's edition of *Travels*.[56] From Montgomery, Roland guided Francis along segments of Bartram's journey southward along the current Alabama and Florida border to Pensacola.[57] They often drove on remnants of earlier roads and at times hiked on ancient Indian trading paths.

---

[55] Francis summarized his 1939 exploration trip, which he began calling "Bartram trail, " from various locations along the way in a series of letter reports to Charles F. Jenkins with carbon copies to Mrs. Bayard Henry (Mary Gibson Henry) and Dr. Pennell. They represented his sponsors, the Penrose Fund of the APS, the John Bartram Association, and the ANSP, respectively. Harper often added handwritten postscript notes for Pennell about plant specimens (Harper to Jenkins, 20 May 1939, ANSP Archives, JB Papers [15C], 1, 3–14).

[56] Roland's version of events and the trip to Tallahassee is summarized by Shores, *On Harper's Trail*, 123–25, based on Roland's notes.

[57] Shores has detailed this segment of their journey in *On Harper's Trail*, 117–23. Francis Harper's letters, notes, and memorabilia are curated at the ANSP, Kansas State University, and the University of North Carolina in Chapel Hill and await the dedicated time and research that Shores spent on Roland Harper. Here, we refer mainly to Francis Harper's published works and resources available in Philadelphia and Florida along with Shores's *On Harper's Trail*. Francis Harper's reports to his sponsors, now collected in the

Roland provided detailed scientific descriptions as the two collected specimens and photographed sites that they believed Bartram had described in *Travels*. Francis reported, "Between Montgomery and Mobile we felt that we were right on the Bartram track in various places."[58] Later, "we passed over probably the same high, gravelly ridge from which Bartram had a view of the Mobile Delta." Unlike Bartram, they did not go to Mobile, Alabama, nor did they travel by boat for a two-day stay in Pensacola. Instead, they drove to Pensacola, where they explored possible Bartram sites. They then continued northeast, across the current Florida border into Georgia, and on to Tallahassee by way of Thomasville, Georgia.[59] While Roland and Francis were in Tallahassee, Roland introduced Francis to Herman Gunter,[60] J. Clarence Simpson,[61] Herman Kurz,[62] and other botanists. These men shared information with Francis that was important for the next leg of his Florida expedition.

ANSP archives, were particularly valuable.

[58] Harper to Jenkins, 25 June 1939, ANSP Archives, JB Papers (15C), 1, 3–14.

[59] Shores, *On Harper's Trail*, 123–25.

[60] Herman Gunter grew up in Florida and studied at the University of Florida under its first geology professor, E. H. Sellards, who became Florida's first official geologist. Gunter joined Sellards's newly created Florida Geological Survey in Tallahassee in 1907. Gunter became Director of the Geological Survey in 1933 and was awarded the honorary degree of Doctor of Science by the University of Florida in 1944. The Herman Gunter building on the campus of Florida State University recognizes his service to Florida geology.

[61] Simpson, a member of the Florida Geological Survey, discovered the Thomas Farm paleontological site near Gainesville in 1931. See also Ray, "An Idiosyncratic History of Floridian Vertebrate Paleontology," http://www.flmnh.ufl.edu/bulletin/raylowres.pdf (accessed 18 September 2018).

[62] Ruth Schornherst Breen, "In Memoriam, Dr. Herman Kurz," www.bio.fsu.edu/faculty-kurz.php (accessed 21 August 2018). Kurz was a pioneering twentieth-century Florida botanist who developed the Department of Botany at the Florida College for Women and later taught biological sciences when this institution became Florida State University. See H. Kurz and R. K. Godfrey, *Trees of Northern Florida* (Gainesville: University of Florida Press, 1962). He and Francis Harper became close friends during Harper's time in Tallahassee. Kurz often chauffeured Francis Harper, who did not drive, on social outings and field trips in the area. Through Kurz's and Godfrey's efforts, the first major research program on fire ecology was established based on Francis Harper's ideas formulated at Tall Timbers near Tallahassee.

Francis Harper departed Tallahassee and traveled eastward from Tallahassee to the Suwannee River and retraced Bartram's tracks to Manatee
Springs: "Authorities disagree as to which spring on the Suwannee River Bartram called the Manatee Spring. But I am sure it is the one still bearing that
name, about 7 miles west of Chiefland, Levy County. It fits his descriptions
as no other does." He continued on and explored Long Pond near Chiefland
before traveling east to Gainesville.[63] With two professors from the University
of Florida, Francis reported that the "Alachua Savanna—the modern Payne's
Prairie—affords a vast and impressive spectacle."

Francis Harper's trip from the Alachua Savanna to the St. Johns River
was successful: "After a number of false leads, Bartram's route between the
St. Johns River and the Alachua Savanna has been determined with a reasonable degree of definiteness and the identification of 'Halfway Pond.'" He visited and photographed Bartram sites along the St. Johns River, from Jacksonville to Lake Harney, writing, "Perhaps the climax of the whole trip was
the identification of the very lagoon where the younger Bartram had his ter-
rific adventures with alligators, and of the near-by shell mound where he
camped!"[64] Further upriver, "On the west side of Lake George the aromatic
Illicium, so frequently and fondly referred to by Bartram, was found bearing
simultaneously its dainty yellow blossoms and its wheel-shaped green fruit."
In a summary letter to his Philadelphian sponsors, Francis Harper noted, "It
is simply impossible to cover the entire Bartram route in a thorough going
manner in six or eight weeks, but the present trip serves at least as a reconnaissance and has brought results of distinct interest and value."[65]

Francis Harper made extensive notes and collections of plant and animal
specimens, which he sent back to the Academy. Some specimens, such as
those in his shipment of fish to Henry Fowler, were subjects for immediate
publication.[66] Harper's article, "The Bartram Trail through the Southeastern

---

[63] *FHBT*, vi. In late June through mid-July 1939, he traveled to the Suwannee,
Manatee Springs, and Long Pond near Chiefland, east to Gainesville, the Alachua
Savanna and Bartram sites along the St. Johns River, including Silver Glen Springs,
Spalding's Lower and Upper Stores, Lake George and Lake Dexter, etc. (Francis Harper
to Charles Jenkins, 25 June 1939, ANSP Archives, JB Papers [15C], 1, 3–14).

[64] Harper, "The Bartram Trail through the Southeastern States," 61.

[65] Francis Harper to Charles Jenkins, 25 June 1939, ANSP Archives, JB Papers
(15C), 1, 3–14.

[66] Fowler, "A Collection of Fresh-Water Fishes Obtained in Florida," 227–44;
Harper, "The Bartram Trail through the Southeastern States," 54–64. The title includes
the first use of the term "Bartram Trail."

States," which he published in the *Bulletin of the Garden Club of America*, included the term "Bartram Trail," which he often used in his letters to describe the piecing together of segments linking sites visited by William Bartram.

Francis Harper on the Bartram Trail in Florida, 1940

In 1940, Francis Harper embarked upon a second comprehensive exploration devoted to the Bartram Trail through the Southeastern states.[67] He and E. Perot Walker, assistant curator of botany at the Academy, left Philadelphia in late February. After many stops (Washington, the Carolinas, and Georgia), Francis Harper and Walker began the Florida segment of their journey in early March ("In Florida we picked up the Bartram trail at King's Ferry on the St. Marys").[68] In reports to his sponsors, which were addressed to Charles Jenkins, Francis Harper again provided detailed accounts about travel, Bartramian subjects, the individuals he met, and their conversations.[69]

After entering Florida, Francis Harper and Walker continued to Green Cove Springs on the western side of the St. Johns River to Palatka and then further southward upriver. At the Ocklawaha River, a tributary of the St. Johns, they made a westward side excursion, driving toward Ocala and Silver Springs. Next, they explored the St. Johns to a point above Lake Harney then returned northward along the river to visit Jacksonville, Amelia Island, St. Augustine, Gainesville, and the Suwannee River.

Several passages from Francis Harper's 31 March report to Jenkins from Palatka reveal the range of the data collection during the early part of the 1940 Florida exploration:

---

[67] *FHBT*, vi. The 1940 timing of their trip coincided with increased interest in *WBT* after Van Doren's edition of *WBT* had been recently reissued in paperback. Bartram's travels were now of interest to natural history scholars and amateurs as well as poets, writers, and the general public.

[68] The trip lasted from early March through mid-April 1940. Sites included many along the St. Johns River, Green Cove, Picolata, Lamb's Bluff, Lake Beresford, Drayton Island, St. Augustine, Amelia Island, and others. The westward trip passed through Alachua Savannah, Kanapaha Sink near Gainesville, and the New Clay Landing on the Suwannee River (F. Harper to Jenkins, 31 March 1940, ANSP Archives, JB Papers [15C], 1, 3–14).

[69] F. Harper to Charles F. Jenkins with cc to Mrs. Bayard Henry, Mrs. Edward Cheston (secretary of the John Bartram Association), and Dr. Francis Pennell, often with handwritten notes (ANSP Archives, JB Papers [15C], 1, 3–14). The letters document conversations with John Swanton and others regarding their willingness to write or edit annotations for Harper's forthcoming publications about Bartram's Trail.

At Hibernia, a few miles north of Green Cove Springs, we inspected a live-oak with a recent spread of 154 feet! It must have been here when the Bartrams passed by. At Green Cove Springs we saw Miss Mary Pyle...who has been investigating and publishing a little on William's route along the lower St. John's...very enthusiastic and helpful.

At Palatka...Mr. Watkins extended to us the hospitality of his camp on the Oklawaha for several days. Here we found several especially interesting Bartramian plants, including tallow-nut (*Ximenia Americana*) and coontie (*Zamia*). Meanwhile we worked out in much better detail than before the Bartram route between the St. John's and the Alachua Savanna. I am pretty well satisfied that the Cowpen Lake, which I visited last year, is the Halfway Pond.

We visited the Indian mound from which Bartram first viewed Tuskawilla Lake, on which the present town of Micanopy is located. We are satisfied that Cuscowilla was either a quarter of a mile east of Micanopy, or at Micanopy itself.

We spent a few minutes visiting Marjorie Kinnan Rawlings at her home.... I had sent her a copy of last year's Bartram paper, and she had written me of her interest in tracing Bartram's route.[70]

The pair traveled north and spent a weekend, as Harper noted, "in the Okefinokee installing my family for a six-week stay" before leaving for Jacksonville. Then,

we have inspected Amelia and Fort George Islands. The Indian mounds on the former, mentioned by William Bartram, have been practically obliterated for road material.... Along the St. John's between its mouth and Jacksonville we have identified a number of Bartramian points.... Between Jacksonville and St. Augustine we were able to follow the Old Kings Road for part of the way.[71]

In St. Augustine, Harper and Walker enlisted the enthusiastic help of the librarian of the Historical Society and her husband in locating maps and images of the area and the buildings mentioned by the Bartrams. They drove to Picolata on the St. Johns along the route taken by Say, Ord, and Peale during the Academy's 1817 expedition, which was now cleared and paved.

---

[70] Francis Harper to Charles Jenkins, 31 March 1940, ANSP Archives, JB Papers (15C), 1, 3–14. Rawlings had lived at Cross Creek since 1928. She received the 1939 Pulitzer Prize for *The Yearling*, published in 1938.

[71] Ibid.

Harper and Walker encountered vestiges of the Fort Picolata observed by Bartram and the Florida Four.

Walker and Francis Harper traveled upriver once more, spending a great deal of time from Lake George to an area slightly above Lake Harney: "At Lake Beresford we located the Indian mound that William Bartram remarked on as the largest he had seen in Florida."[72]

Next, they moved on to Winter Park to visit several professors at Rollins College who had been involved in the Bartram bicentennial celebration and who were very helpful in providing maps and specimen information. They also invited Harper and Walker to join a houseboat party and "cruise up the St. John's above Lake Monroe, and we thus examined a number of points that had not been otherwise accessible." In Winter Park, the two also "had the pleasure of a brief visit with Mrs. Mary Francis Baker, author of 'Florida Wild Flowers.'"[73]

In Gainesville, professor T. H. Hubbell of the University of Florida and E. C. Herlong of Micanopy guided them to several Bartram sites, including the site of the trading store Bartram had visited on the southern margin of the Alachua Savanna. From there, Harper established that "Bartram's route westward from the Alachua Savanna to the Suwannee River has been worked out as follows...."[74] As Harper exclaimed, "Perhaps the most remarkable find was Bartram's 'Alligator Hole,'" which they identified along the route. Harper concluded his letter of 19 April to Charles Jenkins with: "Altogether, we feel that we have been reasonably fortunate in retracing the Bartram routes in Florida."

In a later summary, Harper noted, "We also took advantage of the different season of the year in adding very materially to the botanical collections. Special attention was given to the St. John's River region and to William Bartram's route across northern Florida to the Suwannee River. Amelia and

---

[72] Harper to Jenkins, 19 April 1940, ANSP Archives, JB Papers (15C), 1, 3–14.

[73] Ibid.

[74] "Kanapaha Prairie-Archer-Watermelon (or Generals) Pond-Waccasassa River-Long Pond (near Chiefland)-Talahasochte (4 miles by river above Manatee Spring (at the present New Clay Landing))." Harper to Jenkins, 19 April 1940, ANSP Archives, JB Papers (15C), 1, 3–14.

Fort George Islands and St. Augustine were new points visited along the Florida coast."[75] In mid-April, Harper and Walker returned separately to Philadelphia.[76]

In 1939, Francis Harper followed up the publication of his earlier article with Leeds on Bartrams' exploration with a brief article about the Bartram Bicentennial and also one about his 1939 expedition along the "Bartram Trail" in West and East Florida for the *Bulletin of the Garden Club of America*.[77] After the 1940 Bartram trail trip, Francis Harper concentrated on publications to connect his field and historical research that he had promised in his *Scientific Monthly* article: "a lengthy and highly significant manuscript of William Bartram's which throws new light on his published 'Travels'; likewise the publication of John Bartram's diary of his 1765-66 trip (hitherto largely unpublished)."[78]

Francis Harper and Arthur Leeds's archival research in Philadelphia coupled with that conducted in London by Francis Pennell and Professor Ernest Earnest of Temple University during the course of Pennell's literary and biographical research had identified Bartramian manuscripts and copies that had received little previous study. They also made finds in the archives of the Historical Society of Pennsylvania: John Bartram's diary of 1765–1766 and a Photostat copy of William Bartram's 1773 and 1774 journals, which had been sent to Dr. Fothergill. These documents provided valuable geographic, biological, and seasonal data that aided Francis Harper in his historical analysis linking his field exploration to Bartram's tracks.[79] Harper's historical research was aided by the meetings and conversations he had with local residents during his Bartram exploration. Their specialized knowledge provided him with information and assisted him in preparing the critical comments and annotations that would make his publications unique and very valuable to scientists, Bartram scholars, and enthusiasts.

---

[75] JB, "Diary of a Journey," 8.

[76] *FHBT,* vii.

[77] Harper and Leeds, "A Supplementary Chapter," 1–13; Harper, "*William Bartram's Bicentennial*," 380–84; Harper, "The Bartram Trail," 380.

[78] Harper, "William Bartram's Bicentennial," 383.

[79] JB, "Diary of a Journey," 3; Cappon, "Retracing and Mapping the Bartram's Southern Travels," 507–13.

Francis Harper completed his comprehensive editing of John Bartram's manuscript, "Diary of 1765–66," including the "hiatus" or missing time period that was published in London in the appendix of Stork's *Account of East Florida*. As promised, Francis Harper also published his annotated edition of John Bartram's "Diary of a Journey through the Carolinas, Georgia, and Florida 1765–1766" in *Transactions of the American Philosophical Society* in 1942.[80] Harper's detailed geographical, historical, other comments and the annotated index are similar in page length to the Bartram diary. Although he edited Bartram's diary for punctuation, Francis Harper chose not to "whitewash it." Historical maps and a generalized depiction of John Bartram's route from Pennsylvania to Florida as well as his return accompany many location photographs taken by Harper during his 1939–1940 travels. Francis Harper included many acknowledgments and a special "In Memoriam: Arthur Newlin Leeds":

> It was my great privilege to be associated with him in several of the early efforts of 'rediscovering' the Bartram trail.… It was the cherished plan of Arthur Leeds and myself to work jointly on the present undertaking, in which his special botanical knowledge would have been a contribution of the highest value. But destiny did not permit him to go beyond the initial steps. It has devolved upon myself to carry the program forward, with a very great deal of generous assistance from others; yet the result is doubtless far short of what it might have been with his direct personal attention and devotion.[81]

Francis Harper's second major undertaking, William Bartram's report to Dr. Fothergill, involved similar detailed editing and annotation. Harper concluded that *Travels* and the report to Fothergill cover the same general ground; however, they are far from being duplicates, and the report is more reliable than *Travels* on most of the points where the two do not agree.[82] This assessment is reasonable since the *Report* was written shortly after the events. *Travels* was completed much later and was therefore subject to editing first by Bartram and then by the publisher, without Bartram's review. Harper regarded the report as "a far fresher document than the *Travels*" that "supplies additional information or throws new light on various puzzling species, on

---

[80] This article is often quoted and cited in ch. 1, "The Bartrams' Exploration," of this book.

[81] JB, "Diary of a Journey," 12.

[82] WB, "Travels…: A Report," 123.

his itinerary."[83]

William Bartram's report manuscript is divided into two volumes. He briefly describes his arrival in Charleston from Philadelphia, followed by a section about his travels in Georgia and also the journey across southern Georgia en route to Florida.[84] The second half of volume 1 is "Florida" and covers Bartram's first trip up the St. Johns River as well as his travel westward with traders to the Little St. Juan (Suwannee River) with extended exploration of the Alachua Savanna, which continues into "Florida" of volume 2. "Some days after my arrival at the Store, I began My second trip up the S^t. Johns River," begins volume 2 with his exploration of Mt. Royal, various springs, and the region beyond Lake George. The last section includes detailed records and descriptions of the animals and plants of east Florida.[85] Twenty-six plates of illustrations follow, including a map of William Bartram's travels, historical maps, and Francis Harper's photographs of many Florida sites, as well as Bartram's drawings of Florida plants and animals.

Epilogue

Francis Harper initiated a scientific renaissance of interest in the Bartrams and their Southeastern exploration with his annotated editions of John Bartram's "Diary of a Journey through the Carolinas, Georgia, and Florida, 1765–1766," and William Bartram's "Report to Dr. John Fothergill, 1773–1774." Over the next decade, Francis Harper wrote many articles about his Florida exploration and the Bartrams, particularly about William and his plant and animal nomenclature. At the same time, he used his biologist's point of view along with his scholarly analysis and synthesis to author *The Travels of William Bartram: Naturalist's Edition* based on the first edition of *Travels,* which had been published in Philadelphia in 1791. Francis Harper commented in the preface, "A long-standing need for students of American natural history has, in truth, been a fully annotated and indexed version of Bartram's justly celebrated *Travels....* The inadequacy of the previous dozen or so editions has been felt less by literary scholars than by devotees of the natural sciences."[86]

The 1958 Yale University press edition of Francis Harper's *The Travels*

---

[83] Ibid.

[84] Ibid., 134–44 (Georgia); 145–54 (Florida).

[85] WB, "Travels...: A Report," 154–71 (vol. 2, Florida and Florida animals and plants).

[86] *FHBT,* v.

of William Bartram: Naturalist's Edition included Bartram's text and illustrations along with his original pagination. Francis Harper added notes and commentary, an annotated index, maps, a bibliography, a general index, and even an index of Bartram's errors of spelling, punctuation, and grammar. Bartram's accounts of personal observations were transformed by Harper's scientific knowledge of natural history into an edited guidebook for contemporary biologists, historians, and anthropologists, both professional and amateur. Francis Harper's work also provided a case study for academics in various fields, including literary scholars because he "employed a practical, interdisciplinary methodology well before the invention of ecocriticism."[87]

Ralph Palmer stated at the time of Francis Harper's death that his three major Bartram works were "a monument to the Bartrams and to the scholarship of Francis Harper."[88]

The efforts of Francis Harper produced a contemporary interpretation of and a guide to the Bartrams' natural history observations and also serve as sources for future naturalists and Bartram enthusiasts to follow and refine William Bartram's geographic and scientific tracks.[89] In brief, Francis Harper recreated and stimulated interest in the "Bartram Trail" throughout historic West and East Florida and today's southeast. Harper's *Naturalist Edition* of *Travels* became a guidebook, along with his earlier publications about Bartram, for future Philadelphia connections to Bartram and also for the establishment of the historic Bartram Heritage Trail.

Bartram Trail Conference, Bartram Heritage, Bartram Trail…

The Bartram Trail Conference was created by the governors of eight Southern states as part of America's bicentennial observance in 1976.[90] The organization focuses on William Bartram and his travels, which began (1773)

---

[87] Sturges, "Text and Trail," 19.

[88] Palmer, "Obituaries: Francis Harper."

[89] See especially, Sanders, *Guide to William Bartram's Travels*. This extraordinary book with maps, photos, and contemporary detailed descriptions picks up where Francis Harper left off in many areas and has been added to the library and backpack of Bartram scholars and enthusiasts.

[90] NC, SC, GA, FL, AL, LA, MS, and TN. Established in 1975, the Conference is a regional organization that coordinates Bartram Heritage efforts throughout the southeast. *Bartram Heritage*, a report prepared under a contract between the Bartram Trail Conference and the Heritage Conservation and Recreation Service of the U.S. Department of the Interior, was developed to consider and present a wide range of heritage-related ideas to recognize William Bartram's many contributions to America's natural and cultural history.

and ended (1777) at the historic Bartram's Garden in Philadelphia. The Bartram Trail Conference's initial goals included locating and marking the route William Bartram described in *Travels* through the Carolinas, Georgia, and East and West Florida (the latter now a part of Tennessee, Alabama, Mississippi, and Louisiana). These objectives also required identifying William Bartram's contributions to American and southeast heritage to develop a proposal for a national heritage project (the Bartram Heritage Project) that would recognize and memorialize William Bartram in the natural, historical, and cultural areas he explored. The conference built on Francis Harper's exploration; it also reviewed the contributions of those who preceded Harper at the Academy and those who had followed him through the eight Southern states where Bartram had traveled and also in Philadelphia.

The Bartram Trail Conference was incorporated to develop a proposal for the Bartram Heritage Project; it included two citizen members appointed by the governors of each state as well as any other individuals who wanted to join.[91] The members elected a board of managers to administer the project and to hire three temporary staff members.[92] Robert McCracken Peck, who was on leave as special assistant to the president of the Academy, became the technical director for the project report of the Bartram Trail Conference.[93] In 1977 and 1978, Peck retraced William Bartram's 2400-mile journey through eight Southeastern states on behalf of the National Park Service, U.S. Department of the Interior, the eight state governors, and the Bartram Trail Conference. Peck selected, organized, and coordinated the work of independent volunteer researchers and then assembled their studies and data along with his work into *Bartram Heritage*, the conference's report for the U.S. Department of the Interior's Heritage Conservation and Recreation Service in 1978.[94] *Bartram Heritage* was analyzed and used by the U.S. Department

---

[91] The Bartram Trail Conference is now a not-for-profit corporation registered in the state of Georgia. The officers, board of directors, and other current information are available at www.bartramtrail.org.

[92] Bartram Trail Conference temporary staff at the time: Jerome F. Anderson, project administrator; Robert M. Peck, technical director; and Ann S. Cooper, administrative assistant.

[93] After completing *Bartram Heritage* (U.S. Department of the Interior and the Bartram Trail Conference, 1978), Peck returned to the ANSP as special assistant to the president (Thomas Peter Bennett, 1976–1986) and later became a senior fellow of the institution. Peck is now a distinguished explorer and author of many books and publications, including several about William Bartram.

[94] *Bartram Heritage* was printed in an edition of 1,000; it has since been reissued by the Bartram Trail Conference and is available on its website, www.bartramtrail.org.

of Interior to determine the feasibility of a National Historic Bartram Trail. For the Bartram Trail Conference and Bartram enthusiasts and scholars, *Bartram Heritage* became the guidebook that established Bartram Trail locations, signs, memorials, and sites related to William Bartram's *Travels* throughout the Southeast. The publication of *Bartram Heritage*, which relied heavily on Francis Harper's work, was another landmark in natural historical exploration.

To underpin Peck's preparation of *Bartram Heritage,* some sixty technical studies related to the specific objectives of the Bartram Trail Conference were identified by the staff, academics, government agencies, and laypeople with an interest in and knowledge of William Bartram and his travels. During the course of Peck's work, many of the study units were combined with others; some were deemed unnecessary or not possible and therefore dropped, and a few were also added. Ultimately, thirty technical studies were conducted, and technical reports on the studies were filed with the conference as supporting documents for the report. Conference staff researched and authored a significant number of technical studies. Several of the authors of these materials were associated with the Academy: R. Tucker Abbott, Helen Cruickshank, and Alfred E. Schuyler . The technical authors supplied much of the original material contained in *Bartram Heritage* and thus broke new ground in the field of Bartram scholarship.

Bartram Heritage offered a "string of pearls" concept of a series of sites within a fifty-mile corridor along the approximate route that Bartram traveled from March 1773 to January 1777. Like pearls, Bartram's discoveries and sites were linked by segments of paths he traveled, creating "a string of pearls." The report identified twelve National Landmarks and 101 sites on the National Register of Historic Places in the twenty-two counties within the Florida Bartram Trail Study Corridor.

The National Park Service and the U.S. Department of the Interior collaborated with an Interagency Field Study Task Force, which included the Florida Department of Natural Resources, to determine whether designating a Bartram national scenic or historic trail was feasible and desirable.[95] Their study consulted and analyzed the recommendations of *Bartram Heritage*. A draft of their Bartram trail study was circulated for official comments from

---

[95] The 1968 National Trails Systems Act authorized and provided criteria for reviewing the establishment of national trails of scenic, historic, natural, and cultural value. An amendment to the Act directed the study of eight potential trail routes, one of which was the Bartram Trail.

the southern governors and heads of pertinent federal agencies.[96] The comments of Florida governor Bob Graham are representative of those of seven other governors and agency heads:

> We in Florida support the National Park Service in its efforts to recognize the importance of William Bartram's travels and his accounts of the natural heritage of the Southeastern United States.
>
> We concur with the task force's conclusion that the Bartram Trail does not strictly meet the criteria for designation as a National Historic or Scenic Trail. Other actions, such as the six supplemental actions you have proposed, would serve to appropriately memorialize Bartram's travels. In particular, action six, the concept of the Bartram Heritage Project, would enhance participation by interested parties and would allow for greater flexibility in satisfying local desires for acknowledging Bartram.[97]

Since the *Bartram Heritage* and *Bartram Trail* reports endorsed the "local desires for acknowledging Bartram," many "interested parties" continued or began participating in ventures to memorialize Bartram's travels. The Florida Federation of Garden Clubs led the way by designing the Bartram Trail markers, which are placed within a fifty-mile-wide corridor along the path of Bartram's travels; there are now more than twenty-five such markers in Florida alone.

The William Bartram Scenic and Historic Highway, which was named in honor of his travels in Florida, runs along the east side of the St. Johns River from Jacksonville. This area and the west side of the river include hiking and canoe trails constructed and maintained with the assistance of the Bartram Trail Society of Florida, the Boy Scouts of America, and other local volunteer groups. In Putnam County, a Bartram program staffed by volunteers maintains St. Johns River natural sites and landmarks, such as the Spalding Stores.[98] Early leads were taken in the Bartram Lecture series at Florida State University, naming of buildings such as Bartram Trail High School and

---

[96] *The Bartram Trail: Alabama-Florida-Georgia-Louisiana-Mississippi-North Carolina-South Carolina-Tennessee* (National Park Service, Department of the Interior: National Scenic/Historic Rail Study, February 1982).

[97] Governor Bob Graham to Robert Herbst re: Bartram Trail Report, 14 November 1980, *The Bartram Trail*, 120.

[98] The Bartram Trail in Putnam County website (bartram.putnam-fl.com, accessed 18 September 2018) summarizes ongoing dedicated exploration and research by local citizens and provides interactive maps for Bartram sites called "William Bartram Story Maps," photographs, text, and maps. The YouTube link on that page leads to introductory videos about the trail and many stops along the way.

Bartram Hall for Biological Sciences at the University of Florida, in memorializing William Bartram, his travels, and his residence in Florida. Many sites and markers are named for Bartram, located from the St. Johns River, west to the Alachua Savanna (now Paynes Prairie), to Manatee Springs and the Suwannee River. Bartram memorial gardens and/or arboreta have been dedicated in many Florida locations, including Gainesville, Winter Park, Trenton, and Pensacola. These are just a few of the pearls in a Bartram Heritage Trail string as suggested in *Bartram Heritage*:

> The development of a Bartram Heritage Trail revolves around: (1) a sense of William Bartram, the man; (2) a sense of the places he visited; (3) a sense of the historical times in which he lived. As only the physical places remain today, they must be sensitively developed to evoke the feelings of the other two categories: "the man" and "the times." In many cases, the literal tracing of Bartram's footsteps is not the most appropriate way to commemorate his travels. Where the environment of the actual trail has been irrevocably altered, for example, the development of the trail in its historical location would fail to properly evoke the spirit of Bartram, his times, or even the land as he knew it.[99]

---

[99] Peck, *Bartram Heritage,* 120.

ACKNOWLEDGMENTS

I am grateful for the institutional support received during my tenure as professor and administrator at Florida State University, the Academy of Natural Sciences, the Florida Museum of Natural History, the University of Florida, and the South Florida Museum. I thank these institutions for their backing of and assistance with my work on this project and their staff and faculty members, curators, librarians, and my students, including several coauthors on articles and books related to *Florida Explored*: David Johnston, Dennis Carr, and Ben McFarland.

My special thanks go to Robert (Bob) McCracken Peck for his thoughtful guidance and criticism over many years as well as his shared interest in the Bartrams and their travels.

The hospitality and support of the staff as well as the resources of several other Philadelphia institutions were essential to my research: Bartram's Garden, the Wagner Free Institute of Science, the American Philosophical Society, the Library Company of Philadelphia, the Pennsylvania Historical Society, the College of Physicians, and the University of Pennsylvania. I offer my appreciation to Joel Fry, Susan Glassman, Earle Spamer, John van Horne, and many others associated with these institutions.

I thank the Florida Museum of Natural History staff members for contributing in many different ways: Kurt Auffenberg, George Burgess, Kathleen Deagan, Richard Franz, Douglas Jones, Bruce MacFadden, William Maples, William Marquardt, Jerald Milanich, Roger Portell, Charlotte Porter, Greg Shaak, Sharon Thomas, Thomas Webber, David Webb, Norris Williams, and Elizabeth Wing. My appreciation also goes out to the South Florida Museum staff, Brynne Anne Besio, Tiffany Birakis, Jeff Rodgers, and Matt Woodside, as well as Jennifer Hamilton Tucciarone, John LoCastro, and Mary Francis Weathington. Thanks also to Michael Gannon, Christopher Still, and other friends and colleagues for their many interpretations of Florida's history. Dan Blalock, Jr., friend and continuing supporter of my research and writing about Florida and Georgia natural history, also shared my Bartram enthusiasm.

For my work in Georgia, I am indebted to the creativity and support of Dorinda Dallmeyer, Caroline Harrington, Philip Juras, Brad Sanders, Sara L. Van Beck, and members of the Le Conte-Woodmanston Foundation. Many thanks to Marc Jolley, editor, director, and Bartram scholar, and to

Marsha Luttrell and the Mercer University Press staff.

Copious praise and thanks go to William Bartram and the naturalists inspired by his *Travels*. For over two hundred years, they have explored, studied, and published on Florida's natural history and its changing ecosystems. So too, accolades for the Bartramia efforts of members of the Garden Clubs of America and the Bartram Trail Conference.

My unlimited thanks to Gudrun Dorothea Bennett, who has long supported and shared in my delights of exploring in Bartram's tracks.

APPENDIX

AUDUBON'S BIRDS, MAMMALS, AND PLANTS

TABLE 1

Audubon's Florida Birds[1]

Becalmed, 1826
Dusky Petrel, Plate CCXCIX 184–185, 3:620–641

East Florida

American Coot, Plate CCXXXIX, 97–101, 3:291–94
Anhinga [Snake-Bird], Plate CCCXVI, 122–132, 4:137–50
Black Skimmer [Razor-Billed Shearwater], Plate CCCXXIII, 157–61
Blue Heron [Little Blue Heron], Plate CCCVII, 231–35, 4:58–62
Caracara Eagle, Plate CLXI, 91–94, 2:350–52, ANSP
Common Gallinule, Plate CCXLIV, 138–42, 3:330–33, ANSP
Florida Jay, Plate LXXXVII, 147–50
Glossy Ibis, Plate CCCLXXXVII, 142–44
Great Blue Heron, Plate CCXI, 168–77
Herring Gull, Plate CCXCI, 102–104, 3:592–94
Louisiana Heron [Tricolored Heron], CCXVII, 187–91, 3:136–39
Night Heron, Plate CXXXVI, 161–67, 3:275–80 ANSP

---

[1] Entries based on reference to Florida in Audubon's *Ornithological Biography*. Bird names and plates are numbered according to Audubon in *Birds of America*. Page citations are for Proby, *Audubon in Florida*; volume and page citations are to *Ornithological Biography*. ANSP indicates that an Audubon specimen is in the collections of the Academy of Natural Sciences. In some cases, the birds were observed and have been discussed in both East Florida and Florida Keys locations. In this table, they are listed only once, in the area most commonly cited in the Audubon entry. Area information from Dwight, *Audubon, Watercolors and Drawings*, 44–47; Proby, *Audubon in Florida*, 39–40, 85–307, Audubon, *Ornithological Biography*.

Orange-Crowned Warbler, Plate CLXXVIII, 117–19, 4:449–50

Ruddy Duck, Plate CCCXLLIII, 104–107, 4:326–28

Schinz' Sandpiper, Plate CCLXXVIII, 101–102, 3:529

Scolopaceous Courlan [Limpkin], Plate CCCLXXVII, 229–31, 4:543–44

Whooping Crane [Sandhill Crane], Plate CCXXVI, Male, 177–82, 3:205–210; CCLXI, Young, 182–83, 3:441

Wilson's Plover breeding plumage, Plate CCIX, 144–47, 3:73–75 Also in Keys

Wood Ibis [Wood Stork], Plate CCXVI, 150–56, 3:128–31

Yellow Red-Poll [Palm Warbler], Plate CLXIII, 94–96, 2:360

White-Headed Eagle, Plate CXXVI, 134–138, 2:160–64

Florida Keys[2]

American Flamingo, Plate CCCCXXXI, 241–44, 5:255–57

Black headed Gull [Laughing Gull], Plate CCCXIV, 287–94, 4:118–26

Blue Headed Pigeon or Quail Dove, Plate CLXXII, 261–62, 2:411–12

Booby Gannet [Brown Booby], Plate CCVII, 271–77, 3:63–67

Brown Pelican, Plate CCLI, 107–17, 3:376–85

Cayenne (Royal) Tern, Plate CCLXXIII, 87–91, 3:505–509

Florida Cormorant [Double-crested Cormorant], Plate CCLII, 216–23, 3:387–94

Frigate Pelican [Magnificent Frigate bird], Plate CCLXXI, 295–302, 3:495–501

Great Blue Heron, Plate CCXI, 168–177, 3:87–95

Great Marbled Godwit [Marbled Godwit], Plate CCXXXVIII, 304–307, 3:287–88

Great White Heron, *Plate* CCXXIX, CCLXXXI, 191–200, 3:542–50

Greenshank, Plate CCLXIX, 186–87, 3:483

Ground Dove, Plate CLXXXII, 253–55, 2:421–74

Key West Pigeon [Key West Quail-Dove], Plate CLXVII, 267–71, 2:382–86

Louisiana Heron [Tricolored], Plate CCXVII, 187–91, 3:136–39

Mangrove Cuckoo, Plate CLXIX, 265–66, 2:390–91.

Mangrove Hummingbird [Black-throated Mango], Plate CLXXXIV, 262–64, 2:480–81

Noddy Tern, Plate CCLXXV, 277–80, 3:516–18

Pipery Flycatcher [Gray Kingbird], Plate CLXX, 208–12, 2:392–95

Red-Backed Sandpiper, Plate CCXC, 132–35, 3:580

Reddish Egret, Plate CCLVI, 200–208, 3:411–17, ANSP

Roseate Tern, Plate CCLX, 213–16, 3:296–98

Roseate Spoonbill, Plate CCCXXI, 256–61, 4:188–93

---

[2] "Audubon Visits the Florida Keys"; Proby, *Audubon in Florida*, 39–40, 85; Audubon, *Ornithological Biography*.

Sanderling [Ruddy Plover], Plate CCXXX, 120–22, 3:231–32
Sandwich Tern, Plate CCLXXXI, 302–304, 3:531–33
Semipalmated Snipe [Willet], Plate CCLXXIV, 244–47, 3:51–13
Sooty Tern, Plate CCXXXV, 280–86, 3:263–68
Tropic Bird [White-tailed Tropicbird], Plate CCLXII, 286–87, 3:442
White Ibis, Plate CCXXII, 235–40, 3:173–77 ANSP
White-headed Pigeon [White-crowned Pigeon], Plate CLXXVII, 247–52, 2:443–48
Zenaida Dove, Plate CLXII, 223–28, 2:354–59

TABLE 2

Florida Mammals Described by Audubon and Bachman[3]

Volume 1

Florida Rat (*Neotoma Floridana*, Say et Ord) [32][4] Plate IV

[32] "*Synonymes. Mus Floridanus, Ord, Nouv.Bull.de la Societé Philomatique, 1818; Arvicola Floridianus, Harlan, Fauna Amer., p.142; Arvicola Floridianus, Godman, Nat Hist., vol. ii., p. 69; Neotoma Floridiana, Say et Ord, Journ. Acad. Nat. Sciences, vol. iv., part 2, p. 352, figure.*"

[34] "*In Florida, they burrow under stones and the ruins of dilapidated buildings...*"

[36] "*It was brought from East Florida by Mr. Ord, in 1818, but not published until 1825. It was then supposed by him to be peculiar to Florida and received its specific name from that circumstance. We had, however, obtained a number of...*"

[36] "*On a further examination of Bartram's work...we find his descriptions of the habits of this species very accurate...*"

Carolina Gray Squirrel (*Sciurus Carolinensis*, Gmel.) [55] Plate VII

[62] "*It is the most abundant species in Florida...*"

Common American Shrew Mole (*Scalops Aquaticus, Linn.*) [81] Plate X

[91] "*The Shrew Mole is found inhabiting various parts of the country...and is abundant in...Florida.*"

Marsh-Hare (*Lepus Palustris, Bachman*) [151] Plate XVIII

[156] "*We received a living specimen from Key West, the southern point of Florida.*"

[156] "*We did not publish a description of the species until 1836. In the following year, GRAY, who had not seen the Transactions of the Acad. Of Natural Sciences of Philadelphia, in which our description was contained, described it under the name* Lepus Douglassii.*"

Gray Fox (*Vulpes Virginianus, Schreber*) [162] Plate XXI

[172] "*It exists plentifully in Florida...*"

[166] *and...in the Southern States, the cotton –rat, and Florida rat, constitute no inconsiderable portion of its food.*"

Gray Rabbit (*Lepus Sylvaticus, Bachman*) [173] Plate XXII

[173] "*We have traced this species through all the higher portions of Florida.*"

---

[3] Audubon and Bachman, *The Viviparous Quadrupeds of North America*. Replica published for the National Audubon Society (Kent, Ohio: Volair Books, 1979) or *The Complete Audubon: A Precise Replica of the Complete Works of John James Audubon, Comprising the Birds of America (1840–44) and the Quadrupeds of North America (1851– 54) in Their Entirety*, 5 vols. (New York: National Audubon Society, 1978–1979).

[4] The [page number] is in the volume that is indicated. They provide references for the reader.

[180] Discusses Harlan's & Godman's work and notes: *"In 1827, we proposed the name of Lepus sylvaticus, and assigned our reasons for so doing in a subsequent paper (See Journ. Acad. Nat. Sc., vol. viii, part 1, p.75)"*

Common Flying Squirrel (*Pteromys Volucella, Gmel.*) [216] Plate XXVIII

222 *"...we obtained specimens in Florida..."*

Cotton-Rat (*Sigmond Hispidum, Say and Ord*) [227] Plate XXX

[227] Preface discusses the controversy and has dental work. *"Synonyms"* *"The Wood-Rat, Bartram's Travels in East Florida, 1791, p. 124."*

[230] *"They fight fiercely, and one of them will overpower a Florida rat twice its own size."*

[231] *"...when captured it is far more savage than the Florida rat."*

[232] *"Ord obtained specimens in Florida in 1818, and it was generally supposed that it was not found further to the north. In the spring of 1815, three years earlier than Mr. Ord, we [Bachman] procured a dozen specimens in Carolina, which we neglected to describe. Say and Ord, and Harlan, described it about the same time, (in 1825,) and Godman a year afterwards. We prefer adopting the name given to it by the individual who first brought it to the notice of naturalists.... The genus Sigmond, at the time it was proposed [Say and Ord], was strongly objected to by Harlan and Godman; we have, however, after a good deal of investigation, concluded to adopt it, although our plate of the Cotton-Rat was lettered Arvicola hispidus."*

Mink (*Putorius Vison, Linn.*) [250] Plate XXXIII

[255] *"We once saw a Mink issuing from a hole in the earth, dragging by the neck a large Florida rat."*

American White-Footed Mouse (*Mus Leucopus*) [305] Plate XL

[304] *"Dr. Leitner, an eminent botanist, who, whilst acting as surgeon in the army, was unfortunately killed in the Florida war, informed us that whilst on a botanizing tour through Florida a few years ago, he was frequently kept awake during a portion of the night by the White-footed Mice which had taken possession of the huts of the Indians and the log cabins of the early white settlers."*

[305] *"We received specimen from Florida by Dr. Leitner"*

American Beaver (*Castor Fiber, Linn.*) [347] Plate XLVI

[357] *"Bartram, in his visit to Florida in 1778 (Travels, p. 281) speaks of it at that time existing in Georgia and Florida. It has, however become a scarce species in all the Atlantic States, and in some of them has been entirely extirpated."*

Volume 2

Virginian Opossum (*Didelphis Virginiana, Shaw*) [107] Plate LXVI

Black American Wolf (*Canis Lupus, Linn.*) [126] Plate LXVII

[130] *"All packs of American Wolves usually consist of various shades of colour...in Florida the prevailing colour of the wolves is black."*

Fox Squirrel (*Sciurus Capistratus, Bosc.*) [132] Plate LXVIII

[138] "*It exists in...Florida...*"

Le Conte's Pine-Mouse (*Arvicola Pinetorum, Le Conte*) [216] Plate LXXX

[219] "*...we have specimens sent to us from...Florida.*"

Common American Deer (*Cervus Virginianus*, Pennant) [220] Plate LXXXI

[225] "*It is a remarkable, but well ascertained fact, that in Alabama and Florida, a majority of fawns are produced in November.*"

[238] "*It [Deer] is rather common in...and Florida, especially in barren or swampy regions, of which vast tracts remain uncultivated.*"

Red Texas Wolf (*Canis Lupus, Linn.*) [240] Plate LXXXII

[243] "*To the south, in Florida, the prevailing colour is black...*"

Common Mouse (Mus Musculus, Linn.) [277] Plate XC

An early report of an invasive species.

[280] "*The Common Mouse is not a native of America, but exists in all countries where ships have landed cargo, and may be said to tread closely on the heels of commerce.*"

The Cougar—Panther (*Felis Concolor,Linn.*) [305] Plate XCVII

[312] "*...it is quite abundant in Florida...*"

———

Volume 3

American Black Bear (*Ursus Americanus, Pallas*) [187] Plate CXLI

[196] "*The Black Bear has been found throughout North America in every wooded district from the north through all the States to Mexico, but has not hitherto been discovered in California...*"

Rice Meadow Mouse (*Arvicola Oryzivora, Bach.*) [214] Plate CXLIV

[216] "*Dr. Leitner brought us a specimen obtained in the Everglades of Florida.*"

[216] Audubon comments that the specimen, after being shipped to Dr. Pickering at the Academy, was stolen by Dr. Harlan, who named it in a publication in the New York Annals. Here they revert to the name given by the original describer, Rev. Dr. Bachman.

Southern Pouched Rat (*Pseudostoma Floridana*, Aud. and Bach.) [242] Plate CL

[244] "*This species is found in the high pine barren regions, from the middle of Georgia and Alabama to the southern point of Florida, as far as the elevated portions of that State extend south.*"

TABLE 3

Audubon's Florida Botanicals[5]

East Florida[6]

American Coot, CCXXXIX; 3:291–94. Grassy margins head of the St. Johns near Dexter Lake.

Anhinga [Snake-Bird], CCCXVI; 4:136–60. Trees along the St. Johns River.

Blue Heron [Little Blue Heron], CCCVII; 4:58–67. River grasses with pine lands in the background.

Boat-Tailed Grackle [Great Crow Blackbird], CLXXXVII; 2:504–10. Live Oak with strands of Spanish Moss by Lehman. Reference to the "Live Oakers" and description of trees.

Caracara Eagle, CLXI; 2:350–53. Tree branch.

Common Gallinule, CCXLIV; 3:330–35. Marsh grasses.

Florida Jay, LXXXVII; 3:87–97. Persimmon Tree.

Great Blue Heron, CCXI; 3:87–97. Marsh grasses.

Louisiana Heron [Tricolored Heron], CCXVII; 3:136–41. Swamp with Sabal Palms, right.

Mangrove Cuckoo, CLVIX, 2:390–391 "The Seven Years Apple...found on all the Florida Keys...the outer inlets and the mainland."

Night Heron, CXXXVI; 3:275–382. Mangroves. "In the Floridas, they are partial to mangroves."

Orange-Crowned II:e Warbler, CLXXVIII9; 2:449–51. Huckleberry. "This plant...is very abundant in the pine barrens of the Floridas, where it is in full flower in February, and attains a heights of from four to eight feet."

Pipery Flycatcher CLXX, 2:392–95 "The branch...rather rare on the Florida Keys...blooms during the season when this bird builds its nest."

Whooping Crane [Sandhill Crane], CCXXVI, Male; 3:202–13; CCLXI, Young; 3:441 "...situated in the vicinity of large marshes, covered with tall grasses...and

---

[5] Audubon, Lehman or Maria Bachman illustrated plants for some of Audubon's bird plates. The quotes are Audubon's. For some birds, Florida plants or habitats are discussed in *Ornithological Biography*. Some descriptions are also replicated in the plates. Plates are numbered according to Audubon/Havell. Entries are based on their references to plants in *Ornithological Biography*. The birds are also listed in Table 1. Plates with Audubon's foliage comments are included here with brief quotes. Plates with foliage but without his comments are shown here without quotes. Plates without foliage or comments on by Audubon are not listed in this brief summary.

[6] Proby, *Audubon in Florida*, 20.

other plants." "…William Bartram, when speaking of this species, must have mistaken the Wood Ibis for it…"

Wilson's Plover breeding plumage, Plate CCIX; 3:73–76. Unidentified plant. Audubon mentions his meetings with Wilson and "nothing worthy of his attention was procured."

Wood Ibis [Wood Stork], CCXVI; 3:128–35. Cypress swamp/lake with grasses. "…through cane-brake, cypress-swamp, and tangled wood…on the margin of a dark water bayou…"

Yellow Red-Poll [Palm Warbler], CLXIII, Adult & Young; 2:360–61; Plate CXL, Male & Female; 2:259–62. "In the plate you will find a branch of the wild orange, with its flowers…indigenous in many parts of Florida…in the wildest portions of that wild country."

Florida Keys[7,8]

Blue Headed Pigeon or Quail Dove, Plate CLXXII, 2:411–12. "The beautiful Cyperus [wild Poinsettia] represented in this plate is quite abundant on all the dry Keys of the Floridas, and is also found in many parts of the interior of the peninsula." Tall plants to the right rear.

Booby Gannet [Brown Booby], Plate CCVII, 3:67–68. On a branch view from Island toward land of another island near Tortugas.

Brown Pelican, Plate CCLI; 3:376–86. Special end section "The Mangrove" discusses the Red Mangrove represented in the plate and Land [Black] Mangrove, which he has seen on Key West.

Florida Cormorant [Double-crested Cormorant], Plate CCLII, 3:387–95. Inlet with mangrove islands

Great Marbled Godwit [Marbled Godwit], Plate CCXXXVIII 3:287–90. Grasses mud-bar

Greenshank, Plate CCLXIX, 3:483–85. Describes as collecting on Sand Key yet landscape bkgd is Castillo St Augustine

Ground Dove, Plate CLXXXII, 2:471–75. Wild orange (*Citrus aurantium*) branch

Key West Pigeon [Key West Quail-Dove], Plate CLXVII 2:382–86. Sea Grape leaves?? "The plants represented in this plate grew on Key West…purple flowers are a Convolvulus, the other an Ipomaea."

Mangrove Cuckoo, Plate CLXIX, 2:390–91. "The Seven Years' Apple" "The plant on a twig of which I have represented the Mangrove Cuckoo, is found on all the Florida Keys…on the mud flats that exist between the outer islets and the mainland."

Mangrove Hummingbird [Black-throated Mango], Plate CLXXXIV, 2:480–82.

---

[7] Proby, *Audubon in Florida*, 39–40
[8] "Audubon Visits the Florida Keys."

The Trumpet Vine or Creeper (*Campsis radicans*) as drawn by Maria Martin who called it "Bignonia."

Pipery Flycatcher [Gray Kingbird], Plate CLXX, 2:392–96." A species rare on the Florida Keys...blooms during the season when this bird builds its nest."

Reddish Egret, Plate CCLVI, 3:411–19, ANSP. Marsh grasses and broad-leafed plant

Roseate Spoonbill, Plate CCCXXI, 4:188–97. Grasses, flats low tide. "along the marshy and muddy borders of estuaries, the mouths of rivers, ponds or sea island..."

Semipalmated Snipe [Willet], Plate CCLXXIV, 3:510–15. "Grasses rocks...partially submersed islets of the Floridas called Duck Keys...scantily covered bushes and some mangroves."

White Ibis, Plate CCXXII, 3:173–80, ANSP. "Sandy Island. The vegetation consists of a few tall mangroves, thousands of wild plum trees, several species of cactus...more than twenty feet high, different sorts of smilax, grape-vines, cane, palmettoes, Spanish bayonets..."

White-headed Pigeon [White-crowned Pigeon], Plate CLXXVII, 2:443–48. Rough-leaved Cordia. Geiger Tree. Section at end. Cordia sebestena is a West Indies shrub that grows in the Keys and also in the author's back yard. From the yard opposite Dr. Strobel: "grew in a yard opposite to that of Dr. Strobel, through whose influence I procured a large bough, from which the drawing was made, with the assistance of Mr. Lehman."

Zenaida Dove, Plate CLXII, 2:354–59. Purple-flowered Anona. "This plant [Pond apple or custard apple] is very abundant on many of the outer Keys of the Floridas."

ARCHIVES

General Archives

Leidy, Joseph. Papers. College of Physicians of Philadelphia (CPP), Philadelphia, PA.

Moore, Clarence Bloomfield. #9181. Division of Rare and Manuscript Collections, Cornell University Library.

Peale Family Papers. Historical Society of Pennsylvania, Philadelphia, PA.

Peale Scrapbook, 1820[?]–1850[?], Titian Ramsay Peale Collection, Rare Book Collection, American Museum of Natural History Research Library, New York, NY. Cited as L. Peale manuscript.

Torrey, John. Papers. New York Botanical Garden (NYBG) Archives. The Bronx, New York City, NY.

The following collections are housed at the Archives of the Academy of Natural Sciences, Philadelphia, Pennsylvania (ANSP). Each collection comprises a wide variety of documents, and these are specified within the notes.

Bartram, John (1699–1778). Papers, 1757–1941. Collection 15. Cited as ANSP Archives, JB Papers.

Brown, Stewardson (1867–1921). Papers, 1882–1906. Collection 168. Cited as ANSP Archives, Brown Papers.

Collins, Zaccheus (1764–1831). Correspondence, 1805–1827. Collection 129. Cited as ANSP Archives, Collins correspondence.

Expeditions. Papers, 1819–1969. Collection 113. Cited as ANSP Archives, Expeditions.

Fowler, Henry Weed (1878–1965). Correspondence, 1894–1941. Collection 220. Cited as ANSP Archives, Fowler correspondence.

———. Illustrations, 1900–1960. Collection 197. Cited as ANSP Archives, Fowler Illustrations.

————. Journal, 1885–1948. Collection 199. Cited as ANSP Archives, Fowler Journal.

————. Papers, 1894–1960. Collection 117. Cited as ANSP Archives, Fowler Papers.

Huber, Wharton (1877–1942). Huber-Stone correspondence, 1875–1949. Collection 186. Cited as ANSP Archives, Huber-Stone correspondence.

Le Conte, John Eatton (1784–1860). Papers, 1818–1826. Collection 531. Cited as ANSP Archives, Le Conte Papers.

Leidy, Joseph (1823–1891). Correspondence, 1839–1891. Collection 1. Cited as ANSP Archives, Leidy correspondence.

————. Memorial Albums, 1846–1892. Collection 12. Cited as ANSP Archives, Leidy albums.

Meetings, Minutes, 1812–1927. Collection 502. Cited as ANSP Archives, Meetings.

Memberships, Nominations, 1817–1929. Collection 115. Cited as ANSP Archives, Memberships.

Pennell, Francis Whittier (1886–1952). Biographies of botanists, n.d. Collection 221. Cited as ANSP Archives, Pennell biographies.

Publicity, Papers, 1880–1957. Collection 417. Cited as ANSP Archives, Publicity.

Say, Thomas (1787–1834). Letters to the Melsheimers, 1813–1825. Collection 13. Cited as ANSP Archives, Say letters.

BIBLIOGRAPHY

Adicks, Richard, ed. *Le Conte's Report on East Florida*, by John Eatton Le Conte. Orlando: University of Florida Presses, 1978.

Agassiz, Elizabeth Cary, ed. *Louis Agassiz: His Life and Correspondence*. Boston: Houghton, Mifflin, 1890.

Agassiz, Louis. *Florida Reefs, Keys and Coast. Annual Report of the Superintendent of the Coast Survey During the Year Ending November, 1851, Senate Documents, No. III,* 32 Cong., 1ˢᵗ Sess., Appendix No. 10, 145–60.

———. *Methods of Study in Natural History*. Boston: Ticknor & Fields, 1863.

———. *Report on the Florida Reefs, Memoirs of the Museum of Comparative Zoology at Harvard College*. Vol. 7, No. 1., edited by Alexander E. R. Agassiz and L. F. Pourtales. Cambridge: MCZ, 1880. (Note that this is a later edited version of *Florida Reefs, Keys and Coast (1851)*, above.)

Aiton, William. *Hortus Kewensis: or, A catalogue of the plants cultivated in the Royal Botanic Garden at Kew*. Vol. 3. London: His Majesty for George Nicol, Bookseller, 1789.

Anonymous. "The Audubon of Turtles." *Georgia Alumni Record* 51 (1972): 15–18.

Anonymous. "Explorations in Florida." *Philadelphia Inquirer*. 7 July 1887. WFIS Archives. Coll. 89-040, 1:34.

Anonymous. "Florida Explorations." *Philadelphia Inquirer*. 3 October 1887. WFIS Archives. Coll. 89-040, 1:24.

Anonymous. *Members and Correspondents of the Academy of Natural Sciences of Philadelphia* (facsimile of the 1877 edition printed for the Academy in Philadelphia). Charleston, SC: BiblioLife, 2010.

Anonymous. "New Publications—Geological Florida." *New York Times*. 30 January 1888. WFIS Archives. Coll. 89-040, 1:25A1.

Anonymous. "Scientific Intelligence: III. Botany and Zoology." *AJS* 30 (November 1860): 137.

Armes, William Dallam, ed., and Joseph Le Conte. *The Autobiography of Joseph Le Conte*. New York: D. Appleton and Company, 1903.

Aten, Lawrence E., and Jerald T. Milanich. "Clarence Bloomfield Moore," in *Philadelphia and the Development of Americanist Archaeology*, edited by Fowler and Wilcox, 113–33. Tuscaloosa: University of Alabama Press, 2003.

Audubon, John James. *The Birds of America*. 5 vols. Philadelphia: E. G. Dorsey, 1843.

———. *The Complete Audubon: A Precise Replica of the Complete Works of John James Audubon, Comprising the Birds of America. 1840–44 (and the Quadru-*

peds of North America. 1851–54) in Their Entirety. 5 vols. New York: National Audubon Society, 1978–1979.

———. *John James Audubon: Writings and Drawings.* Edited and introduced by Christoph Irmscher. New York: Library of America, 1999.

———. Letter to the editor (William Featherstonhaugh). 12 January 1832. *Monthly Journal of Geology and Natural Science* 1/10 (June 1832): 535.

———. *The Original Water-Color Paintings by John James Audubon for the Birds of America.* New York: Crown Publishers, Inc., 1966.

———. *Ornithological Biography, Or an Account of the Habits of the Birds of the United States of America.* 5 vols. Edinburgh: Adam & Charles Black, 1834.

Audubon, John James, and Rev. John Bachman. *The Imperial Collection of Audubon Animals; The Quadrupeds of North America,* edited by Victor H. Cahalane. New York: Bonanza Books, 1967.

———. *The Viviparous Quadrupeds of North America.* Replica published for the National Audubon Society. Kent, OH: Volair Books, 1979.

Audubon, Maria R. *Audubon and His Journals.* Vol. 1. New York: Chelsea House, 1983.

Baatz, Simon. "Philadelphia Patronage: The Institutional Structure of Natural History in the New Republic, 1800–1833." *Journal of the Early Republic* 8 (Summer 1988): 128–30.

Bachman, John. "On the Migration of the Birds of North America." *American Journal of Science* 30 (1836): 81–99.

Bailey, J. W. "Discovery of an Infusorial Stratum in Florida." *American Journal of the Sciences and Arts,* ser. 2, 10 (1850): 282.

Barnhart, John Hendley. "John Eatton Le Conte." *American Midland Naturalist* 5 (1917): 135–38.

———. "Nathaniel Ware [biographic footnote]." *Journal of the New York Botanical Garden* 24 (1923): 21.

Bartram, John. "Diary of a Journey through the Carolinas, Georgia, and Florida." Annotated by Francis Harper. *Transactions of the American Philosophical Society* 33/1 (December 1942) i–iv; 1–120. Cited in-text as JB, "Diary of a Journey."

Bartram, John, and William Bartram. *Catalogue of American trees, shrubs, and herbaceous plants: most of which...* (1783). Philadelphia: Bartram & Reynolds, 1807.

The Bartram Trail: Alabama-Florida-Georgia-Louisiana-Mississippi-North Carolina-South Carolina-Tennessee. National Park Service, Department of the Interior: National Scenic/Historic Rail Study, February 1982.

Bartram, William. "Travels in Georgia and Florida, 1773–74: A Report to Dr. John Fothergill." Annotated by Francis Harper. *Transactions of the American Philosophical Society* 33/2 (November 1943) 121–242. Cited as WB, "Travels...: A Report."

————. *The Travels of William Bartram: Naturalist's Edition.* Annotated and indexed by Francis Harper. Athens: University of Georgia Press, 1998. First published 1958 by Yale University (Cambridge). Cited in text as *FHBT*.

————. *Travels through North & South Carolina, Georgia, East & West Florida, The Cherokee Country, The Extensive Territories of the Muscogulges, or Creek Confederacy, and the Country of the Chactaws: Containing an Account of the Soil and Natural Productions of those Regions, together with Observations on the Manners of the Indians.* Philadelphia: James and Johnston, 1791. WBT

Beall, Walli. *The Seasons of Goodwood.* Tallahassee: Beall and Goodwood, 2015.

Bedini, S. "Andrew Ellicott, Surveyor of the Wilderness." *Surveying and Mapping* (June 1976): 113–35.

Belleville, Bill. *River of Lakes.* Athens: University of Georgia Press, 2000.

Bennett, Thomas Peter. "The 1817 Florida Expedition of the Academy of Natural Sciences." *Proceedings of the Academy of Natural Sciences of Philadelphia* 152/1 (2002): 1–21.

————. *A Celebration of John and William Bartram: In Philadelphia and Florida.* Indianapolis: AuthorHouse, 1993.

————. "The History of the Academy of Natural Sciences of Philadelphia." In *Contributions to the History of North American Natural History.* Edited by Alwyne Wheeler. 1–14. London: Society for the Bibliography of Natural History, 1983.

————. *The Le Contes: Scientific Family of Woodmanston.* Bradenton, FL: Johnson Printing, 2014.

————. *The Legacy: South Florida Museum.* Lanham, MD: University Press of America, 2011.

————. "The Peales and Science in Philadelphia." *Proceedings of the Peale Symposium, Independence National Historical Park.* Philadelphia, PA. April 11, 1980. Independence National Historical Park, National Park Service. Copy also at ANSP Library.

Benson, Keith R. "From Museum Research to Laboratory Research: The Transformation of Natural History into Academic Biology." In *The American Development of Biology.* 49–83. New Brunswick, NJ: Rutgers University Press, 1991.

Berkeley, Edmund, and Dorothy Smith Berkeley. *The Life and Travels of John Bartram: From Lake Ontario to the River St. John.* Tallahassee: University Presses of Florida, 1982.

Binney, Amos, ed. *The Terrestrial Air-breathing Mollusks of the United States, Vol. 1.* Boston: C.C. Little & J. Brown, 1851–1878.

Böhlke, Eugenia B. "Catalog of Type Specimens in the Ichthyological Collection of the Academy of Natural Sciences of Philadelphia." Special Publication 14, ANSP, 1984.

Bonaparte, Charles L. *American Ornithology; or the Natural History of Birds inhabiting the United States, not given by Wilson.* Engravings by Alexander

Lawson. Original hand coloring by A. Rider. 4 vols. (vol. 1, 1825; vol. 2, 1828; vol. 3, 1828; vol. 4, 1833). Philadelphia: Carey, Lea & Carey, 1825–1833.

———. "An Account of Four Species of Stormy Petrels." *JANS* 3 (pt. 2, 1824): 227–33.

———. "Descriptions of Two New Species of Mexican Birds." *JANS* 4, pt. 2 (1824–1825): 387–90.

———. "Further Additions to the Ornithology of the United States and Observations on the Nomenclature of Certain Species." *Annals Lyceum Natural History, New York* 2 (1828): 154–60.

———. "Supplement to the Genera of North American Birds and to the Synopsis of the Species Found within the Territory of the United States." *Zoological Journal* 3 (1827): 49–53.

Bonnemains, Jacqueline. *Charles-Alexandre Lesueur en Amérique du nord (1816–1837): catalogue des documents du Muséum d'histoire naturelle du Havre.* 2 Vols. No. 35 of Annales du Museum du Havre. Le Havre, France: Muséum d'Histoire Naturelle, 1986.

Braley, Rance O. *Nineteenth Century Archer: The Archer Story.* Archer, FL: Archer Historical Society, 2012.

Braund, Kathryn E. Holland, and Charlotte M. Porter, eds. *Fields of Vision: Essays on the Travels of William Bartram.* Tuscaloosa: University of Alabama Press, 2010.

Brinton, Daniel Garrison. "Artificial Shell-deposits of the United States." *Smithsonian Institution. Annual Report. 1866.* Washington: Smithsonian Institution, 1867. 356–58.

———. "A City Gone to Seed." *Yale Literary Magazine* 12 (June 1857): 261.

———. "Discussion," *PAPS* 35 (November 1896): 433–48.

———. *A Guide-Book of Florida and the South.* Introduction to facsimile reproduction of the 1869 edition by William Goza. In the Bicentennial Floridiana Facsimile Series, edited by Samuel Proctor. Gainesville: University of Florida Press, 1878.

———. *Notes on the Floridian Peninsula.* Philadelphia: Joseph Sabin, 1859.

———. "Report of the Professor of Ethnology and Anthropology." *PANS* 45 (1893): 570.

Brose, David S., and Nancy Marie White, eds. *The Northwest Florida Expeditions of Clarence Bloomfield Moore.* Tuscaloosa: University of Alabama Press, 1999.

Brown, Robin C. *Florida's First People.* Sarasota, FL: Pineapple Press, 1994.

Buker, George E. "Lieutenant Levin M. Powell, U.S.N., Pioneer of Riverine Warfare." *The Florida Historical Quarterly* 47/3 (January 1969): 253–75.

Burgess, Edward S. "The Work of the Torrey Botanical Club." *Bulletin of the Torrey Botanical Club* 27/10 (1900): 552–58.

Burtt, Edward H. Jr., and William E. Davis, Jr. *Alexander Wilson: The Scot Who Founded American Ornithology.* Cambridge: Harvard University Press, 2013.

Callomon, Paul. "Henry A. Pilsbry and Yoichiro Hirase, with a translation by Tokubei Kuroda," "In Memory of Dr. H. A. Pilsbry: Pilsbry and the Mollusca of Japan," *PANS* 153/1 (2003): 1–6.

Carter, H. J. "Catalogue of Marine Sponges, Collected by Mr. Jos. Willcox, on the West Coast of Florida." *PANS* 36 (1884): 202–209.

Cashin, Edward J. *William Bartram and the American Revolution on the Southern Frontier.* Columbia: University of South Carolina Press, 2000.

Chapman, A. W. *Flora of the Southern United States: Containing an Abridged Description of the Flowering Plants and Ferns of Tennessee, North and South Carolina, Georgia, Alabama, Mississippi, and Florida: Arranged According to the Natural System.* New York: Ivison, Phinney, and Co., 1860.

———. "List of Plants Growing Spontaneously in the Vicinity of Quincy, Florida." *Western Journal of Medicine and Surgery* 3 (June 1845): 461–83.

———. "*Torreya taxifolia*, Arnott. A Reminiscence," *Botanical Gazette* 10/4 (1885): 250–54.

Conant, R. "Henry Weed Fowler 1878–1965." *Copeia* 3 (1966): 628–29.

Conrad, Timothy. "Catalogue of Shells Inhabiting Tampa Bay and other Parts of the Florida Coast." *American Journal of Science and Arts*, ser. 2, 2 (1846): 393–400.

———. "Descriptions of New Species of Organic Remains from the Upper Eocene Limestone of Tampa Bay." *American Journal of Science and Arts*, ser. 2, 2/6 (1846): 399–400.

———. "Observations of the Geology of a Part of East Florida, with a Catalogue of Recent Shells of the Coast." *American Journal of Science and Arts* 52 (1846): 36–45.

———. "Observations on American Fossils, with Descriptions of Two New Species." *PANS* 17 (1865): 184.

———. "Observations on the Tertiary and More Recent Formations of a Portion of the Southern States." *JANS* 7, pt. 1 (1834): 128–29.

Corgan, James X., ed. "Early American Geological Surveys and Gerard Troost's Field Assistants, 1831–1836." In *The Geological Sciences in the Antebellum South.* Tuscaloosa: University of Alabama Press, 1982.

Corning, Howard, ed. *Letters of John James Audubon, 1826–1840.* 1930. Two vols. Reprint edition. New York: Kraus Reprint Co., 1969.

The Correspondence of Thomas Carlyle and Ralph Waldo Emerson, 1834–1872. Boston: Houghton, Mifflin, [1884].

Coues, Elliott. "Fasti ornithologiae redivivi.—No. 1, Bartram's 'Travels,'" *Proceedings of the Academy of Natural Sciences* 27 (1895): 338–58.

———. "General Notes." *The Auk*, New Series, 16 (1899): 84.

Croom, H. B. "Botanical Communications." *AJS* 25/1 (1834): 69–77; *AJS* 26/2 (1834): 313–20; *AJS* 28 (1835): 165–67.

———. *A Catalogue of Plants, Native or Naturalized, in the Vicinity of New Bern, North Carolina: with remarks and synonyms.* New York: G. P. Scott, 1837.

————. "Observations on the genus SARRACENIA." *Annals of the New York Lyceum of Natural History* 4 (1848): 96–104.

————. "Some Account of the Agricultural Soil and Products of Middle Florida, in a Letter to the Editor." *Farmers Register* 2/1 (June 1834).

Cruickshank, Helen G., ed. *John & William Bartram's America: Selections from the Writings of the Philadelphia Naturalists*. New York: Devin-Adair Co., 1957.

Cushing, Frank Hamilton. "Discussion," *PAPS* 35 (November 1896): 433–48.

————. "Exploration of Ancient Key Dwellers' Remains on the Gulf Coast of Florida." *PAPS* 35 (1896): 329–448.

————. *Exploration of Ancient Key-Dweller Remains on the Gulf Coast of Florida*. Edited by Randolph J. Widmer. Foreword by Jerald T. Milanich. Gainesville: University Press of Florida, 2005.

Dall, W. H. "Notes on the Geology of Florida." *AJS* 34 (1887): 161–70.

Dall W. H., and G. D. Harris. "Correlation Papers." In *Bulletin of the U.S. Geological Survey* (1892). 85–158.

Dallmeyer, Dorinda G., ed. *Bartram's Living Legacy: The Travels and the Nature of the South*. Macon, GA: Mercer University Press, 2010.

Daniels, George H. *American Science in the Age of Jackson*. New York: Columbia University Press, 1968.

Darlington, William. *Memorials of John Bartram & Humphry Marshall: With Notices of Their Botanical Contemporaries*. Philadelphia: Lindsay and Blakiston, 1849.

————, comp., *Reliquiae Baldwinianae: Selections from the Correspondence of the Late William Baldwin*. Introduction by J. Ewan. New York: Hafner, 1969. First published 1843 by Kimber and Sharpless (Philadelphia).

Davis, Jack E. *The Gulf*. New York: Liveright Publishing, 2017.

Deagan, Kathleen, and Darcie MacMahon. *Fort Mose: Colonial America's Black Fortress of Freedom*. Gainesville: University of Florida Press, 1995.

Diamond, William. "Nathaniel A. Ware, National Economist." *The Journal of Southern History* 5/4 (1939): 501–26.

Dietz, R. "Description of a Testaceous Formation at Anastasia Island, Extracted from Notes Made on a Journey to the Southern Part of the United States, during the Winter of 1822 and 1823." *JANS* 4, pt. 1 (1824–1825): 73–80.

Doskey, John S. *The European Journals of William Maclure*. Philadelphia: American Philosophical Society, 1988.

Doty, Franklin A. "Florida, Iowa, and the National 'Balance of Power,' 1845." *Florida Historical Quarterly* 35/1 (1956): 30–59.

Doughty, J., and T. Doughty. *Cabinet of Natural History and Rural Sports*, vol. 2. Philadelphia: J. & T. Doughty, 1832.

Dupree, A. Hunter. *Asa Gray: American Botanist, Friend of Darwin*. Baltimore: Johns Hopkins University Press, 1959.

Durant, Mary B., and Michael Harwood. *On the Road with John James Audubon*. New York: Dodd, Mead and Company, 1980.

Durnford, C. D. "The Discovery of Aboriginal Rope and Wood Implements in the Mud in West Florida." *American Naturalist* 29 (1895): 1032–39.

Dwight, Edward H. *Audubon, Watercolors and Drawings.* Utica NY: Munson-Williams-Proctor Institute and the Pierpont Morgan Library, 1965.

Egerton, F. N. "A History of the Ecological Sciences, Part 38A: Naturalists Explore North America, mid-1820s to about 1840." *Bulletin of the Ecological Society of America* 92/1 (January 2011): 64–91.

Ellicott, Andrew. *The Journal of Andrew Ellicott....* Philadelphia: William Fry, 1814.

England, Joseph W., ed. *The First Century of the Philadelphia College of Pharmacy, 1821–1921.* Philadelphia: Philadelphia College of Pharmacy and Science, 1922.

Ewan, Joseph, ed. *William Bartram: Botanical and Zoological Drawings, 1756–1788.* Philadelphia: American Philosophical Society, 1968.

Ewan, Joseph, and Nesta Dunn Ewan. *Benjamin Smith Barton: Naturalist and Physician in Jeffersonian America.* St. Louis: Missouri Botanical Garden Press, 2007.

———, ed. *A Short History of Botany in the United States.* New York: Hafner, 1969.

Fairbanks, Charles H., and Jerald T. Milanich. *Florida Archaeology: New World Archaeological Record.* New York: Academic Press 1987.

Fairhead, Elizabeth, and Nancy E. Hoffmann. "William Bartram's Garden Calendar." In *William Bartram: The Search for Nature's Design: Selected Art, Letters, and Unpublished Writings,* edited by Thomas Hallock and Nancy E. Hoffmann, 462–80. Athens: University of Georgia Press, 2010.

Featherstonhaugh, G. W. *The Monthly American Journal of Geology and Natural Science* 1 (July 1831): 285, 484.

Fishman, Gail. *Journeys through Paradise: Pioneering Naturalists in the Southeast.* Gainesville: University Press of Florida, 2000.

Fisher, George P. *Life of Benjamin Silliman, M.D., LL.D.* New York: Charles Scribner, 1866.

Ford, Alice. *The 1826 Journal of John James Audubon.* Norman OK: University of Oklahoma Press, 1967.

———. *Audubon's Animals: the Quadrupeds of North America.* New York: Studio Publications, 1951.

———. *John James Audubon: A Biography.* New York: Abbeville Press, 1988.

Foster, John T., and Sarah Witmer Foster. *Calling Yankees to Florida: Harriet Beecher Stowe's Forgotten Tourist Articles.* Cocoa: The Florida Historical Society Press, 2012.

Fowler, Don D., and David R. Wilcox, eds. *Philadelphia and the Development of Americanist Archaeology.* Tuscaloosa: University of Alabama Press, 2003.

Fowler, Henry W. "Description of a New Scorpaenoid Fish (*Neomerinthe hemingwayi*) from Off New Jersey." *PANS* 87 (1935): 41–43.

————. Fishes from Deep Water Off Southern Florida." *Notulae Naturae* 246 (1952): 1–16.

————. "Some Cold–blooded Vertebrates of the Florida Keys." *PANS* 58 (1906): 77–113.

Fries, Waldemar H. *The Double Elephant Folio: The Story of Audubon's Birds of America*. Chicago: American Library Association, 1973.

Fry, Joel T. "An International Catalogue of North American Trees and Shrubs: The Bartram Broadside, 1783." *The Journal of Garden History* 16/1 (January– March 1996): 3–66.

————. "John Bartram and His Garden: Would John Bartram Recognize His Garden Today?" In *America's Curious Botanist: A Tercentennial Reappraisal of John Bartram 1699–1777*, edited by Nancy E. Hoffmann and John C. Van Horne, 155–83. Philadelphia: The American Philosophical Society, 2004.

Gambel, William. "Contributions to American Ornithology." *PANS* 4 (December 1948): 127–30.

Gannon, Michael. *Florida: A Short History*. Gainesville: University Press of Florida, 2003.

————. *Michael Gannon's History of Florida in 40 Minutes*. Gainesville: University Press of Florida, 2007.

————, ed. *The New History of Florida*. Gainesville: University Press of Florida, 1996.

Gifford, George E. Jr. "Edward Fredrick Leitner (1812–1838), Physician-Botanist." *Bulletin of the History of Medicine* 46/6 (November–December 1972).

Gilliams, Jacob. "Description of Two New Species of Linnaean Lacerta." *JANS* 1, pt. 2 (1818): 460–61.

Gilliland, Marion Spjut. *Key Marco's Buried Treasure: Archaeology and Adventure in the Nineteenth Century*. Gainesville: University of Florida Press/Florida Museum of Natural History, 1989.

————. *Material Culture of Key Marco, Florida*. Gainesville: University Presses of Florida, 1975.

Glassman, Susan, Eugene A. Bolt, Jr., and Earle E. Spamer. "Joseph Leidy and the 'Great Inventory of Nature.'" *PANS* 144 (1993): 1–19.

Goza, William. Introduction to *A Guide-Book of Florida and the South* (facsimile of the 1869 edition) by Daniel Garrison Brinton. In the Bicentennial Floridiana Facsimile Series, edited by Samuel Proctor, xiii–lviii. Gainesville: University Presses of Florida, 1978.

Graham, Mary. "Reminiscences of Major John E. Le Conte." *Pittonia* 1 (1887– 1889): 303–11.

Graustein, Jeanette E. "The Eminent Benjamin Smith Barton." *Pennsylvania Magazine of History & Biography* 85 (1985): 423–38.

————. *Thomas Nuttall, Naturalist: Explorations in America, 1808–1841*. Cambridge, MA: Harvard University Press, 1967.

Gray, Asa. "A Pilgrimage to Torreya." *American Agriculturist* 34 (1875): 266–77.

———. "Some North American Botanists. IV. John Eatton LeConte." *Botanical Gazette* 8/4 (April 1883): 197–99.

Grunwald, Michael. *The Swamp: The Everglades, Florida, and the Politics of Paradise.* New York: Simon & Schuster, 2006.

Guthrie, William. *New Geographical and Commercial Grammar.* London: Vernon and Hood, 1808.

Hagen, Hermann. "The History of the Origin and Development of Museums." *The American Naturalist* 10 (1876): 80–90.

Hallock, Charles. *Camp Life in Florida: A Handbook for Sportsmen and Settlers.* Forest and Stream Publishing Company, 1876.

Hallock, Thomas, and Richard Franz, eds. *Travels on the St. Johns River: John and William Bartram.* Gainesville: University Press of Florida, 2017.

———, and Joel T. Fry. "Preliminary List of Illustrations by William Bartram." In *William Bartram: The Search for Nature's Design,* edited by Thomas Hallock and Nancy E. Hoffmann, 499–514. Athens: University of Georgia Press, 2010.

———, and Nancy E. Hoffmann, eds. *William Bartram: The Search for Nature's Design: Selected Art, Letters, and Unpublished Writings.* Athens: University of Georgia Press, 2010. Abbreviated as HH in the footnotes.

Hamy, E. T. *Travels of the Naturalist Charles A. Lesueur in North America, 1815–1837,* translated by Milton Haber, edited by H. F. Raup (Kent, OH: Kent State University Press, 1968).

Harlan, Richard. *Fauna Americana: Being a Description of the Mammiferous Animals Inhabiting North America.* Philadelphia: Finley/Harding, 1825.

———. *Medical and Physical Researches: or Original Memoirs.* Philadelphia: Lydia R. Bailey, Printer, 1835.

———. "On a Species of Lamantin resembling the Manatus Sengalensis (Cuvier) inhabiting the Coast of East Florida." *JANS* 3, pt. 2 (1823–1824): 390–424.

Harper, Francis. "Arthur Newlin Leeds." *Journal of Mammalogy* 20/2 (1939): 282–83.

———. *The Travels of William Bartram: Naturalist's Edition.* Annotated and indexed by Francis Harper. Athens: University of Georgia Press, 1998. First published 1958 by Yale University (Cambridge). Cited in text as *FHBT.*

Harper, Francis, and Arthur Leeds. "A Supplementary Chapter on *Franklinia Altamaha.*" Bartonia 19 (1938): 1–13.

Harris, Edward. "Meeting for business, May 18, 1844." *PANS* 2:65.

Harris, G. D. "A Reprint of the Paleontological Writings of Thomas Say." *Bulletin of American Paleontology* 1/bulletin 5 (1896): 3–84. Available online: <www.biodiversitylibrary.org/item/96050#>.

Hart-Davis, Duff. *Audubon's Elephant.* London: Orion House, 2004.

Heilprin, Angelo. "A Comparison of the Eocene Mollusca of the Southeastern United States and Western Europe in Relation to the Determination of Identical Forms." *PANS* 31 (1879): 217–25.

———. "Explorations on the West Coast of Florida and to the Okeechobee Wilderness." *TWFIS* 1 (1887): i–ii.

———. "Notes on Some New Foraminifera from the Nummulitic Formation of Florida." *PANS* 36 (1884): 321.

———. "On Some New Eocene Fossils from the Claiborne Marine Formation of Alabama." *PANS* 31 (1879): 211–16.

———. "On the Occurrence of Nummulitic Deposits in Florida and the Association of Nummulites with a Fresh-water Fauna." *PANS* 34 (1882): 189–93.

———. "Report of the Professor of Invertebrate Paleontology." *PANS* 36 (1884): 345.

Hemingway, Ernest. "Genio after Josie: A Havana Letter." *Esquire* 2/5 (October 1934): 21–22.

———. "On the Blue Water: A Gulf Stream Letter," *Esquire* 5/4 (April 1936): 31, 184–85.

———. *Selected Letters 1917–1961.* Edited by Carlos Baker. New York: Scribners, 1981.

Herrick, Francis Hobart. *Audubon the Naturalist: A History of his Life and Time,* 2 vols. New York: Dover, 1968.

Hoffman, Nancy E., and Thomas Hallock. *William Bartram: The Search for Nature's Design: Selected Art, Letters, and Unpublished Writings.* Athens: University of Georgia Press, 2010.

Hoffmann, Nancy E., and John C. Van Horne, eds. *America's Curious Botanist: A Tercentennial Reappraisal of John Bartram 1699–1777.* Philadelphia: The American Philosophical Society, 2004.

Holbrook, John Edwards. *North American Herpetology: Or, a Description of the Reptiles Inhabiting the United States.* Philadelphia: J. Dodson, 1836.

Holthius, L. B. "Thomas Say as a Carcinologist." In (facsimile reprinting of Say's) *An Account of the Crustacea of the United States,* v–xv. *Historiae Naturalis Classica,* 73. Lehre: J. Cramer, 1969.

Howell, Arthur H. *Florida Bird Life.* 1932. Edited and updated by Alexander Sprunk. New York: Coward-McCann, Inc., 1954.

Hrdlička, Aleš. *The Anthropology of Florida; With Introduction to the New Edition by Jeffrey M. Mitchem.* Tuscaloosa: University of Alabama Press, 2007.

———. "Physical Anthropology in America: An Historical Sketch." *American Anthropologist* 16 (1914): 508–54.

Hughes, Arthur F. W. *The American Biologist through Four Centuries.* Springfield: Charles C. Thomas, 1976.

Hunt, Roy, and Peter Bennett. Foreword to *Key Marco's Buried Treasure: Archaeology and Adventure in the Nineteenth Century,* by Marion Spjut Gilliland, ix–x. Gainesville: University of Florida Press/Florida Museum of Natural History, 1989.

Hunt Thomas C., and James C. Carper, eds. *Religious Higher Education in the United States.* New York: Garland Publishing Co., 1996.

Hunter, Clark, ed. *The Life and Letters of Alexander Wilson*. Philadelphia: American Philosophical Society, 1983.

Irmscher, Christoph. *The Poetics of Natural History: From John Bartram to William James*. New Brunswick, NJ: Rutgers University Press, 1999.

Isely, Duane. *One Hundred and One Botanists*. Ames: Iowa State University Press, 1964.

Johnston, David. "Additional 16th-Century Bird Reports from Florida." *Florida Field Naturalist* 30/1 (February 2002): 1–20.

Johnston, David W., and Thomas Peter Bennett. "A Summary of Birds Reported from the 1817–18 and 1824–25 Expeditions to Florida." *Notulae Naturae* 482 (March 2010): 1–7.

Jones, Douglas S. "The Marine Invertebrate Fossil Record of Florida." In *The Geology of Florida*, edited by Anthony F. Randazzo and Douglas S. Jones, 89–117. Gainesville: University Press of Florida, 1997.

Kastner, Joseph. *A Species of Eternity*. New York: Alfred Knopf, 1977.

Kautz, James. *Footprints Across the South: Bartram's Trail Revisited*. Kennesaw, GA: Kennesaw State University Press, 2006.

Kehoe, Alice Beck. "Philarivalium." In *Philadelphia and the Development of Americanist Archaeology*, edited by Don D. Fowler and David R. Wilcox, 181–87. Tuscaloosa: University of Alabama Press, 2003.

Kimball, Winifred. "Reminiscences of Alvan Wentworth Chapman." *Journal of the New York Botanical Garden* 22/253 (February 1921): 1–12.

Kolianos, Phyllis E., and Brent R. Weisman, eds. *The Florida Journals of Frank Hamilton Cushing*. Gainesville: University of Florida Press, 2005.

———. *The Lost Florida Manuscript of Frank Hamilton Cushing*. Gainesville: University of Florida Press, 2005.

Kral, R. "*Baptisia simplicifolia Croom*." In *A Report on Some Rare, Threatened or Endangered Forest-related Vascular Plants of the South*, edited by R. Kral, 642–45. Atlanta, GA: USDA Forest Service, Southern Region, Technical Publication R8-TP 2, 1983.

La Plante, Leah. "The Sage of Biscayne Bay: Charles Torrey Simpson's Love Affair with South Florida." *Tequesta* 55 (1995): 61–82.

Leal, José. "Celebrating a Long Life: *The Nautilus* Turns 120!" *Nautilus* 120/1 (2006): 1–7.

Le Conte, John Eatton. "Description of a New Species of the Pacane Nut." *PANS* 6 (1853): 402.

———. "Description of North American Tortoises." *Annals Lyceum of Natural History of New York* 3 (1830): 91–131.

——— "Descriptions of Three New Species of Arvicola, with Remarks upon Other North American Rodents." *PANS* 6 (1853): 404–15.

———. "An Enumeration of the Vines of North America." *PANS* 6 (1853): 269–74.

———. "Memoir of John Le Conte, 1818–1891." Read before the National

Academy of Sciences. April 1894.

———. "Notice of American Animals, Formerly Known, but Now Forgotten or Lost." *Proceedings of the Academy of Natural Sciences of Philadelphia* 7 (1854): 8–14.

———. "Observations on North American species of the Genus Viola." *Annals Lyceum of Natural History of New York* 2 (1828): 135–58.

———. "On the North American Plants of the Genus Tillandsia with Descriptions of Three New Species." *Annals of the Lyceum of Natural History of New York* 2 (1828): 129–33.

———. "On the North American Utriculariae." *Annals of the Lyceum of Natural History of New York* 1 (1824): 72–99.

Le Conte, Joseph. "On the Agency of the Gulf- Stream in the Formation of the Peninsula of Florida," *Proceedings of the AAAS* 10, pt. 2 (August 1856): 103–19; reprinted in *AJS*, ser. 3, 23 (May 1857): 46–60.

———. "The Reefs, Keys, and Peninsula of Florida." *Science* 2/45 (1883): 764.

———. '*Ware Sherman: A Journal of Three Months' Personal Experience in the Last Days of the Confederacy.* Baton Rouge: Louisiana State University Press, 1999.

Leffmann, H., J. Willcox, and S. T. Skidmore. 1908. "The Wagner Free Institute of Science of Philadelphia." Reprinted with some modifications from Founder's Week Memorial Volume in *TWFIS* 10 (1923): 1–6.

Leidy, Joseph. "Caries in the Mastodon." *PANS* 38 (1886): 38.

———. "Description of Some Mammalian Remains from a Rock Crevice in Florida." *TWFIS* 2 (1889): 13–17.

———. "Descriptions of Vertebrate Remains from Peace Creek, Florida." *TWFIS* 2 (1889): 19–31.

———. "An Extinct Boar from Florida." *PANS* 38 (1886): 36–38.

———. "Fossil Vertebrates from the Alachua Clays of Florida." Edited by F. A. Lucas. *TWFIS* 4 (1896): vii–viii, 1–61.

———. "Mastodon and Llama from Florida." *PANS* 38 (1886): 11–12.

———. "Notes taken on a visit to White Pond, in Warren County, New Jersey [and a list of ten species of fossil shells collected there]." *PANS* 2 (1845): 279–81.

———. "Notice of Some Fossil Human Bones." *TWFIS* 2 (1889): 9–12.

———. "On the Fossil Horse of America." *PANS* 3 (1847): 262–66.

———. Preface to *TWFIS* 3, pt. 1 (1890): i–ii.

———. "Remarks on the Nature of Organic Species." *TWFIS* 2 (1889): 51–57.

———. "Rhinoceros and Hippotherium from Florida." *PANS* 37 (1885): 32–33.

———. "Vertebrate Fossils from Florida." *PANS* 35 (1884): 118–19.

Lesueur, C. A. "Descriptions of the Five New Species of the Genus Cichla of Cuvier." *JANS* 2, pt. 2 (1822): 214–21.

———. "Descriptions of Several Species of the Linnean Genus Raia, of North America." *JANS* 4, pt. 1 (1822): 100–10.

———. "Descriptions of Three New Species of the Genus Sciaena." *JANS* 2, pt. 2

(1822): 251–56.

———. "New Genus and Several New Species of Freshwater Fish, Indigenous to the United States." *JANS* 2 (1821): 2–13.

Linzey, A. V., R. A. Jordan, and G. Hammerson, contributors. *Neotoma floridana* (2008): IUCN 2011. IUCN Red List of Threatened Species, Version 2011.2, www.iucnredlist.org/details/42650/0 (accessed 10 October 2018).

Long, Robert W., and Olga Lakela. *A Flora of Tropical Florida: A Manual of the Seed Plants and Ferns of Southern Peninsular Florida.* Illustrated by Linda Baumhardt. Miami: Banyan Press, 1976.

Lurie, Edward. *Louis Agassiz: A Life in Science.* Chicago: University of Chicago Press, 1960.

MacFadden, Bruce J. "Famous 'Horseologists'—Joseph Leidy (1823–91) and the Florida Connection." *Pony Express, Florida Fossil Horse Newsletter* 1/2 (1992): 9.

———. *Fossil Horses: Systematics, Paleobiology, and Evolution of the Family Equidae.* Cambridge: Cambridge University Press, 1994.

Maclure, William. "Essay on the Formation of Rocks, or An Inquiry into the Probable Origin of Their Present Form and Structure." *JANS* 1, pt. 2 (1818): 261–76.

———. "Observations on the Geology of the United States, Explanatory of a Geological Map." *Transactions of the American Philosophical Society* 6 (1809): 411–28.

———. "Observations on the Geology of the United States of North America." *Transactions of the American Philosophical Society* 1 (1818): 1–91.

Magee, Judith. *The Art and Science of William Bartram.* University Park: Pennsylvania State University Press, 2007.

Marshall, Humphry. *Arbustrum Americanum: The American Grove, or an Alphabetical Catalogue of Forest Trees and Shrubs, Natives of the American United States, Arranged according to the Linnean System.* Philadelphia: Joseph Cruikshank, 1785.

Martin, William. *Outlines of an Attempt to Establish a Knowledge of Extraneous Fossils Based on Scientific Principles.* London: Macclesfield, 1809.

Mathews, Catharine van Cortlandt. *Andrew Ellicott: His Life and Letters.* New York: Grafton Press, 1908.

McGinty, Thomas L. "Dr. Henry A. Pilsbry in Florida." *The Nautilus* 71/3 (1958): 97–100.

Mearns, Barbara, and Richard Mearns. *Audubon to Xántus: The Lives of Those Commemorated in North American Bird Names.* New York: Academic Press, 1992.

Mears, James. "Guide to Plant Collectors Represented in the Herbarium of the Academy of Natural Sciences of Philadelphia." *PNAS* 133 (1981): 141–65.

Meigs, J. Aitken. *Catalogue of Human Crania in the Collection of the Academy of Natural Sciences of Philadelphia.* Philadelphia: Merrihew & Thompson, 1857.

Merrill, E. D. "Unlisted Binomials in Chapman's *Flora of the Southern United States.*" *Castanea* 13 (1948): 61–70.

Meyers, Amy R. W., and Margaret Beck Pritchard, eds. *Empire's Nature: Mark Catesby's New World Vision.* Chapel Hill: University of North Carolina Press, 1998.

Meyerson, Martin, and Dilys Pegler Winegrad. *Gladly Learn and Gladly Teach: Franklin and His Heirs at the University of Pennsylvania, 1740–1970.* Philadelphia: University of Pennsylvania Press, 1978.

Michaux, Francois André. *The North American Sylva, or A description of the forest trees, of the United States, Canada and Nova Scotia.* 2 vols. Paris: C. D'Hautel, 1817–1819).

Milanich, Jerald T., ed. "Clarence B. Moore." In *Philadelphia and the Development of Americanist Archaeology,* edited by Don D. Fowler and David R. Wilcox, 113–33. Philadelphia: University of Pennsylvania Press, 2003.

———. *Famous Florida Sites: Crystal River and Mount Royal.* Southeastern Classics in Archaeology, Anthropology, and History. Gainesville: University Press of Florida, 1999.

———. *Florida's Indians from Ancient Times to the Present.* Gainesville: University Press of Florida, 1995.

———. "The Bartrams, Clarence B. Moore, and Mount Royal." In *Fields of Vision: Essays on the Travels of William Bartram,* edited by Kathryn E. Holland Braund and Charlotte M. Porter, 117–36. Tuscaloosa: University of Alabama Press, 2010.

———, and Charles H. Fairbanks. *Florida Archaeology.* New World Archaeological Record. New York: Academic Press, 1987.

———. *The West and Central Florida Expeditions of Clarence Bloomfield Moore.* Tuscaloosa: University of Alabama Press, 1999.

Miller, Lillian B., ed. *The Selected Papers of Charles Willson Peale and His Family.* 5 vols. New Haven: Yale University Press, 1983–2000.

Mitchem, Jeffrey, ed. Introduction to *The East Florida Expeditions of Clarence Bloomfield Moore.* 1–53. Tuscaloosa: University of Alabama Press, 1999.

Mitchem, Jeffrey M. "The Willcox Copper Plate from Florida." *Expedition: The Magazine of the University of Pennsylvania Museum of Archaeology and Anthropology* 43/2 (2001): 5–6.

Moore, Clarence Bloomfield. "Certain Aboriginal Remains of the Florida Central West Coast. Part II." *JANS* 12 (1903): 123–358.

———. "Certain Antiquities of the Florida West Coast." *JANS* 11 (1900): 351–94.

———. "Certain Sand Mounds of the St. John's River, Florida, Part II." *JANS* 10 (1894b): 129–246.

———. "Certain Shell Heaps of the St. John's River, Florida." *American Naturalist* (in 5 parts): *AN* 26 (1892): 912–22; *AN* 27 (1893): 8–13, 113–17, 605–624, 708–23.

———. *The East Florida Expeditions of Clarence Bloomfield Moore*. Edited and introduced by Jeffrey Mitchem. Tuscaloosa: University of Alabama Press, 1999.

———. "The Northwestern Florida Coast Revisited." *JANS* 16 (1918): 514–80.

Morton, Samuel George. *Crania Americana, or a Comparative View of the Skulls of Various Aboriginal Nations of North and South America*. Philadelphia: J. Dobson, 1839.

Nolan, Edward J., ed. *An Index to the Scientific Contents of the Journal and Proceedings of the Academy of Natural Sciences of Philadelphia, 1812–1912*. Philadelphia: The Academy of Natural Sciences, 1913.

Nolan, J. *A Short History of the Academy of Natural Sciences of Philadelphia*. Philadelphia: Academy of Natural Sciences of Philadelphia, 1909.

Norment, C. J. "Francis Harper (1886–1872)." *Arctic* 53/1 (March 2000): 72–75.

Nuttall, Thomas. "An Account of Two New Genera of Plants; and of a species of *Tillaea*, and another of *Limosella*, recently discovered on the banks of the Delaware, in the vicinity of Philadelphia." *JANS* 1 pt. 1 (1817): 111–22.

———. "A Catalogue of a Collection of Plants Made in East Florida, during the Months of October and November, 1821. By A. Ware. Esq." *AJS* 5 (1822): 286–304.

———. "A Description of *Collinsia*, a New Genus of Plants," *JANS* 1, pt. 1 (1817): 189–93.

———. "A Description of Some of the Rarer or Little Known Plants Indigenous to the United States, from Dried Specimens in the Herbarium of the Academy of Natural Sciences in Philadelphia." *JANS* 7 (1834): 61–115.

———. *The Genera of North American Plants, and a Catalogue of the Species to the Year 1817*. 2 vols. Philadelphia: D. Heart, 1818.

———. *A Manual of the Ornithology of the United States and of Canada: The Water Birds*. Boston: Hilliard, Gray, and Company, 1834.

———. "Observations on the Genus *Eriogonum*, and the Natural Order *Polygoneae* of Jussieu." *JANS* 1, pt. 1 (1817): 24–30, pt. 3 (1817): 33–37.

Odgers, Merle M. *Alexander Dallas Bache, Scientist and Educator*. Philadelphia: University of Pennsylvania Press, 1947.

Oleson, Alexandra, and Sanborn C. Brown, eds. *The Pursuit of Knowledge in the Early American Republic: American Scientific and Learned Societies from Colonial Times to the Civil War*. Baltimore: Johns Hopkins University Press, 1976.

Ord, George. "An Account of the Florida Jay of Bartram." *JANS* 1 (1818): 345–47.

———. *Biographical Sketch of the Life of Alexander Wilson, Father of American Ornithology*. Philadelphia: Harrison and Hall, 1922.

———. "Biographical Sketch of William Bartram." In *Cabinet of Natural History and Rural Sports 2*, edited and published by Doughty and Doughty. Philadelphia: J. & T. Doughty, 1832.

———. "De Blainville, H, Sur une nouvelle espece de rongeur de la Floride par M. Ord de Philadelphie." *Bulletin des Sciences par de la Societe Philomatique de Paris* (1818): 181–82.

———. "Memoir of Charles Alexander Lesueur." Read before the American Philosophical Society April 6, 1849. *AJS* 58 (1849): 189–216.

———. "Observations on Two Species of the Genus Gracula of Latham." *JANS* 1, pt. 2 (1818): 253–60.

———. "Alexander Wilson, 1766–1813." *Pennsylvania Monthly* 10 (1813): 433–58.

———. *Supplement to the American Ornithology of Alexander Wilson: Containing a Sketch of the Author's Life, with a Selection from His Letters; Some Remarks upon His Writings; and a History of Those Birds Which Were Intended to Compose Part of his Ninth Volume.* Volume 9 of Wilson's American Ornithology. Philadelphia: J. Laval and S. F. Bradford, 1825.

Orosz, Joel J. *Curators and Culture: The Museum Movement in America, 1740–1870.* Tuscaloosa: University of Alabama Press, 1990.

Ott, Mark P. *A Sea of Change: Ernest Hemingway and the Gulf Stream: A Contextual Biography.* Kent, OH: Kent State University Press, 2008.

The Papers of Benjamin Franklin. Volume 3, edited by Leonard W. Labaree. New Haven: Yale University Press/American Philosophical Society, 1961.

Paul, Harald, Alfred Rehder, and Beulah E. Shields Bartsch. *Bibliography and Short Biographical Sketch of William Haley Dall.* Washington: Smithsonian Institution, 1946.

Pauly, Philip J. *Biologists and the Promise of American Life.* Princeton, NJ: Princeton University Press, 2000.

Pearson, Charles E., Thomas C. C. Birchett, and Richard A. Weinstein. "An Aptly Named Steamboat: Clarence B. Moore's *Gopher*." *Southeastern Archaeology* 19/1 (Summer 2000): 82–87.

Peattie, Donald Culross. "Alvan Wentworth Chapman." In volume 4 Chanfrau–Cushing) of *Dictionary of American Biography*, edited by Allen Johnson, 16–17 (New York: C. Scribner's Sons, 1930.

Peck, Robert McCracken, ed. *Bartram Heritage: A Study of the Life of William Bartram.* Montgomery, AL: US Department of the Interior and the Bartram Trail Conference, 1978.

———. Introduction to *Travels*, by William Bartram, vii–xviii. Salt Lake City, UT: Peregrine Smith, 1980.

———, and Patricia Tyson Stroud. *A Glorious Enterprise: The Academy of Natural Sciences of Philadelphia and the Making of American Science.* Philadelphia: University of Pennsylvania Press, 2012. Bicentennial edition.

Pennell, Francis Whittier. "Historic Botanical Collections of the American Philosophical Society and the Academy of Natural Sciences of Philadelphia." *PAPS* 94/2 (1950): 137–51.

———. "Travels and Scientific Collections of Thomas Nuttall." *Bartonia* 18 (1936): 1–51.

Phillips, Maurice E. "A Brief History of Academy Publications." *Proceedings of the Academy of Natural Sciences* 100 (1948): x–xl.

Phillips Venia T., and Maurice E. Phillips, eds. *Guide to the Microfilm Publication of the Minutes and Correspondence of the Academy of Natural Sciences of Philadelphia, 1812–1924.* Philadelphia: Academy of Natural Sciences of Philadelphia, 1967. Special Publication (Numbers 7 and 9).

———. "Writings of Henry Ward Fowler, Published from 1897 to 1965." *Proceedings of the Academy of Natural Sciences* 117 (1965): 173–212.

Pilsbry, H. A. "Conservators Report." *PANS* 51 (1899): 541–42.

———. "Descriptions of a new Hydrobia, with notes on other Rissoidae." *PDANS* 5 (1886): 33–34.

———. *A Manual of Conchology, Structural and Systematic: with illustrations of the species.* Vols. 11–17. Philadelphia: Conchological Section, Academy of Natural Sciences, 1889–1898.

———. "On the Orthalicus in Florida." *Nautilus* 8/4 (1894): 37–39.

———. "Report of the Conchological Section." *PANS* 46 (1894): 473–75.

———. "Report of the Special Curator of the Department of Mollusca." *PANS* 56 (1899): 816–17.

Pilsbry, H. A., and C. W. Johnson. "A New Floridian *Viviparus*." *The Nautilus* 26/4 (1912): 48.

Pitzer, Donald E. "William Maclure's Boatload of Knowledge: Science and Education into the Midwest." *Indiana Magazine of History* 94 (1998): 110–37.

Poesch, Jessie. *Titian Ramsay Peale, 1799–1885, And His Journals of the Wilkes Expedition.* Philadelphia: The American Philosophical Society, 1961.

———. "Titian Ramsay Peale: Artist-Naturalist." Master's thesis, University of Delaware, 1956.

Porter, Charlotte. "Following Bartram's 'Track': Titian Ramsay Peale's Florida Journey." *The Florida Historical Quarterly* 61/4 (April 1983): 431–44.

———. *John James Audubon: Florida Travels, 1831–1832.* Gainesville, FL: Florida State Museum, c.1985.

Potts, E. "Report upon Some Fresh-Water Sponges Collected in Florida by Jos. Willcox, Esq." *TWFIS* 2 (1889): 5–7.

Powell, John W. "In Memoriam: Frank Hamilton Cushing." *American Anthropologist* 2 (1900): 354–80.

Powell, Levin Myne. *Survey of the Coast–Apalachicola to the Mouth of the Mississippi.* Washington, DC: House of Representatives Doc. No. 220, 1842.

Pratt, W. H. "Curators Report." *PDANS* 5 (1887): 235.

Proby, Kathryn Hall, *Audubon in Florida: With Selections from the Writings of John James Audubon.* Coral Gables: University of Miami Press, 1974.

Putnam, Frank. "Discussion." *PAPS* 35 (November 1896): 338–41.

Randazzo, Anthony F., and Douglas S. Jones, eds. *The Geology of Florida.* Gainesville: University Press of Florida, 1997.

Ray, Clayton E. "An Idiosyncratic History of Florida Vertebrate Paleontology." *Bulletin of the Florida Museum of Natural History* 45/4 (2005): 143–70.

Redfearn, D. H. "The Steamboat Home." Excerpt from *Florida Law Journal* 9/5 (May 1935): 405–24.

Reingold, Nathan. *Science in Nineteenth-century America: A Documentary History.* New York: Octagon Books, 1979.

Rembert, David H. Jr. "The Botanical Explorations of William Bartram in the Southeast." Bartram Trail Conference. <www.bartramtrail.org/page-1715747> Accessed 23 July 2018.

Renschler, Emily S., and Janet Monge. "The Samuel George Morton Cranial Collection: Historical Significance and New Research." *Expedition* 50/3 (2009): 30–38.

Reveal, James L. *Gentle Conquest: The Botanical Discovery of North America with Illustrations from the Library of Congress.* Washington, DC: Starwood Publishing, 1992.

Rhoads, Samuel N. *A Reprint of the North American Zoology, by George Ord. …Second American Edition of Guthrie's Geography in 1815. Taken from Mr. Ord's Private, Annotated Copy. To Which is Added an Appendix of the more important Scientific and Historic Questions Involved.* Haddonfield, NJ: Samuel Rhoads, 1894. Also available at www.biodiversitylibrary.org/item/15544#page/9/mode/1up.

Rhodes, Richard, ed. *Audubon: Early Drawings.* Scientific commentary by Scott V. Edwards. Foreword by Leslie A. Morris. Cambridge: Belknap Press of Harvard University Press, 2008.

———. *John James Audubon: The Audubon Reader.* New York: Everyman's Library, Knopf, 2006.

———. *John James Audubon: The Making of an American.* New York: Knopf, Borzoi Books, 2004.

Richardson, Edgar P., Brooke Hindle, and Lillian B. Miller. *Charles Willson Peale and His World.* New York: Harry Abrams, 1982.

Robbins, Christine Chapman. "David Hosack's Herbarium and its Linnaean Specimens." *PAPS* 104/3 (1960): 293–313.

———. *David Hosack: Citizen of New York.* Philadelphia: Memoirs of the American Philosophical Society, 1964.

Rodgers, Andrew Denny III. (1842). 1965. *John Torrey: A Story of North American Botany.* Princeton: Princeton University Press, 1942. Facsimile edition. New York: Hafner Publishing Company.

Rogers, William Warren, and Erica R. Clark. *The Croom Family and Goodwood Plantation.* Athens: University of Georgia Press, 1999.

Rothra, Elizabeth Ogren. *Florida's Pioneer Naturalist: The Life of Charles Torrey Simpson.* Gainesville: University Press of Florida, 1995.

Ruschenberger, W. S. W. *A Notice of the Origin, Progress, and Present Condition of the Academy of Natural Sciences of Philadelphia.* Philadelphia: T. K. & P. G. Collins, 1852.

Samuelson, Arnold. *With Hemingway: A Year in Key West and Cuba.* New York:

Random House, 1984.

Sanders, Albert E., and Warren Ripley. *Audubon: The Charleston Connection.* Charleston, SC: The Charleston Museum, 1986.

Sanders, Brad. *Guide to William Bartram's Travels: Following the Trail of America's First Great Naturalist.* Athens, GA: Fevertree Press, 2002.

Sargent, Charles S. *Scientific Papers of Asa Gray.* 2 vols. Boston: Houghton, Mifflin, 1889.

Savage, Henry Jr., and Elizabeth J. Savage. *André and François André Michaux.* Charlottesville: University Press of Virginia, 1986.

Say, Thomas. *American Conchology; Or, Description of Shells of North America.* New Harmony, IN: School Press, 1830.

———. "An Account of Some of the Marine Shells of the United States." *JANS* 2, pt. 2 (1822): 221–49.

———. "An Account of the Crustacea of the United States." *JANS* 1, pts. 1 and 2 (1818): 57–482.

———. "Account of Two New Genera, and Several New Species, of Fresh Water and Land Shells." JANS 1, pt. 2 (June 1818): 279.

———. *American Entomology, or Descriptions of the Insects of North America.* 3 vols. (Philadelphia: Samuel Augustus Mitchell, 1824–1828).

———. "Descriptions of Some New Species of Fresh Water and Land Shells of the United States." *JANS* 5, pt. 1 (1825–1827): 120–21.

———. "Descriptions of the Myriapodae of the United States." *JANS* 2, pt. 2 (1821): 102–14.

———. "Observations on Some Species of Zoophytes, Shells &c. principally Fossil." *AJS* 1 (1820): 381–87.

———. "On the Fresh Water and Land Tortoises of the United States." *JANS* 4, pt. 2 (1825): 207–208.

Say, T. [Thomas], and G. [George] Ord. "Description of a New Species of Mammalia, Whereon a Genus is Proposed to be Founded." *Journal of the Academy of Natural Sciences of Philadelphia* 4 (pt. 2)/11 (1825): 352–56.

———. "A New Genus of Mammalia is Proposed, and a Description of the Species on Which It Is Founded." *Journal of the Academy of Natural Sciences of Philadelphia* 4 (pt. 2)/11 (1825): 345–49.

Schuyler, Alfred E., and Elizabeth P. McLean. "The Versatile Bartrams and Their Enduring Botanical Legacy." In *America's Curious Botanist*, edited by Nancy E. Hoffmann and John C. Van Horne, 185–201. Philadelphia: The American Philosophical Society, 2004.

Schmidt, Walter. "Geomorphology and Physiography of Florida." In *The Geology of Florida*, edited by A. F. Randazzo and D. S. Jones, 1–12. Gainesville: University Press of Florida, 1997.

Schoepf, Johann David. *Travels in the Confederation (1783–1784)*, translated and edited by Alfred J. Morrison. New York: Burt Franklin, 1911, 1968.

Schöpf, Johann David. *Reise durch einige der mittlern und südlichen Vereinigten nordamerikanischen Staaten nach Ost-Florida und den Bahama-Inseln unternommen in den Jahren 1783 und 1784*, translated by A. J. Morrison. Erlangen: Johann Jacob Palm, 1788.

Sellards, E. H. "Fossil Vertebrates from Florida: A New Pliocene Species; the Pleistocene Fauna." Florida Geological Survey. 18th Annual Report. 1916. 77–119.

———. "Geological Section across the Everglades." Florida Geological Survey, 12th Annual Report. 1919. 59–62.

Sellers, Charles Coleman. *Mr. Peale's Museum: Charles Willson Peale and the First Popular Museum of Natural Science and Art*. New York: Norton, 1980.

Sheldon, Craig T., Jr., ed. *The Southern and Central Alabama Expeditions of Clarence Bloomfield Moore*. Tuscaloosa: University of Alabama Press, 2001.

Shores, Elizabeth Findley. *On Harper's Trail: Roland McMillan Harper, Pioneering Botanist of the Southern Coastal Plain*. Athens: University of Georgia Press, 2008.

Silcox, Henry. "Henry Disston's Model Industrial Community: Nineteenth-Century Paternalism in Tacony, Philadelphia." *The Pennsylvania Magazine of History and Biography*, 114/4 (1990): 483–515.

Simmons, William H. *Alasco, an Indian Tale: Two Cantos: with Other Poems*. Philadelphia: Lippincott & Co., 1857.

———. *Notices of East Florida*. 1822. Bicentennial Floridiana Facsimile Series, with an introduction and index by George Buker. Gainesville: University of Florida Press, 1973.

———. *Onea: An Indian Tale*. Charleston: T. B. Stephens, Printer, 1820.

Simpson, Charles T. "Contributions to Mollusca of Florida." *PDANS* 5 (1886): 45–72.

———. *Florida Wild Life*. New York: Macmillan, 1932,

Slaughter, Thomas P. *The Natures of John and William Bartram*. New York: Alfred A. Knopf, 1996.

Small, John K. "Bartram's *Ixia coelestina* Rediscovered." *Journal of the New York Botanical Garden* 31 (1931): 57–66.

Smith, Eugene Allen. "On the Geology of Florida." *AJS* 3/21 (1881): 292–309.

———. "Sketch of the Life of Michael Tuomey." *American Geologist* 20 (1897): 207.

Smith-Vaniz, William, and Robert McCracken Peck. "Contributions of Henry Weed Fowler (1878–1965), with a Brief Early History of History of Ichthyology at the Academy of Natural Sciences of Philadelphia." *PANS* 143 (1991): 173–91.

Snyder, Noel F. R., and Joel T. Fry. "Validity of Bartram's Painted Vulture (Aves: Cathartidae)." *Zootaxa* 3613/1 (February 7, 2013): 61–82.

Spamer, Earle E. "The Legacy of 'Friends of Natural Science': A Systematic look at the Scientific Publications of the Academy of Natural Sciences of Philadelphia, 1817–2000." *PANS* 150 (1997): 3–13.

Spamer, Earle, and Arthur Bogan. "Time Capsule of Carcinology: History and Resources in the Academy of Natural Sciences of Philadelphia." In *History of Carcinology*, edited by Frank Truesdale, 87–89. Rotterdam: A. A. Balkema, 1993.

Spamer, Earle, and C. A. Forster. *A Catalogue of Type Fossils in the Wagner Free Institute of Science Philadelphia, Pennsylvania: with a History of Paleontology at the Institute*. Philadelphia: Wagner Free Institute of Science, 1988.

Spencer, Frank, ed. *History of Physical Anthropology: An Encyclopedia*. Garland Reference Library of Social Science, vol. 677. New York: Garland, 1997.

Spornick, Charles D., Alan R. Cattier, and Robert J. Greene. *An Outdoor Guide to Bartram's Travels*. Athens: University of Georgia Press, 2003.

Sprunt, Alexander, Jr. *Florida Bird Life*. New York: Coward-McCann, Inc., 1954.

Steiner, Bill. *Audubon Art Prints: A Collectors' Guide to Every Edition*. Columbia: University of South Carolina Press, 2003.

Stephens, Lester D. *Joseph Le Conte, Gentle Prophet of Evolution*. Baton Rouge: Louisiana State University Press, 1982.

———. *Science, Race, and Religion in the American South: John Bachman and the Charleston Circle of Naturalists, 1815–1895*. Chapel Hill: University of North Carolina Press, 2000.

Stevenson, J. J. "Joseph Le Conte Obituary." *Annals of New York Academy of Sciences* 14/5 (4 March 1902): 150

Stone, Witmer. "The Work of William, Son of John Bartram." *Bartonia* 12 (1932): 20–23. Special issue.

Stork, William. *An Account of East-Florida, with a journal, kept by John Bartram of Philadelphia, Botanist for His Majesty for the Floridas; upon a journey from St. Augustine up the River St. John's, as far as the lakes*. London: W. Nicoll and Jeffries, 1767.

Street, Phillips B. "The Edward Harris Collection of Birds." *The Wilson Bulletin* 60/3 (September 1948): 167–84.

Stresemann, E. *Ornithology from Aristotle to the Present*. Cambridge, MA: Harvard University Press, 1975.

Streshinsky, Shirley. *Audubon: Life and Art in the American Wilderness*. New York:Villard Books, 1993.

Stroud, Patricia Tyson. *The Emperor of Nature: Charles-Lucien Bonaparte and his World*. Philadelphia: University of Pennsylvania Press, 2000.

———. "The Founding of the Academy of Natural Sciences of Philadelphia in 1812 and its *Journal* in 1817." *PANS* 147 (1997): 227–36.

———. *Thomas Say: New World Naturalist*. Philadelphia: University of Pennsylvania Press, 1992.

Swift, F. R. *Florida Fancies*. New York: G. P. Putnam's Sons, 1903.

Taylor, Walter Kingsley, and Eliane M. Norman. *André Michaux in Florida*. Gainesville: University Press of Florida, 2002.

Tebeau, Charlton W., and William Marina. A *History of Florida*. Coral Gables, FL:

University of Miami Press, 1999.

Thomas, David Hurst. *Archaeology.* Philadelphia: Holt, Rinehart and Winston, 1989.

Thompson, Arthur B., Paul L. McGinty, and Thomas L. McGinty. "Dredging from the Cruiser Triton." *The Nautilus* 65 (1951): 37–43.

Thomson, Keith. *The Legacy of the Mastodon.* New Haven: Yale University Press, 2008.

Thulesius, Olav. *Harriet Beecher Stowe in Florida, 1867 to 1884.* Jefferson, NC: McFarland & Company, 2001.

Torrey J., and A. Gray. "Baptisia." *Flora* 1 (1840): 383.

Torrey, John, and Asa Gray. *A Flora of North America: containing abridged descriptions of all the known indigenous and naturalized plants growing north of Mexico; arranged according to the natural system.* 2 vols. (New York: Wiley & Putnam, 1838–1840).

Trelease, William. "Alvin Wentworth Chapman." *The American Naturalist* 33/392 (1899): 643–46.

Tuomey, M. "Descriptions of Some Fossil Shells from the Tertiary of the Southern States." *PANS* 6 (1852): 192–94.

———. "Descriptions of Some New Fossils from the Cretaceous Rocks of the Southern States," *PANS* 7 (1854): 167–72.

———. "Notice of the Discovery of a Crania of the Zuglodon." *PANS* 3 (1847): 151–53.

———. "Notice of the Geology of the Florida Keys and of the Southern Coast of Florida." *AJS* 2/11 (1851): 390–94.

Van Doren, Mark, ed. *The Travels of William Bartram.* New York: Macy-Masius Publishers, 1928.

Van Tassel, David D., and Michael G. Hall. *Science and Society in the United States.* Homewood, IL: Dorsey Press, 1966.

Vignoles, Charles. *Observations upon the Floridas.* 1823. Facsimile edition edited by Samuel Proctor and John Moore. Gainesville: University of Florida Press, 1977.

Volmer, Stephanie. *Planting a New World: Letters and Languages of Transatlantic Botanical Exchange, 1733–1777.* PhD diss., Rutgers State University of New Jersey-New Brunswick, 2008.

Waddell, Gene, ed. *John Bachman: Selected Writings on Science, Race, and Religion.* Athens: University of Georgia Press, 2011.

Wagner, William. "Description of Five New Fossils, of the Older Pliocene Formation of Maryland and North Carolina." *JASN* 8 (1849): 151–53.

Walker-Arnott, George A. "On the Genus Torreya." *Annals of Natural History* 1 (1838): 128.

Ward, D. B., ed. *Plants.* Volume 5 of *Rare and Endangered Biota of Florida.* Gainesville: University Presses of Florida, 1979.

Wardle, H. Newell. "Clarence Bloomfield Moore (1852–1936)." *Bulletin of the*

Philadelphia Anthropological Society 9/2 (March 1956).

Ware, Nathaniel A. *Harvey Belden: Or a True Narrative of Strange Adventures....* Cincinnati: Printed for the Author, 1848.

———. *Notes on Political Economy, as Applicable to the United States.* 1844. New York: Reprints of Economic Classics, Augustus M. Kelley, 1967.

Warren, Leonard. *Joseph Leidy: The Last Man Who Knew Everything.* New Haven: Yale University Press, 1998.

———. *Maclure of New Harmony.* Bloomington: Indiana University Press, 2009.

Waselkov, Gregory A., and Kathryn E. Holland Braund, eds. *William Bartram on the Southeastern Indians.* Indians of the Southeast. Lincoln: University of Nebraska Press, 1995.

Webb, S. David, ed. *Pleistocene Mammals of Florida.* Gainesville: University of Florida Press, 1974.

Weiss Harry B., and Grace M. Ziegler. *Thomas Say, Early American Naturalist.* Springfield, IL: Charles C. Thomas Publisher, 1931.

Welker, Robert Henry. *Birds & Men: American Birds in Sciences, Art, Literature, and Conservation, 1800–1900.* New York: Athenum, 1966.

Wheeler, H. E. "Timothy Abbott Conrad, with particular reference to his work in Alabama one hundred years ago." *Bulletin of American Paleontology* 23/77 (1935): 1–157.

Wheeler, Mortimer. *Archaeology from the Earth.* Oxford: Oxford University Press, 1954.

White, George W. "William Maclure's maps of the geology of the United States." *Journal of the Society for the Bibliography of Natural History* 8/3 (1977): 266–69.

White, James T. *The National Cyclopedia of American Biography.* 5 vols. New York: James T. White, 1894.

Whitney, Ellie, D. Bruce Means, and Anne Rudloe. *Priceless Florida: Natural Ecosystems and Native Species.* Sarasota, FL: Pineapple Press, 2004.

Willcox, Joseph. "Notes on the Geology and Natural History of the West Coast of Florida." *PANS* 36 (1884): 188–92.

Willey, Gordon A., and Jeremy A. Sabloff. *A History of American Archaeology.* San Francisco: W. H. Freeman, 1980.

Wilson, Alexander. *American Ornithology: or, The Natural History of the Birds of the United States: illustrated with plates, engraved and colored from original drawings taken from nature.* Philadelphia: Bradford and Inskeep, 1808–1814. 9 volumes. George Ord completed volume 8 and wrote volume 9.

Wilson, James G., and John Fiske, eds. *Appleton's Cyclopedia of American Biography.* 6 vols. New York: D. Appleton and Company, 1889.

Woodring, W. P. *William Healey Dall: A Biographical Memoir.* Washington, DC: National Academy of Sciences, 1958.

Wright, John K. "From 'Kubla Khan' to Florida." *American Quarterly* 8/1 (1956): 76–80.

Wunderlin, Richard P., Bruce F. Hansen, and John Becker. "Botanical Exploration in Florida." In *Pteridophytes and Gymnosperms*, vol. 1 of *Flora of Florida*, edited by Richard P. Wunderlin and Bruce F. Hansen, 49ff. Gainesville: University Press of Florida, 2000.

Wunderlin, Richard P., and Bruce F. Hansen, ed. *Flora of Florida*. 6 vols. Gainesville: University Press of Florida, 2000.

Wurtz, C. B. "Dr. Pilsbry and Fresh-water Mollusca." *The Nautilus* 71/3 (1958): 85.

Wyatt-Brown, Bertram. *The House of Percy; Honor, Melancholy, and Imagination in a Southern Family*. New York: Oxford University Press, 1994.

Wyman, Jeffries. *Fresh-water Shell Mounds of the St. John's River, Florida; Fourth Memoir*. Salem, MA: Peabody Academy of Science, 1875.

———. "On the fresh-water shell heaps of the St. John's River, East Florida." *American Naturalist* 2 (1869): 440–63.

INDEX

ABOUT THE AUTHOR

Thomas Peter Bennett, a Florida native, independent scholar, and poet, is now on perpetual sabbatical. The former professor and natural history museum executive has authored many articles and books on the topics featured in *Florida Explored: The Philadelphia Connection in Bartram's Tracks.* This book draws from his work at Harvard, Florida State University, Philadelphia's Academy of Natural Sciences, the Florida Museum of Natural History, the South Florida Museum, and his extensive explorations in Florida and the southeast. Bennett's early interest in William Bartram's *Travels* was fueled by his study of the 1817 expedition of the Academy of Natural Sciences to Spanish Florida "in Bartram's Tracks." His further research on Bartram's influence revealed a plethora of Philadelphia Academy-related naturalists who made environmental discoveries about Florida during the last two centuries. Bennett's recent books include *The Legacy: South Florida Museum* (2010), *The Le Contes: Scientific Family of Woodmanston* (2014), and *Encore Seasons* (2017). He is a member of The Explorer's Club.

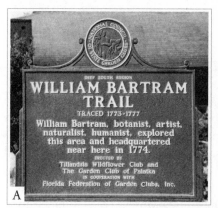

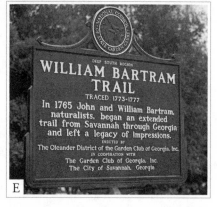

Montage of Bartram Trail signs:
a) Palatka, Florida; b) Gainesville, Florida; c) Picolata, Florida;
d) Fernandina Beach, Florida; e) Savannah, Georgia.

Courtesy of Gudrun Dorothea Bennett and Thomas P. Bennett.